SAFE RETURN
DOUBTFUL

OTHER BOOKS BY JOHN MAXTONE-GRAHAM

Passage East

Titanic *Survivor*

Crossing & Cruising

The Only Way to Cross

Dark Brown Is the River

S.S. Norway

Olympic *and* Titanic

Liners to the Sun

Tribute to a Queen

From Song to Sovereign

Cunard: 150 Glorious Years

SAFE RETURN
DOUBTFUL
THE HEROIC AGE OF
POLAR EXPLORATION

John Maxtone-Graham

Constable · London

This edition first published in the United States of America 1999
by Barnes & Noble Books

First published in Great Britain 2000
by Constable and Company Limited
3 The Lanchesters, 162 Fulham Palace Road
London W6 9ER
by arrangement with Barnes & Noble, Inc.

Copyright © 1988 by John Maxtone-Graham
ISBN 0 094 80330 7

A CIP catalogue record of this book is available from the British Library.

Printed and bound in the United States of America

For Dolf Placzek,
who kept the sledge on course

Contents

Preface

I began assembling material for this book by placing a query in the Sunday *New York Times Book Review*. I had several dozen responses, including proposals from editors at three publishing houses. None pleased me more than a letter from Katharine Lang of Albuquerque, New Mexico. She wrote:

> . . . Last year at about this time, I was in London, loping along the Embankment on a day of wild winds and black rain, and having my usual glorious time doing it. The Thames was roiling—whitecaps! And there, suddenly, was *Discovery*, pitching at her moorings and quite free of tourists for a change. I made my way up the slippery, swaying gangplank with the assistance (unnecessary) of an excessively Naval Gentleman, the Master-at-Arms. He gave me the run of the ship, probably glad for a bit of company, and certainly surprised that an "obviously American" old lady in a mink coat had ever heard of Shackleton and Scott and could ask about minutiae.
>
> When I found myself alone in Scott's cabin and saw his gear—the wooden snow-goggles, the pitiful broken

clogs, the little bits and pieces—I burst into tears. "Are you quite all right, Madam?" asked the Master-at-Arms. I blubbered something about being so moved, treading the very boards that the heroes of my youth had trod. The starch went out of the Master-at-Arms: he was elderly, handsome and had a magnificent pepper-and-salt beard. He put a kindly arm around my shoulders and said, "I quite understand, Madam. This is precisely why I chose to remain in the Royal Navy, rather than to retire. Shall we have a cup of tea?" We talked for hours. . . .

. . . There is a vast audience waiting for you. . . . People are hungry for heroes and we cannot be reminded too often that there were heroes. . . . I am chilled, and that's not a pun, by the tourists who take vacation cruises to Antarctica, insulated against everything, including a sense of the past. Set 'em aboard *Discovery*, *Fram* or *Gjøa*, take away their Nikons and polyester booties and let them have a taste of salt and ice. . . .

Remote, high latitudes have always appealed to me, although I had not—and still have not—ever traveled there. But the men who did left extraordinary records. My correspondent was right: We do need heroes, and each generation has their own. When my children were at school in New York, the student body was divided into three houses: Armstrong, Aldrin, and Shepard. At my English prep school, our three houses were Drake, Raleigh, and Scott. Polar explorers were the astronauts of their day. The great difference was that the men who tried for the poles had no NASA to fund them; they had to struggle for backing just as hard as they struggled over the icy wastes. It seems ironic that those heroes had to beg for the opportunity of being miserably cold and hungry.

A great many people have helped me on my quest. In Norway, I am grateful to Harald Brandsburg, who looked after my Oslovian research so skillfully. I had the pleasure of meeting Bård Kolltveit, now director of the Norsk Sjøfartsmuseum and a firm friend; his colleague, Else Marie Thorstvedt, was adept at ferreting out records and photographs. Toralv Lorentzen at the Fram Museum was invaluable, as were staff at the Oslo University Library and the Ski Museum.

London research was in the capable hands of Pat Hodgson

and Joan Saunders. George Dugdale, former librarian at the Royal Geographical Society, was a tower of strength, as was archivist Christine Kelly. At Cambridge I spent invaluable weeks at the Scott Polar Research Institute; I am indebted to its librarian, Harry King. Thanks are due to Ann Savours and A. W. Pearsall at the National Maritime Museum; also to the Royal Society for allowing me access to the *Discovery* photographs.

Here in the United States, the stacks of the American Geographical Society were a treasure trove, and I am grateful to Roman Drazniowsky for his advice in the matter of maps. At the American Museum of Natural History, archivist Russell Rak was more than helpful. Fred Allis at the Explorers Club is to be thanked for putting the club's archives at my disposal. Dr. William Manger's guidance with the problem of scurvy was invaluable.

In Washington, I am indebted to Mary Raitt for her tireless research. Thomas Smith and Barbara Shattuck of the National Geographic Society were most generous with their time; in addition to providing access to the Peary files and photographs, they were kind enough to pass me on to Admiral Peary's grandson, Commander E. P. Stafford. I received invaluable assistance from Alison Wilson at the Center for Polar Archives. Jerry Kearns, of the Prints and Photographs Division of the Library of Congress, gave unstintingly of his time.

Closer to home, there is no one in the world more selfless about her time and preoccupation on my behalf than my dear wife, Mary. Her contributions to all my books, this one especially, are incalculable. In addition to preparing the index and keeping track of research and pictures, she has smoothed the creative path as only a devoted author's wife can; I am eternally grateful. Dolf Placzek proved, as always, a wise friend, his encouragement never-ending.

I must also extend grateful thanks to Edward T. Chase, my editor at Scribners, for his instantaneous affection for the manuscript. Others who helped are listed alphabetically as follows: Ivo Barne, Calvin Chapin, Elaine Chisman, Laurence Cowles, Theresa A. Czajkowska, Harold Eide, Finn and Charlotte Ferner, Olof Fong, Terry Gacke, David Harrowfield, Wally Herbert, Milton Horowitz, William Hunt, Serge Korff, Matt Larsen, Odd Lindberg, Walter Lord, Canon Gervase W. Markham,

Robert Newman, Einar Ostvedt, Slim Randles, Sir Peter Scott, Mrs. Milton Seeley, Patricia Smith, Carol Spawn, Ethel Thake, Alice Thomsen, Norman Vaughan, Helen Vetter, Elizabeth Stackhouse Wardwell, J. Edward Weems, T. Woodcock, Joan Woodward, and Pat Wright.

And very much appreciated are the excellent maps by David Lindroth.

Perhaps I should explain my title. In advertising anthologies, one prize-winning entry crops up repeatedly. It was said to have appeared in *The Times* of London in early 1907:

> MEN WANTED FOR HAZARDOUS JOURNEY. LOW WAGES, BITTER COLD, LONG HOURS OF COM-PLETE DARKNESS. SAFE RETURN DOUBTFUL, HONOUR AND RECOGNITION IN THE EVENT OF SUCCESS.

The copy has been singled out as a masterpiece of deadly frankness.

Unfortunately, it seems that the advertisement is as spurious as it is famous: It has never appeared in any newspaper any-where. Regardless, the conditions it implies, as well as the spirit it conveys, are so hauntingly evocative that I extracted from it the title for this book.

*   *

Having documented the lives and personas of these larger-than-life figures, one is tempted to select a favorite. It is no easy task, for explorers of the heroic age were a special breed, sprung from a remarkable mold. Those who returned triumphantly from arctic or antarctic were showered with honors, accolades, and publishing and lecture contracts; those that perished in high latitudes were sanctified with emotional paeans of regret.

But delving beyond the medals, extravagant tributes, and memorial statuary, how did those explorers rank in terms of humanity? To find out, we must read between the lines of their diaries and listen to their fellow expedition members and biographers.

The two men credited with attaining the ultimate geographi-cal prizes were, perhaps not surprisingly, the least simpatico.

After eight dogged tries, American Admiral Robert Peary finally planted the Stars and Stripes atop an Arctic Ocean ice floe at the coveted 90° North. Nevertheless, he remains a dour, complex figure, plodding yet pompous, radiating an unrelenting and utterly humorless self-righteousness. Subordinates on several of his expeditions were disenchanted.

His antipodal rival, the man who flew Norway's flag at the south pole, was Roald Amundsen, a similarly cold fish. Though the tenor of his expeditions was less tense than Peary's, I think he shared with the American an overriding preoccupation with image, consumed with ensuring his presumptive niche in polar history. Amundsen's face betrayed nothing more than ruthless austerity; he never married, dedicating his spartan life from adolescence on to relentless polar achievement.

Others might argue that successful attainment of the poles should rightly be predicated on no-nonsense diligence, that popularity or the cult of personality played no part in the polar game. But I am convinced that so much of the day-to-day struggle for high latitude—whether in ship, hut, or tent—demanded tolerance, camaraderie, and inspired leadership of a high order. Confined men living and working under conditions of harsh deprivation required leaders with a sense of compassion and humor that Peary and Amundsen so conspicuously lacked.

In general, the Americans fared worst. Lieutenant Adolphus Greely, the Army officer whose party nearly starved to death at Cape Sabine, was a curious, bookish man, concerned for his enlisted men but consistently at odds and unpopular with his officers. And how to evaluate mystical, enigmatic Charles Francis Hall, poisoned mysteriously in the arctic aboard his scandalously lax *Polaris*? Lieutenant George Washington De Long, the Navy officer whose *Jeannette* was destroyed by the arctic ice, I liked better; but almost more, his chief engineer George Melville, whose competence, courage, and ultimately, devotion to his dead chief proved exemplary.

Among the Scandinavians, one cannot help but admire the spirit of Salomon August Andree, the stubborn Swedish aeronaut determined to fly to the north pole. Yet however congenial, Andree was essentially naive, too willing to sacrifice the lives of junior colleagues in pursuit of his hare-brained scheme.

Fridtjof Nansen rates highly, a Viking of a man whose sangfroid, elegance, and effortless fortitude augured well for two extraordinary expeditions. He followed history's first trek across Greenland with an unconventional near-miss of the north pole. Nansen was one of a kind, idolized by not only his fellow Norwegians but also the English, whose debonair insouciance he emulated. A crack skier, a first-class scientist and seemingly indestructible, Nansen was also a born leader.

Of the two English polar immortals, it is hard to extricate Captain Robert Scott from the aura of posthumous sanctity surrounding him to this day; he and four companions, bested by Amundsen at the south pole, lost their lives returning to base. Scott had been an impoverished Royal Navy officer, burdened with supporting a widowed mother and unmarried sisters; as a result, his polar ambition was freighted with financial desperation. In the field, he adhered to strict, Royal Navy protocol, engendering a prickly detachment from subordinates. Sharing Peary's and Amundsen's preoccupation with self-image, he was often short-tempered and impatient; childhood wraiths of self-doubt, insecurity, and depression dogged him into maturity.

Years before his death, Scott took bitter, professional umbrage with a former sledging companion when he first sensed that the latter's polar ambition might be as adamantine as his own. The companion was Ernest Shackleton, a former Merchant Navy officer inured to the hardship of Cape Horn sailing vessels. Recruited by Scott for his first antarctic expedition, Shackleton would return seven years later at the head of his own.

Of all the impressive roster of polar commanders, Shackleton remains incontrovertibly the most appealing. As a bluff Irishman, he was full of the best possible blarney, boasting a keen penchant for poetry (alone among his exploring peers, I suspect), as well as an affable, bulldog—but never forbidding—determination. Steel ambition was not masked, in his case, by a steely exterior—one senses that on Shackleton expeditions, there were unanimous good spirits with "The Boss," as he was called affectionately by his men, or "Shackles" by his peers.

Shackleton's most incredible adventures occurred several years after the discovery of both poles, hence outside *Safe Return Doubtful*'s parameters. Unable to reach the pole in 1909, Shackleton sailed south seven years later intent on sledging completely across Antarctica, stopping at the pole *en passant*.

But tragically, the expedition could not land; his ship *Endurance* (never was a polar vessel more appropriately christened!) was savaged and sunk by Antarctica's notorious ice pack. There followed a hair-raising epic of endurance and survival, across ice and raging antarctic waters in small boats, including one final, incredible journey to and then across mountainous South Georgia for help. Not one life was lost and, throughout, it was the charismatic, endearing figure of Shackles that brought it off, combining incomparable seamanship and leadership. *Endurance* expedition photographer Frank Hurley described him as having "an eye to everything & so considerate to the party to neglect himself."

When Shackleton came to New York to lecture in 1910, he addressed the Explorer's Club at the Belleclaire Hotel on Broadway at 76th Street. Though the hotel is now a faded simulacrum of its former self, Sir Ernest still illumines the annals of the heroic age, a commander *sans pareil* who throws less a long shadow than a beacon of grit, competence, warmth, and charm.

One unanticipated effect of this explorer ranking may be to have whetted readers' appetites for the expeditions that follow. So button up and buckle down for an arduous but, I trust, rewarding slog.

—John Maxtone-Graham
New York City, 1998

MAPS

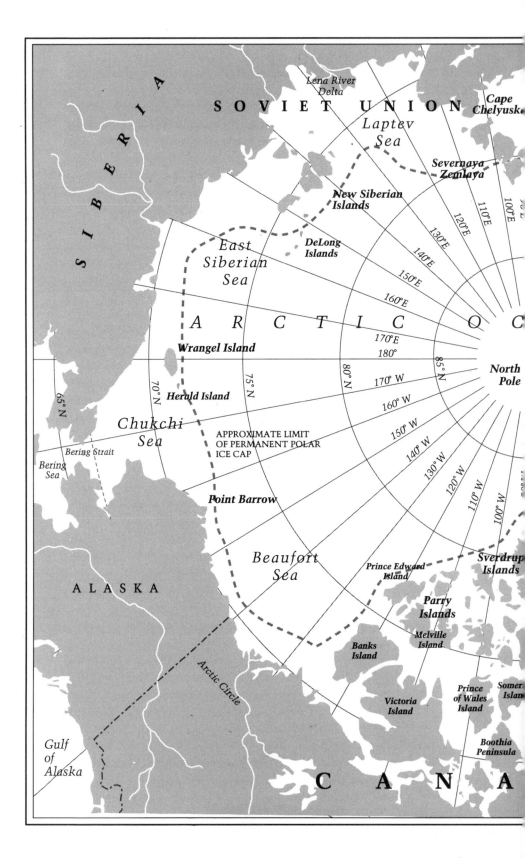

Kara Sea

Barents
Sea

White
Sea

Kara
Pen.

FINLAND

Novya
Zemlya

70°E

60°E

50°E

40°E

30°E

20°E

10°E

0°

North
Cape

Franz Josef
Land

SWEDEN

A   N

NORWAY

Spitzbergen
Islands

10° W

APPROXIMATE LIMIT
OF PERMANENT POLAR
ICE CAP

Norwegian
Sea

20° W

30° W

40° W

50° W

° W

Lincoln
Sea

ICELAND

Cape
olumbia

re Island

Arctic Circle

G R E E N L A N D

evon
land

Baffin Bay

NORTH
ATLANTIC
OCEAN

d Hecla
ait

0   500 Miles

D   A

Baffin Island

Davis Strait

0   500 Kilometers

Foxe
Basin

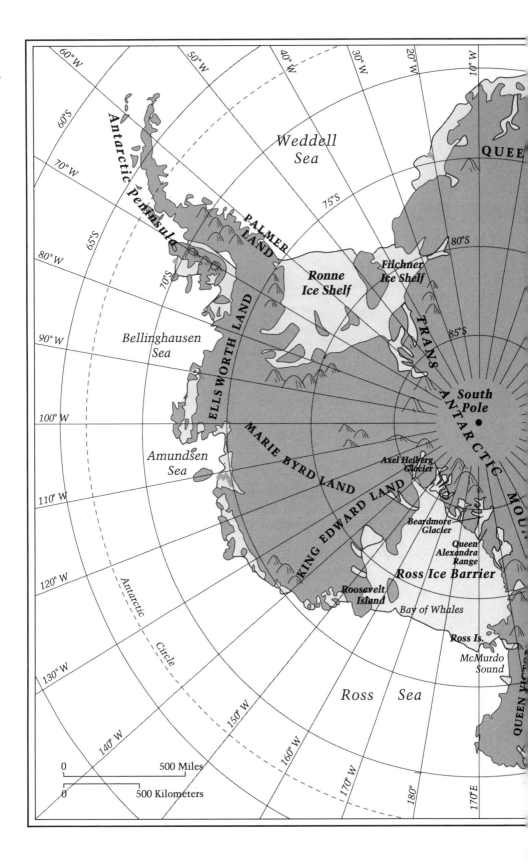

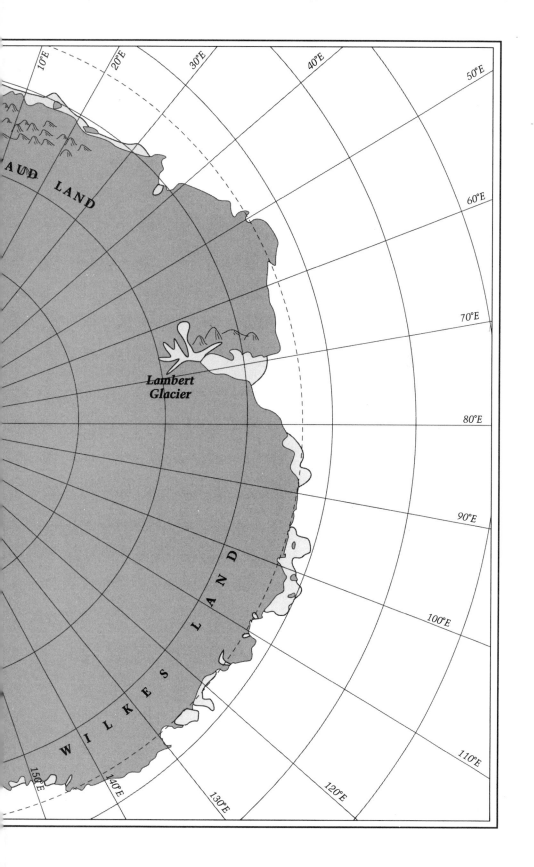

SAFE RETURN
DOUBTFUL

1

THE BRITANNIC EXAMPLE

The iron camaraderie of the North.
—John Buchan

On the night of January 30, 1916, a frail, white-haired gentleman retired to the bedroom of his house in London's Eccleston Square. Once undressed, he swung expertly into a hammock and, as he had done for more than seven decades, read himself to sleep in traditional Royal Navy fashion: One hand held his book, the other a candle, exactly as he had learned as a midshipman in 1844.

But on this occasion, fatigue overcame him with a rush. The burning candle slipped from his fingers and toppled among the bedclothes. Oblivious, the old gentleman slept as charred linen blossomed into flame that ignited the blanket. Dense smoke filled the room. Before anyone in the house could intervene, Sir Clements Markham, then in his eighty-sixth year, dozed into eternity. The following day, he was dead. Directly over his smoldering hammock hung a perfectly good electric light.

So died the doyen of Great Britain's geographical fraternity or, as a colleague was to suggest posthumously, "an Instigator of Polar Enterprise." Both poles had been achieved a few years earlier, the north by Peary and the south at the expense of Captain Robert Scott, Markham's lamented protégé; Amundsen, the Norwegian spoiler, had reached it first. Shackleton, the last of the immortals, whom Sir Clements could not abide, was at that moment beset on board the doomed *Endurance*. There would be no more momentous sledge journeys. A new kind of exploration was just over the horizon: dirigibles and airplanes would quarter the wastes of high latitude with an insolent ease quite alien to those indomitable giants who had shown the way on foot. The air was at hand, the heroic age was over.

It was an age with which Sir Clements's long life was inextricably entwined. He died as it ended; the year of his birth—1830—saw the establishment of the Royal Geographical Society, that prestigious organization of which he would assume the presidency for an unprecedented dozen years. The Clements Markham motif recurs persistently throughout the polar *opera seria*. His tireless, entertaining, sometimes choleric but formidably well-informed voice was heard time and time again. Markham's expertise was a touchstone of the age. His first love was Peru, but polar exploration and the Royal Navy tied for second place; and the overriding force that shaped Markham as well as his immense literary output was a discipline sadly neglected in the present, the science of geography.

Clements Robert Markham was the second son of a Yorkshire clergyman. He grew up in the village of Stillingfleet and was by all accounts frighteningly precocious. Before he was seven, he started a journal, entering the name, appearance, and manner of all who called at the rectory. Moreover, he would detail from memory the floor plan, furniture arrangement, and even picture selection of every house he visited, documenting as well the characteristics of its occupants. "A long neck, an eager little face, and voice like a cockatoo" he described one lady; perhaps this talent served as inspiration for the nursery charades and theatricals that absorbed the four Markham children for hours.

When he was eight, Clements went to a preparatory school at Cheam. In 1843 he moved on to public school at Westminster, where he became coxswain of an eight-oared racing shell, responding to the challenges of seamanship and teamwork. But his Westminster stay was brief. In 1844, at a dinner party, he met Admiral Sir George Seymour, who suggested he join the Royal Navy as a cadet. Markham accepted. An elderly Navy surgeon instructed Clements to write out the Lord's Prayer and then punched him in the stomach, asking if it hurt. He was passed as fit, morally and physically, and reported for training to HMS *Vincent* at Portsmouth.

Markham relished his new life. By the time he joined HMS *Collingwood* in the South Pacific Squadron, he had applied his unremitting journalistic skills to everything and everybody on board. Deck plans and remarkably accurate sketches of rigging and armaments filled his journal. The mania for human observation continued, too. Markham not only reproduced all seventy officers' coats of arms but penned devastating thumbnail biographies as well: "An old fellow with a large stomach, sly and deceitful, but outwardly a jolly old boy." He excelled at every assignment and was given responsibility for the ship's dinghy, a demanding appointment conscientiously assumed. Promotion to midshipman followed.

Markham passed four busy years on HMS *Collingwood;* he taught himself Spanish and traveled extensively throughout Chile and Peru. The remains of the Incan civilization fascinated him and, in later years, a firsthand knowledge of Peru and its flora was to pay significant dividends. Markham was as high-spirited as he was popular: A favorite game ashore was racing from one end of Lima to the other, contestants restricted to the city's rooftops.

After duty in the Mediterranean, he volunteered for a year's special service on board the bark *Assistance*. Under the command of Captain Erasmus Ommaney and in company with the *Resolute*, another search vessel, she sailed for the Canadian North in the spring of 1850. That voyage would initiate a lifelong preoccupation with voyages of exploration in high latitudes.

The two ships had been assigned to the Admiralty's massive Franklin Sea Search, its objective the lost expedition of Sir John Franklin. The disappearance of this celebrated commander had become the Royal Navy's overwhelming concern by midcentury. Sailing to resolve one mystery—the route of the Northwest Passage—Sir John became another mystery himself: The explorer, together with two stout ships and 129 officers and men, had vanished completely.

Born in 1786, Franklin had entered the Royal Navy at age sixteen. After the Congress of Vienna and a three-year hiatus at half pay, Franklin embarked on three expeditions to the arctic. The first and least successful was by sea: In 1818, he sailed from Spitsbergen in command of the *Trent* in a vain attempt to reach the north pole. Subsequently, Franklin led two separate overland expeditions along the frozen shores of northwestern Canada. He almost starved to death on the first but returned to the field three years later to map the Canadian/Alaskan coast as far west as the Bering Strait. So successfully did Franklin explore the desolate tundra west of the Mackenzie River that he was knighted on his return to England. When the Admiralty's arctic fervor cooled temporarily in 1827, Sir John accepted the post of lieutenant governor of Van Diemen's Land, the island south of Australia we now call Tasmania.

But one last arctic quest remained. In 1843, back in England, Franklin sought command of a two-ship expedition that was to solve, once and for all, the puzzle of the Northwest Passage. Lord Haddington, first lord of the Admiralty, suggested to Franklin that, at sixty, he might be too old for arctic service. Sir John protested stoutly: "No, my Lord, you have been misinformed, I am only fifty-nine."

Sir John was given the post. In the spring of 1845 he sailed from Portsmouth in command of the *Erebus* and *Terror*, the first arcticbound ships equipped with screw propellers. In Franklin's cabin was a new three-chart locker, labeled "Home," "Arctic," and "Pacific" waters. Captain Dannert, master of the Hull whaler *Prince of Wales*, last saw the two vessels in Disko Bay that summer, moored to an iceberg while the crews shot and salted hundreds of plump auks. Then the arctic swallowed them up: Neither Sir John, his crews, nor his ships were ever seen again.

Dozens of ships were dispatched to locate the vanished champion. Both *Erebus* and *Terror* had carried hundreds of watertight tin canisters for leaving messages; not one was ever found. Relief ships advertised their presence diligently: Minute guns were fired on schedule, bottles stuffed with encouraging instructions were strewn throughout Lancaster Sound. Messages were sent aloft by ingenious balloons that scattered dozens of flyers over the icy wastes. Foxes were trapped and banded with copper collars on which bulletins of hope had been inscribed. But there was no response.

Not until late August 1852 did hard evidence come to light.

Several ships, British as well as American, discovered the remains of Franklin's first winter encampment on Beechey Island, an encouraging yet mystifying find. The camp had been abandoned in haste, perhaps as spring ice receded; a pair of officer's white cashmere gloves had been set out to dry, weighted with stones, and never retrieved. Although three cairns had been constructed—two on Beechey and one on adjacent Devon Island—they contained no messages whatsoever.

Cairns are the traditional *postes restantes* of the arctic. Explorers or sea captains erected them on conspicuous headlands, usually pyramidal towers built of stone slabs. They had to be visible from the sea and as indestructible as possible. Placed inside them were messages sealed in brass tubes or glass bottles. According to Admiralty tradition, whoever found a cairn was at liberty to appropriate whatever written memoranda it contained, on condition that a complete facsimile be left in its place—a sensible proviso, for the finder might well perish himself.

The lost explorers had left wooden headstones on Beechey Island over the last resting place of three seamen: John Torrington, John Hartnell, and William Braine. Torrington, his gravestone informed, had died "on board Her Majesty's Ship *Terror*," indicating to the finders that the ships had *not* been wrecked that winter but were only missing.

However, one of Franklin's Beechey Island cairns did convey a message of sorts: It was constructed entirely of gravel-filled cans of the kind that had contained the expedition's meat, each one labeled "Goldner's Patent." There were over 700 of them, far more than would have been consumed by 139 men over one winter, indicating that quantities of the expedition's supplies must have spoiled. In the absence of any written record, it was deduced that Franklin, having discovered the damage, had examined all the cans, then ordered defective ones opened and their contents destroyed. This was the significance of that metallic cairn.

Within a year of his return from the arctic, Clements Markham resigned his commission. A voracious reader despite his abbreviated schooling, he set out to become a first-class geographer. Before settling down, he traveled once more to Peru to explore Incan ruins around Cuzco, the ancient capital. Then, at age twenty-two, Markham entered the Civil Service.

Six boring months at the Department of Inland Revenue followed, relieved only by a transfer to liaison duties with the East India Company. Among Clements Markham's proudest accomplishments was assuring the Empire of a new, cheap supply of quinine. In 1859 he was asked to head a small expedition to retrieve, surreptitiously, cinchona plants from the Peruvian highlands for transfer to plantations in India. With a party of five companions—four botanists and his recent bride, Minna—Markham found the plants and, after much derring-do (one of Sir Clements's favorite words), spirited them safely out of the country. Later he oversaw their successful cultivation in India.

But even before that adventure, he made his mark on London. Within a year of disembarking from the *Assistance*, Markham had published *Franklin's Footsteps*, his first book, forerunner of dozens more. Authoritative conviction characterized every phrase. People took note. Sir Roderick Murchison, president of the Royal Geographical Society, invited him to become a fellow. Within ten years he was elected honorary secretary, a position he would hold for a quarter century.

The RGS was the second of two great royal societies. The Royal Society, the first, had been chartered in 1662 by Charles II "for the improvement of natural knowledge." It was inevitable that this scientific body should be succeeded by one devoted exclusively to geography, largely due to the exhaustive peregrinations of one of the Royal Society's earliest fellows, Captain James Cook. Geography's time was ripe, internationally, too: Within a ten-year period, from 1820 to 1830, a trio of European societies was founded: the Société de Géographie in Paris, Berlin's Gesellschaft für Erdkunde, and, in 1830, Britain's Royal Geographical Society.

Markham's forebears had explored and conquered the globe; now he and his contemporaries were preoccupied with tidying it up, exercising an understandably proprietary interest in a map one quarter of which was shaded imperial red. An astute, methodical, and articulate man, Clements Markham fitted in well. He had not only the right credentials—ex-service and an old arctic hand—but a keen awareness of the nuances of rank and privilege as well: Heraldry and genealogy were two of his areas of expertise.

Polar exploration preoccupied him not merely because of his

spell on the *Assistance* but also because, toward the end of the nineteenth century, little else of the globe remained unexplored: Africa was no longer the Dark Continent, and there were almost no blanks on the maps of South America and the Far East. Apart from Tibet and Mount Everest, the poles were the last unclaimed geographical prizes, intriguing unknowns in a world that sought to know everything. Markham's encouragement of true polar exploration was like a breath of fresh air; for too long, Britain's explorers had been distracted by that enduring chimera, the Northwest Passage. This was the quest on which Franklin's men had perished and, though they might as easily have died en route to the pole, their dispatch northwest rather than north was significant, the death rattle of a malady that had afflicted Britain's maritime establishment for centuries.

From the sixteenth century on, a host of English sailors—Frobisher, Davis, Baffin, and Hudson among them—had packed their holds with trade goods for the Chinese and set off for the East. Sailing on behalf of royal patrons, they had probed the Canadian arctic for "a Northwest Passage to Cathaia and lands Orientall."

The earliest explorers hoped that North America could be pierced in temperate latitudes. Years later, after it had been established that North America was indeed a continent, the idea persisted that a waterway to the East lay somehow through the islands that make up the Canadian archipelago. On today's maps, the route looks absurdly easy: due west along the seventy-fourth parallel from Baffin Bay, through Lancaster Sound, Barrow Strait, Viscount Melville Sound, and McClure Strait. But the map is deceptive, for it indicates sea where, in fact, a conventional sea does not exist. The arctic cold confounds matters, obstructing or obliterating those northern arterial routes into ice-choked culs-de-sac. Explorers bound for Cathay grappled with a tantalizing land/sea maze. Ice and snow hampered not only a mariner's progress but his sense of perception as well: Inlets masqueraded as straits, straits as defiles, the frozen sea as terra firma. Cloudbanks produced mountain ranges where none existed. Frost smoke and summer fog are sometimes so thick, according to Lord Dufferin, a nineteenth-century arctic yachtsman and geographer, that "you could almost cut it like cheese."

In fact, the visionaries were right: A navigable Northwest Passage does exist—and was known to exist—long before it was first negotiated after the turn of the twentieth century. But it has been transformed by ice into such a treacherous, laborious route that it boasts no commercial advantage whatsoever, save for those whalers and sealers bold enough to fish its eastern and western approaches. Those frozen Canadian waters are, to all intents and purposes, permanently nonnavigable, no less for powerfully engined tankers than for the wooden sailing ships that preceded them. McClure Strait is choked with such a profusion of ice that the vast *Manhattan*, driven by an abundance of horsepower, ground to an ignominious halt there in 1968, convincing her oil consortium sponsors that the legendary route was impractical even for strengthened supertankers. As a result, Alaskan oil flows south through a controversial pipeline instead.

But regardless, the British continued to press their search for it. The ancient, illogical lure persisted and, in 1815, Sir John Barrow, second Admiralty secretary as well as a founder of the Royal Geographical Society, agitated for a renewed attack. Parliament authorized a twenty-thousand-pound reward— four times, interestingly, the amount promised for the pole— for the man who negotiated it, although, in truth, grandiloquence and scientific curiosity rather than profit were the motives now. The prestige of the world's premier naval power was said to be at stake. Moreover—and was this the real reason?—Sir John had the means at his disposal. Excess tonnage from the Napoleonic Wars clogged the Portsmouth and Chatham roads, and there were many young officers anxious for adventure and promotion. Thus, from 1818 onward, British expeditions were dispatched regularly to the Canadian arctic, an assault sustained with increasing expectation of success until Sir John Franklin's baffling disappearance in 1845.

The Franklin debacle, in fact, serves as the Admiralty's explorational watershed: Until 1845, Their Lordships had been obsessed with passage or pole; after that, they hunted almost exclusively for Franklin. The Arctic Council, that distinguished Admiralty think tank charged with the massive quest, sent out a dozen vessels in 1850 alone, the peak year of the search, determined to dispel what Clements Markham called Franklin's "halo of romantic uncertainty." American as well as British ship captains and sledgers scoured miles of coastline, penciling in new ones on their charts. But although Canada's arctic wilderness came to light—like some gigantic mosaic unearthed from snowbound antiquity—nothing was found. In 1857, after a decade of fruitless searching, the Admiralty stood down. But where the Royal Navy had failed, private enterprise was to succeed.

All the Admiralty expeditions had been dispatched toward the Far North, in the mystical proximity of Beechey Island's encampment. But Dr. John Rae, a civilian employee of the Hudson's Bay Company who had explored the coastline of Victoria Land on foot, suggested to Lady Franklin that traces of her husband might be found nearer the Canadian mainland. Together with powerful friends in the Royal Geographical Society, she urged Their Lordships on yet another search mission; the Admiralty refused. So the determined widow raised ten thousand pounds for a private charter. Two thirds of the funds came from her own purse, the remainder from a private subscription donated by several families of officers lost on board the *Erebus* and the *Terror*. Allen Young, a Merchant Navy officer and independently rich yachtsman, contributed five hundred pounds on condition that he be signed on as sailing master. The vessel selected was the little steam yacht *Fox*; in command was one of Clements Markham's shipmates on the *Assistance*, Captain Leopold McClintock, "discoverer of the naval sledge." He was instructed to explore the shores of King William Land—now known to be an island—just north of the Canadian mainland and far from the Admiralty's area of concentration around Lancaster Sound. Although resigned to her husband's death—the *Fox* sailed a dozen years after the *Erebus* and the *Terror*—Lady Franklin was understandably anxious for firsthand information about his fate. When the *Fox* left England in June 1857, flying from her main truck was her patron's motto "Hold Fast."

McClintock's second-in-command, Lieutenant Hobson, must be credited with discovering the Franklin Expedition's only written record. In a cairn at Point Victory, along the desolate western shore of King William Island, he unearthed a brass box. Inside it was a single paper, bearing two consecutive messages. The first, dated May 1846, was routine, recording the wintering over at the Beechey Island encampment found in

1852. It had been written on what was called a "bottle paper," the Admiralty's standard multilanguage flyer.

But a desperate addendum, scrawled around the margins two years later, told the full tale: After having been beset offshore by the ice for eighteen months, both *Erebus* and *Terror* had gone to the bottom. The surviving crews—105 men in all—had set out south for the mainland, dragging boats and supplies. (One of these boats as well as three bodies and some relics were later found.)

The Franklin riddle had finally been solved. McClintock returned to England with the electrifying if doleful news. He was also able to report to his widowed patron that her husband had died of natural causes on board the *Erebus* long before she had sunk, content, at least, that he had discovered the route of the Northwest Passage. Sir John's funeral is recorded in stone on the plinth of his statue in London's Waterloo Place, hooded crews lining the sledge-borne coffin of their leader. McClintock was knighted and Franklin was said to have discovered the route of the Northwest Passage.

It seems remarkable that those nineteenth-century sailors survived the arctic at all. Their wooden sailing vessels offered primitive conditions: heat, light, and ventilation were inadequate, and a monotonous diet revolved exclusively around biscuit and salted meat. Sickness, injury, or death were inevitable concomitants of the sailor's life. Though ships were strengthened for arctic service, there was little protection for the crews who manned them. The only perks extended were box-cloth jackets—the heavy wool fabric worn by coachmen driving on the box—and, standard arctic incentive, double pay. But it is doubtful whether those extra shillings were adequate compensation for several years' arctic exile, frozen rigging, spume that literally sheathed seamen in icy cuirasses, the continual risk of frostbite, or descent, off-duty, to a cavelike messdeck that alternately dripped and froze.

The success of those British expeditions lay in the fortitude of their officers and crews. Royal Navy sailors had the versatility of Renaissance men. When Lieutenant Scott was recruiting for the *Discovery* in 1899, the qualifications of his candidates convey Jack Tar's diverse resourcefulness: A not atypical applicant listed among his talents sewing, carpentry, sailmaking, netmaking, shoemaking, and barbering, as well as proficiency on three musical instruments. Royal Navy volunteers for Nares's expedition of 1875 were asked bluntly: "What can you do for the amusement of others?"

Indeed, all-roundedness, the ability to cope with crisis, has been a traditional Royal Navy attribute. An interservice triumph was scored in South Africa during the Boer War when a Royal Navy brigade came ashore and, manhandling field guns overland, broke the siege of Ladysmith 150 miles inland, an epic feat of arms celebrated to this day by gun-crew races at the Royal Tournament. Perhaps Britain's ultimate naval accolade was bestowed at Windsor's railway station in January 1901 when a Royal Artillery mount hitched to the gun carriage bearing Queen Victoria's coffin shied and broke the traces. A Royal Navy honor guard was pressed instantly into service: Sailors knotted hand loops into spotless white hemp pirated from the funeral train's communication cord and, formed into detachments fore and aft, set course on foot for St. George's Chapel.

The sight of sailors harnessed to a gun carriage was, quite simply, subliminally reassuring. Eighty years of northern exploration had implanted firmly in the popular imagination the concept of Royal Navy officers and men yoked in democratic tandem to their sledges. For manhauling—"pully-hauly," in the argot of the messdeck—was a polar constant. When expeditions were dispatched from immobilized vessels, sailors transferred from ship to snow. The conveyance they drew was nautical. Although McClintock's venerated prototype had been a rigid, upright sleigh, those that Nansen perfected later took their shape from the Eskimo original, lower and narrower, lashed rather than screwed together so that they adapted sinuously to the wavelike undulations of hummock and ridge. Lines and toggles abounded, loads were roped on board, and canvas sails could be bent onto bamboo masts to capitalize on a following wind. Banners and pennants fluttered from sledges on ceremonial occasions and, like the ships that had borne them north, they were christened with questing names: Markham's sledge in 1875 was *Marco Polo*, while one of his brother officers called his *Hercules*.

Oceangoing celestial navigation was a necessity for sledging. Compass and sextant were invaluable as polar officers reckoned longitude and latitude to determine achievement or destination. A sledger's nautical skills were vital during passage across glacial icecaps when sledge parties crossed wind-furrowed white expanses out of sight of "land," the rocky outcrops that pierced their icy mantle.

The heroic age's greatest explorers had maritime links, from Amundsen to Peary to Shackleton to Scott. The norm was nautical, arctic and antarctic exploration remaining an inextricable blend of ship, sledge, and sailor. Philip Wales, surgeon general of the United States Navy, wrote in 1870:

> The seaman class is the best from which to select arctic sledders. First, it comes more in their line of business. Second, seamen can adapt themselves to circumstances probably better than any other class of man.

When Julius von Payer explored Franz Josef Land in 1872, his alpine *jäger* proved unequal to the mountaineering feats cheerfully accomplished by the expedition's sailors. "Seamen," recorded von Payer, "are better capable of maintaining discipline under such circumstances than members of any other profession." One of Nares's commanders, Lieutenant Aldrich, slogging back to the *Alert* in 1876, reported of his failing sledgers: "It will be observed that it is the bluejackets who hang out; the marine, shipwright and blacksmith being disabled. . . ."

Manned by these stalwarts, Royal Navy arctic vessels were officered just as competently. Promotion during the Napoleonic Wars had been accelerated: Officers were young, blessed with schoolboy dash and determination. They brought to northern exploration a splendid élan. Inspired amateurism had built the Empire, and precisely this same spirit infused polar officers; small wonder they made a go of arctic exploration. Who but an Englishman, Apsley Cherry-Garrard, who paid for the privilege of serving with Scott on his last expedition, could have written: "Polar exploration is at once the cleanest and most isolated way of having a bad time which has ever been devised"?

The ships were adaptable, too. The strongest hulls were nicknamed "bomb" ships, so called because their decks had been strengthened to support mortars for coastal bombardment. These floating ordnance platforms boasted beams and scantlings ideal for work in the ice. Franklin's ships, *Erebus* and *Terror*, were bomb ships of about 350 tons.

Other ships also performed well in the arctic: transports, brigs, barks, yachts, and, of course, the redoubtable whalers. In 1829, James Ross had sailed in command of a Mersey River ferry, the *Victory*, first paddle steamer to brave the arctic; the fragile paddle wheels proved particularly vulnerable to ice and, together with their engines, were scrapped on the shores of Boothia Peninsula. Screw propellers made more sense as long as their blades lasted. All expedition ships of the heroic age were powered by combined steam and sail. Their profiles were relentlessly similar: three-masted craft—bark-rigged—with a single tall funnel between main and mizzen (masts number two and three). Long after the age of sail, they remained hybrids with good reason: Dispensing with canvas would have required enormous coal-carrying capacity, while relying on wind alone deprived captains of an invaluable weapon for charging the pack.

Over the arctic winter, propulsion became academic, for ships undertaking long arctic voyages spent more months immobilized than under weigh. Expeditions bent on deep arctic penetration played a kind of seasonal leapfrog. Sea travel was possible only during the brief arctic summer, when some of the Canadian pack breaks up. Ships would nose through Baffin Bay in June and July and force their way west or north during August. In September, rather than fight their way home again, they would hole up for the winter, held fast but in prime position to continue the following summer.

Wintering in was usually a race against time, the ideal haven a sheltered bay where ice movement was minimal. Those coastal waters froze first: Arctic sea water, sweetened near shore by summer runoff from rivers or meltwater, congeals earliest, its freezing point nearly four degrees higher than conventional sea water's 28.6° Fahrenheit. Crews would have to be sent over the side to cut a channel into a likely bay. A line of holes a ship's width apart would be chopped in the ice, and twelve-foot ice saws, weighted at the bottom, were dropped through, suspended from a tripod of spars. The ice saw's blade could cut through a yard of six-inch ice in a minute. The ice blocks cut free were cut again into triangular fragments and then towed, poled, or sometimes sailed down channel as the ship's hull advanced inland. If, however, the channel's water refroze astern, blocking egress of these superfluous ice chunks, they were tipped up and forced under the ice margins to either side, for all the world like troublesome dust swept under the carpet.

Once the vessels were inshore, conventional anchors were useless: A frozen-in hull could neither rise with the tide nor swing on shortened cable. Ice anchors were used instead—four-inch iron bent pins were frozen into holes cut in the pack. The ship's upperworks were stripped. All running rigging was unrove. Topmasts, topgallants, and boats were stacked on adjacent floes; ropes and sails were put onshore to prevent damage from rot. Shrouds that remained in place to support the lower masts were slacked off.

The decks were spread with a foot of fresh snow as insulation. The lowest spars were turned fore-and-aft to serve as a composite ridgepole the length of the ship. Plank rafters bridged the gap between bulwark and spar. Then wagon cloth or, as it was called, wadding tilt, was draped and tacked over the peaked framing, snugging in the entire deck so that only stovepipes and one midship companionway protruded. Handsome sailing vessels were thus transformed into childlike representations of Noah's ark.

From October through February, the arctic sun never rose. Frigid, endless night prevailed, relieved only by periodic, brilliant moonlight. Traditionally, wintering in was regarded as the arctic's most ominous ordeal, "the mercury solid all the time," as Clements Markham has put it. The Norwegians call this winter darkness *mørketiden*—literally, murky time. Norwegians are ambivalent about their long winter's night, shrugging it off as merely a latitudinal inconvenience, yet refining elaborate stratagems to combat it. More ambivalence: Either extra hours of sleep are indulged, or parties continue on a nonstop basis. Four days before Christmas, northern Norwegians celebrate Midwinter Day, the moment when the absent sun passes its apogee and starts back.

Mørketiden and its indoor corollary, *mørkesyke*, or cabin fever, were seen by explorers as traditional northern bogies. Men cooped up for its duration supposedly risked madness, disease, or both. But Royal Navy crews discovered that arctic winters could be survived and made tolerable as well. The only distressing side effects were pale complexions, lassitude, and a tendency, in dank quarters housing threescore men customarily never below at one time, for abrasive temperaments to clash. The trick was to keep everyone active and amused.

Active was easy. At a quarter before nine each morning, there was a "beat to divisions," a muster on deck under the lamplit awning. Violent exercise followed: The entire ship's company thundered clockwise around the snow-packed deck while the captain and the surgeon inspected the vacant mess-deck below. At ten, all hands went over the side, required to circumnavigate the vessel until noon. They trod a nocturnal Rotten Row, named after Hyde Park's fashionable riding road, the limits of which were outlined with ice pylons connected by halyards.

Only duty cooks were excused from exercise. Their galley was the center of light and warmth on board, dispensing clouds of steam that crystallized into hoarfrost everywhere below decks. Excess water vapor was the arctic's obtrusive curse, whether billowing from cooking pots or exhaled and sweated by toiling sledgers; it froze onto everything from messdecks to mustaches. Men in hammocks fared better than officers in bunks abutting the frosted hull. A fixed warm zone ran inboard the length of the keel; outboard spaces were glacial. Cooks learned to move frozen stores amidships days ahead of anticipated consumption. Ships were inspected rigorously for correctible sources of damp. Each week, berthing spaces were fumigated with "devils," a noxious composition of powders and vinegar purported to smoke out infection, damp, and disease.

The battle against moisture was unending. The galley was enclosed with curtains of Fear-Nought, a kind of oilcloth. Central heating was employed in the form of Sylvester Stoves, from which sprouted pipes and radiant plates. Stovepipes were angled ingeniously through living spaces, although distorting the chimney played havoc with ventilation. Severe cold curtailed vertical draft; vented smoke would not rise up but went obstinately sideways. Promenading officers literally miles from the ship were sometimes stifled by chimney fumes traveling laterally over the ice.

After the noon lunch hour, the crew remained on board. Make and mend, the Royal Navy's conventional recreation, occupied the afternoon. At six, after the drums had rattled another beat to divisions, the men stood down for supper while the officers repaired to the wardroom for tea. There was more to those long evenings than yarning or chitchat: If hard exercise consumed the arctic hand's morning, an equally ruthless regime of amusement dominated his evening. Royal Navy arctic manifests included musical instruments, costumes, scene paint, makeup, and playscripts. Elaborate theatrical entertainments were scheduled. Constant rehearsal echoed belowdecks, newspapers were published, singsongs were organized, and officers held classes for messdeck illiterates. Wintered-in ships were hives of improvisation.

One of those sailor/impresarios never forgot. In 1875, Griffin & Company, of London and Portsmouth, published a slim volume titled *"The Arctic Navy List, or A Century of Arctic and Antarctic Officers*, Attempted by Clements R. Markham."* Markham's only tour of arctic duty had been memorable. Play-acting was a firm Royal Navy tradition and, for Markham in particular, an echo of charades from his Stillingfleet nursery. His nostalgia for those riotous evenings in the *Assistance*'s messdeck theater is obvious: His *Arctic Navy List* records each officer's performance on the boards as well as on the ice. Markham prefaces his work: "The most valuable qualifications for arctic service are aptitude for taking part in those winter amusements which give life to the expedition during those months of boredom—"; then, almost as an afterthought, "—and for sledge traveling."

The author rates half a page: "Markham, Clements R." had not only edited *"The Minavilins,* An Arctic Newspaper,"* but was an active member of the Royal Arctic Theatre as well, playing Fusbos in *Bombastes Furioso* and Gustavus de Mervelt in *Charles XII*. Sledging accomplishments follow: "Twenty days, one hundred and forty miles (temperature $-31°$ Fahr.) . . ."

Walter May, mate on board HMS *Resolute*, was scene painter for the Queen's Arctic Theatre, early evidence of a talent later employed designing bas-reliefs for Franklin's London memorial. Sherard Osborn, a shipmate from HMS *Collingwood* in the Pacific, served on HMS *Pioneer* as editor of the *Illustrated Arctic News* as well as actor/manager of the Arctic Philharmonic Entertainments. On board HMS *Hecla* during the winter of 1821, Lieutenant George Lyon produced nine plays and, in one, earned Markham's undying admiration for playing "through the last act with two fingers frostbitten." Captain Hoppner of HMS *Fury* had already been sanctified in *Franklin's Footsteps:* "The gallant inventor of the amusement kept up the disguise of a one-legged fiddler during the whole of the evening."

One of the notable officers whose extraordinary career was outlined in *The Arctic Navy List* is William Edward Parry, who sailed in command of four separate expeditions between 1819 and 1827. Parry was, according to Markham, "the prince of Arctic navigators." The third son of a Bath surgeon, Parry was efficient, daring, and yet curiously self-effacing, naturally suited for arctic exploration, combining polish and dash to a fine degree. Two juxtaposed entries in *The Arctic Navy List* tell the tale: ". . . Acted Sir Anthony Absolute in *The Rivals.* Discovered the passage into the Polar Sea. . . ." Youth was on his side: When he took his first ship to the arctic, he was still in his twenties.

On his first expedition, in 1819, Parry mounted the Royal Navy's first arctic overland excursion, a fourteen-day outing from the icebound *Hecla* and *Griper* at Winter Harbor across to the northern shore of Melville Island. A dozen officers and men set out with primitive equipment: "Horsemen's tents" were improvised, blankets draped over boarding pikes. The tents, together with eight-hundred pounds of provisions and fuel, were carried on a cart adapted from a gun carriage by Captain Edward Sabine of the Royal Artillery, the expedition's astronomer. Wheels were sometimes superior to runners during arctic summers. When its axle broke on the eleventh day out, Parry's men cooked ptarmigan over the blazing wreckage, setting an arctic precedent of burning surplus impedimenta for fuel.

Less important than Parry's means were the principles he established: A landing party on foot could survive the arctic outdoors, exploring territory unreachable by ship. It was a first step that would culminate in the conquest of both poles.

Parry's last expedition—in 1827—was more ambitious if less successful. He forsook the Northwest Passage for the pole. Once again it involved bluejackets on foot. His inspiration came from Admiralty archives of half a century earlier. In 1773, the Royal Society had proposed to Their Lordships that a route to the Indies might lie across the pole. Accordingly, *Racehorse* and *Carcass,* under the combined command of Captains Constantine Phipps and Skeffington Lutwidge, were sent to the ice margin north of Spitsbergen. Predictably, they were stopped short by the pack: 80° North represented the highest latitude that could reasonably be achieved by vessels in arctic waters; anything higher had to be accomplished on foot. *Racehorse* and *Carcass* were imprisoned by the ice, their crews expecting to be crushed. Phipps ordered loaded boats put out on the ice. A spare studding sail was cut into strips to make towing belts for the sailors. (This was the first mention of the Royal Navy's canvas manhauling harnesses, the same devices that Scott would use in Antarctica as late as 1912.)

The expedition returned to England intact, credited with discovery of the Seven Islands, one of which bears the name of Captain Lutwidge's young coxswain, a supernumerary named Horatio Nelson. But a relatively minor discovery from the *Racehorse*'s log intrigued Parry. Captain Lutwidge had examined the pack's surface through a glass from the masthead, describing it as "one continuous plain of smooth, unbroken ice, bounded only by the horizon." Lutwidge suggested that "a coach and four could have driven unimpeded to the pole," a concept that electrified Parry. Lutwidge's "smooth, unbroken ice" north of Spitsbergen seemed a far cry from the chaos of upended floes north of Canada.

With the Admiralty's blessing, Parry ordered two specialized vessels from the Woolwich Naval Dockyard. These were flat-bottomed "troop boats," twenty feet by seven feet, framed with hickory and ash as lightly as possible: Ribs only an inch square were set one foot apart. Mr. Lang, Woolwich's master shipwright, devised a system of elastic planking—a sandwich of oak and fir was separated by felt and lined with a coat of pitch and Macintosh Cloth. (Charles Macintosh, a Scottish chemist, had first patented his celebrated waterproof canvas in 1823.) Parry's flexible boats were designed as amphibians with metal-shod runners, to which were attached horsehair ropes. (Horsehair cordage will not absorb water and hence stays lighter.) The explorers could either paddle through water or drag over the ice. A third motive option employed detachable wheels five feet in diameter mounted port and starboard amidships, converting Parry's troop boats into vehicles akin to the invalid chairs of his birthplace. They were christened *Enterprise* and *Endeavor*.

In April 1827, Parry's North Pole Expedition sailed from the Nore on HMS *Hecla*. First port of call was Hammerfest, where eighteen reindeer and bales of moss fodder were embarked. Parry hoped to replace sailors with beasts of burden. A month later, *Hecla* was maneuvered into a summer anchorage on Spitsbergen's northern coast.

Enterprise and *Endeavor* were lowered onto the ice for a disappointing test run. They would not roll on the wheels, nor could reindeer drag them on runners. (Santa's legendary octet notwithstanding, reindeer make poor teams: Lapps use them singly, never in tandem.) The reindeer were relegated to ice-hauling chores around the ship. Even dragged by fourteen bluejackets, the troop boats moved at a snail's pace. Parry estimated that he would manage no better than a mile a day.

Weight was the villain. Empty, each hull tipped the scale at 1,539 pounds. Loaded, the weight more than doubled; and at 3,753½ pounds—sledge weights are totaled with scrupulous exactitude—each sailor was pulling 268 pounds. Years later, explorers found that manhauling's optimum load was 200 pounds. It is tempting to conclude that Parry was indulgent with provisions. In fact, he was not. Only a quarter of his 4½ tons of supplies was food, 71 days' rations for 28 men. Each man's daily allowance was 10 ounces of biscuit and 9 of pemmican. (Pemmican is an explorer's staple to this day, a concentrated travel ration that originated with North America's Indians. Lean buffalo meat, sun-dried, was pulverized to a nutritious powder, then mixed with animal fat and preserved in blocks. Sometimes it was leavened with raisins or chocolate.) Parry's pemmican was made of beef, put up by a Mr. J. P. Holmes of Old Fish Street, who had learned the trick while a surgeon with the Hudson's Bay Company. To drink, Parry's men would be issued a daily gill of rum as well as an ounce of cocoa powder supplied by Messrs. Fortnum & Mason. By later standards, Parry's was a lean ration, too lean for the strenuous work he demanded.

They started north at the end of June, sledging by night to avoid snow blindness and sleeping during the comparative warmth of the day. When they stopped each dawn, their boats were parked side by side on the ice, stern to the wind. Paddles standing upright in special slots through the thwart served as a framework for canvas awnings that converted each troop boat into a closed dormitory. After supper, the sailors changed into "camblet sleeping dresses" lined with raccoon skin, and dry socks. Once under their blankets, the entire detachment lit up clay pipes. (Three ounces of tobacco was issued weekly to each man.) The resultant fug dried out the overhead awnings. Pipes extinguished, all hands slept save one, who kept watch for predatory bears or threatening ice conditions. After brewing breakfast cocoa—on a seven-wick stove that burned spirits of wine—he roused both boatloads with a bugle.

Parry encountered a devastating surface. Never once, with but one half-mile exception, did his sweating crews encounter Lutwidge's "smooth, unbroken ice." Often, all twenty-eight men relayed one boat at a time. One night it took two hours to drag the boats 150 yards. Manhandling the heavily laden craft over hummocks was dangerous: Parry's second-in-command, Lieutenant James Ross, who would win an antarctic knighthood a dozen years later, injured his back as one hull lurched downhill, pinning him to the ice.

It poured rain—more, Parry reckoned, than had fallen the last seven summers combined—and his men splashed for miles through freshwater lakes, most too shallow even for the negligible draft of the *Enterprise* and the *Endeavor*. As it turned out, transforming sledge to boat and back to sledge was time-consuming: Each had to be unloaded, launched, reloaded, paddled across, unloaded anew, beached, and reloaded. The rain had rotted the pack's surface into what the sailors christened "penknife ice," ice shards that cut their Eskimo boots to ribbons.

Parry finally called it quits at 82°45′ North. During the final day's march, celestial sightings had indicated negative progress: His men were laboring poleward on a diabolical treadmill that floated south faster than they were traveling north. But a month's incredible effort had not been wasted: Parry had marched through three full degrees of northern latitude—180 nautical miles—a farthest-north record that would stand for half a century. Moreover, Parry's historic polar attempt would establish principles of arctic methodology invaluable to his successors.

First, although committing sailors to the ice on foot made

sense, marching over the open polar sea did not. From that frustrating effort dated future explorers' preoccupation with north-trending coastlines: Though mountainous, crevassed, or larded with impassable glaciers, at least they stayed put.

Second, travel over the pack in high summer was impractical: The ice breaks up or moves or, at best, is corroded by thaw and rain. June, July, and August were prime months for navigation by ship but too late for explorers on foot. Peary—who kept his sledge teams at work throughout the winter months— achieved the north pole in early April, when the ocean ice was more solid.

Third, it was apparent that ice conditions from year to year, even from day to day, were cruelly inconsistent. What Lutwidge had seen eluded Parry fifty-four years later. Spitsbergen ice was no smoother than arctic ice anywhere: The polar traveler's great dilemma was, continually, the appalling surface of ocean ice.

Fourth, small boats—loaded, empty, or runnered—were hopeless. A host of explorers in both arctic and antarctic would learn the same bitter lesson, that boats are cumbersome, unwieldy sledges at best.

Parry's ultimate legacy combined inspired leadership and Royal Navy grit. Despite hardship and short commons, he and his men struggled to a record latitude and back without complaint. Parry was knighted after that final expedition, and his exploits bring us back full circle to young Clements Markham: When he was confined to the Cheam School sanatorium with mumps, it was Sir Edward Parry's memoirs that fired his polar ambition; Parry's son Edward, moreover, was one of his schoolmates.

The roots of the heroic age, then, lie in the imperishable example of Britain's sailors, who set a standard of courage, improvisation, and skill for others to follow. But Franklin's loss unnerved them: Even McClintock's and Hobson's momentous find of 1858 could not rekindle Their Lordships' enthusiasm. Arctic derring-do was put firmly aside. The Royal Geographical Society closed the Franklin chapter in 1860 when they presented a gold medal to his widow for her gallant husband's contribution to the work of the society, of which he had been a founding member. Fifteen years would pass before

Britain's northern finale under Captain George Nares, an expedition thrust to the fore by Clements Markham and the arctic old guard, all of them veterans of the Franklin searches.

In that interim, two American explorers filled the northern vacuum admirably.

2

THE AMERICAN WAY

Let the stately polar bears,
Waltz around the Pole in Pairs
. . . All ye icebergs make salaam,—
You belong to Uncle Sam!

—Bret Harte

Where Greenland rubs shoulders with the Canadian archipelago, an elongated body of water connects Baffin Bay to the Arctic Ocean. During the nineteenth century, this succession of sounds, basins, and channels was called the American way to the pole, a water route protected from the ice that surges southward out of the polar ocean.

It is shaped like a north-pointing wine bottle. Near its hypothetical cork at Robeson Channel, just above 82° North, it is less than twenty nautical miles wide. Just as slitlike windows in castle walls protect occupants from incoming arrows, so Robeson Channel's narrow defile reduces the ice onslaught from the Arctic Ocean.

Since Parry's momentous failure on foot in 1827, the polar game was to force a ship as far north as possible before proceeding via sledge. The American way offered unparalleled advantage in this respect, and early arctic maps reflect it: U.S. Navy hydrographic charts of 1885 offered specific details as high as 83° North, at Greenland, whereas portions of Franz Josef Land, discovered in 1873 by the Austrians, remained cartographical mysteries, their northern shorelines tantalizingly undelineated.

Navigation elsewhere in the Canadian arctic is severely curtailed. West of the American way, in the absence of a protective island screen, the pack is crushed into year-round immobility. McClure Strait, between Melville Island and Banks Island, seems a direct link in the Northwest Passage. But Captain Robert McClure labeled it on his chart: "A Great Water Space in which the Ice appears to have accumulated very much for want of an outlet." Indeed, so devastating is the accumulation that McClure, first to negotiate passage from Pacific to Atlantic, could do so only on foot.

Hence the appeal of the American way. Yet it is a difficult route, no more so than at its broadest. After an easy start through Davis Strait between Canada and Greenland, the American way bulges northward into Baffin Bay. William Baffin first circumnavigated the body of water that bears his name in 1616. By hugging the shore, he avoided the bay's huge, rotating wheel of ice called by his successors Middle Pack, formed by ice discharged from Baffin Bay's four great sounds, Lancaster, Jones, Smith, and Whale.

Different kinds of ice move in contrasting ways: Shallow pack ice responds to wind pressure, whereas icebergs, with most of their bulk under water, travel at the whim of tidal currents. Icebergs sometimes surge directly into the teeth of a gale, smashing through pack ice traveling, wind-impelled, in the opposite direction. Middle Pack is kept rotating counterclockwise by wind and tide working together. Prevailing polar westerlies turn the north end, polar easterlies the south end. Two currents add their own turning moment, the West Greenland Current and the Labrador Current.

Occasionally, Middle Pack would fragment, and bold captains dared sail directly across it. But the safest course was around its perimeter. This conforms with a standard arctic dictum: Northward progress is best accomplished near shore, since open channels—called leads—often appear between fixed shore ice and moving offshore ice. Two forces produce these leads: ebbing tides and, during summer, meltwater running off inland glaciers.

So ships bound up the American way hugged the sweep of Greenland shore from Upernavik to Cape York, sailing through leads along the great ice wheel's northeastern quadrant called Melville Bay. The danger lay in Middle Pack's tendency to conflict with the shore ice, for moving pack to grind against fixed pack like gargantuan millstones, the closing ice shearing through hulls like a hot knife through butter. One whaler was once completely sliced through at the waterline, her planking embedded in ice jaws below while the balance of the ship, apparently unscathed, remained on top of the ice. This epic destruction, away from protective headland or inlet, was commonplace. Between 1820 and 1850 a total of 210 whale ships came to grief in Melville Bay.

Yet, despite the toll, a line of whalers could be found every spring, waiting for a lead to open at the entrance from the south. Small wonder that arctic sailors traditionally doffed their caps in superstitious respect within sight of Devil's Thumb, a towering pinnacle that marks the entrance to the notorious bay.

Passage past Cape York—Melville Bay's western exit—gave entry into the northern water, an ice-free (in summertime) region above the Middle Pack. This geographical paradox—unobstructed water after fearsome ice—lulled early explorers into optimistic expectations about the nature of the trio of Baffin Bay sounds ahead: Lancaster Sound, to the west, offered access to the Northwest Passage; Jones Sound was merely an ice-choked cul-de-sac; and Smith Sound, due north, led to the pole. Its narrow entrance is bounded by Capes Isabella and Alexander.

Another Englishman, Captain Edward Inglefield, ventured into Smith Sound briefly in 1852 on board the *Isabel*, chartered by Lady Franklin. Inglefield, a reputable naval captain and talented artist, sailed for one day only across the threshold of what he believed to be the "polar basin." He found the waters free of ice, and his elaborate sketch of what he saw before autumn gales drove him south convinced him—as well as a host of others—that Melville Bay's ice was merely a prelude to extensive open seas.

It was the last British incursion into that "polar basin" for two decades. But there would be an American presence instead. Although Captain Inglefield hoped to return to Smith Sound the following summer, he was beaten to the draw by the United States' first arctic explorer. Inglefield's "polar basin" is called today Kane Basin after a redoubtable Philadelphian, Dr. Elisha Kent Kane.

He had been born in 1820, the eldest of seven children of an eminent lawyer. Young Kane was, most notably, fearless, tackling bullies or even gangs of bullies in single combat. He also relished clambering at night among chimneys, derring-do in the tradition of Midshipman Markham's Peruvian high jinks. At sixteen, Kane entered the University of Virginia to train as a civil engineer. His studies were disrupted by attacks of rheumatic fever, a recurring malady that would dog him for life. The prognosis was bleak: "You may fall, Elisha," cautioned the doctor to his eighteen-year-old patient, "as suddenly as a musket shot." His father urged: "Elisha, if you must die, die in the harness."

Kane's self-imposed "harness" was unremitting. Turning from engineering to medicine, he was apprenticed to a Philadelphia surgeon. After Kane obtained his degree in 1841, his father entered him for the post of assistant surgeon with the Navy. Awaiting his first assignment, young Dr. Kane circled the globe, serving in Macao, the Philippines, and Egypt. The breakneck pace of his life was firmly established; never once did he submit to infirmity. He ended a tour of African duty invalided home with malaria. Once recuperated, he was wounded with the marines in Mexico before returning to Philadelphia with typhus.

Kane contracted a common, worldwide affliction, Franklin fever, spread to America by Sir John's resourceful widow. Lady Franklin directed her appeals to the White House in 1849. President Zachary Taylor's first response was lukewarm, a promise of American prayers and an assurance that arctic whalers would keep a lookout for Sir John. (Since every arctic hand knew that Parliament offered a twenty-thousand-pound reward for Franklin's rescue, this last presidential directive seems patently redundant.) But in January of the following year, the president asked Congress for an appropriation for an American relief expedition. A New York shipping merchant, Henry Grinnell, offered the government two of his ships, the strengthened brigs *Advance* and *Rescue*. His offer was a measure of popular response to Lady Franklin's plea. Congress was, in effect, shamed into action.

By May 1850, a resolution passed both houses authorizing Navy personnel to man both donated vessels. Unfortunately, Grinnell's generosity established a crippling precedent for

America's arctic explorers: all of them—Kane, Hall, De Long, Greely, and Peary—would rely largely on the private sector. Washington traditionally provided scant support. The United States seemed more preoccupied with westward expansion than northern exploration.

The two vessels sailed that same month. In command was Lieutenant Edwin De Haven, later to be christened "Mad Yankee" by admiring Royal Navy colleagues in the North. The only thing he resented about his command was the diminutive, sickly doctor assigned to the *Advance* as surgeon. It was, of course, Elisha Kent Kane. En route to Greenland, Kane seemed so frail that De Haven asked him to resign; predictably he refused, and his captain never had reason to regret it.

Passage across Melville Bay was infuriatingly slow. Between July 14 and 15 Kane recorded: "The American expedition advances half a ship's length." The two vessels were often warped or heaved through the ice. One end of a hawser, attached to an ice anchor, was buried far ahead and the onboard end taken up on the ship's windlass, forcing the bow into a crack in the ice that would suddenly, miraculously part, "twenty acres of ice" moving silently aside. But if a gale blew up, icebergs posed serious danger: Kane described one as "a mass as large as the Parthenon bearing down on you before a storm wind."

The Canadian arctic was crowded with ships that summer, for 1850 marked the peak year of what the Admiralty called the Franklin Sea Search. The Americans joined ten British vessels. In addition to this sizable Royal Navy fleet, Lady Franklin had her own ships in the field, including the schooner *Felix*, under Sir John Ross. Kane visited the *Felix* and was struck by how well the Britishers were disposed, physically and emotionally, for the rigors of the polar winter. *Felix*, *Resolute*, and *Assistance*, as well as the American *Advance* and *Rescue*, were all in on the momentous find of Franklin's first winter encampment on Beechey Island.

But no further discoveries were made. In September both American ships were beset and nine months passed drifting aimlessly down Lancaster Sound and out into Baffin Bay. Over that harrowing winter, Kane learned to cope with scurvy, cold, and confinement, an invaluable arctic primer that would serve him well three years hence. Amazingly enough, his health flourished in the arctic: An absence of cold germs kept his rheumatic fever at bay. The American flotilla returned to New York at the end of September 1851, having been away for sixteen months.

Back in Philadelphia, Kane prepared the expedition's history. But he was, at best, a distracted author. In between bouts of writing, he agitated for another rescue effort. The fate of Franklin's men obsessed him: "I think of them ever with hope. I sicken not to be able to reach them." He was convinced that some of them—by then, seven years vanished—clung to life somewhere in unexplored Smith Sound.

He approached Grinnell again, asking for the use of the *Advance*, promising to serve in any capacity. "My dignity will not suffer," he begged, "if I go as cook." But Grinnell, although willing to part with the *Advance*, argued that the government should be the sponsor. He also proposed that Kane assume command himself. Kane did so, successfully petitioning Secretary of the Navy John Kennedy for support: ". . . that the same reasons which prompted one attempt, are in force as to a second."

Kane had hoped that his Second U.S. Grinnell Expedition would sail in 1852. But fund-raising, writing chores, and the glacial pace of Washington's bureaucracy made it impossible. His timetable was further disrupted by the death of his fifteen-year-old brother, Little Willie. So upsetting was his loss that Rensselaer, the Kanes' new suburban house, was sold; none of the family could bear to stay there.

Not until December 1852 did Secretary Kennedy authorize ten naval personnel for the *Advance*. The ship was victualed at the Brooklyn Navy Yard, her holds stocked with salted pork and beef "of the Navy Ration." From Texas came a new invention, Borden's Meat Powder Biscuits, which had been tested as convict fare aboard the prison hulk *Tenedos* in Bermuda and pronounced admirable by Royal Navy surgeons. Once more confined to bed by illness, Kane fretted about the cost of pemmican: "If we could procure a malt-kiln for a single week, I would undertake the matter."

By spring the *Advance* sailed north, a framed portrait of Sir John Franklin hung in her tiny wardroom. In fragile health, Kane spent his time on deck during the day in a specially built bunk shrouded in buffalo robes. He was terrified that Inglefield and the *Isabel* would preempt him at Smith Sound, for the

Isabel was propellered while the *Advance* was not. But, in fact, Inglefield was in command of the storeship *Phoenix* that summer, sailing with Edward Belcher's squadron in Lancaster Sound. Kane would have Smith Sound to himself.

The *Advance's* seventeen-man crew were a mixed lot; Kane recalled that "the men had been shipped from the ordinary class of sailors in port." This kind of potluck impressment was ill-advised for polar exploration. Finding a good crew for any voyage was difficult; recruiting for the arctic required the most scrupulous selection. Lieutenant George Washington De Long, an American explorer to follow, suggested picking a crew thus:

> Single men, perfect health, considerable strength, perfect temperance, cheerfulness, ability to read and write English, prime seamen, of course. . . .

Then ethnic selectivity took over:

> . . . Norwegians, Swedes, and Danes preferred. Avoid English, Scotch, and Irish. Refuse point-blank French, Italian, and Spaniards. . . .

Few of Kane's enlisted men fitted De Long's esoteric profile, and some of them ranked low on his table of national preferences: Pierre Schubert, the cook, was French. Carl Petersen and carpenter Christian Olsen were Danish sailors who boasted prior northern experience. But old arctic hands can sometimes be destructive, and both were as scornful of Kane's inexperience as they were frightened by his daring. Kane's intemperate Yankee zeal led him to push recklessly north into the ice.

Crewmen on board the *Advance* were subject to only three regulations: total subordination, no intoxication, and no profanity. "We had no other rules," recorded Kane simply. Distaste for the fo'c'sle's fluent vulgarity seems to have been an expedition constant in either hemisphere from any century. Clause 12 on board Sir Hugh Willoughby's ships attempting the Northeast Passage in 1533 read:

> Item, that no blaspheming of God, or detestable swearing be used in any ship, nor communication of ribaldrie, filthy tales, or ungodly talks to be suffred [*sic*] in the company of any ship.

In 1901, Edward Wilson, Scott's surgeon on board the *Discovery*, wrote disdainfully after examining the men for scurvy:

> There is no sign of it in any one, as far as I can see. The gums of many are red and swollen, but it is the redness and swelling of slight inflammation, rather than scurvy congestion and to my mind is to be attributed to clay pipes, strong tobacco, coarse feeding, neglect of the tooth brush and *the constant use of foul language.* [Italics mine.]

Commander John Ross, wintering in on board the *Victory* in 1830, so flooded the messdeck with "sermons, prayers, and tracts" that his crew, *he* claimed, relinquished swearing completely.

Insubordination proved a recurring problem. Seaman John Blake—neither Frenchman, Italian, nor Spaniard—was a chronic troublemaker who refused to obey orders and once threatened to kill the expedition's dogs. Kane had him tied hand and foot and, together with another troublemaker, confined on deck in the latticed booby hatch, fed only on bread and water. After four days, they were released because, according to Kane, they "promised to be good boys."

Melville Bay was negotiated and, on August 6, 1853, came the momentous day: Kane sailed through the northern pillars of Hercules, Capes Isabella and Alexander, into Smith Sound. Grim, thousand-foot headlands loomed over the little *Advance*. But there was no "open polar sea." For more than a month, Kane battled his way up Greenland's coast through tremendous ice obstacles. More than once, Kane ordered his ship's spars turned fore and aft so the schooner could slip through canyons of floating ice. Men went over the side and, "toggled to the warp," pulled the *Advance* north with tow ropes tied to canvas slings across their chests. (Kane's people called these "rue-raddies," a term for the British harness never used elsewhere.)

At 78°38' North, Kane stopped for the winter in a protected harbor he called Rensselaer Bay. No ship had ever wintered that far north.

Preparations for spring exploration began at once. Sledge

parties continued up the coast; instead of dragging a 140-ton schooner, their rue-raddies were tied to a broad-runnered British Admiralty–model sledge called *The Faith*. Kane was laying depots northward along the Greenland *eis-fod* or icefoot, a negotiable shore path adhering to the land safely above the motion of the sea ice. Sixty miles north they were stopped by the margin of an enormous glacier that Kane named after the geographer Humboldt.

On shorter outings, Kane preferred a dashing hickory sledge, which he christened, sentimentally, *Little Willie*. Drawn by four dogs, it ran circles around the heavier *Faith*. However, its use that autumn was curtailed following a rash of fatal illness among the dogs. Kane diagnosed it first as epilepsy, later terming it "arctic cholera." It was a canine epidemic only too familiar to many expeditions: restlessness, frothing at the mouth, convulsions, erratic hither and yons, and then lockjaw and death, the helpless animal torn to pieces by the rest of the pack. The Eskimos called it *piblokto*. Kane's dog, Tiger, succumbed the following winter: "He ran into the water and drowned himself like a sailor with the horrors." All but six of Kane's dogs died that first fall.

But the ship's rat population throve. Extermination proved ineffectual. Brimstone, leather, and arsenic were ignited 'tween decks; the ship's crew slept on the ice while poisonous fumes permeated their cabins. The rats flourished apace. Sterner measures were employed: Four glowing charcoal braziers were distributed belowdecks, and every hatch and companionway was sealed with oakum. Schubert, conscientious cook that he was, slipped below to season his soup and was felled by carbon monoxide; he was rescued in the nick of time. Then one of the braziers set the planking beneath it alight. The fire was extinguished promptly with seawater lifted up by bucket brigade from the "fire hole," chopped open daily, a sine qua non of every arctic ship wintering over.

Kane finally called it quits and learned to live with his invincible rodents. In fact, rations were so short the following winter that rats became invaluable additions to his menu. Kane called them arctic deer and, alone on board, devoured them without a qualm. An entry from the *Advance*'s log in December 1853 offers a glimpse of catering on board:

December 5th, 1853: Health of brig improving. Scurvy cases better. Dr Kane scorbutic and rheumatic. Commenced eating puppies.

Kane's genius as an explorer lay in his talent for borrowing from both Eskimos and Royal Navy alike. That first winter on board, he followed Ross's example on the *Felix*: The *Advance* was overdecked with canvas, and a program of regular exercise was instituted. He published a ship's newspaper, *The Ice Blink*, and staged theatricals to divert the crew. (With a ship's complement of eighteen, it is a wonder that there were players and spectators enough to go around.)

Relations with the local Eskimos started badly. A vociferous deputation had visited the *Advance* before winter set in, scornful that the Americans had embarked on so ambitious a journey without their wives. The Eskimos stole almost everything they could lift. Kane dispatched a posse to their camp and kidnapped a brace of ladies for ransom: The stolen goods were returned, and peace reigned.

It was a profitable truce. Kane learned much from his involuntary neighbors and soon was kitted out in their full winter regalia. Next to his skin he wore a shirt made from the breasts of five hundred tiny auks, the down turned inward. Over this he donned a *kapetah* or foxskin jumper, topped by a sealskin hooded jacket called a *nessak*. Sensibly button-free, the *nessak* was pulled over the head and exists to this day as the parka. Kane wore bearskin breeches—*nannooke*—which, in the local fashion, were cut low over the hips. Eskimos seem impervious to cold in the groin and small of the back: Although otherwise admirable for retaining body warmth, the Eskimo *nessak* gaps from *nannooke* whenever the wearer bends over. Kane amended this shortcoming with an additional waistband.

Fur clothing has one disadvantage: It is almost too efficient. Running behind or pulling a sledge, let alone manhandling it over hummocky terrain, is hot, sticky work. Kane put it succinctly: "sweating along at eight miles an hour." For this reason, many explorers preferred the relative perviousness of wool. Perspiration will work its way through layers of wool and can be brushed off as hoarfrost. Sealskin retains the moisture and becomes hard as iron. The Eskimos countered this by sleeping naked under animal skins while their furs dried overnight in the heat of the blubber lamp. But explorers, who used drafty tents rather than igloos, slept in their clothes and thus found wool a perennial favorite. But woolen nap collects an inordinate amount of blown ice or snow crystals; a smooth outer cloth is essential. After the turn of the century, an English draper, Thomas Burberry, perfected a lightweight, closely woven fabric that repelled damp while admitting air. Burberry christened his invention gabardine, after the Jewish cloak of the same name, but Edward VII's habit of calling impetuously for "my Burberry" passed the maker's name into legend. Nansen, Scott, Shackleton, and Amundsen all swore by Burberry gabardine windproofs; Amundsen even had his tents made of the stuff.

Kane's penchant for warm clothing apparently stopped short of the feet. His men's boots and moccasins were woefully inadequate, and frostbite, even more than scurvy, quite literally crippled them. Half a party of eight on a mid-March sledging excursion were so incapacitated by frostbitten feet that their four companions left them in a tent and returned for aid to the *Advance*. Kane himself led a rescue mission and, under conditions of the most appalling hardship, brought them back to the ship. Two of the four invalids died from the gangrenous aftereffects.

During the summer of 1854, his second in the ice-locked bay, Kane replenished his depleted kennels by judicious barter with the Eskimos. Thus reequipped, he implemented a scheme of fast, lightweight sledging. Dogs draw sledges in two configurations: spread in a fan or in an extended line, single or double file, known as the tandem hitch. The Greenland Eskimos favored the former, each dog attached with a long sealskin trace called an *atlunak:* these were cut from a seal's corpse in spiral strips for maximum length. Then women chewed, greased, and seasoned them in the arctic sun.

Explorers favored the tandem hitch for a variety of reasons: One man could blaze a trail ahead of the team, and dogs in line did not tangle the traces so badly. Spread in a fan, Eskimo dogs often changed lanes, vaulting into the midst of the pack out of whip range, weaving the traces into Gordian knots every few miles. Unraveling these meant periodic agony with bare hands. Men would often cut rather than sort out the tangle, retying the severed ends. This shortened the traces so that dogs ultimately ran with the sledge on their heels. Dr. Isaac Hayes, the *Advance*'s surgeon, once cut his traces so short that he was reduced to pirating strips of sealskin from his jacket to supply the missing footage.

Kane streamlined his loads as well, taking his cue once more from the Eskimos. His sledgers carried only a tent, a fur sleeping bag, pemmican, and a portable stove. This was logistical pioneering—fast, dog-drawn sledges carrying a minimum of impedimenta, the gospel Peary would preach decades later. Kane's two separate sledge trips were highly successful, exploring both western and eastern shores of the Kane Basin.

Surgeon Hayes and crewman William Godfrey left the *Advance* in May 1854 and, crossing the frozen basin, landed on the Canadian shore for the first time. They called it Grinnell Land in honor of their patron. Miles of new coastline were explored in a fruitless search for signs of Franklin. Returning home, they outlasted their pemmican and, for the last seventy miles, subsisted on sealskin slivers cut from their clothing. They clambered aboard ravenous and nearly blind from the glare.

Along the eastern shore, another two-man expedition set Kane's northern record. One of the two was an Eskimo, Hans Hendrik, who would sail later with Hall and Nares. The second man was William Morton, the *Advance*'s steward-cum-yeoman. Kane remained with the sick, selecting Morton to go in his place: "He is my last throw." It was a good choice. The two men raced up the coast. Resupplying from pemmican cache number 3, set out the previous autumn, they circumvented the Humboldt Glacier by detouring out over the frozen basin at its foot. They nearly lost their way, for the route lay through an icebound flotilla of icebergs recently calved from the glacier, so densely packed that passage between them was a labyrinthian nightmare. Morton and Hendrik coaxed their terrified dogs through a maze of echoing, icy clefts before emerging at the northern limit. Farther up the virgin coast, they named successively Capes Clay, Jackson, Madison, and Jefferson. Across Lafayette Bay, their icefoot road petered out. Morton called that final eminence Cape Kane; Kane would rename it Cape Constitution. From its summit, for as far as the explorers could see, the waters of a narrow, north-trending offshoot of Kane Basin were completely free of ice. Breakers thundered onto the cliffs at their feet. Morton was convinced that he had found his chief's "open polar sea." That terminal camp lay 33' north of 80°; shy of Parry's record, it was an American farthest north.

They arrived back at the *Advance* in time for an ugly crisis. August had passed and it was apparent that the expedition would have to spend a second winter frozen into Rensselaer Harbor. Eight of the crew, led by Hayes, the surgeon—including Petersen and Olsen, the Danish malcontents—decided to walk south, leaving Kane and the invalids to make the best of it. Their departure—save for Olsen, who changed his mind at the last minute—dramatizes a vital issue facing leaders of expeditions in jeopardy: If survival is at stake, should a portion of the command—of necessity, the strongest—abandon those either unwilling or unable to face the trek? A small number going for help would not have been unusual. But the deserters constituted half the ship's complement, the healthier half at that. Their departure was less a quest for assistance than a disgraceful *sauve-qui-peut*.

But in December the dissidents were back, starving and crippled, rescued by the Eskimos. Privately gratified at their failure, Kane was magnanimous in welcoming them back on board. This unsavory episode, unique in polar exploration, points up the desperation of hungry, frightened men and the alarming state of discipline on board the *Advance:* Hayes's dereliction was matched by Kane's apparent inability to prevent his departure.

Kane set about preparing for his second winter. The ship's belowdecks were reworked into a single cabin for all hands—a huge igloo—insulated all around. Forage parties were sent to gather arctic greenery: Even the sickest men labored with crowbars, prying clumps of grass, heather, and willow from neighboring rocks. Once the cabin had been lined with moss, the floor was caulked and covered with two inches of oakum, then carpeted over with canvas. A low tunneled entrance was contrived, inspired by the Eskimos' snowhouse doorway, to conserve heat. Kane improvised, in fact, an identical scheme of shipboard insulation that Nansen would perfect forty years later.

Save for the critical central chamber, the rest of the *Advance* was written off. Coal was exhausted, so Kane charged Olsen, the ship's carpenter, to cut away all that could conceivably be spared from the vessel against its possible extrication in the spring. Spars, railings, bulkheads, writing desks—even portions of the greenheart sheathing—were cut and stacked, to be fed into the stove, which was to be kept alight only during waking hours.

Bunked together in Kane's 'tweendeck "dormitorium," sixteen men would survive a harrowing winter. Rations were tight, fresh meat a rarity. A few bears were killed, but game grew progressively scarce: Hans Hendrik, their champion hunter, managed only a few rabbits before he decamped back to his own people. The huddled, shivering men of the *Advance* survived on a starvation diet: breakfast coffee, sweetened with molasses, was three parts beans to one of grounds; at midday, biscuits were spread with fat rendered from salted beef; stewed apples comprised their entire evening meal. All but five men had scurvy. Kane—the only one who would eat rats—was the fittest of the lot, turnabout for a chronic invalid.

He was determined to break out in the spring. If the *Advance* were not freed, he would sledge to the ice margin and sail south to civilization. The long winter days were passed in methodical preparation. Olsen fabricated a trio of special sledges, each designed to carry a ship's boat, which, in turn, would contain supplies and invalids. Kane galvanized the sick into a tailoring cooperative. To replace worn-out boots, Belgian carpeting and the ship's leather chafing gear were fashioned into uppers, stitched to sealskin soles. Wool curtains were quilted with eiderdown and fashioned into jackets. Canvas provision bags, fitted to the boats' bilges, were made watertight with paste and flour. Sailcloth bread bags were double-walled, interlined with pitch, then roped and becketed on the outside. New cookers were hammered out of stovepipe sections. And empty food cans, with handles braised on, served as mugs.

The ice still held them fast in the spring. Kane's choice of anchorage had been too wise: Throughout two winters, the *Advance* was never threatened by ice movement but was permanently imprisoned as a consequence. Kane had to sledge out for his pains. So the little brig was abandoned in May 1855. Ship's company assembled on deck, Kane read a prayer—written by a New York bishop two years earlier—and the agonizing trek began. The last item removed from the derelict hull was Franklin's portrait, cut from its frame and rolled beneath Kane's jacket.

Two decades later, Austrian polar explorer Julius von Payer was to recall his efforts while quitting the doomed *Tegetthoff* near accidentally discovered Franz Josef Land in 1874:

> . . . After the lapse of two months of indescribable effort, the distance between us and the ship was not more than nine English miles. . . .

Kane's first day seemed like a gloomy preview of von Payer's experience. Three of the *Advance*'s strongest men hacked a trail over twenty-foot pressure ridges while their shipmates, rueraddies cutting into emaciated shoulders, dragged the boat in their wake, provisions belowthwarts, invalids above. By nightfall they had relayed the boats only a mile from the *Advance*. While his crews sweated at the ropes, Kane and the dog-drawn *Little Willie* scouted ahead through the mist, depoting provisions in the path of his projected advance.

Sometimes they converted their hybrid craft into iceboats, bending on sail and skimming over blessed smooth patches. Steering was erratic, and the windblown boats often dug their bows into snowbanks. Extricating them necessitated massive exertion, so much so that Olsen died from the strain. His sorrowful companions buried him in the bedrock of Littleton Island.

The ice extended eighty miles southwest of the *Advance*, but circuitous detours more than doubled their journey. After two hundred weary miles, the thunder of surf gave promise of open water, the first those haggard sailors had seen for two years. But so chaotic were sea conditions at the ice margin that Kane had to order a retreat, back onto the pack that he so fervently wished to quit. When his men finally clambered aboard their boats, during one waterborne day they covered the same distance it had taken them a month to achieve on foot.

Once clear of Smith Sound, they hugged the Greenland shore, navigating a reciprocal, eastbound course through notorious Melville Bay. Wildlife was plentiful. On Dallrymple Rock nested a colony of eider ducks so spectacularly fecund that the explorers were surfeited with eggs, eaten raw because of a critical fuel shortage; Kane issued a rum ration, and his men toasted their commander with fiery eggnog. The *Little Dinghy*, slowest of their three craft, was broken up and burned, a rotisserie for dozens of birds. Accommodated in small boats, Kane's shipwrecked command negotiated Melville Bay far more safely than they had on board the *Advance:* Threatening ice could be dodged with ease, running for shore or hauling boats out onto the ice before they could be nipped.

On August 4 they were picked up by a Danish trading vessel, and their eighty-six-day rout ended at Upernavik. In the absence of the governor, subordinates were unable to succor the American castaways, such were the ironclad regulations of Denmark's colonial bureaucracy. No one but the absent governor could issue from public stores. Food, clothing, and bedding were withheld until His Excellency's return.

Although he found no traces of Franklin, Kane's record was exemplary. He had explored a third of the American way, reached a farthest north, and brought out his command and scientific results. He had perfected techniques of travel, clothing, and survival, invaluable additions to arctic lore; Peary's debt to Kane would be immense. Marred only by Hayes's mutinous desertion, Kane's leadership was enviable, at times inspired: Perfect discipline had been maintained throughout the retreat from Rensselaer Bay.

Sadly, he explored no more: Within two years of his triumphal reception in New York, Elisha Kent Kane was dead at thirty-seven, struck down by the rheumatic fever that had plagued him for half his life. He completed an account of the expedition, although the labor of producing nine hundred pages in six months initiated what turned out to be his final malaise: "The book, poor as it is, has been my coffin." (Poor it was not: Kane's account of the Second U.S. Grinnell Expedition was one of the great moneymakers of all nineteenth-century polar memoirs.)

Weakened by New York's summer heat wave of 1856, Kane sailed for London. The Royal Geographical Society awarded him their Founder's Medal, and Lady Franklin insisted that he take command of a search expedition on her behalf. Stricken anew by London's cold, Kane dismissed her entreaties out of hand, and McClintock would assume command of the *Fox* the following summer. Failing, Kane sailed for Cuba and the warmth of the tropics. He died in Havana on February 16, 1857, with William Morton, his faithful steward from the *Advance*, at his side. His funeral was national in scope, a reflection of the respect his name inspired. Once disembarked at New Orleans, Kane's coffin lay in solemn state there and in three other cities—Louisville, Cincinnati, and Columbus—before reaching Philadelphia, where America's first polar explorer was laid to rest.

The ice-free channel that Morton and Hendrik had seen from Cape Constitution extends over the northern horizon for eighty miles before ballooning into a second great basin, which would be named by Kane's immediate successor, Charles Francis Hall. It was he who extended Kane's penetration of the American way; but he died at his farthest north and so never enjoyed the kudos of his countrymen. Hall was as enigmatic as his death—certainly the most unconventional of America's arctic fraternity. His arctic impetus sprang from a familiar, mystical obsession. Only one reason sufficed for a successful publisher to abandon business, home, and family for three hazardous journeys—two among King William Land Eskimos and his last on the polar ocean: the compelling lure of the lost men of Sir John Franklin.

Hall was a year younger than Kane, born in 1821. Hall grew up in northern New England, apprenticed to a blacksmith. He married and drifted west, as far as Cincinnati, where he found work with an engraver. Within two years, the quondam blacksmith/engraver was peddling an irregular broadside in the streets of Cincinnati called, appropriately, *The Occasional*. There followed a more ambitious publication, *The Daily Press*, which achieved a respectable circulation as well as a respectable reputation for its publisher.

Enter Lady Franklin. Hall's arrival in Cincinnati in 1849 had coincided with news of Grinnell's first relief expedition. By the time Kane's funeral cortege wound its way through the Midwest—Hall was doubtless among the Cincinnati mourners—her mission held the publisher in hopeless thrall. Once McClintock and the *Fox* had returned to England with the contents of the cairn on Point Victory, Hall was off and running. He sold the paper, obtained funding from Henry Grinnell—a recurring touchstone for both of America's arctic pioneers—and sailed north. He sailed cheaply, hitching rides on northbound whalers and living among the Eskimos. Along King William Land's western coast, killing ground for Franklin's castaways, he recovered some 150 relics. Franklin's people had carried impossible burdens: The *Erebus* and *Terror* survivors had trudged to their death encumbered by useless silver and books.

Hall was condemned to these amateur, one-man expeditions because of the Civil War, during which there was scant federal concern for arctic exploration. Hall lived from hand to mouth—borrowing, writing, and lecturing. He had brought an Eskimo couple south with him—Ebierbing and Tookoolito, patronizingly renamed Joe and Hannah by the whalers—and Hall kept body and soul together for years by exhibiting them in full Eskimo regalia as part of his "Lecture on Life Among the Esquimaux."

It was not until midsummer of 1870 that Hall obtained government backing—fifty thousand dollars—for a proper expedition of his own. He had a new objective as well. Just before his departure, Lady Franklin, then an old woman on an American tour, met with him in Cincinnati; but by then, Hall's infatuation with her husband's fate had been superseded by the conviction that he could reach the pole.

He was given the *Periwinkle*, a Navy tug of 387 tons, which was rechristened the *Polaris* and refitted at Washington's navy yard. She was rigged as a foretop-sail schooner and boasted a single funnel between her two masts. Equipped for the ice, she carried a lifesaving canister buoy topped by an electric beacon, sophisticated hardware for the times. But the expedition was top-heavy with scientific demands from its federal sponsor. No longer a solo traveler, Hall seemed swamped in organizing this first, formal undertaking. There was also a problem with his shipmates as, yet again, an American polar effort was plagued by aberrant personnel.

The *Polaris* was to be manned by a crew of common sailors subject to Navy regulations; she would carry, in addition, a trio of scientists. The scientists' qualifications, professionally impeccable, fell woefully short of the mark in terms of congeniality. Dr. Emil Bessels, chief scientist, was an intense, bearded medico from Heidelberg. However distinguished as an academic, he was temperamentally unsuited for the arctic. Both Bessels and Sergeant Frederick Meyers, the expedition's meteorologist, were German, as were three quarters of the fo'c'sle.

The seamen were unreliable: Four jumped ship in Brooklyn and had to be replaced in New London. Among the new recruits was William Jackson, a black cook, the first of his race to serve in the arctic. There was a happier link with Kane: William Morton signed on as second mate and, at Disko, Hans Hendrik and his family came on board, joining Ebierbing and Tookoolito, who traveled as Hall's servants.

Even the vessel's master was to prove a liability. Captain Sidney O. Budington, a respected New London whaler, had been the man under whom Hall had served his arctic apprenticeship ten years earlier. But in the interim, the captain had become a secret drinker. He would indulge his addiction by raiding the ship's supply of medicinal spirits, kept under lock and key by teetotaling Hall. Budington's alcoholism destroyed his command responsibility: He cared little for Hall, the pole, or his crew, openly slandering his commander. Whereas a loyal captain could have bridged the gulf between commander and dissident scientists, the lamentable Budington served instead as a third, conflicting party. By the time the ship reached Disko Harbor, the hostility between Hall and Bessels necessitated Captain Davenport of the accompanying naval supply ship *Congress* rebuking the scientists like so many errant schoolboys, hardly an auspicious send-off.

Apart from Morton, the most reliable officer on board seems to have been George Tyson, assistant navigating officer. Tyson had had years of whaling experience and knew shipboard vibrations uncommonly well. Only days out of New York, he had penciled in his diary:

> I see there is not perfect harmony between Captain Hall
> and the scientific corps, nor with some others either. I
> am afraid things will not work out well.

That last sentence might have been the epitaph of the expedition.

Hall set his course northward through what Kane had called Kennedy Channel, entered Hall Basin, and then passed through Robeson Channel, sandwiching his name between those of two U.S. secretaries of the Navy. Miraculously, those northern waters were free of ice, a deceptive state of affairs from which Greely would profit a decade later. Unobstructed, the *Polaris* steamed boldly into the polar ocean—Hall called it the Lincoln Sea—the first ship in history to do so, achieving, on August 30, 1871, a northing of 82°11′, only thirty-four miles short of Parry's ancient record.

But such abnormal accessibility could not last. Within days, blizzards and a merciless current drove the little tug southward. Budington finally took refuge in a winter anchorage along Greenland's coast. Hall called it Thank God Harbor, the arctic's most expressive cognomen. The *Polaris* was moored in the lee of a huge, grounded iceberg named Providence.

Six weeks later, act one of Tyson's gloomy prognosis was played out. Charles Francis Hall succumbed to a mysterious, violent illness that some, to this day, believe to have been purposely inflicted. Chauncey Loomis, Hall's biographer, has attempted to solve the mystery by forensic science. He flew to Thank God Harbor in the summer of 1968 in company with Dr. Franklin Paddock to exhume Hall's remains. The grave, marked with a bronze plaque left by Nares in 1876, was still intact. Loomis opened the coffin to reveal Hall's body, shrouded in the Stars and Stripes; the flag's blue dye had imparted to the bearded features a bizarre maritime hue. Apart from his projecting stockinged feet, Hall's lower extremities were encased in ice. But his upper torso was accessible. Working awkwardly, stooped over the open grave, Paddock made an incision, only to find that Hall's internal organs had long since been absorbed into the abdominal wall. But a lock of hair and one fingernail were returned to the States for analysis. The tests proved overwhelmingly positive: Hall had ingested fatal quantities of arsenic just before death. Since his first symptoms appeared following a restorative *après*-sledging mug of coffee, a presumption of murder is tempting. However, the Victorian pharmacopoeia leaned heavily on controlled arsenic dosage, so Loomis's discovery is tantalizingly inconclusive. Hall could have been poisoned or could have died, inadvertently, by his own doing. A Navy Board of Inquiry had never fixed any blame other than natural causes.

Both Bessels and Budington were heard to remark that Hall's death did not distress them at all. However, it very clearly distressed the remainder of the crew. Hall's presence had ensured a sense of cohesion and purpose on board; with his passing, everything deteriorated. Seaman Gustavus Lindquist would testify in Washington: ". . . We put discipline along with him in his grave." Captain Budington's supreme inadequacy that winter, apart from his drunkenness—which spread like a plague throughout the wardroom—was ignoring the crew's morale. Conventional shipboard routines were curtailed and Sunday's divine services discontinued a month after Hall's funeral. Admittedly, the late commander had been overbearingly pious to the point of irritation; but Budington's suspension of formal worship over Thanksgiving and Christmas seems unfeeling. In fact, the master seemed intent on discouraging organized activity of any kind. One can poke fun at the Royal Navy's preoccupation with winter theatricals, but it was the absence of this indulgent concern that led to a destructive torpor on board *Polaris*. Abrasive personality conflicts intensified. Nathaniel Coffin, the ship's carpenter, retreated into a state of severe paranoia, terrified that someone was intent on murdering him. Tyson confided on paper just before that first Christmas:

> Nothing occurring that is pleasant or profitable to record. I wish I could blot out of my memory some things which I see and hear. Captain Hall did not always act with the clearest judgment but it *was heaven to this*.

Even their anchorage was in jeopardy. A gale had driven the *Polaris* onto an underwater spur of the Providence berg, and her timbers were wrenched and strained with each ebb and flow of Thank God Harbor's tide. So disconcerting had been the racking of the hull that the entire Eskimo contingent camped on shore. Later, Hans's wife, Merkut, gave birth to a son, the only positive episode of that dreary summer. He was christened Charles Polaris, after the late commander and his ship.

A halfhearted attempt to sail poleward in the ship's boats was made in August but aborted when Budington managed to work his weakened ship free of the ice. The party was hastily recalled, and the *Polaris* crept out of the harbor. But the waters to the south were obstructed, and the ship progressed only at the whim of the packed floes surrounding her. They were held fast for two months, during which Budington made a cautionary depot of supplies on the adjacent ice.

Things were quiet until October, the anniversary of Hall's death. On the night of the twelfth, a gale struck and the ice surrounding the *Polaris* was pounded by heavy seas. The chief engineer reported fresh seawater in his bilges—scarcely a novelty on that leaking tug—and a contagious panic took hold. More than half the ship's complement was sent scurrying over the side with orders to move threatened supplies away from the hull onto firmer ice. Two lifeboats were also lowered.

Only just in time: Moments later, the floe next to the stern broke off. The *Polaris* swung free, attached now by a bow ice anchor. Then that mooring parted and those on the ice saw their ship vanish into the blizzard. Fortunately, among them was George Tyson. He took charge at once, single-handedly rescuing several men adrift on neighboring floes as well as distributing blankets to the women and children. He noted that able-bodied sailors with him made no move to help. While they slept, Tyson stood solitary watch during a cold and fearful night.

At dawn, he took stock. There were nineteen souls on the ice, including all nine Eskimos, the infant Charlie Polaris among them. Still on board the *Polaris*, if indeed she remained afloat, were Budington, Bessels, and a dozen crewmen. On the ice, they had some food, a handful of dogs, two lifeboats, and two kayaks. Their involuntary refuge was topographically variegated, dotted with lakes and hillocks. Tyson paced it out at a mile across. However, the dimensions of drifting floes are seldom constant. New salt ice is sometimes called rubber ice because it reflects, with commendable elasticity, the wave motion beneath it. But older, thick ice is brittle and vulnerable to severe pounding. Tyson and his people were shipwrecked on just such an uncertain haven, in constant danger of having it fragment beneath their feet.

They launched the lifeboats and tried rowing for the nearby Greenland shore, but the sea was so thick with ice that they gave up. Reembarked on their original floe, they spied *Polaris*, only eight miles away, sails set, funnel belching smoke, with not a soul on deck. Tyson signaled frantically but could arouse no response. The ship vanished and, with it, all hope of immediate rescue. The *Polaris* castaways were abandoned on an ice pan, drifting south along the American way.

Severe hardship arouses different responses in different men. Tyson was distressed to find that his men's despondency had blossomed into truculence, a legacy of Budington's monstrous indifference. That survival was at stake made no difference: They seemed determined never to exert themselves for the common good. Had it not been for the Eskimos, undoubtedly all would have perished. Hans Hendrik and Ebierbing, excellent hunters, put their talent to a brutal test that winter. Tyson was also ill-served by Sergeant Frederick Meyers of the Army Signal Corps. He remained mutinously allied to his fellow Germans.

The obliging Eskimos built a complex of igloos to house the entire party. Tyson bunked in with Ebierbing and Tookoolito, and the sailors established an armed camp on the opposite side of the floe. Literally "armed"—after Hall's death, Budington had issued each man on board a pistol, ostensibly for hunting. All of Tyson's icebound command were armed while he was not. Later, when appetites grew sharper, Ebierbing feared for the Eskimo children and slipped Tyson a weapon: Cannibalism was not uncommon among shipwrecked sailors. But even armed, Tyson was an equivocal leader of men. Germans respect discipline, and a show of force might have established his authority. But none was forthcoming: The Eskimos hunted while the men lay about their snow huts, yarning and playing cards.

They had a limited supply of rations but abundant drinking water. Abandoned anywhere else, the *Polaris* castaways, had they avoided drowning, would inevitably have perished from thirst. However, ice floes are covered with a mantle of snow; additionally, frozen seawater loses its salinity by a process of alternately thawing and freezing and is potable. That phenomenon of drinkable salt ice proved a godsend. Blue-topped pinnacles on the floe indicated the purest drinking water.

Food ran short. The dogs were eaten by the Eskimos in the first few days. Three of the sailors pilfered Tyson's slender food reserves daily; he knew the culprits but had no way of stopping them. So the castaways' hand-to-mouth existence depended exclusively on hunting seals. Whenever Hans or Ebierbing killed one, it was instantly butchered and devoured by the floe's nineteen ravenous inhabitants. Nothing went to waste. They drank the blood and then divided the flesh and organs. Flammable blubber provided heat and light, and bristly strips of skin were preserved as iron rations. The youngest children were awarded the seals' eyes as a delicacy; even the intestines were scraped and saved. Tyson's New Year's dinner on the first day of 1873—a lean period between kills—was dried apples and two feet of frozen seal entrails.

The continuing disintegration of the ice that carried them accelerated in the spring. On April 1, the "fools of fortune," as Tyson had ruefully christened his fellow castaways, rowed to a new refuge in the single boat that remained. (The other had been cut up for fuel by the insubordinate sailors.) It was a hazardous passage. Ebierbing and Hans paddled their precious kayaks while the remaining seventeen piled on board the overburdened craft. So little freeboard remained that precious reserves of seal meat and ammunition had to be abandoned. Their new floe, although larger, was no improvement: It soon split beneath their encampment, and breakfast dropped into the sea.

Adverse weather followed, and chronic thirst became a problem. They were trapped on a small floe so lashed by continuous heavy seas that all drinking water was contaminated. Wet, cold, thirsty, and terrified, they lived, as it were, on top of a volcano, never knowing when the ice beneath their feet might rupture and hurl them into the sea. Physical attrition set in. Seals were getting scarce and, by the eighteenth of April, only one day's ration of bread and pemmican was left.

But a worse peril was upon them. Two days later, a violent spring gale fragmented the surrounding pack. Periodic, massive waves deluged their floe. The first washed tent and clothing away; it seemed probable that the boat would go next. Tyson bundled the children beneath its thwarts and rallied the balance of his command along both gunwales. Together they dragged the boat to the ice's windward margin, awaiting the next wave. Twenty minutes later it struck, boiling up over the ice, sweeping the boat and those desperate souls hanging on to it clear across their icy domain. Brash ice in the flood tore at them and, when the fury subsided, more than half the keel's length hung over the malevolent sea to leeward. At once the boat had to be wrenched and skidded back to windward, awaiting the next onslaught.

The storm continued for twelve hours and, when it had passed, miraculously, they were able to kill a polar bear, inexplicably far south for that season. "Poor polar," recorded Tyson, "he meant to dine on us but we shall dine on him." They quenched their thirst with the warm blood.

Rescue came finally at the end of April. They saw their first sealer on the twenty-eighth, while in transit between floes. Once landed, they ringed their new home with pans of burning bear's blubber. Although it was a clear, moonlit night, their signals evoked no response. When another vessel passed the next morning, Tyson mustered his men on a hummock and fired a triple fusillade from all available weapons. The anonymous vessel returned their salute but could not penetrate the ice to reach them. She disappeared. A third ship went by and, despite one ragged signal volley after another, sailed blithely out of sight.

At five o'clock on the morning of April 30, Tyson spotted a fourth vessel, bow on, approaching through the mist. Taking no chances, he ordered Hans Hendrik to paddle his kayak under her bows. She was a sealer, the barkentine *Tigress* out of Newfoundland; in command was Isaac Bartlett, whose nephew, Robert, would captain Peary's ship toward the pole.

Tyson's castaways were taken on board, their epic, involuntary voyage completed. They had drifted, throughout an arctic winter, for five months and fifteen hundred miles, from their abandonment near Littleton Island southward to the sealing grounds off Labrador. That all nineteen were rescued alive is remarkable but, in one sense, not surprising: Their enforced Eskimo diet, however sparse, had been nutritionally sound. Only after they were saved did scurvy manifest itself. All of them suffered the familiar pangs of stiff and swollen legs en route to New York.

No sooner had the *Tigress* tied up in Brooklyn than the government chartered her as the official *Polaris* relief ship, refitting her on the spot. Her new skipper, Commander James Greer, USN, must have been a persuasive recruiter: Four *Polaris* survivors signed on, including Acting Lieutenant George Tyson.

But while Greer sailed north, a preliminary *Polaris* search was already under way. A ship of the line, the USS *Juniata*, dropped anchor at Upernavik in mid-July. Unwilling to continue farther, her commanding officer dispatched his largest steam launch instead. The *Little Juniata*, as she was christened, was just that—only thirty-two feet long, her stem strengthened with steel plate and an iron basket enclosing her propeller. She was swamped with coal, four tons of the stuff, and towed an additional half ton in a dinghy. In command was the indubitably American George Washington De Long, a wardroom volunteer. With a crew of seven, Lieutenant De Long steamed north from Upernavik on the second of August. He found no sign of the *Polaris*, though crossing notorious Melville Bay to within sight of Cape York.

There his open launch was battered for thirty hours by the worst the summer arctic could offer in the way of gale-driven rain; under sail alone—more than half his coal was expended—De Long fought his way through a flotilla of massive bergs. When the storm subsided, the *Little Juniata* was awash, bunkers flooded, and everything, matches included, wringing wet. But the resourceful officer dried a single match next to his skin, lit a fire, coaxed his boilers to life, and steamed back toward Upernavik. En route he encountered Greer and the northbound *Tigress* and was able to report conclusively that the *Polaris* was nowhere to be found in Melville Bay. De Long's impromptu search on board the *Little Juniata* was his arctic baptism, the start of a literally fatal infatuation with the North.

The *Tigress* negotiated Melville Bay in turn and rounded Cape York into Smith Sound. By late August she had reached the waters off Littleton Island where Tyson and his companions had been marooned on the ice floe. Nearby, on shore, Greer's landing party found a deserted, snowbanked hut built of ship's timbers and canvas, its walls lined with fourteen bunks; apparently all hands remaining on board the leaking *Polaris* had made it to land. Neighboring Eskimos at Etah confirmed that they had given the shipwrecked Americans food and clothing in return for the promised gift of the wrecked *Polaris*. (They never collected: She was broken up and sunk by winter storms.) In the spring, Budington and his men had salvaged enough saloon paneling to fashion a pair of launches— nail holes were a constant problem—and they sailed south along Greenland's coast, following Kane's example of two decades earlier. Within two weeks they were picked up by the Dundee whaler *Ravenscraig*.

So all the *Polaris*'s people came home, all save their late commander. America's second polar venture was over, its most memorable aspects an arctic whodunit, the survival of two separate lots of castaways and, overall, an aura of incompetence and dereliction. The *Polaris* had steamed closer to latitude 90° than any ship in history, yet, sadly, Hall's exploring potential had never been realized. Had he not died, much of the Arctic Ocean coastline subsequently charted by the British would have been trodden first by Americans. But Hall's death ended all that: Mission and morale crumbled under the incompetent pair who succeeded him in command. Of the two, Emil Bessels fared better, emerging professionally unscathed from the Navy Board of Inquiry's investigating the loss of the *Polaris;* he would assume the mantle of distinguished arctic expert. Captain Sidney Budington never sailed in command again, and his record of ineptitude continued to the end of the *Polaris* affair. Although no explanatory cairn had been left at his hut on the shores of what he called Lifeboat Cove, Budington *did* leave the mutilated log of the *Polaris;* Captain Greer found it abandoned among the litter of the campsite. Significantly, the pages concerning Hall's illness and death had been torn out, and there was no mention of the storm off Littleton Island that had led to the loss of more than half his command on the ice.

Between them, Kane and Hall had opened up the entire American way, delineating the three hundred miles between Smith Sound and the Arctic Ocean. Although "an open polar sea" was nonexistent, it was clearly the way to the pole, the same route that Peary would make his own toward the turn of the century. In common, both Kane and Hall were bold, innovative leaders; also in common, they had been plagued by unreliable subordinates. An ominous precedent was established: American arctic crews would repeatedly fall short of the mark. Nevertheless, Americans had broken Great Britain's monopoly in the waters north of Canada and, not unexpectedly, their success reawakened old ambitions at the Royal Geographical Society.

3

IN WANT OF LEMONS

> . . . The scurvy flew through the
>   schooner's crew
> As they sailed the Arctic Sea;
> They were far from land and their food
>   was canned
> So they got no vitamin C.
>
> —"C.H.A." in St. Bartholomew's Hospital
>   *Journal*, January 1928

The whale ship *Ravenscraig*, overburdened with Budington's castaways in midseason, transferred them to the
Arctic, bound home for Scotland with a full hold. The *Arctic*
already carried one supernumerary, Lieutenant Albert
Markham, Clements Markham's cousin. On leave from the
Royal Navy and under orders from the Royal Geographical
Society, he had signed on to observe the performance of modern screw steamers against the pack and "to report on the
present state of the ice in the direction of those northern
sounds." The RGS hoped for a renewal of Royal Navy arctic
exploration. The unexpected addition of *Polaris* crewmen on
board was a bonus for the young officer and, during passage
back to Scotland, he heard firsthand reports of their ordeal
and, even more intriguing, the ease of their entry the previous
summer into the Arctic Ocean.

The disembarkation of yet another party of *Polaris* survivors
at Dundee on September 9, 1873, created a sensation in the

United Kingdom, in marked contrast to America's response the previous spring. When Tyson's ice-floe castaways had come home, *The New York Times* lamented: "The death of Hall and the loss of the *Polaris* adds another to the long list of arctic failures." But London's *Observer* saw things differently: "The rude wooden monument to the intrepid American, standing alone in the polar solitude, is at the same time, a grand memorial, a trophy and a challenge." Franklin was forgotten, and polar fever, long dormant, broke out anew. The British Association for the Advancement of Science called on Parliament to send an expedition to the arctic.

But Lieutenant Markham's sponsors had beaten them to the draw. Clements Markham became honorary secretary of the Royal Geographical Society in 1863, and agitation for a renewed arctic assault dates from that appointment. He was a formidable proponent. Hugh Robert Mill's description of Markham on the podium catches the man's fire: "As he spoke, he seemed the embodiment of the romance of Geography; his bosom swelled, and his shirt front billowed out like the topsails of a frigate." Moreover, he was backed by dozens of Franklin Search veterans within the society, identified by the amiable generic Old Arctics.

Old Arctic Admiral Sherard Osborn had read a paper on the arctic in 1863 and, two years later, the society's president, Sir Roderick Murchison, had approached the Duke of Somerset, first lord of the Admiralty, proposing an expedition above Spitsbergen. His Grace had demurred, suggesting that the British await the results of Nordenskjöld, at that moment heading a Swedish expedition in the same area. The first lord's caution was justified: The Swedes came home having achieved only 81°42'; reaching the pole above Spitsbergen was patently no easier for them than it had been for Phipps in 1773 or Parry in 1827.

Rebuffed but undismayed, the society tried again. In April 1872, Admiral Osborn read yet another paper, provocatively titled "New Lands Within the Arctic Circle." Markham formed an Arctic Committee, which produced a new proposal. He had enlisted a powerful ally—the Royal Society—with some persuasive, long-range strategy. There would be a transit of Venus in 1882, best observed from Antarctica. A cadre of experienced polar officers would be invaluable on that occasion: Why not train them on an arctic expedition in the interim? Sir Joseph Hooker, the surgeon/botanist who headed the Royal Society (and an "Old *Ant*arctic" who had sailed south with Ross in 1840), needed no urging. A joint committee of the Royal Societies was formed, with Clements Markham once again in the chair.

The joint committee framed an impassioned appeal. England, it was said, had watched polar explorers of other nations "not without a feeling of shame." Now the time had come "to assert our old pre-eminence." Since 1818, it was recalled, arctic expeditions

> have redounded to the national honour and repute and have in no small degree contributed to keep alive, through a long period of peace, that spirit of courage, enterprise and self-denial which is so essential to the character of the seamen of a great maritime nation. . . .

Without actually articulating the name Franklin, the report argued that "steam navigation was now so advanced" that little risk was entailed. Markham had already averred that "a wretchedly equipped little schooner" and "a mere river steamer of small power" (*Advance* and *Polaris*, respectively) could not compete with a pair of stout, Dundee-built oak vessels manned by Royal Navy crews.

In December 1872, Major Sir Henry Rawlinson, who had succeeded Murchison as president, presented the joint societies' proposal for a try up the American way to the chancellor of the Exchequer and the first sea lord. Within a fortnight, a reply came back in the—regretful—negative. The disqualifier this time was a shortage of funds occasioned by the recent dispatch of HMS *Challenger*, history's first oceanographic research vessel. (The eighteen-gun Royal Navy corvette would roam the world's oceans for four years; six times the length of that extensive voyage would be consumed assimilating and publishing the expedition's findings.) *Challenger* was commanded by an Old Arctic, Captain George Nares, who had served as mate on the *Resolute* with Kellet in 1852. Rebuffed again, the society filled the time by dispatching Lieutenant Markham on board the *Arctic* for a private reconnaissance.

After Markham's return with the Budington castaways, the

society was abuzz. In November, Clements Markham read a paper on Hall's accomplishments. It was scarcely enthusiastic. Hall was dismissed as "a man without education, in no sense a seaman" but, rather, "an enthusiastic and gallant leader." The *Polaris*'s officers and crew were, for the most part, "advanced in years . . . without any zeal for discovery." Although stopped by the ice at 82°14'—their record—"old Buddington [*sic*] had seen a water sky to the north" and yet refused to proceed. The crew, continued Markham with Royal Navy disdain, were "without discipline or control and in a position in which every man considered himself as good as his neighbors." Someone proposed that a private British expedition should be mounted, but Admiral Sherard Osborn differed: It should be "under government auspices, with naval discipline, naval order, and naval *esprit de corps*, to carry them through the labors of an arctic winter and spring."

Curiously, it was an electrifying discovery on the other side of the arctic that finally tipped the scales. In 1871, two Austrian officers, Lieutenant Julius von Payer of the Army Engineers and Lieutenant Karl Weyprecht of the Imperial Navy, had hired a small vessel to explore Novaya Zemlya, that long, caterpillar-shaped island stretching north from Russia's arctic coast. They had encountered open water and were convinced that perhaps an entire Northeast Passage might be possible. The news excited such enthusiasm in Austria that a full-scale expedition was mounted by public subscription. The 220-ton screw steamer *Admiral Tegetthoff*—named after the naval hero who had trounced the Italian fleet in 1866—was provisioned for three years and sailed in June 1872 with a crew of twenty-one sailors and mountaineers.

But the open water had vanished and the *Admiral Tegetthoff* was soon beset, drifting first northeast, then northwest. After a year's imprisonment, the explorers saw, looming above August cloudbanks, mountains only fourteen miles away. For two months, the ship was worked within three miles of shore. Then von Payer and Weyprecht disembarked onto new, arctic terra firma, which they named Franz Josef Land, after their emperor. They stood at 79°54', at the southern fringe of a mountainous archipelago that stretched invitingly north, on the threshold of that almost featureless white disc atop the world's maps enclosed by the eightieth parallel of latitude. They traveled overland as far north as 82°30′, within forty miles of Parry's record of 1827. Subsequently they had to abandon the *Admiral Tegetthoff* and walk south on foot ("two months of indescribable effort" for nine miles of progress), to be picked up by the Russian schooner *Nicolai*.

Von Payer addressed a packed meeting of the Royal Geographical Society in November 1874. The response of those scientists, geographers, and Old Arctics was predictable; but quite unexpected was the impact of von Payer's discovery elsewhere in Britain's establishment. An undiscovered landmass offering apparent access to the pole persuaded the newly elected prime minister, Disraeli, to accede to the joint societies' proposal, held so long *in suspenso* by his predecessor, Gladstone. Parliament endorsed it, even though the old Smith Sound route it espoused bore not the remotest geographical relationship to Franz Josef Land. Polar fever had gripped Whitehall: After two decades of indifference, ships were to be dispatched to forestall other nations that might be emboldened by Austria's discovery. Disraeli's letter of approval was dated November 17, 1874.

The Royal Navy leaped into the fray. Within a week, the Admiralty had appointed an Arctic Committee, composed of three rear admirals: McClintock, Osborn, and Richards, all from the Royal Geographical Society and all Old Arctics. Lieutenant Markham was officially signed to the expedition, and in turn signed on six ice quartermasters from Scottish whaling ports. McClintock, now admiral superintendent of Her Majesty's Dockyard at Portsmouth, supervised the refit of two vessels in the Steam Basin: the *Alert*, a seventeen-gun steam sloop of the line; and a Dundee whaler, the *Bloodhound*, bought in Dundee for eighteen thousand pounds and rechristened *Discovery*, the fifth Royal Navy ship to bear the name. The *Alert* was given new boilers and machinery; thus engined, she would serve as the advance ship. Both vessels had strengthening timbers added athwartship. The crews' quarters were encapsulated in felt, and ice-melting reservoirs jacketed each galley chimney. A specialized arctic chandlery was loaded on board—sledges, ice saws, ice anchors, and wagon-cloth awnings—unused since the Franklin searches. Patent trusses and reefing and furling gear were added as well, the very latest in maritime hardware.

Captain George Nares was recalled from HMS *Challenger* to assume command. He sailed home by fast steamer from Hong Kong, an old-school sailor with a beard and a high-domed, bald head; he was the author of *Seamanship*, a perennial Royal Navy backlist. Both he and his second in command, Captain Henry Stephenson—transferred from the royal yacht *Albert and Victoria* to command the *Discovery*—were contemporaries of Clements Markham, men in their mid-forties. Although Nares boasted sledging experience, Stephenson had none; it was not considered a prerequisite. Departing from tradition, expedition and ship commanders would remain on board, leaving the hard work on the ice to younger men. Albert Markham would lead one sledging division, and an officer who had returned from the *Challenger* with Nares would lead another: Lieutenant Pelham Aldrich, who was a talented watercolorist and musician. He had never seen arctic service, but his uncle, Captain Robert Aldrich, had sailed on board the *Resolute*, consort to Clements Markham's *Assistance*, in 1850. The third sledge commander was to be Lieutenant Lewis Beaumont, recalled from the Mediterranean. Two crews—fifty-two for the *Alert* and fifty-nine for the *Discovery*—were selected from thousands of eager Royal Navy volunteers—"a fine willing set of fellows," reported Albert Markham.

At the February 1875 meeting of the Royal Geographical Society, with the Prince of Wales in the chair, Admiral George Richards proposed the thanks of the society "to our able and unwearying secretary." Just as he would, single-handedly, agitate for a joint societies' expedition to the Antarctic a quarter of a century later, so Clements Markham had labored for a decade to see that Britain reentered the arctic lists.

Although Franklin's name appears nowhere in the Admiralty's instructions to Captain Nares, the specter of his lost expedition was everywhere. The *Discovery* and the *Alert* were ordered to winter no more than two hundred miles apart—preferably closer—and one hauntingly explicit directive was stressed:

> I need scarcely remind you that it is impossible to leave too many notices of your movements, intentions and any alterations in the latter.

Determined to remedy the complacency of their predecessors in 1845—who had waited three years before sending ships after Franklin—Their Lordships secured the cooperation of Allen Young, who would be sailing to the arctic for that summer only on his steam yacht *Pandora*. Backed by Lady Franklin and James Gordon Bennett, publisher of the *New York Herald,* he was hoping to explore Franklin's projected Northwest Passage route. Nares was ordered to leave cairns along each shore of the American way, and Allen Young was asked to inspect the southernmost ones on his return, bringing any dispatches home to the Admiralty.

Their Lordships' caution was not shared by fellows at the RGS. Sherard Osborn pooh-poohed all the fuss: the worst that could happen was that one ship might not survive; in that event, both crews could double up in the surviving hull. Another Old Arctic observed that more men—twenty-four in all—had been lost climbing the Alps than during all the Franklin searches. Markham stressed the power of the new ships: *Alert* and *Discovery* were double the size of *Erebus* and *Terror* and appropriately engined. Admiral Richards remarked: "One of the cardinal laws of arctic navigation is never to turn a corner if it can be avoided." Franklin had turned two corners—west into Lancaster and south into Prince Regent Inlet—and had vanished. Nares would hold course due north, in waters already charted by Kane and Hall. As a final clincher, Albert Markham reported that the ice was much reduced during the *Arctic*'s cruise; it had taken only sixty hours to negotiate dreaded Melville Bay.

Coincidentally, a new painting called *The North-West Passage* by Pre-Raphaelite John Millais was hung at the Royal Academy. The model for its central figure was a celebrated sea captain, Edward Trelawney. He posed seated in a seaside cottage, a young lady visitor at his feet; her bonnet and gloves lie on the table. She is reading to Trelawney, one hand on his. Yet restlessness belies repose: The sailor's gnarled hands are clenched, his eyes far away. The artist's props reflect his preoccupation: an open chart; water-stained logbooks; flags—perhaps sledge banners?—in a corner; a print of Nelson and another of an ice-beset frigate; and, through the window, a sloop under sail. The obvious recall of a heroic struggle relinquished must have struck a responsive chord in the hearts of all Old Arctics who saw it. Pole had supplanted passage; there would be another expedition.

On May 19, 1875, after a visit from the Prince of Wales, *Alert* and *Discovery*, in company with the steam frigate *Valorous*, a paddle-wheeler laden with coal, sailed from Portsmouth. An Army band played "Auld Lang Syne" from ashore, and Her Majesty telegraphed blessings from Balmoral. Clements Markham, the expedition's godfather, would sail as far as Greenland, returning on the *Valorous*. He was berthed on board the *Alert*, a vessel so crowded that Markham swung his hammock in a makeshift cabin, five feet square, off the wardroom. It also housed festoons of the expedition's Christmas puddings, some of which splashed into Markham's hip bath during the "wet and uneasy" crossing. The weather was foul: Whaleboats on both expedition ships were smashed in their davits, and the brave new rigging gear came to grief, "all iron gimcracks carrying away," reported traditionalist Markham smugly; but he comforted his shipmates by suggesting that the same gales buffeting them were doubtless scouring ice from Baffin Bay. He was doubly delighted to be on board, revisiting his beloved arctic for the second and last time as well as rejoicing amid the evocative camaraderie of a Royal Naval warship once more. One young officer wrote home that the RGS honorary secretary was "a peripatetic encyclopaedia." When the flotilla reached Disko Harbor, the two expedition ships' bunkers were topped up with coal, and Markham transferred to the *Valorous*. He ordered a signal aloft: FAREWELL, SPEEDY RETURN, which Nares acknowledged with a constrained THANK YOU; below, Markham's cabin had already been transformed into the *Alert*'s printshop and darkroom.

After touching at Upernavik to take on dogs, Nares turned his ships' bows northwest, across Melville Bay and around Cape York. Obligatory cairns were left at the Cary and Littleton islands before both ships sailed into Kane Basin, the first British presence there since Inglefield's maiden entry in 1852. The waters that summer were more congested than Hall had found them, so the more powerful *Alert* towed the *Discovery* through ice jams when necessary. By late August both vessels had negotiated Kennedy Channel and were well north of 81°.

The *Discovery* wintered on the western shore of Hall's Basin, in what was named Discovery Bay on the northern shore of

Lady Franklin Strait, invaluable protection against marauding ice. With his fallback ship in prime position, Nares departed to continue north on August 26. He left just in time: New ice was forming and, only three miles from her consort, the *Alert* was beset, precisely the dangerous proximity Their Lordships had forbidden. But Nares freed his ship a week later and, by early September, had rounded Distant Cape into Robeson Channel, the final segment of the American way. An autumn gale roared out of the south, fragmenting and driving the pack north. At ten knots, the *Alert* swept unobstructed through the channel's embouchure into the polar ocean.

Hall's latitude was surpassed. Nares sought a winter anchorage on the virgin coast trending northwest along Ellesmere Land. Finding an "Alert Bay" was not easy: Robeson's cliffs had degenerated into shelving lowlands that afforded scant protection. Finally, north of Capes Union and Sheridan—glimpsed and named from a distance by Hall—Nares selected a north-facing bay protected by a rampart of grounded icebergs. He called it Floeberg Harbor. Ice anchors were taken ashore, connected to the vessel by chains that were draped across a series of casks to keep them safely above accumulating snow. The *Alert* was moored at a record—for a ship—latitude of 82°30'. Within weeks, Lieutenant Pelham Aldrich's dog sledge *Challenger* would go one better, surpassing Parry's northern mark of 82°45'.

Nares's ships were only eighty miles apart. Eight men from the *Discovery* under Lieutenant Wyatt Rawson had sailed north on the *Alert* with the intention of sledging south to their own ship before darkness set in, carrying news of the *Alert*'s location. But the icefoot along Robeson Channel was impassable, and they wintered on the advance vessel instead.

Every extra hand was welcome. Nares divided his command into two divisions: One laid depots to the north, the other emptied the *Alert*'s holds. Fuel, provisions, rigging, powder, and instruments were taken ashore and stored in Markham Hall, a 50-by-12-foot warehouse made of ice and canvas. Nearby, three underground snow caves were dug, connected by 150 feet of tunnel that would ease the task of the scientists taking daily readings over the winter; that little complex was called Kew.

Cold September sledging began. On one outing, candles were inexplicably left behind: Rations were eaten in the chill gloom of the tent, and Markham risked frostbite as he wrote diary entries outdoors with bare hands. The going was hard for dogs and men alike. Sailors hauled the sledges with canvas loops—similar to Kane's rue-raddies—shifting them from shoulder to shoulder as the skin chafed. Temperatures inside the eight-man tents were bitter and, despite their mooseskin boots, the men's feet were cold all night. Those who did doze off were continually awakened by the noise of benumbed heels drumming against the floor cloth to restore circulation.

The fifty sledge dogs taken on in Greenland were a disappointment. Perhaps they were indulged too much. The Danes had recommended bleakly:

> Don't feed them more than twice a week; and if they show any sign of insubordination, knock them down with a marlinspike. If they attempt to come near you, kick them; it is the only way to prevent them from biting you.

Predictably, the British ignored this advice. Surgeon Belgrave Ninnis on board the *Discovery* reported happily that the men fed and petted the dogs so that "they became as sociable and decorous as if brought up in a cottage." The *Alert*'s surgeon, Edward Moss, was less sanguine, suggesting that Greenland dogs were "merely wolves that have found slavery convenient." They devoured everything and anything, including their own puppies. A dog named Michael swallowed canvas harness and even part of a tin ladle. Later the British learned to thwart this appetite for harnesses by coating them with tar.

Pelham Aldrich was put in charge of the *Alert*'s pack, and he rated the dogs' performance mediocre. The British sledges' iron-shod runners disappeared beneath the deep coastal snow. The animals themselves sank up to their muzzles and would not move without continuing assists from the men. Dogs alone cannot manage a standing pull, that vigorous wrench that lurches buried sledges forward, so the exhausted dog-drivers had to do it themselves. Once, while Aldrich was coaxing his dogs along, he could hear, five miles away, "One, two, three—*haul!*," the hoarse litany of the standing pull. Sometimes Markham's men varied it with "Main, top, sail—*haul!*" But whatever the refrain, the dogs did not help: When sledges bogged down, the teams would sit, tails curled over forefeet, and await human assistance. Significantly, no dogs were taken on any of the sledge journeys the following spring. By then, half of the dogs on both ships had succumbed to *piblokto,* the same "arctic cholera" that had ravaged Kane's kennel. Manhauling won out, and the seeds of British disillusionment with sledge dogs were planted, bitter fruit to be harvested in Antarctica after the turn of the century.

Winter darkness engulfed the *Alert* on October 12. By that time, a cache of fuel and provisions had been established thirty-four miles to the north, at Cape Joseph Henry, an eminence named by Hall five years earlier after the president of the U.S. Academy of Science. It was from there that Lieutenant Albert Markham would lead the expedition's polar thrust on a pioneering trek out over the Arctic Ocean's ice.

Outdoor exercise was taken along a half-mile promenade where the snow had been trodden down and outlined with meat cans and barrels. Nares's men dressed for the winter in either duffel or yellow sealskin tunics and trousers, their hands protected by long, fur-backed mittens suspended from the neck on lampwick that were known popularly as "elbow bags." On their heads, all hands wore "Eugénies"—knitted wool Berlin helmets that had been presented, along with playing cards, to the expedition by the French empress in exile. "Eugénies" made excellent nightcaps as well, although they itched terribly; Markham remembered that what he most enjoyed about coming in from sledging was a hot bath and a chance to brush his hair. Instead of using socks, feet were wrapped in blanket squares thrust into open-heeled canvas leggings that laced up the back. On board, feet were shod in carpet boots with thick cork soles.

The weather was bitterly cold, an all-winter low of −73° that mirrored the Empire's high of 132°, recorded in India. Candles on deck burned only in the center, leaving intact a frozen, lacy sleeve of wax around the circumference. Whiskers were trimmed to avoid freezing them to woolen scarves. Men coming indoors removed excess snow with a housemaid's brush kept on deck, then descended through double doors, preceded by clouds of water vapor; outer clothing was removed quickly to discourage condensation. Cabins were either coated with hoarfrost—"ice buttons" adorned boltheads extending through the planking—or dripped ceaselessly as temperatures rose. One officer, in an attempt to dry his quarters, tried burning fifty candles at once. But cleverer was his colleague who simply put up his umbrella: He slept longer than any of his fellows, who were awakened not by the clatter of coal in the wardroom stove, nor by the aroma of fresh bread or curried sardines, but by the infuriating drip of melting frost.

But the expedition's health seemed sound. Every man had a weekly hot bath, and a cup of lime juice—laced with 10 percent rum as a preservative—was dished out daily from a tub on the messdeck in the presence of an officer. Members of the wardroom were issued two glasses of claret each evening; to ensure a full glass despite the *Alert*'s continual shoreward list, officers leveled their glasses with tiny wooden wedges. Through oversight, salt had been omitted from the *Alert*'s stores; however, crystallization of the brine dripping from thawing flanks of salted beef served instead.

Guy Fawkes Day—on November 5—was celebrated by parading a sledge-drawn dummy around the *Alert*. Its blouse was stuffed with rockets and fireworks so that, when put to the torch, the "Guy" made a splendid show, as did a tissue-paper hot-air balloon that caught fire as it rose into the arctic night. The Royal Arctic Theatre was reopened—"temporarily closed" since 1854—and Albert Markham, billed as "The Wizard of the North," proved a master conjurer. Pelham Aldrich composed and played the music for several pantomines as well as thumping out endless polkas, waltzes, and a gallop for the Christmas dance held on deck under the awning. Chaplain Henry Pullen entertained one February evening with "A Few Words on Arctic Plants."

By April, at the start of spring sledging, spirits were high. Two sledge parties would set out from the *Alert*, one headed by Markham for the pole, the second under Aldrich to proceed west along the coast. From the *Discovery*, far to the south, Lieutenant Beaumont would lead his party across Hall's Basin to investigate Greenland's northern shore. Everything presaged success.

As it turned out, records were achieved. But all three divisions suffered grievously—in some cases, fatally—from scurvy, supposedly eradicated from the Royal Navy since Nelson's day. That it could have ravaged an expedition as late as 1876 seems incomprehensible.

Scurvy afflicts those species that cannot synthesize ascorbic acid—vitamin C—from glucose, a disparate group including all primates, guinea pigs, the red-vented bulbul, and certain bats as well as rainbow trout and Coho salmon. It had long decimated navies. Half of the 2,000 men who circumnavigated the globe with Admiral George Anson in 1740 died from scurvy. The same plague killed 100 sailors out of a ship's complement of 160 on Vasco da Gama's voyage around the Cape of Good Hope. Hawks, a British privateer, once boarded a derelict Spanish galleon on which every man had perished from scurvy. Yet Eskimos, who knew neither vegetable nor citrus, avoided scurvy with a high carnivorous intake, consumed raw: Fresh meat is loaded with vitamin C.

No one has ever discovered why a deficiency of this vitamin should cause extravascular bleeding. Cumulative hemorrhages break out all over the body in crippling succession. The earliest ones are so surreptitious as to escape detection. Blood vessels around hair follicles of the scalp rupture: tiny red halos appear and then vanish. Subsequently, identical red blushes surface on calves and thighs. Symptoms proliferate. Ankles swell and discolor, severe pain nags at knee joints and hamstrings. Gums become inflamed; teeth loosen. Victims experience lassitude, shortness of breath, and emotional distress. Old wounds re-open. Walters, surgeon of the *Centurion*, recounted one bizarre case history:

> . . . Of this there was a remarkable instance in one of the invalids on board the *Centurion* who had been wounded about fifty years before at the battle of the Boyne, for though he was cured soon after, and had continued well for a number of years past, yet on his being attacked by the scurvy, his wounds in the progress of the disease, broke out afresh and appeared as if they had never been healed: nay, what is still more astonishing, the callus of the broken bone, which had been completely formed for a long time, was found to be completely dissolved and the fracture as if it had never been consolidated.

Although contemporary doctors concede that scurvy retards the healing process, they do not subscribe to Walters's diagnosis of retroactive wound decay. But documenting advanced scurvy cases in the twentieth century is harder than in the eighteenth, and there are too many similar accounts to dismiss the phenomenon. Elisha Kane had observed a man sick with scurvy: "Every old scar was a running ulcer." Significantly, in 1875, when Nares's men were recruited, one Admiralty surgeon specified that no sailors with "old wounds" would be accepted.

In its terminal stages, scurvy reduces the human body to bloated yellow flesh daubed with purple, red, and green blotches. The tortured skin itches fiendishly and, where scratched, bursts into suppurating ulcers. The flesh literally rots away, reeking of putrefaction.

For years a variety of treatments were hazarded. Complicating matters was ignorance that scurvy was a deficiency disease. Some doctors posited that, since so many overcrowded and underfed poor contracted scurvy, it was doubtless transmitted as a germ. Scurvy sometimes was cured by consumption of *Cochlearia officinalis*, scurvy grass, a small, white-blossomed plant similar to the mustard plant that grows, conveniently, as far north as the arctic. Treatment at sea included consumption of spruce beer, potatoes, sauerkraut, bottled fruits, onions, and cloudberries. What all these semi-effective antidotes contained were varying amounts of ascorbic acid or vitamin C, a correlation that escaped detection until the twentieth century.

The best remedy was pioneered in 1747, when James Lind, a Royal Navy surgeon on board HMS *Salisbury*, fed different diets to six pairs of scurvy victims. In addition to their regular ship's ration, two drank a daily mug of cider, two others vinegar, two more seawater, and so on. One lucky pair were given two oranges and a lemon. They responded so remarkably that one of them, according to Lind's report, was "appointed nurfe to the reft of the fick." Despite this conclusive proof, the Admiralty did not adopt Surgeon Lind's recommendation until 1803, when a daily ration of lime juice was finally prescribed for all hands. Scurvy disappeared from the fleet, and British sailors were nicknamed "limeys."

Better that they had been christened "lemoneys" or even "orangeys." The choice of "limeys" betrayed a woeful ignorance. Two centuries earlier, Woodall had written: "In want of lemons, use limes . . . ," damaging nutritional advice. Lemons and oranges contain fifty milligrams of ascorbic acid per hundred grams of fruit, limes only half that amount. Black currants, grown in temperate England, contain two hundred milligrams per hundred grams of fruit but, regrettably, were never adopted as the Royal Navy's antiscorbutic. Lemons and limes were, lumped together as scurvy's grand specific, and a fatal confusion resulted. When scurvy broke out on the *Investigator* in 1848, Sir James Ross suggested that his lemon juice had been improperly preserved. So the Admiralty sent a special representative to Sicily to oversee the procedure: although he dealt exclusively with lemons, he was dubbed "inspector of lime juice."

Subsequently, that inspector was transferred to the Caribbean. Sicilian lemons were to be supplanted by West Indian limes. Lime juice was enjoying a vogue among Victorian Britons. Yet the fragrant lime is a second-rate antiscorbutic. Scurvy resurfaced. Admirals, victualers, surgeons, and explorers alike concluded that Lind's classic experiment, as well as the Royal Navy's lemon juice edict of 1803, had somehow been erroneous. After 1850, scurvy was once again established as the voyagers' plague. Among the first to suffer were sailors aboard the *Britannica* in the Crimea; next came the resolute men who sailed with Nares. Since almost no one was familiar with symptoms of the long-vanished disease, the crews of the *Alert* and the *Discovery* ignored early manifestations that their sailor grandfathers would have recognized with ease.

During March, a month before their departure, prospective sledgers had their lime ration doubled; but it was too late. Moreover, there was little fresh meat. Game near the *Alert* had proved elusive, though the *Discovery*'s crew dined regularly on musk-ox steaks (which, the surfeited messdeck complained, tasted musky). But, regardless, the *Discovery*'s sledgers were to suffer just as harshly as their colleagues to the north.

April 3 marked the send-off of the northern and western divisions from the *Alert*. Fifty-three officers and men assembled on the ice next to the snowbanked hull. Every departing sledge boasted an individual banner. *Marco Polo*'s had been stitched personally by Lady McClintock; others were *Victoria, Alexandra, Bulldog,* and *Bloodhound*. The two boats that Markham would haul over the ocean ice had been painted a dark color to reduce glare. The back of every man's Holland overall had been decorated to relieve the visual monotony of those trudging behind: Union Jacks, freemason symbols, pictures of the *Alert*, even Lady Franklin's motto—"Hold Fast!"—were emblazoned on the men's backs. Chaplain Pullen spoke a prayer and, doffing their "Eugénies" in the chill breeze, the explorers responded with a doxology. Three cheers were echoed by shipmates lining the rail, and the great cavalcade set off.

Northern and western parties traveled together as far as Cape Joseph Henry. There, Markham and his sixteen-man polar party continued north, the first time that sledges had ever been committed to the Arctic Ocean. Reaching the pole was Nares's primary mission, and in Lieutenant Albert Markham he was served by an officer of the highest resolve. Aldrich continued along the coast to the west, charged with mapping the northern shores of Ellesmere Island (at the time called Ellesmere Land); within days he had named James Ross Bay, Cape Hecla, and Clements Markham Inlet. Far to the south, Beaumont's party set off from the *Discovery* to touch base first with the *Alert* before crossing Robeson Channel and investigating Greenland's northern coast. Nares's triple assault was launched.

Scurvy manifested itself almost at once. Two days from land, Markham's seaman John Shirley reported stiffness in his legs. Within a week his knees and ankles were so painful that he could no longer pull. He and a fellow sufferer, marine gunner George Porter, were "relieved of duty." They stayed roped to the sledge; it was easier to keep up in harness.

The same lameness—tertiary symptoms of the disease—afflicted all three parties. Sledge officers presumed at first that those aching muscles were the result of winter's inactivity. Moreover, for Markham in particular, suffering was to be expected over such appalling terrain, the ice as notoriously obstructive as Parry had found it fifty years before. A trail was often cut with pick and shovel.

Aldrich and Beaumont's land parties, slogging along the coastline, had things no easier. Ellesmere Island's and Greenland's northern shores are indented with inlets where the prevailing west wind's scouring action is negligible; snow accumulates in undisturbed abundance. Although winter crusts might have borne men and sledges, spring snows did not. In a passage from his sledge journal, Lieutenant Beaumont details conditions:

> . . . no longer crisp and dry but the consistency of moist sugar; walking was most exhausting, one literally had to climb out of the holes made by each foot in succession, the hard crust on top, which would only just *not* bear you, as well as the depths of the snow preventing you from pushing forward through it, each leg sank to about three inches above the knee, and the effort of lifting them from their tight-fitting holes, soon began to tell on the men. William Jenkins, Peter Craig and Charles Paul complained of stiffness in the hamstrings, and all of us were very tired. . . .

Inadvertently, Beaumont has identified the culprit: For "stiffness in the hamstrings" he could have written "scurvy." Yet, regardless, their days were punishing: At what point did aching legs outweigh conventional sledging miseries? The explorers shivered as they waited—an hour and a half—for tea. "Did it boil?" was the impatient, repetitious query each night as they retired, kicking down into frozen sleeping bags coiled stubborn as mainsprings. (Moisture accretion again: Although ration and fuel consumption reduced sledge weights, Aldrich's loads remained constant, accumulating damp offsetting diminished provisions.) But sadly, it was not only fatigue and cold that "began to tell on the men"; scurvy was taking its toll.

Markham gave up first. On May 10 he stopped his division at what would be their northernmost camp. They had struggled over the ocean ice to 83°20′26″, dragging sledges and boats thirty miles from Cape Joseph Henry. It was a world's record. Camp was made as usual, two tents pitched side by side, each guyed with one end to a loaded sledge, the other to a pick handle jammed in the snow. While the men piled snow blocks along the tents' edges, two duty cooks disappeared into their "kitchens," canvas appendages that had been sewn onto the tents, coaxing their inadequate cookers into life-giving warmth. The bacon, as always, was frozen so hard that the men had to melt it in their tea, chilling what should have been a hot restorative. A Union Jack fluttered between the tents, lashed to Markham's lancewood flagstaff, which boasted a naval crown and polar star in silver. On it was inscribed:

> I may do all that may become a man;
> Who dares do more is none.

an echo of Macbeth's resolution.

One of the tents was actually a hospital. Six of its eight occupants were incapacitated with scurvy. The condition of these invalids rather than the appalling surface of the ice had made up Markham's mind. Ten days earlier, he had confided in his journal: "Porter's symptoms appear to be scorbutic."

Even *in extremis*, that Royal Navy detachment celebrated its achievement. Somebody produced a box of Havanas, and Markham spliced the main brace with the customary rum as well as a magnum of whiskey, a present from the dean of Dundee, with instructions that it be drunk at Markham's highest latitude. So pemmican, bacon, biscuit, and tea were washed down by the fiery spirits, sparking an impromptu singsong. Since the party was not accommodated under one canvas, choruses were roared contrapuntally between tents. Over four hundred miles short of the pole, a third of them crippled, those plucky Britishers sang "God Save the Queen"; "The Union Jack of Old England"; and a rollicking standard from the previous winter, Chaplain Pullen's "Grand Palæocrystic Sledging Chorus," to the tune of "The Shannon and the Chesapeake":

> Here's a health to all true blue
> To the officers and crew
> Who man this expedition neat and handy-o
> And may they ever prove
> Both in sledging and in love
> That the tars of old Britannia are dandy-o!

Clements Markham would have approved.

A desperate retreat began the next morning. Markham's sledges had to travel the same ground twice, first with provisions, then with the sick. Although they were following the same route in reverse, retracing arctic steps is painful: Searching the shadowless white void for tracks aggravates the eyes cruelly. But whereas snow blindness was treated with spirits of opium, the scurvy proliferated unchecked. Markham recorded wryly that of thirty-four legs on the expedition, only eleven were unafflicted.

No open water was ever encountered. One large cutter had already been discarded during the northbound advance. Their remaining smaller boat served only as a cumbersome litter, and it, too, was abandoned, on May 27. It is an indication of their dire prospects that it served as a midocean cairn, complete with message detailing the reason for its abandonment. Neither British boat was ever launched. Peary would have sold his soul for one thirty-three years later at that same spot.

By the time they reached Cape Joseph Henry, only six men and two officers were left in harness. Among them they dragged five invalids, while four of their comrades, pulling themselves along on alpenstocks, crawled in their wake. Only Lieutenant Alfred Parr, Markham's second-in-command, was fit enough to go for help, a thirty-four-mile solo trek to the *Alert*. Before he returned with a rescue party, Gunner Porter was dead. His weeping comrades buried him in the snow, fashioning a cross out of an oar and a sledge batten.

Far to the west, Aldrich's men were afflicted with identical leg pains, which, sportively euphemistic, he called "game leg." But on April 30 an even gamier leg was submitted for inspection:

> The Sergeant Major has just shown me a very ugly-look-
> ing red patch or blotch just above the ankle; the limb is
> slightly swollen

reads Aldrich's sledge journal. He administered turpentine liniment.

He and his men persevered westward as far as longitude 85°33' West—again, a record. That evening, marine James Doidge asked: "Is scurvy ever got while sledging, sir?," betraying his belief that the disease was dispelled by fresh air and exercise.

The next morning, Aldrich turned back. By the time they reached Cape Joseph Henry, he and another man dragged six others. Scouting ahead, Aldrich discovered and removed the self-explanatory cross from Porter's grave so as not to alarm his invalids en passant.

As both the northern and western divisions regained their vessel, Chaplain Pullen greeted them with reams of couplets that began:

> Welcome home to the wished-for rest
> Traveler to North, and traveler to West. . . .

The desperately sick men were carried belowdecks. Their recovery took weeks. Among all three divisions, the officers remained unafflicted, although certainly not for lack of exertion. Admiral Sir Leopold McClintock had laid down the polar officers' ground rules in that regard: "The officer in charge of a sledge party," the father of the modern naval sledge had written, "not only leads the party, he is its very pulse."

The severest toll was taken of Lieutenant Beaumont's Greenland division, men who had supposedly benefited from the *Discovery*'s enriched game diet. Again, at first, the struggle through deep snow seemed ample reason for shortness of breath and aching legs. To avoid sinking into the drifts, Beaumont's sailors sometimes dragged sledges on hands and knees and made better progress. Every fifty yards they halted, panting for breath.

But resting would prove as ineffectual as had Chaplain Pullen's vacuous rhymes. On May 19, a week before turning back, Lieutenant Beaumont confessed:

> I did not encourage the inspection of legs and tried to make them think as little of the stiffness as possible, for I knew the unpleasant truth would be forced on us. . . .

But within three days, Craig and Jenkins, confirmed scurvy victims, went back with a support party. Beaumont continued with five men, all of whom declared themselves able to continue. But farther afield, three of this supposedly healthy quintet complained of aching legs. Beaumont admired their courage: "Although tired, stiff, and sore, there is not a word of complaint." Two of those men would die before their comrades staggered back to Discovery Bay.

Shaken by the epidemic, Nares aborted his scheduled second winter's layover and sailed home. Near the end of October, the secretary of the Admiralty received a cable from Ireland's southwestern tip:

ARRIVED AT VALENTIA. ALL WELL. POLE IMPRACTICABLE. NO LAND TO NORTHWARD. OTHERWISE VOYAGE SUCCESSFUL. HIGHEST LATI-TUDE 83°20'. ALERT PROCEEDS TO QUEENSTOWN. DISCOVERY EX-PECTED HOURLY.

—NARES

Scurvy was not mentioned, nor that it had killed three men.

The same band that had played them out serenaded the ships with "Home, Sweet Home" as they entered Portsmouth Harbor. There was a banquet—for officers and men, sepa-rately—at Portsmouth and, later, at the Mansion House in London, where the lord mayor presented each sailor with a pipe and an ounce of tobacco. On December 1, the expedition commander entrained for Windsor and returned to London Captain Sir George Nares. At St. James Hall a week later, the Prince of Wales presided at an overflow meeting of the Royal Geographical Society; the stage was draped with the sledge banners, and the sledge *Marco Polo* was exhibited among some Eskimo artifacts. Clements Markham spoke warmly, and there were even a few verses of the *Alert*'s sledging chorus.

But a day of reckoning was due for the new arctic knight. At the lord mayor's dinner, in response to a toast, Nares had re-ferred to the expedition's "one dark spot"; it was a stain that would not wash out. Questions were asked at Westminster. Though many sailors had succumbed to scurvy on expeditions before, someone must now be held accountable for four deaths. Just as committees had been formed to set the British Arctic Expedition in motion, one was convened to find out what had gone wrong: A Parliamentary Committee of Enquiry was ap-pointed, with five members—three admirals and two doctors. One was Dr. James Donnet, an Old Arctic who had served as surgeon on the *Assistance*.

Their report, delivered in January 1878, criticized Nares for "the absence of lime juice from the sledge dietaries." In fact, Markham had carried small quantities, but reserved them for the sick only. Enough for a daily ration for all was not possible,

due to weight limitations as well as the probability of break-
age. Yet the dean of Dundee's celebratory magnum had survived intact, as had the sailors' daily tot. More controversy:
One letter to *The Times* recommended that in the future, "If
anything should be left behind, it should be the rum and not
the lime juice."

The verdict aroused choleric indignation at the Royal Geographical Society; an Old Arctic network rallied to Nares's
defense. Clements Markham retaliated with *A Refutation of the
Report of the Scurvy Committee* (a title whose penultimate word
might well have doubled as an adjective), in which he argued
that lime juice had never prevented scurvy and that only fresh
meat and/or vegetables would. Admiral Sir Leopold McClintock contradicted the report as well, pointing out that he had
carried no lime juice on his sledges. Another Old Arctic wrote
to *The Times*, asking if any of his readers had ever tried lime
juice "which has become mouldy and covered with a layer of
fungoid growth."

There, unresolved, the matter rested. That Nares was cen-
sured perhaps epitomizes the frustration and disbelief attend-
ing the recurrence of the disease, confusion to be compounded
throughout the heroic age. Not until 1912, the year in which
Britain's last polar champion would contract scurvy himself,
did Sir Gowland Hopkins's discovery of "accessory food factors"—later called vitamins—start to unravel the mystery.

Captain Sir George Nares's published account of the voyage
places the outbreak into blameless context:

> Although the disease had commenced during the out-
> ward journey, it was not known to be scurvy until they
> were halfway on their return to the ship. Then the deso-
> lating scourge proclaimed itself. . . .

His chronology is at odds with the sledge journals of Lieutenants Markham, Aldrich, and Beaumont, none of whom was
ever reprimanded. Nares's dereliction, to my mind, pales in
comparison with his field commanders' disregard for the wel-
fare of their men. All three men knew perfectly well, even
though their men or absent superior did not, the sinister import of those "game legs," warning signals that demanded response. As early as May 2, Markham had recorded:

> The invalids are not improving, and we are inclined to
> believe that they are all attacked with scurvy, although
> we have not been led to suppose that there is any proba-
> bility of our being so afflicted, and are ignorant of the
> symptoms. . . .

Nevertheless, he continued northward. On the ninth, the day
before turning back, he repeated his apparently reluctant conclusion, *fully acknowledged a week earlier*, that "our sick men
are suffering from scurvy."

Similarly, a week before he turned back, Lieutenant Beaumont was certainly aware that scurvy was the villain. He had
to know the symptoms from having read Lieutenant Hobson's
Fox diary. All polar officers committed to memory the accounts of those who had preceded them; for Markham to dis-
semble about recognizing symptoms seems evasive.

Aldrich had prevaricated as well. When Gunner Doidge complained of sore gums at Yelverton Bay, Aldrich told him that
they were caused by insufficient water with which to soak his
biscuit ration. But at least Aldrich did not wait; he turned back
the following day. Yet an illusory self-deception was maintained: The word "scurvy" does not occur in his sledge journal
until June 7, two full months after departing the *Alert*.

Indeed, the posture of all three sledge commanders is perhaps best typified by Beaumont's genuine regret: "It seemed
too cruel to turn back after such hard work." Was it "too cruel"
for the four who perished? Where did ambition end and indifference begin? By today's precepts, the simple preservation of
life would have offered overwhelming reason to turn back; but
in 1876, apparently the expected behavior of Royal Navy
sledge commanders was to press on, regardless. Quitting was
not acceptable. McClintock sets the tone as he lists attributes
of a compleat polar officer:

> . . . Strong sense of duty, and an equally strong deter-
> mination to accomplish it—dauntless resolution and in-
> domitable will, that useful compound of stubbornness
> and endurance which is so eminently British, and to
> which we islanders owe so much.

The polar game was played for keeps, its final score reckoned
in latitude rather than lives. Only by acknowledging that stern

proviso can one sense the ruthless determination goading Markham on. Whatever his professed ignorance of scurvy symptoms, it was not lost on him that, while prevailing northward over that frozen ocean, he was fronting for Queen and Empire, the cutting edge of a national effort renounced since Franklin's time and unlikely to be resurrected again.

None of Nares's sledge commanders was reprimanded; they were promoted instead. As for the pole, Nares was convinced that it could never be reached over what he called the palæocrystic—literally, ancient ice—sea. He had hoped that once his northern division left the land, they would either find another Franz Josef Land—a land bridge to the pole—or that the floes would become smoother. In fact, the very opposite proved true: The floes' surface deteriorated the farther from the shore. His cable from Valentia had said it all: "Pole impracticable. No land to northward."

The British Arctic Expedition of 1875–76 was the last of its kind. Never again would the Royal Navy embark officially for the pole, although Royal Navy grit would characterize privately subscribed ventures in Antarctica. Saddest of all was that the Britannic example, emulated by explorers the world over, never reaped the ultimate reward: The British lion, rampant elsewhere, was foiled at both poles. A dogged officer of another navy—who learned to cope with the palæocrystic sea—was first to reach the north, and an interloper ran away with the south.

4

TRY, TRY AGAIN

*I often contrast ours with the pleasant
relationship of the English officers when
here, and think how much happier we
should be following their example.*
—Lieutenant James Lockwood, U.S. Army,
at Lady Franklin Bay

Although Their Lordships had folded, America raised
the ante for the polar jackpot. Momentum initiated by Kane
and Hall was sustained by the dispatch of two additional expeditions. But both ventures would end catastrophically, cooling
Congress's polar ambition just as effectively as Nares's scurvy
had soured Parliament's. The result was predictable: Washington would deal itself out of the polar game for half a century.

The two Yankee expeditions had much in common. Both
were commanded by scholarly young officers—Lieutenant
George De Long of the Navy and Lieutenant Adolphus Greely
of the Army—who shared enthusiasm, promise, pince-nez, and
the same middle name, Washington. Both leaders, like their
American predecessors, were plagued by disgruntled subordinates, and two thirds of both commands would perish.

George De Long was the only child of a doting mother. He
applied for the Naval Academy when he was thirteen, but a
blow on the ear with a snowball precipitated a long infection,
and his application was withdrawn. Mrs. De Long proposed
that he become a doctor instead, but, apprenticed to a surgeon,

her son fainted during every operation he observed. When the Civil War broke out, young George was underage, and both parents withheld permission for his enlistment. But on his seventeenth birthday he entered the Naval Academy, situated at Newport for the duration.

Four years later, when Midshipman De Long arrived on board the USS *Canandaigua* for his first tour of duty, he found too few bunks in the midshipmen's fo'c'sle. He suggested to the astonished admiral in charge that more be installed; they were. At Lisbon, the impetuous De Long fell in love with an opera singer, proposing while she was onstage in mid-aria. Although a sophomoric prank, the episode was characteristic of a man whose motto was "Do it now." Irrepressible bravado—Markham's derring-do again—was the hallmark of this promising polar officer.

When the *Canandaigua* put into Le Havre for repairs, he fell in love again, this time with an American: Emma Wotton was the seventeen-year-old daughter of a partner in the New York/ Le Havre Steamship Company. He proposed within a fortnight, but the girl's parents, feeling that Emma was too young to become a Navy wife, mandated a two-year cooling-off period. De Long languished in South American waters, receiving only a handful of precious letters postmarked Le Havre and cherishing Emma's keepsake of a little gold cross. Two years later he pressed his suit again, and the couple were married on board the USS *Shenandoah*, anchored off Le Havre, on March 1, 1871.

But De Long's greatest love affair was with the arctic. As first lieutenant of the USS *Juniata* off Greenland, he had volunteered to command the *Little Juniata* during its search for the *Polaris*. He returned to New York a hero with, as Emma put it, "the polar virus in his blood." During a dinner party at Henry Grinnell's, the shipping magnate who had sponsored De Haven, Kane, and Hall, he requested backing for an expedition of his own. But Grinnell begged off, suggesting that De Long appeal instead to James Gordon Bennett, Jr., the heir apparent who had assumed control of the influential *New York Herald* from his father, its founder.

It was an inspired referral. The younger Bennett was a dashing man-about-town, a bachelor rake as outrageous as he was powerful. Four years earlier, in 1869, the playboy publisher had dispatched his ace foreign correspondent, Henry Stanley, in search of a lost missionary: David Livingstone was somewhere in East Africa, originally sent by the Royal Geographical Society to trace the course of the Lualaba River. Although many presumed him dead, Stanley found him alive. "The scoop of the century" rocketed the *Herald*'s daily circulation to over a hundred thousand copies. It was creative journalism of a high order and, as Bennett listened to the earnest young naval officer in January 1874, he envisioned another *Herald* coup.

De Long's proposed route was innovative: through the arctic's back door between Alaska and Siberia. He told Bennett that a kind of Pacific Gulf Stream, the Kuro-si-wo or "black tide," would carry his ship as far north as recently discovered Wrangel Land. De Long subscribed to the theories of Baron Oscar Petermann, a German geographer, who believed that Wrangel Land, Greenland, and also recently discovered Franz Josef Land were all one, not separate islands but southern vestiges of a vast, unknown continent atop the globe. The enthusiastic young naval officer envisioned the start of a land bridge to the pole beginning just north of Alaska.

Bennett was the first press baron to subsidize polar exploration. Others would follow: Fleet Street's Alfred Harmsworth would launch Frederick Jackson's thousand days in Franz Josef Land in the 1890s, and publisher Sir George Newnes's investment allowed Carsten Borchgrevink to winter ashore on Antarctica for the first time, at the turn of the century. In 1909, when Peary and Cook were bickering over the north pole, Commodore Peary was backed by *The New York Times* and Dr. Cook by the *New York Herald*, guaranteeing front-page notoriety to every salvo of that abrasive conflict.

Although Bennett wholeheartedly supported De Long's expedition, five years would pass before it sailed. Both men were awaiting Nares's return from the arctic; the instant they learned that Lieutenant Markham had stopped four hundred miles short of the pole, Bennett gave his unconditional blessing, in November 1876.

Granted two months' leave of absence, De Long searched for a vessel. None could be found in the States, so he sailed for the United Kingdom. But Scottish owners were not selling cheaply: Whalebone and whale oil were in great demand that year, and Dundee profits were enormous. Moreover, word of De Long's prestigious backer had preceded him, and prices were raised accordingly. Of the twenty whalers he inspected, half he condemned as no good; the other half were overpriced.

He returned to America empty-handed. The vessel he most coveted was the first he had inspected, not a whaler at all but the *Pandora*, Nares's "relief ship," moored at Cowes. The owner was Sir Allen Young—knighted for his arctic service—and he refused to sell for a year, capitulating only when Bennett, his recent patron, joined his persuasive voice to De Long's. Sir Allen even tried rebuying the vessel after the sale, but by then *Pandora* was undergoing a preliminary refit at Deptford.

Built originally for the Royal Navy at Devonport in 1863, she had spent four years in African service before Allen Young bought her and transformed her at Southampton into an arctic yacht. She was 124 feet long, 25 feet in the beam, with a shallow draft of 13 feet, a bark-rigged three-master with auxiliary steam engines. From Deptford, De Long cabled Emma to join him; she arrived on the next ship from New York with Sylvie, their six-year-old daughter, and moved on board. Then De Long announced that they would be sailing around Cape Horn to San Francisco that summer.

A week later, a cable arrived from Bennett, who was at Deauville, ordering De Long to suspend the work on the Thames and bring the *Pandora* over to Le Havre to be christened. De Long took the vessel across the Channel and, on July 4, 1878, Bennett's sister, Mrs. Isaac Bell, rechristened the *Pandora* with her own name, *Jeannette*.

Whatever his playboy image, Bennett was a homebody about naming ships: His own yacht, *Henrietta*, had been named after his mother, *Jeannette* after his sister. For a polar ship, it was unconventional. Most had names like *Discovery*, *Endurance*, *Intrepid*, *Endeavor*, *Quest*, or *Fram* ("forward" in Norwegian), to name but a few. Some echoed their intended objective: *Polaris*, *Stella Polare*, and, by coincidence, *Terra Nova*. There were exceptions: *Belgica* espoused nationalism, and Peary's *Roosevelt* would flatter an esteemed patron, although Charcot's *Pourquoi Pas?* was unique, the only ship that carried a question mark on her counter. These last, together with the *Jeannette*, deviated from the heroic norm. Clements

Markham, commenting on what he considered the lamentable business of rechristening expedition ships, once observed that all Franklin search vessels that had changed names were ultimately lost; only the *Fox,* bearing her builder's original choice, survived. Sadly, *Jeannette*-ex-*Pandora* would prove no exception to Markham's melancholy hypothesis.

De Long oversaw another fortnight's shipyard work at Le Havre before departing on the long trek around Cape Horn to San Francisco. For Emma, that six-month, eighteen-thousand-mile voyage, however stormy, was blissful, the longest period that she and her Navy husband had ever shared (and would ever share). Sir Allen had left his polar library on board, and Emma immersed herself in arctic history, growing to share her husband's fascination with the *Jeannette*'s polar quest. After a long, wet struggle up the California coast, they reached San Francisco two days after Christmas, 1878, with exactly one bucket of coal remaining on board. As soon as the *Jeannette* was secured at Mare Island, both De Longs were caught up in another six months' frantic preparation for departure that summer.

The Mare Island Navy Yard's refit was the *Jeannette*'s third under Bennett's ownership, and one wonders at the wisdom of entrusting the work to a trio of shipyards—one English, one French, and one American. Years later, the efficacy of the vessel's readiness for the arctic would become a matter of official scrutiny. At the Naval Court of Inquiry convened after the loss of the Steamer *Jeannette,* Commodore Edmund Colhoun, Mare Island's commanding officer, blamed the hull. "She would be less likely to get clear when nipped in the ice," he observed, even though the vessel's first owner had had firsthand experience to the contrary: Sir Allen Young had, many times, seen his beloved *Pandora* "rise to pressure" admirably. One can only assume that the cautionary hindsight of Mare Island's officers stemmed less from professional judgment than jealousy. De Long enjoyed an enviable celebrity, a young officer accorded highly preferential treatment by a rich publisher and friendship with a Navy secretary who had informed him: "When you sail, you will have the same power that is conferred upon admirals commanding fleets." Small wonder that discomfited superiors ashore might feel antagonistic.

According to George Much, Mare Island's general superintendent, the novice commander was afraid that Bennett's financial patience might wear thin. Although Congress had conferred American registry on the U.S. Exploration Steamer *Jeannette*, the *Herald*'s publisher still footed all the bills, including her purchase, three refits, and wages for her Navy crew, a staggering total of two hundred thousand dollars. Rather than kill the golden goose, De Long had restricted the Mare Island work to new sails and rigging, some new hull sheathing, boilers, and coal bunkers for a modest expenditure of fifteen thousand dollars.

Whatever her structural shortcomings, the *Jeannette* carried some exotic hardware. The *New York Post* concluded that the *Jeannette* "goes out better equipped for her work, it is believed, than any vessel that has ever gone before." Edison sent a generator to power a masthead lamp (which never worked), and Alexander Graham Bell presented De Long with telegraph keys and underwater cable to connect Siberia and Alaska en passant. Bennett spoke grandly of shipping a balloon as well, which De Long tactfully refused.

While the work proceeded in San Francisco, De Long traveled east to find officers and men. With only one exception, the thirty-one he chose proved the most harmonious polar crew yet assembled under American command. The officers were all old friends. Lieutenant Charles Chipp, the executive officer, was a tried shipmate from the *Little Juniata*. Chief engineer George Melville came from De Long's South American ship, the USS *Lancaster;* he had also sailed on the *Tigress* and would see ultimate promotion to engineer in chief of the U.S. Navy. On the messdeck, a former troublemaker had reformed: William Nindemann, one of Tyson's mutinous Germans from the ice floe, became the *Jeannette*'s ice quartermaster. Despite De Long's ethnic prejudice, the cook, steward, and cabin boy were all Chinese. Although the latter was shipped home from Alaska as unsatisfactory, the remaining two performed well, seemingly impervious to the cold.

Three civilians were carried on the rolls as seamen, though they berthed and messed with the officers. William Dunbar, the ice pilot, was a genial New England whaling captain. The *Jeannette*'s naturalist was Raymond Newcomb, a jug-eared mother's boy, immediately nicknamed Ninky. Third was the rotten apple, Jerome J. Collins, expedition meteorologist and correspondent for the *Herald,* Bennett's man-on-board. Collins came highly recommended, having made the paper's weather forecasting the envy of New York's editors. But his personality grated; he was a dark Irishman, unpredictably sensitive. Throughout the voyage he became increasingly upset that he was not carried as a full officer, an anomaly cheerfully accepted in prospect.

Of course, Collins's presence did not cause the loss of the *Jeannette;* she was done in by the pack, and her meteorologist's behavior did not hasten that end. But expedition commanders expect unquestioning loyalty and obedience from all hands, and, in this respect, Collins proved insidiously deficient, obviously unsuited for confinement on any vessel. Yachtsman Bennett should have realized this before assigning him to the expedition.

In June, only weeks before De Long was to sail, a crucial Washington promise was broken: An order assigning a navy collier to accompany the *Jeannette* to Alaska was canceled. Either the Navy Department was dragging its feet, or West Coast brass were trying to sabotage the expedition. De Long had to charter a civilian substitute, the *Fanny Hyde,* an inferior, weather-beaten coastal schooner.

The pressure of these last-minute crises cast a pall over De Long's final days at home, and an irritable gloom preoccupied him. "We may be gone for three years," he told Emma bleakly, "or we may be gone for an eternity." During one of their last evenings together, she wore black velvet to supper in their Palace Hotel suite. He stared at her strangely, suggesting with unnecessary cruelty, "I have been thinking what a pretty widow you would make."

In tune with his mood, storms battered the California coast during the first week of July, but by the afternoon of the eighth, the sun shone. It was the day of the *Jeannette*'s departure, and thousands of San Franciscans ashore and afloat—"from the boatman on the pier to the intelligent millionaire" gushed the *New York Herald*—packed the harbor. A glittering armada from the San Francisco Yacht Club, with Commodore Harrison's *Frolic* in the van, escorted the expedition ship out through the heads. As she passed Fort Point, the 4th Artillery battery thundered a twelve-gun salute from the Presidio. But

Navy ships ignored her: Not a pennant dipped to acknowledge the *Jeannette*'s passing.

Last to disembark was Emma De Long; after shaking hands with the *Jeannette*'s officers, she and her husband clambered down into one of the ship's cutters and were rowed over to the *Frolic*. De Long embraced his wife for the last time, helped her onto the yacht's companionway, and returned to his ship. Once he was back on the bridge, engine room telegraphs shrilled, black smoke poured from the single pipe stack, and the U.S. Arctic Expedition was under weigh.

Passage north was infuriatingly slow; two months would pass before the pack was sighted. The square-rigged *Jeannette* sailed poorly by the wind, consuming too much coal in consequence; slower still, the *Fanny Hyde* was soon left astern. On August 3, De Long put into the Aleutian Island port of Unalaska, where the captain of the revenue cutter *Rush* informed him that the season was "an open one." But a week passed before the *Fanny Hyde* caught up and De Long could set his course to the port of St. Michael to pick up sledges and dogs; an Alaskan kennel joined the four English dogs that had been brought around Cape Horn. Then the two ships crossed to Siberia, bucking the fury of an arctic summer gale. The *Jeannette*'s bunkers were topped up for the last time, and the coaling schooner turned back for San Francisco, carrying De Long's only crew reject, his Chinese cabin boy.

Even after the *Jeannette* had passed through Bering Strait, she was delayed yet again. De Long was under orders from Washington to find out whether Nordenskjöld's *Vega* had completed the Northeast Passage. No cairns were found at Cape Serdze Kamen, but the Chukchi Eskimos informed De Long indirectly that the vessel had indeed passed by; some of them exhibited Swedish Navy buttons, and the word *schnapps* peppered their otherwise incomprehensible patois.

August was over by the time the *Jeannette*'s ironshod bows were turned to the north. De Long had clear sailing at first, utilizing a passage carved, he presumed, by the Kuro-si-wo between the Siberian and Alaskan packs. But one night a week later he ran full tilt into stubborn ice in which the *Jeannette* became firmly imprisoned. She would remain thus for twenty-one months before going to the bottom. Like Shackleton in the

Weddell Sea in 1915, De Long was stopped before he had begun. At a latitude scarcely into the low seventies, the *Jeannette*'s voyage was at an end, his polar dream a shambles. "Truly, this is no pleasant predicament," ran a November entry in his journal.

Long before he had planned to, Melville was ordered to winterize the ship. Boilers and pipes were drained, rudder and propeller shipped inboard, and decks covered over with canvas awnings. For the first two and a half months of her confinement, the *Jeannette* was locked at a fixed, nine-degree list to starboard, scarcely hazardous but cumulatively aggravating: Port-side diners had to negotiate an irritating gap between themselves and their plates; those on the low starboard side risked a deluge of soup in their laps.

Though De Long and his men tried every means to free their ship, nothing worked. Blasting was impossible because neither electric nor flammable fuses would function. They secured halyards from the mast tops to ice hooks far out on the portside ice to career the ship—tip her on her side—but despite the entire crew heaving on the falls, the *Jeannette* remained stubbornly canted in place. A British ice saw was rigged, suspended from the fore yardarms, its low end weighted with an anchor, and dropped through the ice. But after four hours of excruciating toil, the crew had nothing to show for their pains but a six-foot cut and a damaged blade.

In November, suddenly, deliverance seemed at hand. The ice cracked open and a smoking waterway appeared along the starboard side. But with his engine winterized, De Long could not capitalize on that miraculous lead. Almost at once it turned into a liability, transformed by a gale into a millrace for wind-driven floebergs that, tumbling and jostling, threatened to crush the hull. Within a day, new ice gripped them again, the lead's only positive legacy a blessed correction of their list.

Darkness heralded the start of the arctic winter, the first of two they would pass incarcerated. During Christmas and New Year's, the crew improvised a stage in their winter deckhouse and mounted a minstrel show. Collins, an incurable punster, composed some topical riddles, to whit: "Why is that stanchion like James Gordon Bennett? Because it holds up the house." There were *tableaux vivants*, blacksmith Dressler garbed as Vulcan at his forge and, typical of messdeck humor to this day, *Two Sailors Mourning a Dead Marine:* revealed were two crewmen draped lugubriously over an empty brandy bottle, one of four that De Long had issued, full, to greet the New Year. Not quite Royal Arctic Theatre caliber but, warmed by the spirits, the *Jeannette's* crew roared their approval, grateful for anything that jogged their monotonous routine.

Monotony was conjoined with terror a few weeks later. On January 19, a massive wall of ice, fifty feet high, appeared out of the night, grinding relentlessly toward the *Jeannette* as though some subterranean monster were intent on her destruction. Such pressure ridges are inevitable phenomena of the restless, frozen sea. Far beyond the *Jeannette's* horizon, ice had been set in motion by wind or tide: A weak point had fractured, exposing a black ribbon of water. Leads created like this trigger havoc: Torn here, the ocean ice wrinkles there. One of those "wrinkles" became a pressure ridge. Compressed floes erupted, arching, bridging, and toppling in violent confusion. Once spawned, these pressure ridges establish an implacable line of march, raising adjoining ice in contagious upheaval.

Such was the awesome rampart threatening the *Jeannette*. With professional detachment, ice pilot Dunbar clocked its approach at a yard a minute, then paced off the intervening distance to the ship: three hundred yards. The *Jeannette*, he announced to De Long, would be a goner in five hours. But, mysteriously, the onslaught ceased a hundred yards short of the hull; somewhere over the horizon, the pack's stress had been relieved. The incident was not atypical: Logbooks of beset ships threatened by pressure ridges continually anticipate Armageddon only to record miraculous, sudden reprieves.

But worse was in store that day. A restive floe beneath them heaved and tore the *Jeannette's* forefoot. Seawater flooded in through five feet of solid oak, engulfing the fireroom. Only steam pumps would save them, but both boilers were drained. When Melville tried filling the high, portside boiler, he found that the seacock piercing the hull had frozen solid. It would have to be filled by hand.

A stoker clambered atop the frigid boiler and attacked the manhole bolts. They backed off easily—thank God for Bennett's new boilers! Once the cover was off, Melville organized the black gang into a bucket brigade that hoisted up pails of seawater swirling at their feet, bailing fireroom into boiler.

Spillage coated the men with ice, and their booted feet froze to the submerged iron deck.

Contravening Navy regulations, Melville ordered anticipatory fires lit in the firebox. The cold boilers might fracture like glass but that risk was no worse than the peril they faced without steam. Within moments, orange flames crackled in the grate. After eight tons of water had been dumped into the boiler, its sight glass indicated that the crown plates were submerged. Ice was chipped away from the rim, and the cover was rebolted in place. Stokers hurled coal on top of the blazing kindling, and the draft roared as steam was raised. Melville nursed the almost submerged pump into motion. With a hissing groan, the flywheel turned and clattered into motion. White water foamed out onto the surrounding ice through the low-side scuppers. Once again, the *Jeannette* had been saved.

The pump kept up its welcome clangor for weeks as carpenters, working knee-deep in icy water, built a cofferdam across the bow, improvising in desperate haste a transverse bulkhead that should have been part of Mare Island's refit. Then the ingenious Melville constructed a windmill that, geared to the hand pumps, whirred day and night on the bridge. This restricted the inflow enough so he could shut off the steam, drain the boiler, and save his precious coal.

Daylight returned. All but Lieutenant John Danenhower, blinded by a persistent eye inflammation and confined below, rejoiced at the sight of it. Collins, who had dined alone since Christmas, sulked in his cabin, at acrimonious odds with his captain. The sailors shot game, the Chinese flew kites. By the end of summer, after a year beset, the *Jeannette* would have drifted 150 miles. Although a convenient word, "drift" does not adequately describe that agonizingly slow repositioning that De Long could verify only by sextant. Aimless and frustrating as their movement was, at least it tended toward the pole. Explorers on the opposite side of the globe knew only the reverse, a prevailing ice thrust that drove them south. De Long joked that given enough time, he might actually drift to his objective. As it was, his only geographical discovery that year was exposing the fallacy of Baron Petermann's "land bridge to the pole": The *Jeannette* was carried north of Wrangel "Land," proving it nothing more than Wrangel Island.

That summer of 1880 coincided with a mounting expectancy

that the *Jeannette* might be freed. Summer rain showers, it was hoped, were rotting the pack. Additionally, De Long tried a whaler's trick to hasten the process. Ashes and refuse, darker and more heat-absorbing than the ice, were deposited around the hull, turning their promenade into black slush. But it worked: The *Jeannette* rose a few inches. The forward leak was retarded and, joyously, De Long ordered Melville to rig the propeller and rudder. But July 4, his anticipated date for flotation and the second anniversary of the *Jeannette*'s rechristening, passed with no change, as did the balance of that brief arctic summer. De Long and his crew resigned themselves to a second winter beset.

The end came in June of the following year. Ironically, just two days before she succumbed, the *Jeannette* was afloat in a tiny lagoon. But on the twelfth, opposing banks of ice closed in ruthlessly and the ship was wracked over on her starboard beam ends, caught this time in a fatal nip, keel and submerged starboard railing holding *Jeannette* firmly in place, unable to slip upward. The starboard side caved in and the spar deck buckled. De Long, pipe clenched imperturbably under his drooping mustache, stood on the sloping bridge to the end. That evening he had the naval ensign run up to the mizzen truck and, shouting over the death rattle of his broken ship, ordered his men over the side for the last time.

It was a moment long anticipated. A standby camp, with tents, sledges, boats, and provisions for sixty days had already been established three hundred yards away on the ice. After months of false alarms, final abandonment of their ship came as a relief; nothing that lay ahead, it was agreed, could be worse than those anxious months behind them. However, their first night camped on the pack proved unsettling: The ice beneath them parted abruptly, and a man sleeping in midtent awoke to find himself cradled over black water, saved only by the weight of shipmates on either end of their joint ground cloth.

Frank Hurley, Shackleton's photographer on the doomed *Endurance*, captured his ship's destruction on motion picture film. Whereas whalers nipped in Melville Bay capitulated in minutes, ships long beset, like the terminally ill, exert a stubborn hold on life: Death comes not by cataclysm but by awful degrees. Hurley's establishing shot shows the *Endurance*'s hull and superstructure almost indistinguishable from the encroaching ice. From a confusion of buckled timbers rise masts, funnels, and ventilators, all askew. The icescape heaves, sending fatal tremors aloft. Spars twitch, then tumble, lodging precariously in tangled rigging. Stays slacken and a topmast collapses, arcing over and down. Then a halyard snaps, dropping topsail yards like a stone, trailing shrouds of fluttering canvas. The *Endurance* seems savaged by invisible wreckers.

That same devastation consumed the abandoned *Jeannette*. By three o'clock on the morning of June 13, 1881, she had returned upright, momentarily sustained on the surface of the ice that had destroyed her, her hull perforated like a basket and her wracked funneltop awash. Only her masts remained in place because Melville remembers that she disappeared from sight so swiftly that, dropping through the ice, her yards snapped upward—"like a great gaunt skeleton clapping its hands above its head." Then the *Jeannette* was gone, sunk at a paltry 77° North, the end of De Long's vision and Bennett's ambition, five hundred miles from the Siberian mainland and half again as far from the elusive pole.

Nil desperandum—"Nothing is to be despaired of"—reappears continually throughout De Long's journal. Emma had embroidered the same motto on the silk banner that flew from his sledge, *Sylvie*. Surely, if any man had reason to despair, it was Lieutenant George Washington De Long that bleak summer of 1881, his ship gone, his chronometer broken, his men committed to a southern march over the rotting pack, retreating rather than advancing. The ice that had sunk his ship now cut his men's boots to ribbons, and they splashed along in improvised sandals of sealskin and hemp. Danenhower was still blind, Dunbar was crippled with arthritis, and the cantankerous Collins had long since been relieved of all duties, placed under arrest since December. Yet *nil desperandum:* At least his command was intact, food adequate, and the dread scurvy at bay.

After six laborious weeks, the castaways reached and named uncharted Bennett Island, struggling gratefully over its icefoot onto Cape Emma, a barren, basalt beach covered with driftwood and game. It was their first landfall in two years. They camped there for several days, gorging themselves on roasted seabirds. Then they passed on, ever south, sledging or sometimes sailing through the New Siberian Islands. Then, at last, they were free of the pack, navigating in three boats through unobstructed waters.

By a cruel irony, the open sea De Long had sought for two years drowned a third of his command. Within sight of the mainland, the boats were separated by a gale. Melville and the whaleboat made it to shore and, ultimately, civilization; but Lieutenant Chipp's cutter, with Captain Dunbar and six sailors on board, was lost. In hindsight, it might have been kinder had De Long's thirteen men suffered the same fate, a sailor's death by drowning. As it was, they grounded in the mouth of the Lena River. Where it flows into the East Siberian Sea, the river's mouth is a bewildering, fan-shaped delta, wetlands neither solid enough for marching nor deep enough for navigation. De Long and his scarecrow detachment abandoned their boat and trudged inland through knee-deep, icy muck.

They had not progressed far before they halted forever. Hunting parties were sent out, but they only managed to shoot two reindeer, scarcely enough to alleviate the starvation, exhaustion, and cold ravaging the sailors. As a last resort, De Long sent two men to look for the Lena Delta's Eskimos who, thus far, had not appeared. Seamen Noros and Nindemann were selected as the strongest. Obstreperous to the end, Collins demanded that, as *Herald* correspondent, he accompany them; De Long refused, point-blank. Scarcely less debilitated than their comrades, the two sailors disappeared into a blizzard, the last to see De Long or his party alive.

After a nightmare journey, they reached a settlement but were unable to muster help from its inhabitants. Like characters in a fatalistic, Oriental morality play, the two seamen tried communicating their urgency in pantomime. Nindemann borrowed a child's toy boat and, with twigs representing men, reconstructed the drama of the *Jeannette*, the ship beset and sunk, her crew disembarked on the ice, the voyage to shore, and, as a finale, a starving encampment in the wilds.

The Eskimos listened respectfully, seeming to comprehend. But nothing would stir them: Either they nodded out of politeness or they realized the folly of traveling that late in the season. Their indifference reduced Noros and Nindemann to tears of impotent rage. Melville came across them weeks later, bedded down in an infested hut. The two men wept anew, sobbing out the plight of their starving comrades. But by then, Siberia was deep in the grip of winter.

In the spring, James Gordon Bennett sent his promised relief overland. Deprived of the pole for his readers, he was hoping for a dramatic rescue, promising to bring back De Long "dead or alive." John Jackson, the *Herald*'s Paris bureau chief, arrived in Yakutsk with trunkloads of arctic equipment, confident of duplicating Stanley's African coup. But chief engineer George Melville forestalled him: With Nindemann to guide him, he and a party of Eskimos had already sledged north to De Long's last camp.

A kettle, resting incongruously atop the snow, betrayed its location. Nearby, De Long's arm protruded above the drift. Tears freezing on his cheeks, Melville uncovered the bodies. Behind De Long's was his journal, flung over his shoulder to avoid the fire that had burned at his feet. Some of his men had literally crawled into the flames for warmth; their chests were charred from the heat. De Long had become too incapacitated to write on October 30, the 140th day since the *Jeannette* had sunk. His journal petered out with a cryptic rota of deaths: "Collins dying" were the last words De Long wrote. There may have been others, for the journal's next page had been torn out; Melville assumed that it had been intended as a letter to Emma, but he never found it.

They buried the rigid, emaciated bodies in a communal tomb, said a prayer, and departed. Jackson of the *Herald* arrived the following day and, journalistic zeal outweighing respect for the dead, opened the grave in search of papers. But Melville had gathered them all.

Months later, the bodies were retrieved by an official U.S. Navy detail and, by sledge, riverboat, train, and steamship, brought back to New York. Commander George Washington De Long, promoted in absentia, had come home. Still wrapped in an oilskin case across one shoulder was the *Jeannette*'s commissioning flag stitched by Emma that, together with a scrap of the *Polaris*'s ensign, was to have been deposited at the pole. In his pocket was a battered gold cross, young Emma Wotton's betrothal keepsake from Le Havre. Together with five of his crew, De Long was buried in Woodlawn Cemetery. Cold haunted him to the end: It snowed the day of the funeral, and a

Navy monument unveiled at Annapolis in 1889 was fringed with marble icicles.

There were two curious aftermaths, the first a posthumous jab from Collins. Although a Navy Court of Inquiry had already closed its investigation, Collins's aggrieved brother succeeded in having a congressional inquiry convened as well. After reading Jerome Collins's diary, he maintained that De Long so hated his brother that at the Lena camp he had prevented him from saving his own life; he demanded an investigation. Called to testify, Emma De Long quoted a passage from Surgeon Ambler's diary, also recovered by Melville, that refuted Collins's claim; the inquiry was called off.

While Emma was editing her husband's journal, she uncovered a remarkable coincidence: De Long had left his nickel-plated pocket watch with her for safekeeping. She had wound it every day, but after two years of trouble-free accuracy, it had inexplicably broken its mainspring one day in the summer of 1881. As she read through George's journal, she discovered that the pocket watch had broken at exactly the same time as the *Jeannette*'s chronometer had failed.

A disastrous sequel to the *Jeannette* tragedy was already in train back on the American way. Lieutenant Adolphus Greely of the U.S. Army was in command of a detachment at Fort Conger on the shores of Lady Franklin Bay, within a stone's throw of Nares's *Discovery* anchorage of 1875. Their presence at Fort Conger that summer of 1881 resulted from the United States' commitment to the work of the International Polar Commission. Weyprecht, the Austrian explorer, had founded the Commission in 1875 as an instrument for coordinating scientific observations from eleven nations: Fourteen stations, a dozen in the arctic and two in the antarctic, were proposed and established.

As its contribution, the United States had pledged to man one station at Alaska's Point Barrow and another "somewhere in the Canadian archipelago." "Somewhere" proved to be Discovery Harbor, even though the site lay at an unnecessarily high latitude, far higher than any of the others. Its selection had resulted from legislative convenience. The previous year, Congress had voted funds for an extraordinary manifestation of polar fever known as polar colonization: A permanent settlement, complete with women and children, was to be set up on the shores of Discovery Harbor, near a convenient coal seam. It was assumed that the colony's male inhabitants, spared a troublesome annual battle through the ice of the American way, could dash to the pole at will.

This preposterous scheme foundered, but its residual advantage included congressional approval. So Lady Franklin Bay was chosen, for all the wrong reasons, as one of the United States' two weather stations for the International Polar Commission. It was to be manned by Greely and his command.

Unlike De Long, Greely combined success and failure in ambiguous measure. He maintained his post for two successive years, gathering meticulous meteorological data. Even more noteworthy, his second-in-command, Lieutenant James Lockwood, persevered along Greenland's northern coast to 83°23', surpassing Nares's record above Cape Columbia. Yet these stirring achievements were flawed by a subsequent debacle, culminating in the return of only six of his original twenty-five men. It was not Greely's fault: Governmental complacency, adverse weather, bad timing, and the ineptitude of others conspired against him. History has remembered his ordeal south of 79° rather than his glorious record north of 83°; the name Greely is synonymous with starvation and death.

His budget was minuscule—at twenty-five thousand dollars it was one eighth the amount that Bennett had lavished on the *Jeannette*. Three quarters of that sum went to hire the Dundee whaler *Proteus*, merely to transport the detachment north, an inordinately expensive charter. Greely would be land-based; one of the rare generosities extended him was a large, insulated hut, sixty by seventeen feet, that had been prefabricated for the colonization scheme and that would be loaded on board the *Proteus* at Disko. Ashore, Greely would remain invulnerable to treacherous ice movements that plagued ships wintering in.

Greely found that equipping his expedition was no picnic. Army lieutenants have little clout in Washington's bureaucracy. His only trump card was the powerful support of Michigan's senator Omar Conger, whose name was given to the northern encampment in grateful acknowledgment. Even so, Greely was roundly abused. Some of his scientific instruments, promised new, were uncrated rusty and unserviceable. The steam launch *Lady Greely* had a boiler inadequate to handle salt water, necessitating a last-minute replacement at St. John's. He was issued no special cold-weather clothing; although he bought some furs in Greenland, Army quartermasters provided his men with only standard winter woolen issue.

That summer of 1881, while Greely battled an indifferent federal establishment, the chartered whaler *Rodgers* sailed in search of De Long, now vanished for two years. The *Rodgers* found nothing, and she was to burn in Siberia's St. Lawrence Bay the following winter. She had been renamed after Admiral John Rodgers, president of the *Jeannette* Relief Board; her subsequent misfortune served to reinforce Clements Markham's foreboding about rechristening search ships.

Sir Clements, in fact, was also vehemently articulate on the subject of relief ships, pointing out that, had backup expeditions been dispatched promptly in Franklin's wake, the *Erebus* and the *Terror* might have been saved. In 1901, when Scott sailed, Markham made no bones about it. No sooner had the *Discovery* left England than he set about raising funds for a relief ship. Predictably, Her Majesty's government balked. They had expended considerable monies to build one ship; agitation for another seemed deceitful. But Sir Clements differed: Relief ships, he maintained, were an intrinsic part of exploration, and their provision should be implemented with the same priority that had attended the expedition ship. With the specter of Franklin and his lost command looming in perpetual reproof, Parliament predictably gave in. But Congress made no such plans for Greely's relief or, at least, not until long after the *Proteus* had returned.

But relief was only part of Greely's problem. Once again, on this fourth American arctic expedition, personnel proved intractable, this time on a commissioned level. There were only two officers besides Greely, one the efficient Lockwood, the other a Lieutenant Frederick Kislingbury, whose disaffection surfaced before the expedition reached Lady Franklin Bay. Although an old friend, Kislingbury informed his astonished commanding officer that he wished to leave, just as the *Proteus* was weighing anchor. Greely, a stickler for military protocol, demanded a formal letter of resignation; Kislingbury complied. The delay would cost him his life: Captain Pike of the

Proteus, awaiting an opening in Lady Franklin Bay's accumulating ice, departed abruptly before the resigned officer could complete Greely's letter and board the southbound vessel. So Greely was stuck with a former second-in-command who wished fervently to be elsewhere. Although Kislingbury proved an excellent hunter and pulled his weight, his presence at Fort Conger was a source of constant embarrassment and friction.

The expedition's surgeon, Octave Pavy, was openly antagonistic from the start. He was an unreliable hybrid, neither civilian fish nor military fowl, sworn in for Army service on an annual basis, starting at Disko. Pavy had enjoyed a privileged Louisiana upbringing and studied medicine in Paris. In the mid-1870s, he had hoped to mount his own polar expedition, but he had it aborted at the last minute by the death of a crucial backer. Pavy had then dropped out, moving to Kansas City, where he lived for five years in self-imposed poverty and humiliation, surgeon turned itinerant gardener, before joining Greely's expedition. Greely regarded him with hostility and contempt, a man whose "previous Bohemian life" ill-suited him for subordination. Quite obviously, Greely and his doctor were a hopeless, oil-and-water combination, and one queries the wisdom of having recruited a civilian physician who had hoped for his own polar command in a former life. Pavy invariably sided with the disgruntled Kislingbury, often in front of the men. Thus it was that the officers' mess partitioned off at one end of Fort Conger was psychologically subdivided yet again: Greely and Lockwood, service stalwarts, were in continuing disagreement with surgeon Pavy and disenchanted Kislingbury.

The disaffection of two out of three colleagues is revealing. What kind of man was Adolphus Greely? Physically, he was distinctive—tall, thin, and erect, with long, sensitive hands and fingers. His detached, scholarly air was heightened by pince-nez spectacles and a long, flowing beard, grown thus to conceal the ravages of a Confederate bullet on his lower jaw. Greely was all Army, a military ascetic wedded to routine and regulation, yet at the same time abrasive to his peers. Would both Kislingbury and Pavy have proved so intractable serving under a man they admired? Conversely, an overbearing commanding officer does not excuse insubordination. Identifying the traits that brother officers found trying is not easy. Greely

returned from the arctic semicanonized, and documenting be-
havioral deficiencies in Victorian soldier/heroes is notoriously
difficult. But reading between the lines of his two-volume self-
justification—*Three Years of Arctic Service*—one does detect
the author's humorless inflexibility, verging on the pompous, a
commander determined to follow a rulebook that had never
been written for high latitudes.

Passage north was benign: The *Proteus* negotiated the seven
hundred miles between Upernavik and Lady Franklin Bay in a
carefree week. After the ship's departure, Fort Conger's garrison settled down to routine. Lockwood, elevated to second-in-
command by Kislingbury's defection, was ordered to lay depots for the spring expeditions. It was his first exposure to
sledging; like all neophytes, he had to start from scratch, and
he made his share of gaffes in the process. Every polar explorer, however much he has boned up on his predecessors,
undergoes weeks of trial and error before mastering the intricate art of sledge travel.

Lockwood tried building his own sledge to replace the heavy
British Admiralty models that Greely had brought north. He
found his own design equally cumbersome and fell back instead on a light, maneuverable Greenland sledge, similar to
Kane's *Little Willy*, drawn by dogs. The expedition's cook-
stoves, called "Tramp's Companion," proved hazardous. They
had been soldered too close to the flame and collapsed when
hot, deluging waiting diners in floods of burning alcohol,
melted lead, and lukewarm food. Even the sledging pemmican
was specious stuff; it had been laced with lime juice in an
attempt to avoid a repetition of Nares's scurvy. As a result, the
expedition's stews tasted unpleasantly tart; consumed uncooked, frozen lime juice crystals in the meat cut and irritated
the men's gums.

Logistical shortfalls enlivened several early excursions from
Fort Conger. On one, after both cups and spoons had inadvertently been left behind, the soldiers had to eat like Arabs, dip-
ping fingers into the stewpot itself, alternately burning and
freezing them in the process. They learned, as Nares's men
had, to carry spoons on lanyards around their necks. (The British had used massive spoons carved out of horn to prevent
their freezing to the lips.) On another autumnal outing, candles
were mistakenly omitted from Lockwood's sledgeloads.

But before spring arrived, he had become expert. In April 1882, driving dogs at impressive speed, Lockwood set out along Greenland's northern coast in Lieutenant Beaumont's footsteps. In support were four man-hauled Hudson Bay sledges, christened *Kane, Hayes, Hall,* and *Beaumont.* The Americans encountered the same deep snow that had confounded their Royal Navy predecessors six years earlier, but with lighter loads on their tobogganlike sledges, stayed atop the snow's crust.

At the end of April the Americans established a final depot, at Cape Bryant. From there, a three-man assault party pressed on alone: Lockwood, Sergeant David Brainard, and Frederick Christian, one of the fort's two Eskimo drivers. Within three days, Beaumont's farthest north, Cape Britannia, had been surpassed; in another ten, Lockwood's party achieved an additional hundred miles. They stopped for only two reasons: to conserve rations for their return and because they had beaten the record. Lockwood, Brainard, and Christian had sledged farthest north, not merely in the Western Hemisphere but also worldwide, wherever the Royal Navy had left their heroic mark for three centuries.

The Americans spent an entire day rechecking their observations. Their journals would be scrutinized by geographers in Washington and Europe, nowhere more rigorously than in London, at 1 Savile Row, headquarters of the Royal Geographical Society. At a dozen locations, Lieutenant Lockwood flopped belly down in the snow and put one tortured eye to his sextant's leather-rimmed eyepiece. With meticulous patience, he brought the sun's image down to touch the glistening mercury pool of his artificial horizon, the device that all travelers in the arctic's shrouded wilderness must use to gauge their position. Each result, tabulated with the help of Admiralty tables, was gloriously consistent: 83°23' North, three nautical miles better than Markham's record above Cape Columbia of 1876.

Having established his position, Lockwood assigned names to the world's new northernmost geographical features. The island on which he stood became Lockwood Island; Brainard rated a smaller one nearby for himself. Greely's name was conspicuously absent. Although, the following year, Lockwood would christen Greely Fjord in Grinnell Land far to the west, the expedition commander was denied lasting recognition at the farthest north. Was it oversight, or an indication of Lockwood's unspoken reservations about his chief? One compensatory ritual was observed: Mrs. Greely's silken flag was unfurled, the first time Old Glory had ever flown at such an exotic latitude.

The journey home was made at a slightly increased rate of speed. Apart from cold feet and occasional snow blindness, the health of the party was excellent. The dogs suffered most, so ravenously hungry that on several occasions they burrowed under the tent flap to eat scraps of harness.

After sledging a thousand miles in sixty days, the indefatigable Lockwood reported back to his superior at Fort Conger. Greely was ecstatic. Unlike most commanders of the heroic age, he had apparently been content to send a subordinate on the glory march. I doubt that it was a question of ability: Greely was a conscientious exerciser who jogged regularly at Fort Conger, while Lockwood, the instrument of his triumph, toiled up Greenland's coast. Years later, as America's arctic elder statesman, General Greely would be critical of Nansen for heading to the pole on foot, "deserting his command" on the *Fram*. But then, given the parlous state of officer morale at Fort Conger, Greely's preoccupation with minding the store is scarcely surprising.

Lockwood's electrifying achievement that spring was the expedition's psychological highwater mark; thereafter, things deteriorated. The following year, he was prevented from improving his record by impassable open water along the same coastline. By the end of August 1883, the expedition had completed two years at Lady Franklin Bay; but no relief ship had appeared during either intervening summer, though not, it must be admitted, for want of trying. Since Greely's arrival, the American way had reverted to bleak normal. The first summer, the *Neptune* had been unable to battle farther north than Cape Hawks; during the second, the *Proteus* had not only failed to reach Fort Conger but also had been crushed by the ice just north of Smith Sound; she went to the bottom carrying the bulk of Greely's reprovisions. Lieutenant Ernest Garlington, the Army officer in command, left two inadequately marked and protected caches on Littleton Island and fled south. He took with him more than he left for Greely.

With no relief ship in sight for the second successive summer, Greely evacuated his command. The steam launch *Lady Greely* was loaded to the gunwales with two and a half tons of locally mined coal. Divided among three smaller boats in tow were forty days' worth of provisions and all the scientific data. The men were restricted to eight pounds of personal possessions—half the officers' allotment—and the entire command was newly shod in homemade boots of untanned sealskin manufactured by Private Fredericks, whose specialty was saddlery.

Just as Captain Pike had steamed abruptly out of Discovery Harbor to evade the August ice two years earlier, so, too, did Greely, mustering the garrison in midmeal. Abandoned Fort Conger assumed the phantom desolation of a landbound *Mary Celeste*. A fire glowed in the cookstove, laundry was left hanging in the washroom, and food-encrusted plates adorned the mess tables. The only vestiges of life remaining were the dogs, spared rather than slaughtered. There was neither room nor need for them in the boats, but Greely prudently left open the possibility of a return should passage south prove impossible. So the animals were unchained and awarded a rare, gluttonous orgy as Sergeant Brainard broached all the barrels of meat and blubber to sustain them against the foreseeable future. One faithful animal, Flipper, splashed after the departing boats, paddling for miles in their wake before drowning, uncomprehending, in the chill brash of Lady Franklin Bay. Also left crated at Fort Conger were dress uniforms, all save Lockwood's and Greely's. The expedition commander chose the moment of departure for a bizarre, tragicomic gesture: He stood in the *Lady Greely*'s bow accoutered in full regalia, sash, sword, and frock coat, glistening with buttons, incongruous among his ragged command but determined to lend an air of dignity to their retreat.

Whereas the detachment had reached Lady Franklin Bay within a week in 1881, the return journey to Sabine Island consumed two months. It became abundantly clear why relief had been denied them: Kennedy Channel was hopelessly clogged. The launch, with fragile charges in tow, steamed cautiously along the western shore, in continuing peril from the tidal ructions of the ice. On countless occasions, Greely's men avoided having their boats crushed by hauling them out on top of the threatening floes, all save the impossibly heavy, engined

Lady Greely, which mercifully rose above the ice rather than succumbed to the squeeze.

On another occasion, Greely was obliged to pass between the fractured halves of a gigantic floeberg that lay grounded in his path. Floebergs were avoided whenever possible, for they are unstable white leviathans that often topple without warning. The little armada chugged through one, into an echoing cleft scarcely wider than its collective gunwales; to either side, fifty-foot cliffs of dazzling blue ice loomed up—awesome, vaulted majesty that might, momentarily, entomb the entire expedition. No one spoke. Greely threaded his way a hundred yards before emerging, vastly relieved, from the floeberg's southern exit.

By September, after a month afloat, their luck ran out just north of the seventy-ninth parallel. All four boats were hopelessly beset, dragged back north by successive ebb tides. On the nineteenth, Greely abandoned the *Lady Greely* and committed his men to the ice, relaying loaded boats on sledges across the pack toward land. They finally reached Eskimo Point, south of their destination, frozen and already emaciated, a landfall devoid of promise. Sabine's trio of caches, two left by the hapless Garlington and one of Nares's, would provide little more than bare subsistence throughout the winter that followed. It was the detachment's third in the arctic, only this time removed from the comforts of Fort Conger. Now they bedded down in a drafty, stone hut roofed with oars, canvas, and an upturned whaleboat, inshore from Wreck Cache Cove, midway between Cocked Hat Island and Cape Sabine. "Bedded down" quite literally, for once their sleeping bags were spread, no further room remained. There was nothing to do but try to keep warm, talk, think and dream about food, and stay alive. Their winter house was called Camp Clay, after Henry Clay, the silver-tongued American statesman.

That two-month boat journey had wreaked havoc with morale, starting at the top. Greely's dress uniform had been discarded after only one day's wear and, once they were beset, his saber was wrought into a fishing spear. That disposal of ceremonial trappings symbolized Greely's degeneration as well. Away from shore, both he and his men had been dangerously out of their depth. None of them was a sailor: Rope, canvas, cleat, and spar were alien, and, in hindsight, one longs for a whaling man or an able-bodied seaman to have been among them.

As they were adrift in a hostile environment of water and ice, demoralization manifested itself in ugly ways. Sergeant William Cross, the unit's only engineer, drank himself into a stupor on duty belowdecks in the *Lady Greely*'s engine space, so incapacitated that he was relieved by an infuriated Greely. Cross alone was qualified to maintain their steam machinery; worse, his illicit grog was the expedition's cooking fuel, already in short supply.

Other malcontents perseverated as well. Prior to quitting Fort Conger, Dr. Pavy had declined to be sworn in for a third year of service, although he did continue to serve the sick; Hippocrates prevailed where Uncle Sam did not. He also refused to hand over his journal. (Expedition regulations required all its members to keep diaries and turn them in to the commanding officer.) Greely had ordered the surgeon's arrest—surely an arctic first—restricting him to within a mile of the fort, confinement the prisoner promptly violated. In the boats, Pavy's defiance took the form of criticizing Greely's conduct of the retreat. Kislingbury, his ancient ally, joined in the attack. The two men even debated relieving Greely of his command as medically unfit, mutinous talk they shared indiscreetly with the sergeants.

Was their concern justified, or were they pursuing a savage vendetta? Probably the latter. Certainly Greely was distraught. The summer pack is bewilderingly capricious—water one minute, solid ice the next. Negotiating boats or sledges through that chaos has taxed the skill of many a naval officer. For Army-man Greely to have brought off his hazardous maritime gamble was, to my mind, an enviable feat.

Greely parried the insubordinate antagonism of his officers ingeniously: Both were included among a council of officers and sergeants with whom he discussed all major decisions. It was an arrangement that remains at odds with military convention but one that seems the choice of a conciliatory and rational commander: A Bligh or a Queeg would never have compromised their threatened authority, and it is to Greely's credit that he did. Moreover, whatever his method or even shortcomings, he had succeeded thus far in bringing out his entire command intact.

Back in the States, jarred by the loss of the *Proteus*, Washington dithered. Should a third relief ship be sent? One finally was, thanks largely to Lieutenant Greely's indomitable wife. Having dutifully stitched her husband's polar banner, Henrietta Greely was not content to wait prayerfully in San Diego. Rather, in the tradition of Lady Franklin, the determined polar wife whose name graced the waters off Fort Conger, she browbeat a reluctant government. She had no fortune at her command but, instead, influential Washington wives as her friends, as well as the ear of a sympathetic press, Bennett's *Herald* among them. Cleverly, she concentrated her fire on Secretary of the Navy William Chandler, who was openly receptive to the idea of a Navy rescue of an Army calamity.

At the War Office, evasion reigned. Having dispatched two successive relief ships with disastrous results, Secretary Robert Todd Lincoln was not sanguine about mounting a third. "I do not see any use in throwing away more money on dead men," he observed unfeelingly. Henrietta Greely continued to woo the Navy.

President Chester Arthur straddled the service fence and resorted to the time-honored presidential ploy of appointing a commission. Two Army and two Navy officers were convened as a Board of Officers Considering a Relief Expedition to Lieutenant Greely. They spent weeks soliciting the opinion of dozens of expert witnesses, whose names read like an American *Who's Who in the Arctic:* Dr. Bessels, George Tyson, Captains Pike and Greer, as well as Danenhower and Melville, just back from Siberia.

Despite Greely's acknowledged predicament, nothing could be done before the spring of 1884. George Melville advocated a quick September rescue, but whether a ship could have reached Sabine before the ice closed in was debatable. As a result, Congress had at its mellifluous disposal an entire fall and winter to ponder, debate, wrangle, and cajole before reaching agreement.

In mid-February, the House and the Senate hammered out a compatible bill: A Navy expedition was to be mounted, composed of three ships, their crews equipped, if necessary, to winter over as far north as Lady Franklin Bay. Furthermore, Congress authorized a reward of twenty-five thousand dollars to whichever whaling master first reported traces of the lost detachment. Dundee ships were to be purchased, for New Bedford whalemen were not as bold as their Scottish colleagues; neither, in consequence, were their hulls. To President Arthur's credit, American consuls in both Dundee and St. John's were instructed, discreetly, to price available whalers in early January, even though Congress had not yet authorized funds for their purchase. January tenders were essential for, within weeks, all masters and ships would have sailed on their annual sealing/whaling voyages.

A pair of ships was speedily bought, the *Bear* and the *Thetis*, the former a sister of the ill-fated *Polaris*. A third was added to the fleet gratis, a gift from Her Majesty's government. She was HMS *Alert*, Nares's expedition vessel that lay dismantled at Chatham. Her hull was still sound (the stoutest afloat), and she was given a thorough refit on the Thames.

The *Alert* reached New York in late April, only two days before the *Bear* set sail for the North. The *Thetis* followed a week later, and the *Alert* on May 10. All three were cheered down the East River. Although the Royal Navy ensign streamed from the *Alert*'s foremast, volunteers from the U.S. North Atlantic Fleet exclusively served on board. Commodore of the flotilla was Commander Winfield Scott Schley, a can-do line officer; one of his chief engineers was George Melville, hero of the *Jeannette*. It was only regrettable that they had not sailed a year earlier. In awful contrast to the resolve that marked their departure was the desperation awaiting them at Sabine Island.

On January 19, while in Washington senators wrangled over Chandler's appropriation, Camp Clay's first death had occurred. Sergeant Cross, the alcoholic engineer, died from scurvy and malnutrition, a dread diagnosis that Pavy communicated to Greely in French to avoid panicking the others; Greely subsequently lied that Cross had suffered a "dropsical effusion of the heart." He was buried on top of a nearby knoll, selected for no other reason than that its gravel afforded the only possible winter digging. By the time relief arrived, ten additional graves would adorn the plot, each shallower than its predecessor as the strength of the burial parties diminished. Not even the strongest was spared: Lieutenant Lockwood succumbed and was laid out in his dress uniform. So cruelly did winds batter the hilltop cemetery that the gravel-scoured brass buttons along his chest were soon exposed, winking in the arctic sun each time Sergeant Brainard passed en route to bait shrimp traps in the cove.

Death's only beneficial legacy at Camp Clay was that survivors' rations were increased in consequence. Clothes from the deceased were shared so that those remaining alive at the end were cocooned in ragbag layers of underclothing, tunics, and overalls, courtesy of their dead comrades. By spring, sealskin clothing was transmogrified by desperation from fur into food: it was found that boiled sealskin, regardless of age, yielded a nourishing broth.

Food was their eternal preoccupation. One of Camp Clay's enduring time-killers was fabrication of elaborate, imaginary feasts, some of which were recorded. Cooking what they had to eat was an ordeal. Their stove was made from the whaleboat's iron plating, its chimney from interlocking tin cans, its fuel from match-size slivers whittled from planking. Smoke so stifled the detachment that all but the cooks had to withdraw beneath the flaps of their sleeping bags. When ready, portions were weighed out by Sergeant Brainard, each scrutinized to ensure a fair division. A day's ration of bread—some of it moldy dog biscuit—scarcely covered the palm of one hand. Tea leaves, twice used, were devoured eagerly.

In late May, the sun melted the hut's ice and, on Pavy's recommendation, the seventeen remaining alive moved into a tent. By then, formal issuance of rations had ceased: They lived from hand to mouth on netted shrimp and occasional dovekie. These were cooked on a fire outdoors, blubber fuel combined with saxifrage, a kind of arctic heather. Greely's journal records that he dined on tea, sealskin gloves, and *tripe de roche*, lichen scraped from rocks and boiled.

Despite their common peril, some among those starving soldiers had raided the commissariat all winter, pilfering bread, bacon, and alcohol. Greely, according to his outraged account, caught Dr. Pavy rifling the bread can of Corporal Elison, their most helpless invalid. Elison had suffered massive frostbite in a vain attempt to sledge back a load of Nares's cached beef. Gangrene forced the amputation of both feet and hands. Despite his misfortune, he hung cheerfully on to life, feeding himself with a spoon lashed to the stump of one wrist, sustained, ironically, by the devoted care of the same man who tried to steal his rations.

In early June, Greely put a harsh end to thievery by ordering the worst offender shot. Private Henry was incorrigible: Caught red-handed, he was dissuaded by neither threats nor rebukes. Greely invoked the Army's ultimate punishment. He wrote out an execution order in trembling manuscript, observing military protocol even *in extremis*. Three surviving sergeants, Brainard among them, none of them the physical equal of their better-fed prisoner, implemented the sentence, two rifles loaded with blank, one with ball. The body was left on the icefoot; no one was strong enough to bury it.

The men received news of Henry's death approvingly. A posthumous search of his kit revealed a dozen pounds of stolen sealskin. On that same day, June 6, Pavy hastened his own death by swallowing extract of ergot from the medicine chest. He was sorely missed, having compensated for his insubordination by selfless care of the sick.

The Army's ordeal at Camp Clay is one of the blackest in polar annals. Perhaps most awful was their immobility. In 1848, Franklin's men had died just as wretchedly but they, at least, had dropped in harness, dragging their boats toward what they hoped was salvation. Greely's command was denied that heroic struggle. Camp Clay was a cul-de-sac where nineteen soldiers, mostly brave, suffered and starved in contemplation of inevitable death. Their inertia was involuntary. Littleton Island and its food lay beyond their reach, twenty-three miles away; Smith Sound remained obstinately unfrozen. Throughout February and March, when returning daylight made travel possible, observers daily reported whitecaps in the straits: too wet for sledges, yet too icy for navigation. Greely realized that crossing the sound courted an even worse disaster than that which engulfed them, piecemeal, at Sabine Island.

Not surprisingly, Greely shone in defeat. Fort Conger's martinet was honed into the gentle savior of Camp Clay. Near the end, death was commonplace. Men would wake to find corpses sharing their joint sleeping bags. They subsisted on the covers of those bags and saxifrage tea. Even water was scarce. Brainard and one of the other sergeants, the only two still on their feet, were so debilitated that carrying full buckets up to the tent exhausted them. June 20 marked Greely's sixth year of marriage, three of which had been spent in the arctic. "When will this life in death end?" he wrote, a rare *cri de coeur* and his penultimate journal entry. He stopped writing because a gale that was to last for days toppled the tent. Its pole fell across three men, including Greely, pinning them to the ground. No one could lift it up again.

Help was on the way. Once past Upernavik, Schley's search pattern was simple: If Greely were not at Littleton Island, then he had to be across Smith Sound, either at Sabine or farther north along the American way. *Bear* and *Thetis* set out to cross Melville Bay, in company with fleets of whalers bound for Lancaster Sound, also anxious to find Greely en route. (Plagued by engine trouble, the gallant *Alert* never got past Devil's Thumb.) Although new to those waters, Schley won out over dozens of experienced Dundee and New Bedford ice masters and was the first to reach Cape York after a fortnight's battle with the ice. It was mid-June; he had made exceptionally good time.

Littleton was deserted. But across the straits, at Stalknecht Island, Ensign Harlow recovered Greely's cairn left the previous October. Its message included Camp Clay's position and closed with the, by then, improbable assurance "All well." The relief expedition was only six miles from its objective. By nine-thirty on Sunday evening, June 22, *Bear* and *Thetis* approached Sabine's storm-lashed shore, waking the echoes with triple blasts on their steam whistles. They were just in time.

Entombed in their collapsed tent, Greely's men heard something over the gale. Brainard and Long crawled painfully to the bluff's edge but could see nothing. While the sergeant went back to report, Long paused to resurrect the wind-toppled distress signal—shreds of clothing lashed to an oar—that had flown since daylight's return. Then he glanced seaward again and saw, unbelieving, a Herreshoff steam launch heaving around the point of the cove, with a man in its bow waving a flag at him. Long stumbled down to greet his rescuers, a gaunt zombie in tatters and scraps. Long did not even climb back up to the tent with them. After blurting out that Greely and six others were alive, he clambered into the launch.

The first men to reach the tent slit the canvas with a knife. Greely was revealed on hands and knees in a filthy dressing gown and skullcap, groping for his pince-nez. He seemed vague and confused; gently, the sailors helped him back into his sleeping bag. When Schley came ashore, Greely inquired piteously if his rescuers were English, betraying his sense of abandonment by his own country. Then pride surfaced momentarily: "Did what I came to do," he croaked, "beat the best record." Despite the storm, all the survivors were carried outside their dank prison. Lassitude gave way to hunger, and the sailors started feeding them pocketfuls of bread and pemmican they carried. But the Navy surgeon put a stop to it, fearful for his patients' fragile systems; alcohol cookers were set up and warm milk and beef extract administered instead.

The gale raged unabated, as though the arctic were loath to surrender the seven survivors. Five were carried on stretchers over the wave-racked icefoot and lifted into launches; only Private Fredericks, like Long before him, preferred to walk. Sea conditions offshore were hazardous. Laden boats clustered alongside the black hulls, their crews soaked by spray while awaiting a propitious swell on which to hoist the invalids on board to the comfort of warm bunks below.

Once the survivors were on board, a macabre cargo followed. Over Greely's strenuous objections, Camp Clay's bodies were gathered up, from Cemetery Ridge as well as those unburied, including Private Henry, retrieved from the icefoot with a bullet in his brain. Transferring the dead on board was no easier than the living, and two were nearly lost in the process. Its mission fulfilled, Schley's flotilla sailed for home. Only six of the seven survivors reached the States: Elison, the plucky corporal without hands or feet, died en route. Salvation killed him: Nourishment had activated circulation near the stumps of his mortified extremities, and he succumbed to blood poisoning.

Back in New York, the privations of Camp Clay were dramatically underscored by autopsies performed on its cadavers. Many bore identical mutilations, incisions along the ribs on the back, over which skin flaps had been resewn with the skill of a surgeon. A conclusion of cannibalism was inevitable. As it has throughout history, this latest episode of man-eating aroused the opprobrium of the civilized world. The remnants of Franklin's command had been reduced to the same expedient as were a planeload of Uruguayans recently forced down in the Andes. Although no explorer has ever advocated consumption of his expedition's dead, as a last resort it seems justifiable. Perhaps the verdict is best left to those who, dying, are faced with the decision of becoming cannibal or corpse.

Was Greely privy to Camp Clay's grisly secret? Was there more than the violation of sanctified ground that had distressed him about exhuming the dead? It is doubtful that either he or Sergeant Brainard, the expedition's other published survivor, had any inkling of it. Their only culinary experimentation had been restricted to fantasy. They never forgot their hunger. Brainard was commissioned and rose to the rank of general. Every June, he and Greely dined on the anniversary of their rescue; each year, their menu was one of many fabricated in wistful anticipation on Sabine's frozen shore.

Uncle Sam had broken John Bull's farthest north monopoly. But on the heels of both De Long's and Greely's catastrophic losses, polar fever all over the United States subsided, even though the pole still beckoned elusively. By 1884, most Americans were content to relish the polar exploits of their predecessors rather than head north for themselves.

All save one, a boy who grew up in Portland, Maine. Robert Edwin Peary had been born in 1856, a year prior to Dr. Elisha Kent Kane's untimely death. That the lives of these two men overlapped even that little is fitting: Kane and Peary remain stars of the first magnitude in America's arctic firmament. Peary's favorite boyhood reading was Kane's memoirs, an adolescent preoccupation put aside throughout four undergraduate years at Bowdoin and subsequent commissioning in the Navy's Civil Engineering Corps.

His first assignment was scarcely arctic: In 1884, the year of Greely's rescue, Lieutenant Peary was in Central America, on the first of two surveying missions for a transcontinental canal through Nicaragua. Home from the tropics the following year, he was browsing in a Washington bookshop and happened upon a pamphlet about Greenland's icecap; his dormant arctic obsession reasserted itself at that instant. Within a year, with five hundred of his mother's precious dollars, Peary went ashore at Godhavn to reconnoiter, as he called it, the great ice sheet blanketing Greenland's interior. This was the first of two planned expeditions, the second of which, according to Peary's bold timetable, would see him cross the island for the first time, from western coast to eastern. Sledging with him on that first occasion was Christian Maigaard, a local Danish administrator, the assistant governor of Ritenbenk; their equipment was minimal, a light sledge drawn by each man, loaded with three weeks' supplies.

What followed was scarcely more than a vacation outing during which the novice explorers penetrated one hundred miles inland. No important discovery was made—in fact, Baron Nordenskjöld had gone farther three years earlier. Regardless, young Peary's arctic baptism was an unqualified success. His appetite for exploration was whetted by that modest venture, the first of eight increasingly ambitious journeys that would conquer the pole twenty-three grueling years later.

Of all the giants of the age, Peary was unquestionably the most dogged. Never once did he sail under federal sponsorship, and his career as an explorer, although crowned with success at its end, was marred by constant struggles to achieve financial backing. Then, too, disappointment haunted Peary, the first that, before he could mount a second Greenland expedition, a Norwegian unknown crossed the island from the opposite coast, pulling the arctic rug out from under the American hopeful. With that geographical tour de force, Fridtjof Nansen began his extraordinary arctic career, the explorer who has been acknowledged as father of the heroic age.

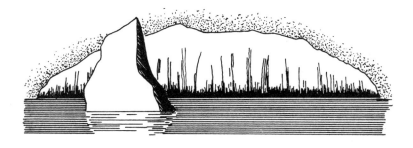

5

VIKING REDUX

*If we know that behind us is nothing, we
must go forward.*

—Fridtjof Nansen

Fridtjof Nansen was a man of extraordinary talents, brains, and brawn in splendid combination. A doctor of zoology, an artist, a humanitarian, and a diplomat, he was also a crack skier, speed skater, and expedition leader par excellence.

Nansen was tall and blond, with piercing blue eyes; as his hair receded, he grew a luxuriant mustache. His clothes were unique, designed for him alone, a simple sporting tunic buttoned high across the chest with a low Tyrolean collar; his hat was worn rakishly over one eye until the day he died.

Whereas Baldur Nansen, his lawyer father, was rigidly strict, his mother, Adelaide, was brimful of energy and independence. She was the daughter of Baron Wedel-Jarlsberg, a social advantage she typically ignored. Her first husband was a baker's son, with whom she eloped and had five children. After he died, Adelaide married Baldur Nansen; two more sons were born, Fridtjof in 1861 and Alexander a year later. But though once again a member of the establishment, Adelaide Nansen never really conformed. Enormously competent in kitchen and garden, she made all her children's clothes and skied at a time when no other women did.

Nansen shared his mother's spirit, and his childhood, on a

farm outside Christiania (as Oslo was then called), was replete with lessons of sturdy self-reliance. Every Norwegian primer to this day includes the following episode of Nansen juvenilia: Sent to the Christiania Fair with money to buy candy, Fridtjof and Alexander returned instead with a utilitarian collection of tools. Sent back with additional pocket money, they reappeared with more tools.

That stubborn tenacity remained part of his character. Resolutely, he swam summerlong in the chill Frogner River, which flowed near his door, as well as fished its waters exhaustively. He hiked and hunted throughout Nordmarka, the forested wilderness surrounding the capital, "inhaling the fragrant breezes, and with them great draughts of courage and energy," he would recall. These were usually solo, Spartan ventures, during which he lived off the land for weeks at a time. He felt himself a Robinson Crusoe, and it is not hard to detect early qualifications for the demands of polar exploration.

Another story about Nansen's single-mindedness has passed into legend. Visiting London as a young man, he stood outside Buckingham Palace, cheering the arrival of one of the royal family. A pickpocket tried lifting the Norwegian's watch; Nansen seized the man's wrist, continuing with his free hand to wave his hat as the royals disembarked from their carriage. Only after they had entered the palace did Nansen turn his captive over to a policeman. The unfortunate pickpocket, nursing a numbed hand, welcomed the law with relief.

It is scarcely surprising that Nansen and his countryman Amundsen were two of the six polar giants. Norwegians have a particular spirit and flair. Historically, they were the renegades of Scandinavia, fierce, truculent, and dedicated to self-determination. Norway's Viking spirit is palpable to the present day, and centuries of domination by neighboring kingdoms foster a fierce sense of independence and pride. Modern Norway emerged out of the complex treaties following the Napoleonic Wars. Four centuries of reluctant liaison with Denmark were to be followed by yet another with Sweden. But, although submerged within Stockholm's dual kingdom, the Norwegian Storting, or Parliament, produced an extraordinary constitution. Written and approved at Eidsvold, a small town in southeastern Norway, with a dispatch that puts our Founding Fathers to shame, this enlightened document abolished both hereditary nobility and primogeniture with a stroke of the pen rather than bloodshed, setting the country firmly along the road to a classless society. This was a unique European phenomenon in 1814, and Constitution Day, May 17, remains Norway's cherished national holiday.

By the end of the nineteenth century, the constitution's drastic prescription had made considerable impact. Norwegian society was refreshingly unified. Transcending all of it was a determination to end the irksome union with Sweden. Seaborne conquest of a more peaceful kind demanded it: Norway, with a merchant fleet triple the size of Sweden's, wanted her own consular representation abroad. Dissolution finally came in 1905. The ancient flag of the kingdom, Norway's traditional red, white, and blue cross, was no longer sullied in its upper left quadrant with the Swedish cross, which Norwegians had christened contemptuously "herring salad."

All four great Norwegian ventures of the heroic age—Nansen's Greenland trek and subsequent voyage over the polar sea, and Amundsen's navigation of the Northwest Passage as well as his dogged victory at the south pole—were characterized by consistent harmony. The absence of an abrupt social gap between commanders and subordinates paid obvious dividends. There is a traditional Norwegian seafaring idiom that underscores relationships on board their ships: *skippertak*—literally, the captain lifts—an admonition that command does not imply exemption from labor. Nansen, for instance, used to load and trim coal on board the *Fram*, willing to roll up his sleeves and get a job finished. Interdependency is woven into the Norwegian character. A farmer interviewed by a sociologist in the 1950s put it succinctly: "You mustn't quarrel, because bad feelings would develop that might never go away . . . the best thing is to forgive and forget as quickly as possible." Thus a variety of factors—classless bonhomie, mutual cooperation, and an inbred wish for harmony—guaranteed equanimity on board Norwegian expedition ships. The legendary demoralization of the polar winter—commonplace on American vessels— never surfaced. "We are all a shirt-sleeved people," one Norwegian ship's officer once observed. Perhaps that was their secret.

Although physically indestructible, Nansen was only a middling scholar for most of his schooling. However, during the succeeding two years of his education, Nansen turned firmly and studiously toward science. He chose zoology, a field that would enable him to capitalize on his love for the outdoors.

One of his professors suggested that a sealing cruise would be an admirable way for him to perfect techniques of research. So, in the spring of 1882, Nansen sailed on board the *Viking*, bound for a six-month expedition into arctic waters. He signed ships articles and, although exempted from full duties by his scientific work, bunked with the crew, taking a turn in the galley, polishing brass, manning the crow's nest, and, although sickened by the carnage, helping shoot and butcher hundreds of seals.

Scientifically as well as personally, Nansen's experience on the *Viking* was an unqualified success: He found that he derived the same tonic effect from the arctic that he enjoyed in his beloved forests at home. But the most significant event of that sealing cruise resulted out of navigational error: For twenty-four days the *Viking* was beset, caught in the turbulent pack along Greenland's eastern coast. Nansen spent hours examining unexplored mountains through a telescope, tantalizing landmarks of a mysterious, unknown world. For Nansen, arctic Greenland seemed the ultimate outdoors.

Greenland is the world's largest island, an enormous triangular catch basin rimmed by mountains on all but a portion of its western side, its center heaped with vast accumulations of snow to a depth of over a mile. This icecap, second only in size to Antarctica's, conceals a variegated topography, hints of which pierce the snow as *nunataks*, an Eskimo word describing a mountaintop reduced to a mere protuberance by the domed expanse concealing it. If Greenland's ice reservoir were to melt, the level of all our oceans would rise by several feet. But it cannot. The runoff is minimal, only surface meltwater in the summer and, year-round, the ponderous descent of glaciers splaying seaward through chinks in the mountainous coastal stockade. Although we know now that its northern coast lies some four hundred miles from the pole, it was thought for centuries that Greenland might be the southern tip of a polar continent straddling the globe.

Eric the Red landed on Greenland's southwestern coast in 983 and, upon his return to Norway, encouraged a convoy of settlers to accompany him back. He called the place Greenland, not only to sweeten the agricultural promise of the new country but also because the western mountains, warmed by the Gulf Stream, actually sprout a green summer mantle of moss, grass, and willows. Colonies were established that lived harmoniously with the Eskimos for five hundred years before vanishing mysteriously in the fifteenth century. Colonial exports included polar bear skins, seals, fish, and hunting falcons for Europe's nobility.

But Greenland's eastern coast could never be settled. Although a few Eskimo encampments could be found, treacherous offshore conditions forbade the approach of any ships save those, like Nansen's *Viking*, imprisoned by the ice. There was a perpetual icy blockade. Some ice broke up in the summer, washed southward by the East Greenland Current; but that same current brought fresh rafts of tough arctic ice out of the north to replace it. Landing on the shore meant passage through a compacted, chaotic jumble of moving pack.

Upon his return to Norway in the autumn, Nansen was offered the post of curator at the Bergen Museum. This was the start of a six-year sojourn on the coast, save for a spring's work in 1886 at the Stazione Zoologica di Napoli, researching new developments in the study of the nervous system of invertebrates. He enjoyed Bergen save for its wet winters and returned to Christiania whenever he could for winter sports. Once, on impulse, he made the journey on skis—the Oslo–Bergen rail link was still twenty years away—and covered 150 miles in six days.

Greenland still haunted him. It was on the occasion of Nordenskjöld's return from a third Greenland expedition the following summer that Nansen's plan for a Greenland expedition of his own crystallized. Nils Nordenskjöld was Nansen's great Scandinavian predecessor. While mapping Spitsbergen's northern coasts in 1864, he had achieved a record northing of 81°42'. But he never got closer to the pole than that, bringing off, instead, another arctic coup: In 1878 he sailed his ship *Vega* east from Norway clear across Siberia to Bering Strait, the first ship ever to navigate the Northeast Passage. He then circumnavigated the entire Eurasian landmass, returning to Stockholm and wild adulation two years after his departure.

In the summer of 1883, the now Baron Nordenskjöld mounted a final overland expedition to probe Greenland's interior. Once again he was not successful, but two of his Laplanders, on skis, did penetrate east over the icecap for a distance of seventy-five miles. Nansen decided that as a maiden exploring venture he would cross Greenland from shore to shore. What made his plan novel was its direction of march: Whereas the Swedes had landed on the inhabited western coast, pressing inland and back, Nansen hypothesized that crossing in the reverse direction, from east to west, would obviate the need to carry supplies enough for a round trip. Despite his logistical advantage, his scheme was fraught with risk: Assuming that he *could* gain a foothold on that perilous eastern coast, he would have absolutely no line of retreat save forward.

He journeyed to Stockholm to consult Nordenskjöld and was cordially received. The baron's *idée fixe* was that Greenland's center was free of ice and snow. This myth of remote, ice-free arctic areas was a persistent geographical fantasy throughout the entire nineteenth century. Kane and Inglefield's "open polar sea" was symptomatic of this fairyland syndrome, a naïve concept—or wish?—that Shangri-la lay somewhere beyond those forbidding wastes. Even scientists were not immune. On the expedition from which Nordenskjöld had just returned, he had instructed his Lapp skiers to bring back samples of all vegetation encountered. Even though they returned empty-handed, the baron remained convinced that the icecap was merely a prelude to greenery. Delighted that Nansen might be the one to reveal such a lush interior (and prove him right), he gave his unconditional blessing.

But Norway's Parliament, approached through the University at Christiania, was less sanguine. Nansen asked for very little—only five thousand crowns—but was informed that there seemed no valid reason to subsidize "a private person to make a pleasure trip to Greenland." However, a Dane, Councilor Augustin Gamél, who would have both a cove and a *nunatak* named after him for his pains, advanced the entire amount. Like most first prospectuses, Nansen's was quite unrealistic: the actual cost of the expedition proved three times as great. Elated Norwegian students raised the outstanding balance when they heard of his triumphal arrival on the western coast.

Like Parry, Nansen toyed with the idea of using reindeer, the traditional Lapp standby, for haulage. But the prospect of off-loading the creatures onto that hostile shore, as well as the problem of carrying fodder, made him abandon the plan. However, he did turn to the Far North for a pair of Finnish Lapps, people renowned for mountaineering skill and their supposedly uncanny sense of direction. Nansen specified that they be over thirty, unmarried, and briefed on the potential dangers of their employment. Two smiling recruits reached Bergen, and it was obvious that Nansen's qualifications had either been overlooked or ignored: Ravna was forty-six and the father of five children, a lazy and phlegmatic mountain Lapp who spoke not a word of Norwegian. Balto, his companion, was a lowlander or river Lapp, twenty-five years old, who could just manage fractured Norwegian and seemed the more imaginative of the two. Neither had the faintest idea where they were going, having volunteered solely in anticipation of the promised salary. When informed of the details of their indenture, both were terrified; inexplicably, Nansen decided to take them anyway.

Three other men, all Norwegian, made up the party. Second-in-command was Otto Sverdrup, a name that would become an arctic byword. Sverdrup, son of a simple farming family, was a sea captain and blacksmith. The two others were Oluf Dietrichson, an Army officer, and Kristian Trana, a young hand from Sverdrup's farm. Sverdrup persuaded Nansen to include Trana, even though, at twenty-four, he fell short of the expedition's age criterion of thirty. But this was hardly enforceable, since Balto and even Nansen himself were both under that age.

Having chosen his men, Nansen set about equipping them. Outfitting arctic expeditions in Norway has its advantages: There is a ready supply of snow, and Nansen spent part of the winter of 1887–88 up in the mountains behind Bergen, testing sledges, tents, and clothing. Much of this equipment he made himself, and his record for successful design is not too bad. But, as we shall see, certain shortcomings emerge only in the field.

Nansen's first problem in Greenland would be to get ashore. He had a special boat built, double-planked with oak and pine, interlined with canvas. It was an amphibian, like Parry's boat/sledges of fifty years earlier: Bracketing the keel were fore-and-aft runners by which Nansen hoped to negotiate the icy passage to shore. Once on land, the boats would be abandoned and supplies shifted onto sledges. These would be manhauled in the British tradition: Dogs were ruled out as too hungry and too expensive. Five sledges were built, modeled on a standard Norwegian vehicle called a *skikjaelke*. They were nine and a half feet long and only two feet wide. Their runners were as broad as skis and shod with steel plates. Nansen planned to sail them when possible, and his six-man patent tent had a detachable floor that could be unlaced and bent onto ski poles as a sail.

A Bergen furrier named Brandt made two oversized reindeer sleeping bags to order, each designed to accommodate a trio of explorers. More warmth for less weight was Nansen's objective. Multiple versus single sleeping bags would remain the subject of heated controversy throughout the history of polar exploration. The primary objection to sleeping three men to a bag was their having to turn over in unison: When one turned, all turned, and this specific inconvenience seemed to outweigh any economies of load; however, the man in the middle was invariably warmest.

Apart from these sleeping bags and some dogskin mittens, the only fur taken across Greenland adorned Balto and Ravna: Their reindeer tunics were conventional winter garb in Lapland. Their feet were shod in *finnesko*, a supple, lightweight boot also made from reindeer. The uppers were cut from the fur of the forelegs, while the tougher hind leg skin provided the soles. The inside was packed with sennegrass, a crinkly, dry arctic grass that insulated the feet from the cold and could be replaced when worn. There is no better footwear for polar work.

Nansen adopted *finnesko* for his fellow Norwegians, but they were clothed entirely in wool—underwear, knickerbockers, sweaters, and short jackets, this latter on the order of Nansen's sporting garb. A thin cotton overgarment was reputed to be waterproof; in practice, it soaked up moisture like a blotter, although it did keep out wind and drifting snow. Snow goggles were essential. Nansen tried out Eskimo models, simple bone discs with a slit, but found that their narrow, horizontal openings prevented his seeing the tips of his skis. So he reverted to European smoked glasses, a thoughtful present to the expedition from Nordenskjöld. For additional protection against glare, they carried another Nansen invention, face veils made incongruously of red silk.

Sir Ernest Shackleton said, after his second return from the

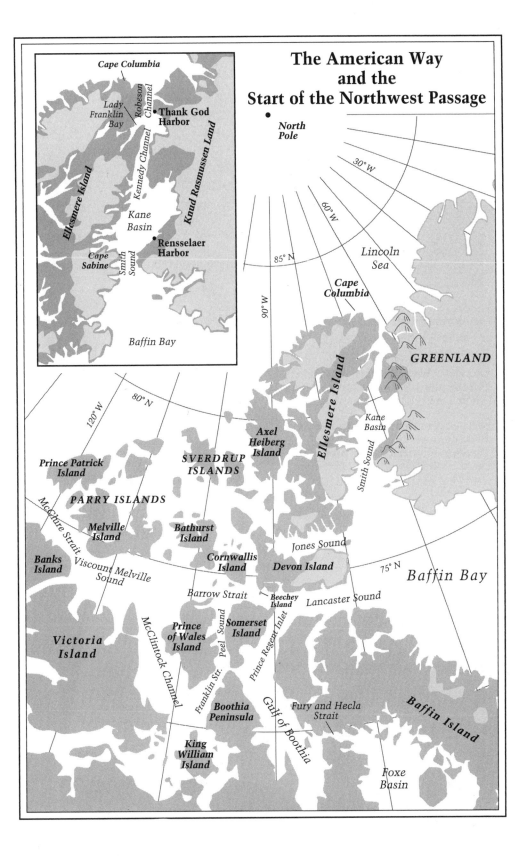

The American Way and the Start of the Northwest Passage

Inset map labels:

Cape Columbia
Lady Franklin Bay
Robeson Channel
Thank God Harbor
Kennedy Channel
Knud Rasmussen Land
Ellesmere Island
Kane Basin
Rensselaer Harbor
Cape Sabine
Smith Sound
Baffin Bay

Main map labels:

North Pole
30° W
60° W
85° N
90° W
Lincoln Sea
Cape Columbia
GREENLAND
Kane Basin
Ellesmere Island
Smith Sound
80° N
120° W
Axel Heiberg Island
SVERDRUP ISLANDS
Prince Patrick Island
PARRY ISLANDS
McClure Strait
Melville Island
Bathurst Island
Banks Island
Viscount Melville Sound
Cornwallis Island
Jones Sound
Devon Island
75° N
Baffin Bay
Barrow Strait
Beechey Island
Lancaster Sound
Victoria Island
McClintock Channel
Prince of Wales Island
Peel Sound
Somerset Island
Prince Regent Inlet
Franklin Str.
Boothia Peninsula
Fury and Hecla Strait
Baffin Island
King William Island
Gulf of Boothia
Foxe Basin

ABOVE: Sir John Franklin on the eve of his final expedition, spring 1845. *Library of Congress.*

AT RIGHT: Franklin's memorial in London's Waterloo Place. Bas reliefs on the plinth show his funeral. *Peter Strachan.*

BELOW: Franklin's cairn on Beechey Island: gravel-filled cans of the spoiled Goldner's Patent preserved meat. *Collection of John Maxtone-Graham.*

Hecla and *Griper* snugged in for the long arctic night at Winter Harbor, July 1827. *American Geographical Society.*

William Edward Parry's troop boats on the ice. The men have roofed over the hulls for the night. *American Geographical Society.*

Elisha Kent Kane, the American arctic pioneer, posed next to one of Franklin's crew's tombstones on Beechey Island. *Library of Congress*.

ABOVE: The only known photograph of Charles Francis Hall. A picture of the *Polaris* hangs behind him. *Chauncey Loomis.*

AT RIGHT: Forensic riddle at Thank God Harbor: Hall's corpse, shrouded in Old Glory, exhumed in 1968. *Chauncey Loomis.*

BELOW: The ice-floe drift party from the *Polaris.* George Tyson stands at extreme left. *The Smithsonian Institution.*

James Lockwood's departure from Fort Conger, April 1882. He stands sixth from right. Adolphus Greely is on far left. *Library of Congress.*

AT LEFT: After the Camp Clay rescue in June 1884, Greely en route home. *Library of Congress.*

ABOVE: Tunic, fedora, mustache, and piercing gaze—all hallmarks of dashing Fridjof Nansen. *Norsk Sjøfartsmuseum, Oslo.*

Nansen and his party ascend the Greenland glacial massif, August 1888. *Universitets-bibliteket in Oslo, Picture Department.*

Nansen and Sverdrup's makeshift coracle. *Harald Brandsburg.*

Group at a Greenland cairn. *Back row, left to right:* Frederick Cook, expedition surgeon; Matthew Henson; Josephine Peary. Her husband was confined to camp with a broken leg. *National Geographic Society.*

Robert Peary in civilian clothes at the start of his arctic career, 1885. *Library of Congress.*

Fifteen years later, Peary poses in the North, wearing a Navy tunic and bearskin Eskimo trousers. *National Geographic Society.*

Antarctic in 1909: "The two great facts of life were food and God." As a practicing agnostic, Nansen paid little heed to the latter but did his best with the former. Most of the expedition's supplies came from Denmark, the pemmican especially made up at Beauvais of Copenhagen, the Fortnum & Mason of the North. Once onto the icecap, Nansen and his companions realized, belatedly, that Dr. Beauvais, opting for a high protein yield, had neglected to add any lard to his product; as a result, all six men craved fat for the duration of their crossing. Nansen would have done well to heed the American, Robert Peary:

> . . . Next to insistent, minute personal attention to the building of his ship, the Polar explorer should give his personal, constant and insistent attention to the making of his pemmican.

Another catering shortfall was Beauvais's *leverpostei*, ground calf's liver: It had a dismal ratio of nutrition to weight. Worse, it froze into veritable marble. When Nansen went after it with an ax, the wretched pâté splintered into shards. Supplies from France included Rousseau's meat powder chocolate; and the venerable English firm of Huntley & Palmer provided meat powder biscuits.

Although he later enjoyed cigars, Nansen did not smoke in 1888 and discouraged it among his men. In fact, he took very few stimulants—only a small supply of coffee, which, together with tobacco for the inveterate smokers, was doled out only on special occasions. Curiously, very little tea, the universal polar brew, was taken. On many expeditions, tea served as a double stimulant: Once infused, the leaves were dried and provided a passable pipeload for short-rationed smokers.

Since they would pull the sledges themselves, Nansen took both skis and snowshoes. In fact, his use of skis on the Greenland crossing would serve to popularize them worldwide; prior to that time, they were little known outside Norway. There is a cave painting in Scandinavia of a stick figure sporting long, thin snowshoes curled up at the point. It was descendants of this troglodytic *schusser* to whom Procopius of Gaza doubtless referred in the sixth century when he described a race of "gliding Finns"—presumably skiing rather than dancing. The only other recorded instances of skiing in Europe occurred early in the nineteenth century: Austrian peasants of the province of Krain used short skis, as did Cumbrians in the North of England. But the custom never caught the popular imagination.

Norwegian Army skis of the late nineteenth century were of differing lengths—the right nine feet long, the left only six, its underside coated with sealskin strips for gripping the snow. The short was for pushing, the long for gliding. *Skilöbbers*, as the Norwegian skiers call themselves, used only one long pole, with no basket at its point.

Two kinds of snowshoes were brought, the conventional paddle-shaped ones as well as some *hester-trugers*—horse troughs—oval shoes of Norwegian origin used traditionally for horses. The *trugers* served the expedition in a way that their maker never predicted: Both Nansen and Sverdrup found that chewing on fragments of their cherry wood relieved the intolerable thirst that plagued the expedition day and night.

Scarce drinking water in the midst of snowy wilderness seems paradoxical. Yet an inescapable reality of the icecap, even in summer, was that every drop of water would have to be melted, consuming a proportionate amount of precious fuel. In Nansen's case this was alcohol, which he prudently rendered unpotable by the addition of wood naphtha. Fuel tippling was a chronic problem on Royal Navy arctic expeditions, for rum was often used; one-half pint of the fiery liquor could boil soup enough for ten men. The British Admiralty's solution was to taint their rum/fuel with camphor.

But, however melted, water in the arctic was perennially in short supply. John Hieel, a Royal Navy seaman, recalled that he was once given Leopold McClintock's wash water to throw away; he took the bowl behind a tent and drank it. Nansen planned to supplement his supply with ingenious "body cookers." Each man carried a curved tin flask, which was filled with snow each morning and hung under his shirt. By the end of the day's march, he was permitted to drink whatever water he had melted.

Nansen perfected his own cooking stove, based on equipment used by Greely's expedition. Multiple cotton wicks burned in the base of Nansen's cooker, similar in principle to the burners used under restaurant chafing dishes. Directly above the flame was a very efficient cooking pot, felt-insulated, with a hole in the middle, like a tall angel-food cake pan. On top of it rested a covered pan in which snow could be melted, with waste heat passing up from the lower container. When perfected, Nansen's cooker at −20° F took one hour to make a gallon of cocoa, using eleven ounces of alcohol. This was a vast improvement over early field trials in the Bergen hills: The first prototype had flickered dismally for hours without bringing water near a boil.

In the spring of 1888, they were ready. As though he had not enough to distract him, Nansen defended his doctoral thesis a few days before departure. Then, on May 2, he departed Norway for the Scottish port of Leith, traveling on the land route via Copenhagen, while the other members of the expedition sailed from Kristiansand with the equipment and stores. At Leith, the reunited party boarded the Danish steamer *Thyra* and sailed for Iceland and a rendezvous with the sealer *Jason*. Her master had contracted to land Nansen's people on the Greenland coast with the understandable proviso that he would do so only between bouts of sealing.

All of June and half of July passed before the *Jason* was in position off Cape Dan, nine miles from shore. From the crow's nest, Nansen spotted a lane of open water on the far side of the pack. It was his first sight of Greenland in six years: "Never have I seen a landscape of more savage beauty, or nature in wilder confusion. . . ."

Regrettably, "confusion" was the operative word. They disembarked on the evening of July 17 in two boats, their own specially built one as well as another from the ship. Both craft were packed to the gunwales with skis, rations, instruments, sledges, tent—everything they would need to cross the icecap. As a farewell present, the *Jason*'s master handed down some horsemeat and a small keg of beer. An icy drizzle began to fall.

The six men started rowing through the pack toward land. But the restless ice closed in and nipped one of the boats so badly that its occupants had to haul out onto a floe for repairs. The larger of their two craft had been holed through in both planking and sheathing. Worse, the canvas interlining had soaked up seawater like a wick, adding critical topweight to an already overladen hull. Any chance of getting through to shore that night was out of the question. Even had they been able to repair the damaged boat, there was suddenly no channel in which to launch it. Cape Dan receded through the sodden twilight, and the explorers retired into their tent. Rain seeped irritatingly through its lacing holes.

They spent the next week and a half camped thus on the ice, the East Greenland Current thrusting them relentlessly south toward the narrowing tip of the island they sought to cross. Their position was perilous. The outer edge of the ice was battered by breakers where current and ocean conflicted. Once, they were so close that surf spray drummed on the tent wall. But most worrisome for Nansen was the passage of time: Crucial summer days were passing without one mile of westward progress to show for them.

The two Lapps were resigned to disaster. While still in sight of the *Jason*, Ravna blurted, "How foolish we Lapps were to leave the ship to die here!" Both refused the raw horsemeat their four companions chewed valiantly, scorning it as fare fit only for heathens. Both Ravna and Balto were recent converts, intensely religious. When the camp was threatened by the sea, both retired to one of the boats, lying beneath its tarpaulin and reading aloud passages from their New Testament.

Finally that interminable southern drift came to an end and the expedition was able to land at Cape Tordenskjold. Nansen celebrated with an issue of hot chocolate, christening the haven Gamél Cove after their Danish patron.

By then it was the end of July and the brief arctic summer was half over. Determined to go on despite the delay, Nansen's party rowed back north, hugging the shore where possible to evade the current. They had to circumvent glacial tongues across their path. This was dangerous business. Several times, Nansen's boats barely missed being crushed by huge fragments of ice thundering into the water, to become newly calved icebergs. They encountered their first Greenland mosquitoes, voracious hordes that harassed them for most of one day. Pleasanter contact was made with some Eskimos who replenished Ravna and Balto's supply of soaked sennegrass. The Lapp duo accepted the gift scornfully, confiding to Nansen that the grass had been picked too early and was improperly cured.

The entire first phase of the expedition, that infuriating, useless trek up and down the coast in search of a landing place, was a severe test of Nansen's perseverance. Rations during that unscheduled detour had to be held to a Spartan minimum so that once uphill manhauling began, the projected daily in-take could be maintained. When they reached Umivik Fjord on August 12, only two thirds of the three hundred miles they had drifted south had been retraced. But it was far north enough. For the last time, both boats were dragged ashore. Balto, elated at being on terra firma permanently, relinquished his Bible to Ravna, convinced that his troubles were over.

The next few days were spent in preparation for the ascent. Rust was scraped from the bottom of sledge and ski. Both boats were left upturned, well above the high-water mark, to serve as a cairn. Under those discarded hulls, Nansen left any-thing he could spare to lighten his load, unfortunately, among them a sailmaker's palm, the sturdy hand thimble used for sewing canvas, which would be sorely missed on the western coast.

On the night of August 15, three and a half months after they had left Christiania, the six explorers set their backs to the coast, shrugged on canvas harnesses roped to their sledges, and started west. Progress was measured in miles of hauling and, eagerly awaited at each halt, meters of ascent. They traveled at night, when the snow surface was hardest, soaked by an appar-ently endless deluge of rain that, however miserable, had the advantage of packing down the snow. Sometimes they simply could not proceed. Between August 17 and 20 they were con-fined to their leaky tent by a violent storm. Finally, on the night of the twenty-second, Nansen realized joyfully that the most difficult climb was behind them. Before him stretched a limitless expanse of white, no longer obstructed by cliff and crevasse. Progress improved at once, and marches of ten miles a day became standard, although half the daily progress that Nansen had optimistically projected back in Norway. But now at least the sledges moved more easily, pulled by one man apiece rather than having to be relayed laboriously uphill.

On higher ground, downpours were replaced by blizzards. They were perpetually thirsty but even during the long rains on the ascent had had no means of collecting rainwater. So they relied instead on the inefficient output of Nansen's body flasks.

Despite the daily attrition of food and fuel, their sledgeloads were still oppressive. Equipment deemed essential back in Bergen was eagerly discarded; if it proved flammable as well as superfluous, so much the better. The oilcloth covers from their sleeping bags were expendable: They burned experimental shreds in their stove in the tent, nearly asphyxiating the party before lukewarm tea could be brewed. The next morning, the rest of the oilcloth was ignited outdoors, a bonfire for a feast of hot soup and lemonade. Nansen concocted a *granita* of lemon oil and snow, adapting an Italian confection so fondly remembered from Naples. Wooden splints from the first-aid kit went for fuel as well.

A daily ration of lemon oil was essential to ward off scurvy. Apart from water, they most hungered for fat because of their inadequate pemmican. Each man's weekly half pound of butter did little to alleviate this craving: Dietrichson gulped his down all at once, a gargantuan, greasy dollop. Sverdrup confessed that he was increasingly tempted to gnaw on his boots, which had been oiled against the damp.

Camping is as arduous as sledging in extreme cold. Arctic explorers retreated inside the tent as soon as possible, huddled around the tiny blaze at the base of their efficient cooking stoves. Over it, they slowly melted snow and simmered thick meat soup (or hoosh, as the British were inclined to call it).

Polar historians are indebted to Herbert Ponting, Scott's photographer on his last expedition to Antarctica in 1910, for some incredible cinematic footage that dramatizes better than words the intricate routine necessary within a four-man tent. The quartet of "actors" in question ultimately perished, so there is added poignancy in the sight of Scott, Wilson, Bowers, and Evans performing for the camera with such good-natured facility. Ponting has captured the entire ritual: The five-legged tent frame is erected over ground cloth, stove, and sleeping bags, ready for its lining and outer canvas shell. While two of the party drape fabric over the poles, the remaining pair are already cutting and carrying snowblocks that will weight the tent's rim against the wind. Softer, granular snow, which produces more water more quickly, is packed into a brace of cooking vessels. Before they enter the tent, all superfluous snow is brushed carefully off outer clothing and boots. (Snow brushes were essential: Among Amundsen's south polar memorabilia preserved in Oslo's Ski Museum is a common household broom, its handle removed and the bristle block split in half to conserve weight. Polar historians have never understood the significance of the clothes brush found with the body of one of Franklin's people: It was not for vanity but to remove superfluous snow.) Once inside the tent, wet clothing is hung to catch heat radiating up from the stove. The duty cook has brought in the ration bags and sets them to melting, while another distributes mugs. Biscuits are circulated while the men await the call of "Hoosh up!"

Most striking about Ponting's footage is the practiced grace—the choreography—of each movement within that impossibly crowded space. Yet more than grace was involved: Dangerous chills might result from any delay in getting the tent erect. Sledging produced incredible body heat. Once the party halted, there was a real urgency to be under shelter before sweat-sodden clothing froze onto one's back.

Ponting's film ends with Scott and his fellow performers squatting about the stove seated on rolled-up sleeping bags. In the field, they would have gotten directly into their bags. Socks changed, pipes lit, *finnesko* arranged for the morrow, diaries in train, the explorers' supper was invariably taken in bed. Tobacco smoke roiled with the fragrant steam clouding the tent's chill interior, freezing into glittering icy spicules that whitened the conical canvas overhead. Nansen's Greenland journal recalls it evocatively:

> However hard the day had been, however exhausted we were, however deadly the cold, all was forgotten as we sat around our cooker gazing at the faint rays of light which shone from the lamp, and waiting patiently for our supper. Indeed, I do not know how many hours in my life on which I look back with greater pleasure than these. . . .

In an attempt to shorten that patient wait, Nansen once tried cooking supper on the sledge as they traveled. Carrying the hot, top-heavy stove into the tent, he inadvertently knocked it over, spilling their precious meal onto the ground cloth inside. At once, anxious hands dove for the four corners, and the entire brew, contained within the filthy canvas, was ladled into gratefully proffered mugs. Predictably, Balto carped at the garnish of reindeer hair in his ration; what he never divined was its potentially lethal seasoning of wood alcohol from the capsized spirit lamp. Balto was the expedition's potwasher, a chore he performed inefficiently with his tongue: Tea leaves often surfaced in the soup, and morsels of the previous night's pemmican sometimes appeared in breakfast cocoa.

As an unpleasant sequel to the overturned cooker, Nansen awoke the following morning to find the tent's interior carpeted white. Wind-driven snow had penetrated the lacing overnight, and everything was full of powder, including their boots. "Nevertheless," he records in his diary, "we spent a very pleasant Sunday morning with coffee and breakfast in bed." At an altitude of a mile and a half, it grew increasingly colder. Seventy degrees of frost were all their thermometers were graduated to record. When a headwind blew, Nansen insulated his solar plexus with a folded hat. He suffered greatly from accumulated frost on his whiskers and would have preferred to be clean-shaven. But they drank all the water they produced; there was none for washing or shaving. To this day, Norwegian mountain climbers sport an evocative facial badge when conditions are bleakest: A completely frost-rimed beard and mustache are known as a "full Nansen."

The direction of a prevailing wind over Nansen's right shoulder caused him to amend their destination from Christianhaab to Godthaab, farther south and, in yachting parlance, an easier reach. With the wind at their backs and their way perceptibly downhill, they experimented with sailing. The first attempt was disastrous: The tarpaulin sails were shredded by the wind, requiring several hours of excruciating labor to repair the damage. Subsequently things went better, and they obtained the best results by lashing their sledges in parallel pairs and stepping them with a tent-pole mast; a single sail was bent on ski-pole spars top and bottom, approximating the mainsail of a square-rigger. The canvas was considerably wider than the paired sledges and acted as a transverse barrier, dividing the crew fore and aft.

One memorable day, near the end of their trek, Sverdrup steered one of their sledge catamarans, perched on the bow. Nansen and Trana were squatting precariously aft, out of sight behind the sail. They raced along before a northeast blizzard, reeling off a dozen miles that morning alone. Fully preoccupied, Sverdrup peered ahead, alert for crevasses. As they rattled along, Nansen leaned forward to tighten a lashing. As he did, a ski came loose beneath him, caught its tip in the snow, and flipped him unceremoniously overboard. The sledge vanished into the blizzard. Nansen plodded along in its wake. He came across some cases of pemmican, bits of clothing, and, finally, young Trana, who had involuntarily abandoned ship as well.

Miles ahead, the last man on board, Sverdrup bowled along at a furious clip, shouting over his shoulder to his absent passengers. Their protracted silence turned his head about: One glance at the empty sledge and he came to a panicky, dropsail halt. The other sledge—skippered prudently by Dietrichson and his reluctant Lapp crew (they were convinced that sailing sledges was the devil's work)—drew up to where Nansen and Kristian Trana waited. The castaways sat patiently on ration boxes, having gathered up all the supplies that had toppled from the sledge. After Sverdrup appeared, dragging his sledge back against the wind, the cargo was reloaded, lashings were double-checked, and the little flotilla continued on its way.

Two days later Balto spotted "land," the first rocks the explorers had seen for weeks. The western coast was nearby. The temperature rose and birds reappeared. They came across a blessed pond of meltwater, flopped down on their bellies, and drank their fill for the first time since the day they had burned the sleeping-bag covers. That night they camped on heather rather than snow. Sverdrup sat contentedly at the mouth of the tent, his pipe packed with fragrant moss, an improvement over the tarred rope fragments he had been smoking for weeks.

The sledges were left behind on the upper slopes as, carrying packs, they descended to the shore. Godthaab lay to the north, unreachable by land; their Greenland crossing would end as it had begun—by water. First they had to build a boat, improvised in one afternoon. The abandoned sailmaker's palm would have been invaluable. The tent floor, no longer needed as a sail, served as the shell of a craft scarcely larger than a bathtub, a coracle of canvas lashed about a rib cage of bamboo stakes and willow branches. (Lieutenant John Franklin had built its prototype to cross the Coppermine River in 1819.) Nansen's, preserved to this day in Oslo's Ski Museum, has the look of a kind of Huck Finn rivercraft. It was paddled with makeshift oars, forked willow branches with canvas blades.

It would carry only two. Leaving the other four explorers,

Nansen and Sverdrup cast off. One bailed, the other rowed. Periodically they splashed ashore and gorged themselves on ripe crowberries. Most trying to Nansen was the lack of a proper thwart: Two bamboo poles from the theodolite stand were poor expedients, "the scantiest seat it has ever been my ill luck to sit upon, and I devoutly hope never again to have to go through a similar penance."

But uncomfortable or not, their little nutshell carried the explorers to the head of Amerilik Fjord after a six-day voyage. They waded ashore at Godthaab on October 3, 1888. A throng of curious Eskimos greeted them. A Dane, Assistant Colonial Superintendent Baumann, shouldered his way through the crowd.

"Do you speak English?" he inquired.

"No, we are Norwegians," replied Nansen in his own tongue.

"May I ask your name?"

"My name is Nansen and we have just come from the interior."

Baumann grinned. "Allow me to congratulate you on taking your doctorate!"

With this surreal greeting, contact was reestablished with civilization.

The last steamer of the season had left Godthaab two months previously. Two teams of Eskimo kayakers were dispatched in its wake. The first, carrying Nansen's dispatches, paddled furiously for Ivigtut, three hundred miles to the south, just in time to catch the Europe-bound *Fox*, the same vessel on which McClintock had sailed to find Franklin's cairn thirty years before. The second brought temporary sustenance to Nansen's four stranded companions, including a welcome pound of tobacco for the smokers. The *Fox* reached Europe on November 9, carrying news of Nansen's triumph home ahead of him.

The expedition settled down to a winter in Greenland. Godthaab's social climate was formidable. At their first dinner, the colonial administrators donned boiled shirts, and their ladies were gowned and gloved as though in Copenhagen; Nansen and his companions made do in borrowed finery. After three and a half months on the icecap, civilization was cloying—the food too rich, the rooms too stuffy, the feather beds too soft. Never idle, Nansen immersed himself in a study of the local

Eskimo life. Over the winter, he gathered enough material for a book and, in the spring, mastered the art of handling kayaks in all weather and sea conditions. He was convinced that the light, maneuverable craft would be invaluable adjuncts to polar exploration.

The international acclaim awaiting Nansen and his companions was delayed until the following summer. They did not sail from Godthaab until mid-May. As the ship neared Christiania, guns roared in salute from Akershus Castle. A motley fleet—tugs, yachts, and fishing craft—obstructed their joyous way. Overwhelmed by the turnout, Dietrichson remarked on the size of the crowds to Ravna. Pining for his northern pasturelands, Ravna responded disconsolately: "Yes, it is fine, very fine, but if they had only been reindeer!"

Within two months, Nansen was engaged to Eva Sars, an opera singer and daughter of zoologist Michael Sars. She was a lively and intelligent companion who loved the outdoors as much as her husband. Legend has it that Nansen's proposal to her contained a prophetic caveat that he planned to try for the north pole; true or not, it was the only subsequent arctic foray that Eva permitted him. Dr. Nansen and his bride were feted all over the Continent. He was immensely popular, admired both by the general public and within learned scientific circles. He had solved the mystery of Greenland's interior, laying to rest Nordenskjöld's tropical fantasy. Nansen had shown that the interior was ice-filled to such a depth that the domed top of the icecap in no way reflects the substratum of terra firma. Dietrichson's meteorological records provided invaluable data about the icecap's role as a huge weather crucible that influences the entire Northern Hemisphere's climate.

But most gratifying was Nansen's personal vindication. He returned a hero, the Storthing's early ridicule forgotten. German geographer Baron Ferdinand von Richthofen was among many who offered encomiums, praising Nansen's "well-weighed and carefully projected plan." But, in truth, most astounding about Nansen's "plan" was that it so hinged on luck: Bad luck extended his eastern coast landing from hours into weeks; good luck saw him win through despite faulty provisions and supplies. The expedition was dangerously under-equipped: Food and fuel were short, no extra clothing was carried, and much of their kit was flawed—sodden water-proofs, ineffectual body flasks, leaking tent, defective skis, and pemmican devoid of fat.

Yet Nansen brought it off and, in the record books, that is all that matters. Had he failed, any one of those logistical short-comings might well have been bemoaned in diaries found with his corpse. But he did not fail, and the Norwegians' exploring *éclat*—resiliency in the face of all odds—served Fridtjof Nansen well. The legend of his invincibility had begun.

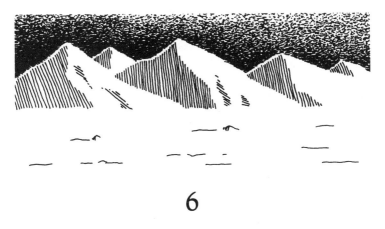

6

A CAPITAL SHIP

Build me straight, O worthy master,
Staunch and strong, a goodly vessel
That shall laugh at all disaster
And with wave and whirlwind wrestle.

—Henry Wadsworth Longfellow,
The Building of the Ship

Nansen incorporated the story of his Greenland experience into two books: *The First Crossing of Greenland* and *Eskimo Life*, gathering material for this latter during his enforced winter in Godthaab. Publishing was important for explorers: Most of them sailed after having incurred crushing debts. Nansen's countryman Amundsen, en route for the Northwest Passage in 1903, would leave Christiania during a midnight downpour to evade creditors. But conversely, a successful return guaranteed brisk international book sales and remunerative lecture tours to follow. Nansen did the reverse: His honeymoon with Eva was a lecture tour as well; then he came home and wrote the books. Peary hated lecturing, referring to the lecture circuit with gloomy disdain as the "great black road," as opposed to the glorious white road of the arctic. But Nansen, charming and magnetic, found lecturing to his taste and did well at it.

Nansen was already plotting his next arctic objective, the north pole itself, as legend tells us he had warned his beloved Eva when proposing marriage. But he was to choose a novel means of approach, a plan that had preoccupied him for years, long before the Greenland crossing. Henrik Mohn, director of the Norwegian Meteorological Office, had written an article for a Christiania newspaper in 1884 about some items that had washed up that summer on Greenland's southwestern tip, at Julianehaab. They included a list of provisions bearing De Long's signature as well as a cap and oilskin breeches, each marked with a crew member's name; one pair was Nindemann's. The finds were, indisputably, flotsam from the wrecked *Jeannette*. What intrigued Professor Mohn, no less than Nansen, was that since she had foundered on the far side of the globe, the relics must have drifted clear across the pole, from Siberia to Greenland. It had taken more than three years, but their arrival at Julienhaab, however slow, confirmed the existence of a hitherto unknown transpolar current.

The more Nansen thought about it—and it was often a topic of discussion with Sverdrup in Greenland—the more sense it all made. The Arctic Ocean is largely landlocked, surrounded by North America, Greenland, and Eurasia. Two of its three openings are tiny, one between Russia and Alaska, another at the top of the American way. The largest opening lies twenty degrees of longitude to either side of the Greenwich meridian, a two-way street divided on either side by Iceland. The Gulf Stream pushes water north, above Norway; and the East Greenland Current, the Arctic Ocean's great drain, spills south, west of Iceland. If it were not continually replenished, thought Nansen, the ocean would be empty. The ocean's inflow is three-fold: river runoff from the Canadian and Siberian river systems as well as the Gulf Stream. Since the inflow is one-sided, a consistent pattern of polar drift is established: northeast from Siberia, across the pole, and then south through Denmark Strait, exactly the route followed by those pathetic oddments from the *Jeannette*.

Nansen had additional clues. The driftwood littering the treeless coasts of Iceland and Greenland comes from Siberia. Siberian ice is young and thin; near Greenland the ice is thick, a frozen agglomeration indicating long life and lengthy passage. Nansen's own analysis of sediment from Greenland's eastern coast ice indicated without question that it had come from Siberia.

Nansen seized on a plan that was as simple as it was bold

and unorthodox: Commit a vessel purposely to the Siberian ice and let the transpolar current carry her across the top of the world. Monumental patience would be required (more, as we shall see, than Nansen himself possessed); even more vital than patience, presuming he could afford it, was a ship that could withstand the ice, a hull impervious to the pressure of the pack.

Although strong, a traditional whale ship hull fell short of the invulnerability that Nansen sought; without it, entering the pack was impossible. No ship, however stoutly braced, can withstand the pressure of polar ice driven by wind or tide. Nansen's theoretical solution was to evade rather than resist, to devise a hull that, cunningly wrought, would slip up out of the ice's grasp, the way a cherry pit squeezed between thumb and forefinger pops into the air. Sverdrup told him of small vessels sailing between Spitsbergen and Franz Josef Land that escaped the pressure in this manner. Might not the same life-saving phenomenon be duplicated on a larger ship? Nansen felt it might. He sketched preliminary plans for an egg-shaped hull with an ungainly three-to-one length-to-beam ratio, its ovoid flanks so sheared that lateral ice thrusts would be deflected, either down toward the keel or up over the bulwarks, but never to pierce or crush the planking.

Nansen shared his drift idea with Christiania's Geographical Society in February 1890. Reaction was so enthusiastic that he approached Parliament the following spring. In contrast to his bleak reception three years earlier, the hero of Greenland was welcomed cordially and awarded a two-hundred thousand-crown subsidy. King Oscar made a personal contribution of twenty thousand crowns, and the balance of the expedition's budget, a total of nearly half a million crowns, was subscribed by a variety of donors, among them the brothers Ringnes, Norwegian brewers, one of whose grandchildren would serve as president of the Fram Museum in Oslo.

His financing assured, Nansen let the contract for his ship to Colin Archer, a Norwegian of Scottish descent. He was one of thirteen children born to a Perth timber merchant who had immigrated to Norway in 1825 and settled at Larvik, down the fjord from Christiania. Colin was a talented naval architect who had perfected a sturdy, decked-over pilot boat for use in Norwegian coastal waters, the popular Hvaler lifeboat, with a stern as pointed as its bow. He had had larger commissions as well, including the comfortable yachts *Venus* and *Storgut*. He was immensely prestigious in Norwegian maritime circles, a white-bearded, patriarchal figure who looked like Noah, the archetypal boat-builder.

So, on the ways at Archer's Larvik yard grew the massive timbered structure that would become the legendary *Fram*, a vessel that Nansen specified must be "as round and slippery as an eel." Prior to her construction, only one other vessel had been specifically built for polar exploration, Leigh Smith's *Eira*, which had succumbed to the ice in Franz Josef Land in August 1881. The *Fram* would have a very special and very strong hull and would do better.

Two balks of American elm, fourteen inches square, made up the keel, to which were attached Italian oak frames, each grown to shape and cajoled by Archer from the Norwegian Navy, in whose yard at Horten they had been seasoning for three decades. Finished frames were twenty inches wide, separated from their neighbors by little more than an inch. Four feet of oak, juniper-doweled, made up the formidable stem and almost identical stern.

The hull was carvel-built, its planking butted edge to edge to avoid any possible purchase by the ice. Three layers of planking covered the hull: First three-inch, then four-inch planks were spiked onto the closely spaced frames. These were sheathed with greenheart, South American laurel of such iron density that it will not float; however, it is astonishingly tough and slippery, standard sheathing for all whalers.

Once the three layers, or trebling, had been hung up on the frames, the interstices between frames were filled with a gooey fudge of coal tar, pitch, and sawdust to keep water out in the event of leakage. The frames were then covered on the inside with yet another skin, four-inch pitch pine fitted carefully about white pine knees, 450 of them, that joined frame to cross-beam to diagonal shoring. Knees are L-shaped timbers cut from trees at the point belowground where the trunk sends out major roots, the forest's strongest right angle. The last task before painting the hull's exterior was to wrap iron straps, Band-Aid–like, around bow and stern.

Poised on the ways, the *Fram* was scarcely graceful: There was nothing trim about those blunt ends and overblown bilges.

She looked like half a coconut. The keel was almost invisible: Greenheart sheathing obliterated all but three inches, its edges rounded to foil the ice. That abbreviated keel would make her unmanageable in heavy seas. But, in compensation, she was enormously strong, solid enough not to cave in before responding upward. "I arrived at the result," wrote Nansen, "that the strength must be several times that necessary to withstand the pressure required to lift her."

Although bow and stern seemed almost interchangeable, the latter was identified by two slots under the counter, each a well into which propeller and rudder could be withdrawn. Nansen cautioned that the stern was "the Achilles heel of ships in the Polar Ocean": Propeller and rudder alike were especially vulnerable. To minimize ice damage, all arctic propellers were designed to stop vertically so that they would be sheltered within the rudder post. Shearing off a blade while under weigh was a common arctic mishap. Another advantage of the twin-bladed propeller was that, disengaged from the shaft, it could be drawn up into the hull for protection or even replacement. Propeller wells were common, but to have a supplementary well for the rudder was almost unique: Only the *Discovery*, Scott's first antarctic ship, to be launched at Dundee eight years later, boasted the same protection. The *Roosevelt*, Peary's Maine-built ship, had no such provision, and he lost his rudder (and nearly his ship) on her first trip north.

Belowdeck, from keelson to main deck, there was a workable interior height of only twelve feet. Divided in half with a 'tween deck, there would not have been height enough for the crew to stand. Rather than raise a deckhouse amidships, Archer fitted a quarterdeck aft that added a supplementary yard of precious interior height to the after two-fifths of the hull. *Fram* was thus divided at the mainmast: Cabins, saloon, galley, and engine spaces were located aft, and a clean spread of deck reached forward to the bowsprit. Her after freeboard was thus increased to six rather than three feet. In fact, the *Fram* was so overloaded by the time she sailed that freeboard forward was woefully small; the first rough weather she encountered raised havoc with deck cargo.

Whereas the ship's sides had been buttressed against the rigors of the pack, her interior bulkheads needed protection against a different kind of ice, if not as lethal as that outside, then nearly as unpleasant. Condensed water vapor would freeze to cabin walls in successive layers of hoarfrost that could thicken indefinitely. On the *Advance* in 1854, Kane had encouraged this ice buildup as a means of caulking his drafty cabin walls. But the ice lining melts in any heat, from a stove, a candle, or even a cabin occupant, dripping and soaking bedding and mattresses nearby. Nansen had suffered these dank conditions on board the *Viking* and was determined to avoid them on the *Fram*. He instructed Archer to insulate the ship's living quarters with multiple layers that included dead air, wood, felt, linoleum, and reindeer hair. (This latter is extremely efficient as an insulator because each hair is hollow.)

The saloon's skylight was triple-glazed. Descent to the saloon from the deck was made through a succession of three doors, each with a twelve-inch sill to exclude cold air and drifting snow when they were opened. Despite all these provisions, Archer could not resist installing, in Nansen's cabin, a hinged device that could move the bunk several inches away from the wall, just in case; Nansen never had reason to use it.

The efficacy of Archer's insulation was amply demonstrated one January afternoon during construction. Nansen had shown some English friends over the ship and, leading the way up the companionway, discovered that workers had locked the door from the outside, inadvertently sealing the visitors belowdeck. For twenty minutes, Dr. Nansen and his fellow prisoners yelled and pounded on the bulkheads, to no avail. Men on deck within a few feet heard nothing and, but for the fortuitous descent of a foreman to retrieve his jacket, the visitors might have spent an involuntary night on board.

Never once did *Fram*'s interior, even those cabins abutting the sides, suffer condensation. If anything, the ship was almost too warm, certainly for English tastes. Edward Wilson, surgeon on both of Scott's expeditions, read about the *Fram*'s average interior temperatures with horror; he used to crank open the *Discovery*'s skylights whenever the temperature reached 60°, to the displeasure of his older shipmates.

Eva Nansen christened the ship on October 26, 1892, bittersweet blessing of a vessel that was to deprive her of a husband for several years. Thousands had gathered at Archer's yard, including whaling masters from all over Norway, come to admire the hull's stubborn lines. Three flagpoles were stepped in place of masts: Fore and aft, the Norwegian flag fluttered, but the center pole was vacant. Fru Nansen smashed a bottle of champagne across the iron-strapped bows and called in a clear voice: *"Fram skal du Hede!"* ("She shall be called *Forward!*"). At the same moment, a huge red pennant bearing FRAM in white letters was run up the central staff, first revelation of the name. It was an obvious choice for Nansen; as in Greenland, no other direction mattered. The black-and-white hull started down the ways, and Nansen took Eva's hand; his eyes filled with tears. The *Fram* plunged into the sparkling waters of Rekkevik Bay. As she tugged at her mooring lines, guns fired a salute from shore, and a great cheer echoed around the hills.

Within a week, Nansen was in London, first on his schedule a formal appearance before the Royal Geographical Society. The arctic old guard was out in force: Sir Francis Leopold McClintock was in the chair that night for "the most adventurous program ever brought under the notice of the Royal Geographical Society." Admiral Sir George Nares expressed misgivings about Dr. Nansen's polar current and fussed about a "line of retreat." Admiral Sir George Richards went further, delivering himself of the astounding theorem that *all* (italics mine) ice moved south from the pole; he further suggested that the *Jeannette* documents found in Greenland were not originals but merely copies lost by another expedition. The venerable Sir Joseph Hooker worried about scurvy and "cabin fever," a sinister malady presumed endemic to arctic incarceration. Was the reward, he wondered, worth the risk?

As McClintock had anticipated, Nansen's was an adventurous program, punctuated by animated but essentially negative discussion; the English were cordial but restrained. They liked Dr. Nansen, and the respect was mutual. Nansen was an inveterate Anglophile and had always idolized the Royal Navy explorers. Long before he was appointed ambassador to Great Britain, he remarked: "If I were not a Norwegian, I had rather be an Englishman than belong to any other nation," an evocative paraphrase that might have been plucked from Sir William Gilbert's *HMS Pinafore*. In truth, Nansen sometimes seemed more English than the English. He spoke their language flawlessly and was welcomed in the most rarefied English drawing rooms and clubs. He was blessed with a blithe, good-natured ease with everybody, from stoker to statesman.

To cultivated Englishmen, he seemed one of them. His clear blue eyes, nonchalant good looks, and aristocratic demeanor charmed everyone, no less provincial hostesses than the crusty upper echelons of London society, who warmed to him without reservation.

Nansen had more to do in London than convince skeptics at the Royal Geographical Society. He bought vast amounts of provisions: Bovril, Cadbury's cocoa and chocolate, Bird's Custard, Rose's lime juice, all those reassuring staples of the Victorian commissariat. He visited the British Army's balloon depot at Aldershot and made a disappointing ascent into a bank of autumnal fog. He arranged for a balloon and hydrogen cylinders to be part of the *Fram*'s equipment but ultimately reneged in the interests of economy and deck space. En route home to Oslo, Nansen stopped at Beauvais's Copenhagen shop and ascertained personally that the *Fram*'s pemmican would boast the required proportion of fat; just to be on the safe side, he ordered six tons of Danish butter as well.

During that winter of 1892–93, preparations proceeded apace. At Larvik, the *Fram*'s fitting out was well in hand. Massive mast stubs were stepped and had their supplementary extensions hoisted into place. She was, officially, an auxiliary screw steamer, rigged as a three-masted, fore-and-aft schooner for easy handling by the smallest possible crew. The *Fram* was engined with a two-hundred-horsepower reciprocal steam engine from the Akers Mekaniske Vaerkstead that would drive her at six knots while consuming nearly three tons of coal each day. A collapsible windmill was designed to power an electrical lighting plant. The saloon was floored with bearskin. Stores and provisions accumulated in a warehouse at Christiania. Nansen wrote a fellow explorer, Baron Edward Von Toll of St. Petersburg, asking for a supply of sledge dogs. Von Toll promised to have the creatures awaiting the *Fram* at Khabarova, the ship's only Russian port of call. Nansen's final order of business, following an English lecture tour in February, was recruiting a ship's crew.

There would be ten in addition to Nansen and Sverdrup, and there was no shortage of applicants. Whereas forty had applied for the Greenland outing, now hundreds of letters poured in from all over the world. Nansen had two favorites, both rejected: one from a thirteen-year-old Swedish boy; the other, the application of a French lady "tired of life" who, before entering a convent, offered her "services" (unspecified) "as a member of the expedition." In fact, the only acceptable female candidate, Eva Nansen, had already been regretfully refused. Nansen had discussed the possibility frankly with Sverdrup. The two men had reached the same wise conclusion: that for the expedition leader to bring his wife was hardly fair to the remainder of the crew, most of whom were also married.

He was determined to eradicate privilege on the *Fram*. Living arrangements on board reflected this predisposition and were relentlessly democratic. The saloon in which all twelve of the ship's people would pass much of their time was only sixteen feet square, pierced by the massive butt of the mizzenmast, its walls peppered with enough doors for a Restoration comedy. There was no wardroom; the only privileged area was a portion of the deckhouse in which Nansen would spread his papers during the warmer months. Off the central saloon were four individual and two multiple cabins. Nansen and Sverdrup each had private quarters, as did Sigurd Scott Hansen, the scientific chief, and Dr. Henrik Blessing, a surgeon botanist in the tradition of Sir Joseph Hooker. Since there was no fo'c'sle, the remaining eight crew members shared two larger cabins just aft of the saloon: Jacobsen (the mate) and three hands in one, and four engineers in the other. Anton Amundsen (no relation to Roald) was chief engineer. The lowest of his subordinates was Frederik Hjalmar Johansen, a member of *Fram*'s crew who would become almost as famous as her commander. Johansen was a university student with a reserve Army commission; he was also an accomplished gymnast. Among his feats of derring-do was an astonishing somersault over forty-two inert colleagues, for which he had been awarded a gold medal in Paris. Such was the crush of applicants for a berth on the *Fram* that Lieutenant Johansen cheerfully accepted the post of stoker. Nor was he alone in assuming an inferior position: Bernt Berntsen, an unexpected thirteenth man, signed on in Tromsø. He had served as mate on other ships; on board the *Fram* he was simply a deckhand. Perhaps the most bizarre crew occupation was that of Ivar Mogstad, sixteen years as a keeper at the Gaustad Lunatic Asylum; but he was, additionally, an accomplished violinist and amateur watchmaker, invaluable talents for the arctic.

A triumvirate of Norwegian tycoons—Axel Heiberg, Thomas Fearnley, and Ellef Ringnes—were the "corresponding owners" of the completed *Fram*. They scarcely had a bargain. The ship's final cost was over two hundred seventy thousand crowns, twice its original budget. She was a plain ship with no unnecessary show, eminently sound. Her only leak, which made its presence known shortly after launch, was tackled at once. Colin Archer put her in drydock, pumped water into the engine room, and looked for outside seepage. He found it before the telltale drip was transformed into an icy stalactite. In fact, it was patched but never completely stopped. What fixed it was the cold north of Siberia: Once *Fram* was frozen in, leakage ceased. A disadvantage of multiplanked hulls is that leaks are extremely difficult to trace. Water that penetrates the trebling may travel far from its initial point of entry before entering the subcutaneous oak.

The *Fram* sailed from Christiania on Midsummer's Day, June 24, 1893. Before departure, she lay at her mooring, the center of an animated fleet. Nansen had ordered his ship gaily painted to combat the gloom of the arctic winter night: She sported a gray hull, green gunwales, and water and petroleum tanks of bright scarlet. On board, cargo was still being stowed belowdecks. The *Fram* carried provisions for six years, and both holds, upper and lower, were jammed, the interstices between barrels filled with firewood. Access to the lower hold was made through small hatches spotted port and starboard the length of the deck, each numbered with a roman numeral. (Shipwrights invariably used roman numerals for, under one hundred, the numbers could be incised with a chisel.) Johansen had devised a master cargo manifest so that anything and everything would be available when needed. (Haphazard loading on board the *America* eight years later would lead to the disappearance of several rifles until the ship was unloaded following her return from the arctic.)

Nansen was the last to board. He and Eva had become new parents six months earlier, and he bade good-bye to his wife and baby girl, Liv, at Godthaab. Now he drew up to the *Fram*, a solitary figure in the sternsheets of the ship's motor launch, his only companion the black mongrel Kvik, a favorite dog from Greenland. Once he was on board, visitors were ushered over the side. Scott Hansen rang the engine telegraph—Sverdrup was to board at Trondheim—and smoke billowed from the single black stack.

Fram left her buoy mooring and, just past noon, made a showy turn for the benefit of the crowds ashore, then puffed away down the fjord. In her wake came a flotilla of boats, their occupants bursting into spontaneous song, "Sons of Norway" and the anthem "Yes, We Love This Country." It had been dry for several days, but now a gentle rain began. As the *Fram* passed Godthaab, a chance ray of sunlight flashed through the murk, illuminating the house and a figure in white who waved. For Nansen, leaving wife and daughter was a terrible wrench, "the darkest hour of the whole journey."

They called in at Larvik the following day, the first of a series of coastal calls en route north. Two lifeboats, each twenty-four feet long, were hoisted on board and lashed in twin cradles constructed over the main hatch amidships. They had been purposely designed oversize to carry the explorers should the expedition ship suffer fatal damage. When the *Fram* left Larvik on the twenty-sixth, Colin Archer stayed on board long enough to steer the vessel he had wrought on the initial mile of her momentous venture. Then he clasped hands all around, clambered into his skiff, and rowed back to shore. Nansen saluted him with a double cannonade from one of the *Fram*'s brass one-pounders.

Once past Kristiansand, they sailed into a North Sea storm. As predicted, the *Fram* behaved abominably. She "rolled like a log," Nansen recorded ruefully between fearful bouts of seasickness. It was an inauspicious and dangerous baptism. The overloaded little ship buried her nose into mountainous waves. Green water thundered over the foredecks, breaking away paraffin casks and balks of timber that threatened to batter the lifeboats to pieces. Finally the loosened deck cargo went over the side, nearly accompanied by Juell, the cook, roused from his nap in a lifeboat and then sloshing around the treacherous deck in pursuit of his sea chest. The *Fram* was unquestionably not a deep-water ship and would pay no design dividends until she encountered the ice.

At Bergen, Nansen personally conducted a party of American tourists, who had boarded without invitation, all over the ship. International preoccupation with Nansen's adventure was intense, and people hounded him everywhere. The special pride of the Norwegians manifested itself in quieter ways. As the *Fram* worked her way north, crowds that gathered at every stop were distinguished by their warmth and a kind of touching, awe-filled restraint. Between ports, along stretches of barren, mountainous coast, where a tiny cottage was a landmark, solitary peasants waved their greeting. Passing ships of every size saluted the *Fram*, none more movingly than the fishermen who doffed caps and bowed their heads.

On July 12, the *Fram* crept into Tromsø through a summer blizzard and took on cold-weather clothing: reindeer cloaks, wolfskin parkas with fur both inside and out, *finnesko*, and bales of sennegrass stuffing. A noisome load of dried fish was winched on board as well, food for the thirty dogs waiting at Khabarova. Bernt Berntsen was signed on at short notice, ostensibly to travel only as far as Russia and return with Ole Christoferson, Nansen's secretary; but Bentzen stayed on for the entire voyage and, if a ship's complement of thirteen excited superstitious dread elsewhere, no mention of it was ever made on board.

Tromsø gave them a heartfelt send-off, prelude to an even more elaborate reception awaiting them at their next and last Norwegian stop, at Vardø, around the far side of the North Cape. The endless banquets, speeches, and toasts began to cloy; Nansen felt that such lionization was dangerously premature. A team of divers from the Governmental Harbor Department scraped an accumulation of mussels and grass from the *Fram*'s bottom. Then commander and crew cleansed themselves with a final sauna in Vardø's bathhouse and, early on the morning of July 20, 1893, the *Fram* slipped out of the harbor for passage east, across the Barents Sea. She would not be seen in Norway for three anxious years.

7

ADRIFT ON THE POLAR OCEAN

*I can now mock at the strength of the ice.
We live, as it were, in an impregnable
castle.*

—Fridtjof Nansen

Nansen had never anticipated entering the pack through Bering Strait in the wake of the *Jeannette.* That would have involved the same punishing trek around the infamous Cape Horn; it had taken the *Jeannette* five and a half months from Europe to San Francisco alone. Nansen chose instead to skirt the northern shores of Europe, in the footsteps of Nordenskjöld, who had first navigated the Northeast Passage fifteen years earlier.

Two geographical obstacles would have to be negotiated. First was the mountainous island barrier of Novaya Zemlya, separating the Barents Sea from the Kara Sea. There are three chinks in this island chain; Nansen, like Nordenskjöld before him, chose the southernmost, Yugor Strait, adhering to the wise arctic precept that passage closest inshore avoids the worst ice. Then, too, his dogs were waiting at Khabarova, the Samoyede settlement on the strait's southern shore.

Within twenty-four hours of leaving Vardø, the *Fram* was

139

engulfed in the bane of arctic summer, a persistent, impenetrable sea mist. Sverdrup pressed on, cautious but blind. Nordenskjöld had been hampered by fog, and his charts were understandably inaccurate. As the *Fram* groped toward the Russian coast, the first ice crunched under her prow, harmless brash that soon turned to solider stuff. This confirmed disquieting reports heard at Vardø on the late disintegration of ice that summer. For the *Fram* to have met so much ice so soon was an ominous harbinger of conditions to the east.

But it was also a triumphal encounter. The *Fram* bulled her way through. In his dispatch from Khabarova, Nansen exulted: "The *Fram* is excellent for ice navigation; she is worked with ease and precision and entered the masses and forced her way in an astonishing manner. . . . She is very powerful and one never hears a crack or a sound while she labors in the ice. . . ." It was a glowing testimonial to Archer's genius.

Battling the ice was hard on ship and crew alike. Sverdrup conned the *Fram* from the crow's nest, bawling commands down to a perspiring helmsman who, in turn, relayed abrupt directions down to Amundsen in the engine room: "Hard-a-port!. . . Full astern!. . . Full ahead!. . . Stop engines! . . ." So it went, hour after hour. There was no rest for those off watch, jarred from any hope of sleep by continuous impact with the ice. Tons of coal were consumed; ramming ice runs riot with fuel economies.

Fram dropped anchor at Khabarova on July 29. First on board was Alexander Ivanovitch Trontheim, Norwegian-born but now a naturalized Russian who had spent years, some enforced, in Siberia. Trontheim was the agent acting on behalf of Baron Von Toll, the man from whom Nansen had ordered his sledge dogs. Thirty-four huskies were waiting ashore, the survivors of forty he had driven over the Urals from Muzhi, three hundred miles inland. The dogs had traveled with a spring caravan of reindeer and were handsome, strong creatures, acceptable save in one critical respect: Most of the males were sterile. Since Russian sledge harness passes under rather than over the back, male Siberian huskies were routinely castrated rather than risk chafing and infection of the scrotum by the traces. Nansen, who had brought Kvik expressly to whelp successive litters, found to his dismay that all but four of the new arrivals were unable to sire puppies. But they pulled like furies, and Nansen had his first exhilarating ride behind a sledge rudely interrupted when the entire team raced off in pursuit of an alien dog and nearly tore it to pieces.

A last-minute rendezvous with the makeshift collier *Urania*, to replenish *Fram*'s coal, had to be aborted: She was held up in the ice. Nansen decided that time was more precious than coal. At every polar explorer's heels thunders "time's winged chariot." Brief arctic summers were crucial to negotiate waters navigable only scant weeks of the year. Such was the urgency that prompted Nansen's Khabarova departure at midnight on August 4, despite depleted bunkers, in order to enter "the dreaded Kara Sea." The sea itself was less frightening than the objective, which lay a thousand miles away at its eastern end: Cape Chelyuskin, Asia's northernmost point and the Northeast's Passage's second great natural obstacle. Chelyuskin thrusts north to 77°; if it was iced in and impassable, Nansen risked cooling his heels there for the winter.

The Kara Sea brought more fog, more ice, and, in the first week of September, contrary winds and waves. But the ice relented and, at 4:00 A.M. on September 10, the *Fram* slipped past bleak, frozen Chelyuskin with all flags flying; firing a triple salute was impossible because of damp cartridges. Despite the hour, an exhilarated Nansen mustered his ship's company for a dawn collation. Medicinal spirits were in such short supply that rounding the notorious cape, passage past which guaranteed their entry into the ice that fall, rated only fruit, cigars, and "Chelyuskin fruit punch."

The rest was plain sailing. Warm water flooding north from Siberia's rivers kept the coastal ice at bay. The only untoward episode was the belated discovery that noncanine creatures also had boarded at Khabarova, presumably from the hems of fur-clad Samoyede visitors: *Fram*'s upholstery swarmed with body lice. All mattresses, blankets, and clothes had to be steamed. They put their clothes into an airtight barrel, but the boiler pressure was so vigorous that the makeshift fumigating tank exploded, scattering their belongings all over the deck.

Nansen finally entered the pack on September 25, foregoing in his haste a supplementary supply of dogs from Olenek left by the accommodating Baron Von Toll. He turned the *Fram* north, riding an ice-free current from the Lena River that had deeply indented the margin of the pack. This was De Long

country, and the Siberian Islands, through which he had
sailed, lay just to the east. Nansen was at pains to avoid them
for, if the *Fram* were prematurely iced in, islands in her drift
path could act like a sieve, straining the ship and leaving her
imprisoned between rock and ice. By turning north at longitude 135° East, Nansen avoided this peril. To my mind, he
would have fared better had he persevered past the New Siberian Islands to Wrangel Island at 180° East. Starting his drift
that far around might have given him the pole. As it was, the
Fram rode the polar current on an arc that peaked just above
the eighty-fifth parallel; catching the polar bus earlier along its
route might have done the trick. It might also have meant an
additional winter, but that seems inconsequential on board a
ship provisioned for six years.

In any event, September 1893 saw the *Fram* firmly embedded in the pack, the first ship in history to embrace rather than
evade its clutches. The rudder was withdrawn but the propeller remained in place, unlikely to be damaged since it would
not revolve for three years. Although spars and shrouds were
left rigged, the *Fram*'s engine was taken completely apart,
cleaned, oiled, and stored away. In its place, Chief Engineer
Amundsen established his machine shop. A carpentry shop was
shoehorned into the crowded hold, and blacksmiths Pettersen
and Sverdrup set up their forge on deck.

The first job was assembly of the windmill generator, now
that no electricity was produced by their dismantled engine.
Once erected, the generator turned out to be a giant contraption, with revolving canvas sails twelve feet in diameter. When
it went into operation, their brilliantly lit saloon was a tonic,
not only to readers but also gamblers, who were able, suddenly, to distinguish hearts from diamonds at a glance. The
windmill was temperamental, requiring the finger-nipping
services of a patient engineer to reef sails when winter winds
blew too hard.

The *Fram* ceased to be a ship at all. She became an arctic
station, self-sustained but inanimate, unable to move even
when the late autumn ice occasionally relented. Like De Long
before him, Nansen debated reassembling the engine when he
found that his ship was suddenly afloat in open water stretching north; but within a day, the ice closed in again. As those
first weeks slipped by, every member of the expedition found

his time fully occupied. An elaborate scientific program was initiated: Temperature, barometer, and magnetic gauges were set up on the ice in a specially louvered shelter; bottom soundings were taken; water temperature and salinity were scrupulously recorded. Nansen set himself the task of analyzing the differing forms and frequencies of the aurora borealis, that stunning sky phenomenon of the arctic night, which Eskimos picturesquely attribute to the cavorting of departed spirits.

There was every comfort. Food was almost too plentiful; Dr. Blessing's physical examinations indicated neither illness nor scurvy, only additional weight on all hands. The stubborn lice surfaced again; since the boiler had been drained, cold rather than heat was prescribed. Infested clothing was left outdoors and new, English winter underwear was issued. Sverdrup, the champion improviser on board, perfected some wooden-soled boots with canvas uppers that he ran up on the sewing machine in his cabin. When a shortage of lamp wicks threatened, he made a miniature loom for weaving replacements.

By mid-October, darkness closed in, the vanished sun only a crimson smear along the southern horizon. The dogs were established in more spacious if chillier quarters on the ice. In fact, huskies need no shelter at all, able to fend for themselves in all but the coldest weather by curling up in the snow. However, they fought savagely and, after Job had been killed by the pack, Nansen ordered them brought back on board. He could ill afford the loss of any dogs; two had succumbed to *piblokto* en route from Khabarova. In November, a polar bear ambled on board, carried a dog away, and ate it; unsated, the brute returned for two more before he was tracked and killed. Shortly thereafter, Kvik produced her first litter, twelve pups in all, eight of which were kept as replacements. One of them died cruelly under the exposed main cog of the windmill.

The first serious test of Archer's hull took place on Friday, October 13. The *Fram* survived a succession of severe pressure squeezes that had destroyed scores of ships before her. But the threatening sea ice passed harmlessly under the *Fram*'s hull. Polar ice is noisy, never silent even in apparent repose. Frank Worsley, master of the *Endurance* under Shackleton in the Weddell Sea, was once examining an imprisoned iceberg and, though all was motionless, he heard "tapping as from a hammer, grunts, groans, squeaks, birds singing, electric trams running, kettles boiling noisily." On board another vessel, the *Karluk*, skippered by Peary's colleague Bob Bartlett, a Scottish crew member heard a "twanging banjo" resonating through the ship's side near his berth, an effect produced by ice grinding miles away. This sound-carrying phenomenon is not restricted to the noise of ice movement. Commander Winfield Schley of the U.S. Navy was in his bunk on the *Thetis* near Cape Sabine and heard cheering; since search parties were ashore hunting for Greely's people, he raced on deck. But the officer of the watch had heard nothing. Below again, Schley distinctly heard cheering and went back on deck in time to see Ensign Harlow semaphoring the joyous news from ashore. Human voices had been transmitted faithfully across a mile of ice, through the ship's side, and into his cabin.

In motion near a ship, the pack's noise is amplified accordingly. Elisha Kane ranked escalating ice noises on a scale of peril: A "humming of bees" was merely a warning, while a "whining of puppies" signaled imminent fracture. On board the *Jeannette*, the same humming and buzzing were climaxed by a jolting *cra-a-a-ck* underfoot. Nansen had planned to bring a recording device to capture on wax for the first time the sound of rampant ice. To him, that first October skirmish on the *Fram* sounded like the full diapason of a manic organist, trembling, howling, thundering, and rumbling. During the worst bouts, the men had to shout in the saloon, that same insulated chamber in which Nansen and his visitors had been unheard when trapped back in Larvik. That the *Fram*'s crew were dining peacefully below rather than agonizing on deck characterizes their sense of security.

Yet they discovered that complacency was ill-advised. The *Fram* might rise to the pressure, but adjacent kennels did not and were buried; so was an ice anchor, under so many tons of ice that its cable had to be cut. Similarly, the water hole, chopped open daily as a fire precaution as well as for scientific soundings, vanished beneath a welter of ice blocks under the stern.

The most severe trial of the *Fram*'s imperviousness came fifteen months later, when cumulative pressure ridges threatened to overwhelm the ship. Such was the onslaught over that Christmas and New Year's of 1894–95 that Nansen ordered provisions, sledges, and boats onto a neighboring floe. Despite the cold, all deck entrances were kept open, ready for escape in the event of inundation. But once again, although awnings were crushed and davits twisted like pipe cleaners, Archer's hull triumphed: The *Fram* jolted stubbornly up, above the ice. Sverdrup was naked, intent on a bath, when that crisis came; that he completed the ritual betrays how little apprehension he felt.

But in the long run Nansen's most insidious enemy was neither ice, hunger, nor hardship; it was, simply, boredom. Having achieved a unique arctic invulnerability, there was nothing left to do but sit out the erratic drift. Seen on the chart, the *Fram*'s progress was a jagged line of fits and starts. Nansen's current existed but was clearly subject to the vagaries of wind and tide. Results from the daily noon observations were eagerly awaited. Typically, although September 29 saw the *Fram* at 79½°, a week later she had regressed south more than a degree, a bitter disappointment where even minutes of northing were cherished milestones.

For Nansen, immobility palled. Scientific work somewhat filled the void and, additionally, there were polar bear hunts, excursions on skis, or driving the dogs. But whatever the diversion, Nansen chafed. Only one month into his voluntary incarceration, his diary read: "How the days drag past!" For his sailor shipmates, life on the *Fram* became a curious maritime contradiction, with no roll or lift of the hull and no sound of water rippling beneath the hull. Their vessel was stationary, perched half in and half out of the ice, occasionally heeling as the pack was wrenched by the eternal pressure.

The first winter passed. Birthdays were celebrated relentlessly: Dr. Blessing's, on September 29, was doubly feted, for the day also marked the *Fram*'s crossing of the seventy-ninth parallel (disappointingly, to be recrossed shortly). A musical gala dinner was given in the saloon, with Johansen's accordion, Mogstad's fiddle, and willing hands at the crank of the ship's patent organ. The menu listed *Potage de Poison* (*sic*), *Pudding de Nordahl*, the electrician's concoction, washed down by "*de la table bière de la Ringnaees* [*sic*]," a welcome donation from their brewer/backer that would be exhausted by February. Over Christmas and New Year's, there were more banquets, and first publication of the ship's newspaper, *Framsjaa*, filled with prose and poetry by all hands.

The long arctic night, which lasts from October to February in those high latitudes, seemed a matter of effortless routine. If frigid British messdecks had echoed to continual theatricals, no plays were produced in the *Fram*'s diminutive saloon. There was neither enough space nor players nor, I suspect, inclination; *mørketiden* (literally, murky time) was an accepted fact of Norwegian life. They had plenty of food and light and no damp. There was a well-stocked library, including every arctic memoir to date. There were endless tournaments of *halma*, a kind of Chinese checkers, and gambling to distraction; losers forfeited weeks of bread ration on the turn of a card.

Sometimes, when the arctic night was bathed in moonlight, Nansen would ski away from the ship, sliding over a lunar landscape. Looking back, he could see the *Fram* in splendid, glittering isolation. There was no light from the skylight, for it had been banked with snow for warmth. But Pettersen's forge glowed on the foredeck, tinting the spars above it orange. A pinpoint of light passing the length of deck and up the shrouds signaled Johansen's ascent to read the crow's nest thermometers; with the boiler drained, stoker Johansen had been promoted to assistant meteorologist. A howl from an insomniac dog would rouse the entire pack to a doleful chorus. Often, the panorama would be capped by northern lights, yellow-blue curtains draped in careless magnificence across the night, paling the moonlit cloud bank below into neutral gray.

After Christmas, one night Nansen roamed far to the north and found sheets of glistening new ice stretching as far as he could see. In his diary that night he mentioned for the first time the possibility of striking out for the pole on foot, "an easy expedition for two men." But on harsher nights, when northern gales tore at the ship, when the windmill clattered like a mad thing, and when swaying rigging showered the deck with icicles, he retired uneasily to his cabin. Adverse winds distressed him; he was convinced they were driving the ship south. He often stayed by himself, surrounded by the familiar noises of the beset *Fram*, the stamp of the firewatch overhead, the murmur of hard-core gamblers in the saloon, and brisk bursts of speed from the treadle of Sverdrup's sewing machine.

But they did creep north, crossing the eightieth parallel on February 2. On the twentieth of that month a festival heralded the sun's return, even though it remained obstinately behind clouds on the horizon. Their festival went on regardless, a shooting competition climaxed by yet another banquet, gluttony their only dissipation. Faces were scrupulously washed for the occasion, and Nansen remarked on the radiant plumpness of his crew.

A month later, summer routine began. They shoveled snow off the skylight and removed the dogs' kennels once more to the ice. Nansen reoccupied the wheelhouse during his working hours, complete with microscope, sketch pad, and Schopenhauer. It had just been vacated by Kvik's first litter of puppies, and the leather bindings of Scott Hansen's scientific volumes were all chewed at the corners.

Although daylight made life pleasanter, Nansen still fretted. From his diary for May 28: "Ugh, I am tired of these endless white plains!" Wet, treacherous snow and sudden leads thwarted progress from the ship in every direction, and excursions common in winter were curtailed. Boating supplanted skiing and, in addition to the longboat, six double kayaks were built and launched. Nansen made a one-man kayak modeled on an Eskimo original, its bamboo framework covered with tallow-impregnated sailcloth. Strong and flexible, it weighed only forty pounds and was short enough to fit onto a sledge.

The end of September marked their first full year in the ice. They had progressed 189 miles as the crow flies, a net gain of nearly three degrees of latitude, about the distance the *Fram* could sail in a day and a half. Nansen theorized that the ice they rode would be forced northward by Franz Josef Land, pushing his vessel still closer to the pole. By mid-December they were at 82°30′, having surpassed the northern record for a ship, achieved in 1876 by Nares on the *Alert*. Nansen hoped for 84° or even 85° by spring.

But he would not wait until then. Indeed, the little kayak he had built over the summer was his first overt preparation for leaving the ship. In November he announced his intention to the crew, ordering preparations for a February departure as their second winter's priority. The immediate question to be settled was which of a dozen candidates should accompany him on the polar dash. Otto Sverdrup was without doubt the most experienced, the only one on board linked to Nansen by an overland expedition. But the two friends agreed that Sverdrup's first duty lay with the *Fram*, a decision accepted without rancor.

The man Nansen chose was Johansen, the indefatigable gymnast, stoker, and, now, meteorologist. Though he had no sledging experience, he was extraordinarily fit and methodical as well as a superb skier. He accepted at once, fitting his own description of the compleat polar explorer: "Sound, whole and hearty and accustomed to face exposure and danger. Temperate and anything but a gourmet and able to eat anything cooked and uncooked." He was, admittedly, a hopeless cook. When his turn in the galley came, he had been unable to light the balky stove; while undertaking its repair, he let that evening's corn beef freeze solid, and dinner was hours late. By unanimous decree, Johansen was excused from all further cookery, a dispensation maintained while on foot with his chief: Nansen did the cooking, Johansen fed the less discriminating dogs.

Typically, Nansen's plan was fraught with risk. Once disembarked, he and Johansen could never regain the vessel, for she would have drifted on, leaving the two explorers to find their own way home via Franz Josef Land. Again, Nansen opted for no line of retreat, characteristic of the man and, fortunately, his comrade as well. Ironically, had they stayed on board, they would have achieved, by effortless if frustrating drift, two thirds of the distance over which they were to struggle on foot.

It was a unique commitment. Characteristic of most polar assaults was their origin from a base that served as logistical supply point as well as return objective. From that base, the previous fall, relays of sledges would have planted caches along the route; moreover, the base would be a source of assistance if the assault team were overdue. But Nansen and Johansen had neither base nor depots and, whether they reached the pole or not, their return to civilization would be longer than their approach. In that sense, Nansen's polar thrust would be merely a preamble to hardship. When Peary, Shackleton, Amundsen, or Scott turned back, they had survived the conventional apogee of risk. Not so Nansen and Johansen: They would abandon their polar attempt on April 8, three weeks after quitting the *Fram*. Fourteen months would pass before they reached safety.

How should they travel over a frozen ocean that, summer and winter alike, can fragment without warning? Nansen realized that no single amphibious conveyance would do. Runner-equipped boats had failed not only his Greenland landing but Parry's abortive polar thrust as well. Instead, Nansen decided to combine sledge and kayak into a temporary whole: *Fram*-built Eskimo craft would be carried on two of Nansen's three sledges, keel and runner readily interchangeable. Afloat, the kayaks could carry sledges, explorers, and their supplies, while on the ice, each kayak would be firmly and ingeniously mounted on its sledge.

During the winter, dozens of cans of pemmican and liver pâté were opened. When thawed, their malleable contents were shaped like Plasticine into cradle blocks, contoured to receive the keel of each kayak. Then these edible chocks were refrozen, encased in canvas, and padded with reindeer fur. This was improvisation of the highest order, a guns-*and*-butter expedient combining sustenance with structure. Furthermore, kayaks served as admirable containers, crammed with food for both men and dogs, along with rope, guns, bilge pumps, clothing, instruments, cameras, tent, double sleeping bag, and, seated neatly in the round body opening, the Nansen cooker, with its nested containers. Since the Greenland crossing, the Swedish Primus stove had been invented, and pressure burners, an explorer's staple to this day, produced far greater heat returns for modest fuel expenditure.

There is a polar bromide about an expedition commander weighing, literally, the merit of packing a certain pocket handkerchief on his sledge. All sledgers made these agonizing decisions. Nansen did carry a trio of Norwegian flags, indispensable props should the pole be reached. But weight restrictions otherwise were harsher. Written messages from their shipmates were confined to a single sheet of paper, covered in tiny script on both sides; Scott Hansen's could be read only with a magnifying glass. Also carried with the two explorers would be copies of all of the *Fram*'s scientific data gathered to date, tacit acknowledgment that either ship or commander might fail to return. Though death was an eventuality on

which none of the Norwegians dwelled, Nansen and Johansen
on foot were given equal chance of survival with those remaining on board. The *Fram* might, after all, remain locked in the
ice forever, drifting like the *Flying Dutchman*.

Nansen's timetable was to travel north for fifty days, a time
factor predicated on the amount of food he could carry for
himself, Johansen, and the dogs. The twenty-eight dogs, nearly
the entire ship's complement, would ultimately serve as their
own fodder, in the practical if grisly food-chain rationale
wherein diminished supplies could be drawn by diminished
teams of animals. They would draw thirty-pound sledges (the
same *skikjelke* used in Greenland), their German silver runner
plates soldered on with silver reclaimed by Mogstad from rendered half crowns solicited from the crew. Blessing put together a compact first-aid kid and demonstrated to Nansen
and Johansen the art of splint-making and shoulder-setting in
the saloon. He also gave them a crash course in amputation in
the event of gangrene following severe frostbite. But as in
Greenland, the medicine chest would be depleted for utilitarian purposes only: Bandages served for blubber wicks, and
wax from the plaster boxes was an effective caulking agent for
the kayaks. Jacobsen made the explorers an ax, its head the
size of a matchbox, as well as a bear spear, which, never used
in anger, saw double duty as a soldering iron instead. Sverdrup
fabricated a combination pocket tool for Johansen, complete
with saw, file, gimlet, and screwdriver. From the wreckage of a
superannuated wind-speed indicator, Amundsen and Mogstad
created an odometer to be dragged behind the last sledge to
record mileage.

How best to organize the dogs, sledges, and drivers occasioned two false starts, the first on February 26. Nansen and
Johansen relayed two sledges each, all of them loaded with 550
pounds. They were too heavy: Within a few miles, after several
cross braces had been broken by ice hummocks, the explorers
returned to rethink and restow. Two days later they tried
again, this time with six sledges carrying lighter weights; but
coping with six separate dog teams was chaotic. They returned
once more and, after two weeks of ruthless reorganization of
weights and loads, set off for the third and final time with three
sledges only at noon on March 14, 1895, 356 miles from the
pole.

Scott Hansen, Hendriksen, and Pettersen accompanied them for one day's march. Sverdrup came along for the first half mile, red-bearded face encircled by a fringe of wolfskin. When he turned back, he shook hands with Nansen and begged him, if he got back to Norway first, to wait for the *Fram* before departing for the south pole! (It was ironic that of Nansen, Sverdrup, and Johansen, only the latter would sail to the antarctic.) Then he waved farewell and skied back to the ship.

That night, as for both previous departures, an arc lamp was hoisted into the rigging, and oakum bonfires were burned in a ring about the ship, a dazzling homing beacon should the party seek to turn back. But the only return this time was that of the three outriders who reported that Nansen and Johansen were already seven miles north. Sverdrup waited another week, then packed Nansen's belongings into the forehold and moved into his chief's cabin. Another year and a half of icebound drift would follow before Sverdrup blasted his ship clear of the summer ice and emerged, exactly as Nansen had predicted, near Spitsbergen.

They made a promising start: seven, nine, and, once, a triumphant twenty-four miles a day, less than Nansen had hoped, but admirable progress over sea ice. After a week, their odometer dropped by the way; they did not bother to retrieve it but guessed all subsequent mileage. They had brilliant sunshine by day and 70° of frost overnight. The mercury of their artificial horizon froze solid. But the stove was a great success; they had so much water that they discarded their india rubber chest flasks. Accumulated moisture was, as always, a persistent nuisance, their crackling clothing, as Wilson would describe it years later, "a cuirass of ice during the day, and wet bandages at night." The ice-laden cuff of Nansen's jacket chafed an open sore on his right wrist that, frostbitten, scarred him for life.

By nightfall, both men were drained by the exhaustion of lifting sledges over hummocks. Sometimes Nansen fell asleep in his tracks, awakening to find himself facedown over the points of his skis. But merely calling a halt was not the end of it: There were dogs to feed and tether for the night; the tent to be pitched; supper to melt, cook, and eat. Their day, in fact, was divided into neat thirds: eight hours sledging, eight hours sleep, and the remaining eight an ordeal of packing and unpacking, kicking down into the frozen coils of their "dear bag," lying, teeth chattering, for an hour or more until the elusive warmth of their supper and consuming fatigue overcame bouts of ague. They worked, ate, and slept in the same sodden, tattered rig. The terrain was hard on everything: Their tunics were torn and ripped, and the kayaks were repeatedly holed as the sledges were dragged over icy pinnacles.

It was the ice that finished them. Two weeks after they had set out, conditions deteriorated and mileage slumped. On April 3, the indomitable Nansen scribbled in his diary: "Beginning to doubt seriously of the advisability of continuing northward much longer. It is three times as far to Franz Josef Land as the distance we have come." Although Nansen did not know it at the time, Johansen, lying next to him in their joint sleeping bag, was writing in *his* diary on that same morning that they should stop.

They were then at the eighty-sixth parallel, 240 miles short of their goal but separated from it by endless pressure ridges. Mileage on April 6 was only four miles, discouraging progress that would hardly get them to 87°. Johansen fell through the ice and was soaked to the waist—"not an unmixed pleasure," observed Nansen. Wet clothing froze solid at once and dried by almost imperceptible evaporation spread over weeks.

On Monday, April 8, they stopped at 86°13' North, their farthest north—if not the pole, a record surpassing Lockwood's. Nansen and Johansen pitched their tent; Johansen fed the animals and then lashed a pair of Norwegian flags onto skis stuck upright in the snow. His chief, without dogs or sledge, pressed on to see if the ice relented. But it did not: He saw nothing but "a veritable chaos of ice blocks."

Nansen stood farther north than any man in history, faced with the intolerable choice of continuing or turning back. It was the agonizing decision that plagued every explorer who had struggled to high latitude and could go no farther. At those terminal camps, ambition was tempered, perforce, with prudence. Nansen customarily ignored caution, and what must have deviled him further was that he and Johansen were still fresh; most polar explorers who turned back short of their goal (and all but three had to) did so under conditions of relative distress.

Nansen's farthest north would be abrogated five years later by Commander Umberto Cagni of the Royal Italian Navy, point man for the incapacitated Duke of the Abruzzi, Prince of Savoy, recuperating back on board the *Stella Polare* with two amputated fingers. Cagni and his assault party achieved their record thanks to days of effortless sledging across level ice, the elusive snow plain that Parry had hoped for in 1827 and within miles of the jagged, upturned fields that had defeated Nansen. One of the rare arctic guarantees is that ice conditions vary from year to year; the Arctic Ocean could be navigable, frozen smooth, or, most likely, chaotic.

It was just as well that the two Norwegians turned back. Petermann Land, their first destination to the south, did not exist! It was merely a hint of mountain range that the *Tegethoff*'s people thought they had seen. Nansen would head, instead, for Cape Fligely, 450 miles away, northernmost tip of the Franz Josef Land archipelago.

Ironically, as soon as they turned back, conditions improved dramatically. Pressure ridges and leads ran parallel to the west-southwest course they followed, and the dogs were driven along for hours at a time with almost no necessity for heaving the sledges over barriers. Their loads were diminishing and, in mid-May, the third sledge was put to the torch. With the reduction in sleds, there was an attrition in dogs as well. All twenty-eight dogs were killed during the ensuing spring and summer. To ease the blow, Nansen and Johansen each dispatched the other's favorites, using a knife after one abortive attempt at garroting; bullets were far too precious. Nansen's loyal bitch, Kvik, collapsed by the end of May. She had done nobly, surviving the punishing trek longer than Barbara and Gulen from her December litter. In one sense, death was a kindness; alive, the creatures suffered cruelly, pulling over impossible terrain, whipped, cursed, and rewarded with either brick-hard pemmican or the dripping haunch of one of their fellows. They were no longer the sleek, bushy pets from the *Fram;* they were lean predators now, fierce to the point of savagery, often gnawing through their night traces and gobbling anything they could find. One had polished off a pair of reindeer-hair socks and another one end of a ski.

Despite weeks of southerly progress, land remained elusively out of sight. Both men forgot to wind their watches within the same day, so no accurate longitudinal observations could be made. Nansen became convinced that they had somehow by-

passed Franz Josef Land and set his mental sights on Spitsbergen instead. The single exception to a vista of unrelenting
white was a trunk of Siberian larch, upended grotesquely in
the ice, mute testimony to the efficacy of Nansen's drift hypothesis. It was frozen in solidly. Unable to extricate it for fuel,
they carved their initials and presumed latitude on it instead.

In fact, the cold was relenting. It was occasionally stifling in
the tent. Johansen once fell asleep in the sun while waiting for
Nansen to retrieve their lost compass. Diaries could be written
bare-handed, and they replaced their worn-out *finnesko* with
kommager, the Lapps' summer leather boot. Nansen found it a
pleasant relief to sleep without having to warm a lump of
damp sennegrass on his chest.

There were disadvantages to higher temperatures. The snow
puddled and, each night, they had to construct a makeshift
palliasse of skis and staffs under their sleeping bags to keep
them out of the damp. They were wet most of the time; Nansen
suffered from recurring attacks of lumbago. Progress was hampered now by a proliferation of open leads as the summer pack
fragmented, necessitating laborious detours. Negotiating these
hazards by kayak was, for the moment, impossible. The fragile
hulls had been pierced repeatedly during their march.

Nansen and Johansen spent much of June holed up in what
they called Longing Camp, "longing" for better snow conditions (which never came) and repairing their damaged kayaks.
They were reduced to an ounce and two thirds of bread for
breakfast and two ounces at night. (A slice of bread weighs
approximately an ounce.) Game became more abundant with
warmer weather. They shot some gulls and auks, although
Nansen was loath to expend the ammunition. They killed their
first seal, dispatched with gun and harpoon. The latter was
essential, for a dead seal will sink like a stone and not resurface
for twenty-four hours. Nansen and Johansen wrestled the massive corpse onto their floe, and both they and the trio of dogs
remaining enjoyed a glut of meat and fat.

Consumption of that initial seal marked a long-overdue
switch to living off the land. Seal meat, particularly the loin
muscle, is excellent, as well as the heart, liver, and tongue.
When cooked, the steaks turn a deep mahogany color with a
strong but not necessarily fishy flavor as long as they are lean.
The inhabitants of the *Discovery*'s messdeck refused to eat seal

meat unless it had been scrupulously trimmed of its blubber to minimize its notoriously rancid flavor.

Waxy, yellow/pink blubber is the seal's insulating fat, between skin and underlying flesh, and is invaluable as fuel. Seal or train oil, burning in soapstone dishes with a moss wick, served as the igloo's candle, stove, and furnace. Nansen improvised his own train oil lamp by turning up the edges of a sheet of German silver (spares for the sledge runners) and igniting within it a scrap of redundant, blubber-soaked bandage. Raw blubber is an Eskimo delicacy that squeamish Europeans invariably abuse through cooking. In its natural state, blubber is almost tasteless, not unlike sweet butter; only when heated does it turn unpleasantly fishy. Leopold McClintock was an early advocate. "This is the first time I have eaten positive *blubber*," he wrote on board the *Fox* in June 1858. "All scruples respecting it henceforth vanish."

Nansen improvised yet another resource from the ubiquitous seal. At Longing Camp, both kayaks were successfully patched with a mixture of stearin and resin. Then the canvas was painted with a gummy macédoine of train oil, soot, and, for good measure, crushed pastel crayons from Nansen's sketching equipment. The kayaks were once more waterproof and, on July 23, were lashed onto the sledges; the pemmican boat blocks, long since consumed, were replaced with pads of folded bearskin. Nansen and Johansen left Longing Camp with vastly reduced loads, each sledge drawn now by one man and one dog.

The next day they spotted land at last, a white wraith on the horizon seen for days but only that morning established indubitably as their long-sought objective. But two weeks passed before they achieved it. During that time they came upon open water after five months on the ice. By then they were wading knee-deep in slush that filled their boots. "Behind us lay all our troubles, before us the waterway home!" exulted Nansen in premature relief on August 5. He and Johansen celebrated with a ration of chocolate. The last two dogs, Kaifas and Suggen, useless encumbrances now, were dispatched with a bullet each.

They launched their kayaks as an improvised catamaran, lashed together by transverse sledges and skis across the decks. Rigged with a sail, they proceeded briskly through the water toward the glaciated slopes ahead. They camped at night either on a drifting floe or the icefoot that fringed an island. After several days of struggling through ice-choked channels, Nansen took the irrevocable step, long envisioned, of cutting each sledge to half size, enabling it to be stowed on the afterdeck of each kayak. Thus the two explorers could proceed independently, with increased maneuverability, to find a passage through the worst of the ice jams.

A week later they landed on terra firma, the first in two years. They slept that night on coarse basalt and flew the Norwegian flag outside the tent once again. Nansen reckoned that they had missed Cape Fligely, the northernmost eminence, and had entered Franz Josef Land from the east and were now skirting its western boundary. For ten more days, the two men sailed and paddled before deciding to hole up, to winter in the open arctic. Eskimos had done so for centuries, but they were bred to it. Nansen and Johansen had completed an arduous, five-month trek and were at the end of their logistical tether, their petroleum exhausted, larder bare, and tent in tatters. In this parlous extremity, they proposed to set up house through a long arctic night.

That decision to winter over on a remote arctic island invites comparison with the most extraordinary feats of survival in history, polar or otherwise. For improvisation, ingenuity, and cold-blooded courage under the most appalling conditions, there are few tales to match it.

In a region of the earth where ghastly conditions are the norm, Franz Josef Land stands out as a paradigm of inclemency. Sir Leopold McClintock called its climate "about the most abominable in the world." A Captain Robertson of the whale ship *Balanea* provided his own pithy epitaph: "Franz Josef Land consists of two black spots: Cape Flora is one and the other is something else and you can't see them both together." Cape Flora was Franz Josef Land's southernmost point and, though remote, was at least accessible by sea. Nansen and Johansen's ice-girt beach was an isolated outpost on the frontier of nowhere, scoured by fearsome winds that welcomed them that August and continued unabated throughout the winter that followed, blowing stone-weighted kayaks uphill and snapping a ski stuck upright in the snow clean in half.

The explorers camped on a pebble-covered beach at the foot

of a cliff. Game was plentiful. Walrus bellowed and hooted in the ice jumble offshore, polar bears with cubs in tow sniffed and pawed inquisitively about their camp, and a plague of foxes, with the kleptomania of jackdaws, made off with critical supplies, including a ball of twine and one of their last remaining thermometers. Food was less of a problem than shelter. Conventional polar expeditions domiciled ashore took along elaborate, prefabricated huts complete with stove, library, and sometimes electric light. Nansen and Johansen wintered over in two successive homemade huts, the first "dreadful den" a drafty, rock-walled bothy roofed with the remains of their silk tent draped over a framework of skis and poles. It was too short, and Nansen's feet stuck out the door. It was also too low, and he could not sit upright in the sleeping bag. Clearly, a more ambitious structure was required.

They set about constructing a permanent winter lair; it was half underground, a pit ten feet by six hacked and clawed a yard deep into the frostbound scree. They had jettisoned their only shovel at Longing Camp and so made do with hunting trophies: Walrus tusk and shoulder blade served as pick and shovel, respectively. Once the pit had been excavated, they surrounded it with a stone wall three feet high. Although driftwood was at a premium, they found a single length of pine, twelve inches in diameter, that Johansen patiently cut to length with Amundsen's miniature hatchet. Then he and Nansen wrestled the waterlogged trunk into place atop their stone walls. (Members of the Baldwin-Ziegler expedition who visited the site five years later were struck by the massive dimension of that ridgepole; the hut's construction seemed the work of "giants.") Their roof was walrus hide. Skinning an entire creature seemed beyond them at first because of sheer bulk. But they found that by butchering one in the shallows, they could roll over the floating carcass and skin it whole. So their roof was capped with a full skin, softened in the comparative warmth of the sea and draped hastily over their dwelling before it froze. The margins were weighed with stones against the wind. A dogleg entrance tunnel, roofed with ice blocks, was dug in a low corner, trapping the minimal interior heat. In another corner, they constructed a crude chimney of ice and snow over a frame of walrus bones.

Along one long wall was laid a stone sleeping bench, preposterously uncomfortable even though padded with bearskins. In their first hut they had tried separate sleeping bags, but after one bone-chilling night had resewn their blankets together and profited from their mutual warmth for the balance of the winter. In fact, the temperature indoors never registered above freezing until spring.

However, the cold had one advantage: Had the hut's interior been any warmer, it would have stunk like an abattoir. A rank bearskin, amateurishly cured, had replaced the greasy, almost hairless reindeer sleeping bag from the *Fram*. Above them sagged the walrus-hide roof, festooned with flesh and blubber. Overall, there was a pervasive stench of train oil and, considerable by then, the reek of their own neglected bodies. Effective hygiene was impossible. They had no soap and, even if they had, precious little water in which to lather it. The closest they came to washing was done in fresh bear's blood, toweling off with remnants of the silk tent. Nansen tried boiling his shirt, but little of its ingrained soot and grease was removed. So he resorted to a simpler solution, reversing it instead, a time-honored explorer's expedient; Shackleton would turn his inside out only for holiday celebrations. Both Nansen and Johansen let their hair and beards grow to preserve precious body heat.

So matted and ineffectual were their clothes that the men seldom ventured outdoors. Instead, they sought oblivion in food-drugged sleep. Years afterward, Nansen dismissed the tribulations of that winter: "Well, perhaps it was a little monotonous." Most revealing was neglect of the diary he had kept faithfully since Christiania. From late August until December of 1895, there was a gap, months of preoccupation with hunting, killing, skinning, and building. Yet once they were ensconced in the completed winter digs, the entries were spasmodic, days and weeks often lumped together. The pages themselves bear testimony to the conditions of their confinement, so black and greasy that penciled notations were practically indecipherable. (Polar diarists seldom used pen, for the ink was forever freezing.)

Relations between Nansen and Johansen were curiously distant. Since they had brought no books from the *Fram*, they talked a great deal, elaborating in the main fantasies about food or clean clothing. The two men were scarcely similar:

Although Johansen was a commissioned officer, he was essentially a simple, phlegmatic fellow with none of Nansen's dazzling intellect. The formalities were quaintly observed. Not until New Year's Eve did Nansen propose that he and Johansen address each other by the familiar *du* rather than *de*. When conversation palled, sleep was the great escape. Instead of driving dogs in his sleep, as he had done on their march, Johansen snored, a common irritation between the most cordial bedmates, even more irritating on a pallet of jagged stones only slightly assuaged by layers of rank bear pelt.

When the sun returned at the end of February, they began preparations to move on. Provision bags and twine were unraveled for thread, and both men stitched new clothes from their blankets. They resoled their boots with walrus skin. Sledge rations buried the previous autumn were exhumed. They had deteriorated badly: The flour was moldy, chocolate destroyed by damp, and even the pemmican had a sinister flavor and color. So their traveling commissariat consisted only of fresh bear steaks and three precious cans of train oil. They lashed abbreviated loads onto abbreviated sledges and departed the hut, left intact as a cairn. Nansen suspended a record of their activities from the ridgepole, secreted in the brass pressure tube of their useless cooker. Then they moved out, southwest toward Spitsbergen.

During that final spring push they seemed in continual peril, as though Fate had saved its cruelest tricks for the end. On more than one occasion, vengeful fleets of walrus attacked the kayaks. Then again, while Nansen pressed ahead of his companion on foot, he fell through the ice: Ski-shod, he was unable to clamber out and, but for Johansen's fortuitous appearance, might have drowned.

On June 12 they switched back to water travel and, during a lunch stop on the ice, suffered a near-catastrophe when both kayaks, caught by the wind, drifted away from the floe on which the horrified explorers were stranded. Remembering to shuck his pocket watch, Nansen dove into the water in pursuit. With superhuman effort, he reached the craft and heaved himself on board and, teeth chattering violently, paddled back to Johansen. It was their closest call.

The astonishing denouement came four days later. On June 16 they heard several loud reports to their front, which they assumed to be cracking ice. In fact, it was Frederick Jackson's hunting party out after auks. Lieutenant Albert Armitage, his second-in-command, had spotted an alien figure through a telescope, and Jackson set out with his dog to investigate. Nansen heard the dog barking before he saw its owner, a slight, civilized figure in cap and tweeds. Their encounter was surreal, Britannic squiredom confronted by a scruffy, long-haired giant in the midst of a white wilderness. They shook hands solemnly; a ritualistic exchange of "How-do-you-do's" followed.

"I'm immensely glad to see you," ventured Jackson, as though in the anteroom of his club.

"Thank you," replied Nansen, teeth glinting against his blackamoor face. The two men fell in step together.

"Have you a ship here?" inquired the Britisher.

"No, my ship is not here," countered Nansen. He noticed how pleasantly the Englishman smelled of perfumed soap.

"How many of there are you?" pursued Jackson.

"I have only one companion, at the ice edge."

Only then did the penny drop. "Aren't you Nansen?"

"Yes, I am."

"By Jove!" cried Jackson. "I *am* glad to see you."

In fact, he had met Nansen in London years earlier but now did not recognize him. The incongruity of the Norwegian's sooty dishabille confounded him, hardly the same as the charming, fair-haired explorer Jackson recalled. I sense, too, in Nansen's reluctance to identify himself, a hint of remorse that he had regained civilization. Filth, hunger, and the limitations of his sledging companion notwithstanding, it seems clear that Nansen sought to prolong his anonymity and, by extension, his adventure. Ahead lay reunion with his shipmates, family, and countrymen, to be followed by publicity, adulation, and reward that would pall.

Nansen was physically affected by his second arctic ordeal; it marked his face and bearing for life. But there were hidden, emotional scars as well, deprivation of another kind. Although he would gain international renown and prestige, further exploration would be denied him. He was leaving the arctic that summer for the last time, and no reward, not even the love of a devoted Eva, would ever supplant the fierce triumph of will he had known during those exacting years. Cherishing that agony seems to have been endemic to all the explorers of that heroic age: Peary, Amundsen, Shackleton, and Scott knew it well. The polar struggle seemed right, and everything afterward somehow second-best.

Jackson took charge. Four shots were fired to alert Johansen, and he and Nansen were escorted to the luxury of the Jackson/Harmsworth base at Cape Flora. Washed, shaved, and clad in his host's trousers and jacket, Nansen took his unaccustomed ease in a folding camp chair. The clothes were a poor fit, for his enforced idleness over the winter had added twenty pounds to his weight; but, he told his host, there was indescribable pleasure in wearing garments that did not stick to him when he moved. His host handed him a soldered tin box of mail brought from England the previous year. Regrettably, there was none from Eva, but a long letter from his brother Alexander reassured Nansen that all was well in Norway.

Jackson initially made no inquiries about the *Fram*, assuming that both vessel and crew had been lost. Only when Nansen himself begged for news of his ship was the subject of the *Fram*'s whereabouts openly discussed. Over the ensuing weeks, the Englishmen and his visitors chattered incessantly; one epic conversation among Jackson, Nansen, and Koettlitz (who, with Armitage, was to join Scott on the *Discovery*) lasted a full forty-eight hours, interrupted only by food. Decompression from months of isolation had begun; not surprisingly, much of their talk centered on the south pole. Nansen stressed to Jackson that any antarctic work must await the return of Adrien de Gerlache on the *Belgica*. He was loath to trespass on another explorer's preserve.

Jackson's relief ship, the *Windward*, was due; she reached Cape Flora at 4:00 A.M. on July 26, after a delay in the ice. Captain Brown, her master, off-loaded Jackson's supplies and departed with Nansen and Johansen on board. Brown drove his ship home through ice-filled waters to the south in a record seven days, reaching Vardø on August 14. Once more on his beloved Norwegian soil, Nansen strode up the street to the telegraph office, where he was recognized only by his signature on the top of a stack of wires. The overjoyed telegrapher, his wife, and his staff spent three full days flashing the joyous news that electrified Norway and the world. Word of Nansen's miraculous reappearance animated the summer crowds that thronged Christiania's cafés. An evening performance of

Bjørnstjerne Bjørnson's *Mary Stuart* was disrupted as the long-awaited news was relayed in whispers throughout the auditorium, creating such a brouhaha that the play was stopped. Soberingly, there was no word of the *Fram*. By appropriate coincidence, staying at Vardø's solitary hotel was Professor Mohn, the man who had first theorized about the polar drift of the *Jeannette* relics. Nansen stormed up to his room, and the two colleagues enjoyed a hilarious reunion, complete with matutinal champagne.

Captain Brown's next stop was Hammerfest, Norway's northernmost town. There Nansen transferred from the *Windward* to the Baden-Powell steam yacht *Otaria*. Sir Robert, founder of the Boy Scouts, and Lady Baden-Powell were en route home from viewing a solar eclipse in Novaya Zemlya. He had proposed to Nansen four years earlier that the *Otaria* would search for him in Franz Josef Land in the summer of 1896; now he was delighted that his proposed mission had been rendered irrelevant. Two among the dozens who clamored to see Nansen were most cordially received on board: first Eva, who had raced north by mail steamer once she had received her Vardø wire; and second the head telegrapher of Hammerfest, who insisted on delivering one of dozens of wires in person. Like a deus ex machina, he handed Nansen a *petit bleu* that resolved the third-act cliff-hanger:

FRAM ARRIVED IN GOOD CONDITION ALL WELL ON BOARD SHALL
START AT ONCE FOR TROMSØ WELCOME HOME OTTO SVERDRUP

The news dispelled Nansen's worry about the fate of his companions and precipitated a second joyful furor the length of Norway. The Norwegian Polar Expedition had returned intact.

Nansen and the *Otaria* made all speed south, hoping to intercept the *Fram* at Skjervøy. But she had already departed and was tied up at Tromsø when the English yacht came in. It seemed unbelievable to Nansen that the icebound derelict he and Johansen had left the year previous awaited him now, grimy but gloriously intact. His crew lined the port bulwarks, cheering like fools. Then they rowed across in the whaleboat and swarmed onto the *Otaria*'s spotless teak. For the reunited thirteen, it was a moving occasion. Nansen found his emotions impossible to describe: ". . . we were together again—we were in Norway—and the expedition had fulfilled its task."

Passage south was a triumphant replay, in reverse, of their northbound farewell three summers previous. The only antipathetic aspect of that final leg was Nansen's curious failure to reberth on the *Fram*, as Johansen had done. Admittedly, it would have meant displacing Sverdrup from the master's cabin, as well as cramped quarters for his wife and himself. Apparently Eva decided matters. In a letter from Tromsø to Liv's nanny, she wrote, "*Fram* is a pigsty," and that she and Dr. Nansen would remain on the yacht as far as Trondheim; there they would transfer their flag to the *Haalogoland*, a government tug.

But Nansen was back on the *Fram*'s bridge when she reached Christiania. Norway's capital pulled out all the stops. *Fram* was escorted up the fjord by three warships. Norwegians packed every vantage point from shore, and cannonades, thirteen of them, echoed from ship to shore, one for each crew member. Then the *Fram* anchored in the Pipervika, maneuvering through a dense cluster of small boats; her long voyage was over.

Nansen, Sverdrup, and Johansen were rowed ashore first, in a state barge. They were received at the flag-draped quay by the full Norwegian establishment as well as an ecstatic three-year-old Liv. The explorers landed and boarded carriages. Their route across Christiania passed under a specially constructed *arc de triomphe*, garnished with fifty sailors and topped by a banner of welcome; on its lower tiers, women gymnasts clutched bouquets of roses that they showered down on the delighted crew. Through Rosenkrantz Gate the procession wound its way, turning at last into Karl Johan Gate, clip-clopping through delirious throngs up to the palace, where a beaming King Oscar was host at a state banquet.

Norway's capital was turned on its ear for a full week, with bonfires, processions, dinners, and a *folkefest* for the crew. Then the explorers went back to their homes and jobs; Sverdrup signed on as master of an excursion ship to Spitsbergen. Nansen had no sooner made friends with Liv (whom Eva had anxiously coached to call him "Father") than he plunged into work on a two-volume account of his voyage, *Fram over Polarhavet*.

Further honors awaited him overseas. Geographic societies all over the world struck gold medals in his honor. The Royal Geographical Society presented theirs in Royal Albert Hall.

Another London chore was some unfinished business at the Savage Club. On the occasion of a farewell dinner three years earlier, Nansen had signed the dining room wall. The sacred patch of plaster had been framed, awaiting the promised addition of a north pole date. For Nansen's return, a boisterous membership packed the club to hear his remarks; the rule forbidding speeches had unanimously been abrogated for that evening. "Brother savages," began Nansen, immediately drowned out by cheers. He spoke of having done without soap for fifteen months and told of the *Fram* and "my comrades," the crew. Then he wrote his farthest north—86°14′—beneath his signature on the wall. In New York, he dined at the Explorers Club and was presented with a comic souvenir, a bear's rib that had been retrieved by an American expedition from the refuse surrounding his Franz Josef Land hut.

Thus Nansen's second and final expedition passed into history. He never tackled the south pole; the pull of home, wife, and an increasing brood kept him from any further attempts at high latitude. His was a hard act to follow. No other figure from the heroic age quite matched him, with the possible exception of Ernest Shackleton. The Swedish playwright Strindberg best put Nansen's appeal into historical perspective, comparing the Norwegian with his own countryman Nordenskjöld. The Swedish explorer had conquered the Northeast Passage, a two-year voyage completed without incident and crowned with success; Nansen had set out for the pole and fallen far short of his goal. Yet Nansen is remembered—nay, immortalized—while Nordenskjöld's feat remains an arctic footnote. Such was the impact of the Nansen persona.

8

BY BALLOON

*Ascensions should not be made when
the thermometer is too low, for there is
then a probability that the caoutchouc
might be affected by the frost, and might
crack. . . .*

—Wilfrid de Fonvieille, aeronaut,
*Best Manner of Preparing Balloons for
Use in the Polar Regions*

If one equates polar ambition with polar success, then Andrée's celebrated balloon expedition seems on a glorious par with Nansen's epic voyage. Andrée was one of a kind, combining vision, determination, and courage in such stubborn quantities that he is an incontrovertible candidate for inclusion among the immortals of the heroic age. His real passion was aeronautics, the infant science of flying. That he saw his airship as a means of crossing the arctic was incidental: If it had not been the pole, he might well have tried a round-trip from Stockholm to Moscow or even a flight across the Atlantic.

Salomon August Andrée was born one of seven children in 1854 at Grenna, a small Swedish village. Andrée *père* was a pharmacist. Salomon proved an inquiring and impetuous student: He quit the local grammar school after only three years and passed final examinations at the age of twenty. After a two-year spell as a draftsman, Andrée traveled to America. His passion for flying began in the New World, at Philadelphia's Centennial Exposition of 1876, where he supported himself by sweeping floors at the Swedish exhibit. He met elderly John Wise, an American balloonist who had once tried crossing the Atlantic. Andrée's first flight came to grief: The balloon's fabric parted and, in the words of the crestfallen Swedish passenger, "the gas went up in the air alone."

On his return to Stockholm, Andrée joined the faculty of the Technical Institute as assistant professor of pure and applied science. Five years later, he was in the arctic. The year 1882 was the year of the International Polar Commission, the event that had dispatched Greely's expedition to Fort Conger. Sweden manned a station in the Spitsbergen islands, and Nils Eckholm, the director, selected Andrée to make the aeroelectrical observations. Andrée kept those records and more: He wrote a paper on whirling snow and, to study the effect of lightless periods on skin color, shut himself in a blacked-out cabin for a month. He emerged, as he suspected he would, with a greenish skin pallor. A comment from his diary shortly before the experiment is revealing: "Dangerous? Perhaps. But what am I worth?" Andrée was ruthlessly curious, determined to try regardless of the consequences. Once committed, he could not be diverted.

In 1885 Andrée was appointed chief engineer at the Royal Patent Office. His dual career, at institute and patent office, kept him au courant with the latest scientific developments, exposed to continuing inspiration from students and inventors alike. Over his desk passed specifications for all manner of contrivances, many devoted to realizing in fact what Jules Verne had long suggested in fancy. The French lawyer-turned-novelist had dominated popular fiction since 1865, and his influence over the late Victorian imagination cannot be overemphasized. By the turn of the century, invention and industry seemed close to implementing the Vernesian imagination. It seemed possible that men might embark on some of his more fanciful *voyages imaginaires:* journeys by balloon, submarine, or rocket; ventures to the moon, the north pole, the center of the earth, or even around it in an astonishing eighty days. Less well known than Verne's famous submarine *Nautilus* was another vessel, which carried her crew straight to the pole; her name was *Forward*, and there is every good reason to presume that it had inspired Nansen's name for his vessel. But it would be Andrée who would first turn Verne's incredible science fiction into bold science fact.

Andrée was nearly forty when, thanks to a grant from the Swedish Academy of Sciences, he bought his own balloon. It was made in France by Gabriel Yon, and Andrée christened it the *Svea*. He first inflated it in the barracks square of the Royal Engineers in Stockholm. For a beginner, some of his flights were ambitious. On one, he ascended to a height of thirteen thousand feet; on another, the *Svea* was carried across the Baltic Sea to the Finnish archipelago, on which it was wrecked and its pilot rescued after "an extremely unpleasant night."

At low levels Andrée experimented with directional flight, anxious to set his course independent of a prevailing wind. Perfection of a "dirigible"—from the French word for "directional"—had obsessed and eluded generations of aeronauts, and a variety of solutions had already been discarded. Oars had proved useless; propellers, turned either by hand or lightweight steam engines, had proved disappointing; jets of heated air had delivered insufficient thrust. A German proposed using captive eagles harnessed to his airship; 'he even patented a system complete with miniature bridles and reins, but the kaiser rejected it out of hand.

Andrée concentrated on using the wind, unlimited power that need not be carried aloft. But sails hung on a balloon are usually ineffectual, since both craft and canvas travel with the wind. A sail-rigged balloon tends to rotate on its axis, all the while moving inevitably to leeward. Andrée's solution was a drag rope, a device first tried by an Englishman named Green years before, but never in tandem with sails. A drag rope, trailed along land or sea, retarded Andrée's speed; thus he traveled *slower* than the wind, a sine qua non for the sailor. Moreover, that tenuous link with the ground gave his craft the advantage of mechanical torque or leverage, with a real resistance to twisting the balloon. After much experimentation,

Andrée found that he was able to steer, if not against, then certainly across the wind. The *Svea*, he discovered, could maneuver 30° to either side of the wind's direction.

All he needed, then, was an opportunity for an aerial expedition. It came, obliquely, from his countryman Nordenskjöld. He and Andrée were walking home across Stockholm one night after a meeting of the Anthropological and Geographical Society and were discussing the possibilities of aerial work in the antarctic. Having circumnavigated Eurasia, Nordenskjöld was considering an antarctic venture and sounded out Andrée on the possibility of surmounting Ross's Ice Barrier with a captive balloon.

Andrée's response was predictable: Why a captive balloon? Why not a free balloon direct to the *north* pole, which was much closer to Sweden? He had, after all, perfected a means of steering. The *Svea* was no longer merely a balloon but also a dirigible. What better use for it than vaulting over the arctic's implacable ice, which had proved the nemesis of so many conventional ships in the past?

Nordenskjöld offered his cautious blessing, and Andrée's irresistible dream was born.

In February of the following year he appeared before the Swedish Academy of Sciences, the same body that had subsidized purchase of the *Svea*. The patent engineer was back, an experienced balloonist now, with a proposal that staggered the imagination.

"These words may seem bold," began Andrée, bursting with optimism, "and even reckless, but I ask you to suspend your judgment on the matter until you have heard my arguments." Then he elaborated to a spellbound academy, describing a huge dirigible poised north of Spitsbergen, filled with hydrogen manufactured *in situ* and housed in a roofless octagonal shed awaiting a propitious wind from the south. She would carry a crew of three provisioned for four months, provided with sledges and a folding canoe as "lifesaving apparatus." His budget was modest, a mere 125,000 Swedish crowns to "explore this white quarter of the globe."

Andrée's timing was fortuitous. Sweden was afire with polar fever, and the balloon seemed perfect for a Swedish try. It was the same all over the world: Earlier defeats forgotten, a new generation of explorers was assaulting the polar bastions. That year, 1896, marked Nansen's third year drifting in the arctic; Britisher Frederick Jackson was nearing the end of his thousand days in the arctic at Cape Flora; Adrien de Gerlache was in Anarctica on the *Belgica,* among his crew a wiry Norwegian mate named Amundsen, and Frederick Cook, a Brooklyn doctor, as surgeon; at the RGS, Sir Clements Markham was planning history's most elaborate polar expedition to Antarctica, to sail under the command of a Royal Navy lieutenant named Scott. The only idle explorer that year was Robert Peary, the dogged U.S. naval officer; he was between tries, having pried the world's largest meteorites out of Greenland's frozen muck. There was a sense abroad that a polar breakthrough might be at hand. Within that climate of anticipation, Andrée's proposal seemed feasible and promising. Besides, thought more than one Swede privately, how marvelous to steal a march on those troublesome Norwegians!

Impressed by Nordenskjöld's endorsement, the academy responded favorably. Investors materialized; the first was Alfred Nobel, rich from his invention of dynamite and already an enthusiastic philanthropist. He and Andrée were not old friends, they were old antagonists who had spent an evening together years before and decided on parting that they agreed on nothing. But the balloon scheme obviously tickled the explosives king, and he would ultimately subscribe half of Andrée's costs. The balance was taken up by two prestigious punters: Baron Oscar Dickson, who had sponsored Nordenskjöld's Northeast Passage expedition, and King Oscar II.

World reaction was mixed, tempered with derision. Although geographical societies in Berlin and Paris rumbled their support, others predicted disaster. Andrée's balloon would be pecked to pieces by birds or shot down by savages. Wise old men assured Andrée gloomily that he would perish either from cold or lack of oxygen. "Andrée is simply a fool or a swindler" thundered the *Neue Freie Presse* from Vienna.

Undaunted, Andrée took his case to the International Geographical Congress in London in the summer of 1895. Heading the American delegation was General Adolphus Greely, who vociferously opposed Andrée's scheme. Britain's explorers also took a dim view of his chances. They had heard it all before, fifteen years before: John Cheyne, a Royal Navy veteran of three Franklin search expeditions, had proposed balloons for a polar attempt, fueled by coal gas from the Spitsbergen mines. Perhaps understandably, Andrée's sole British supporter was a Colonel Watson, late commander of Her Majesty's Aeronautical Corps. But, then, he was a balloonist as well. "It may happen, of course," he allowed, "that Mr. Andrée will never come back, but in spite of that risk, the attempt ought to be made." It might have been Andrée speaking himself.

Meanwhile, European balloon-makers deluged Andrée's office with swatches of fabrics. They were scrutinized by his new assistant, Nils Strindberg, a handsome young physicist and cousin of the playwright. After exhaustive testing for strength, elasticity, and tightness, Strindberg settled on a French maker, Henri Lachambre. Andrée traveled to Paris and, on Christmas Eve of 1895, concluded a contract for his polar balloon, *Le Pôle Nord*, to be delivered, crated, to Gothenburg, no later than mid-May of the following year. Stern penalties were spelled out in the event of delay. Andrée's countdown had begun, his schedule inexorably tied to the brief arctic summer. Every day was precious.

Lachambre's specifications included a sphere of six thousand cubic yards, made of Chinese pongee silk cemented together in double, triple, and occasionally quadruple layers with a patent varnish. In the days before nylon, varnish was all; balloons of any description were only as efficient as the preparation that coated them. The ideal was a finish combining flexibility with airtightness, and recipes were jealously guarded. A hundred years earlier, Captain Coutelle, in command of Napoleon's first balloon corps, had perfected an oil varnish of such enviable reliability that his tethered balloons had been used against the Austrians without refilling for two months. Unfortunately, his formula was lost.

Maintaining airtight integrity was crucial for long-range flights such as Andrée's. Yet it was apparent that Lachambre's sealing technique was faulty: Leakage through thousands of needle holes along the balloon's seams was never satisfactorily contained despite repeated applications of Arnoul's varnish inside and out.

Lachambre first assembled and inflated his creation in the thirty-meter gallery of Paris's Palais du Champ de Mars, vacant since the Universal Exposition in Paris in 1889 but traditionally a focal point for aerial spectaculars. The brothers Montgolfier had made several ascents there. *Le Pôle Nord* was inflated with air for a pressure test. It held its shape with no significant leakage and was then collapsed, varnished once more, and reinflated to dry. During the four-day drying period, thirty thousand Parisians, led by the president of the Republic himself, trooped through the hall for a look.

There was more to see than the vast orange globe. Adjacent to it hung the woven net that would enclose the silk, a meticulously wrought web with no knots in it at all: Where each length of hemp crossed another, a ligature of fine twine was tied. All the cordage was infused with vaseline to prevent its absorbing moisture from the air.

The last component exhibited in the hall was the passenger compartment. Although made of wicker, the vehicle suspended beneath all balloons is—and should be referred to as—the car, never the basket. Andrée's car was a partially enclosed duplex, with sleeping quarters for one crewman and a darkroom on its lower deck. Suspended above the load ring were skis, rifles, tent, canoe, sledge, and dozens of linen pockets for provisions. There was space as well for wicker cages full of carrier pigeons. Other means of communication from high latitude were a dozen cork buoys, painted blue and yellow, Sweden's colors, the tops of which contained a message receptacle. A thirteenth buoy, larger than the others, was reserved as the polar buoy, to be dropped either at latitude 90° North or at the expedition's farthest north.

Andrée was besieged by applicants from all over the world, eager to accompany him. The student body of the Royal Technical Institute volunteered en masse. Some were signed on as crew members of the *Virgo*, the Hull/Gothenburg ferry that had been chartered as the expedition ship. As on the *Fram*, even the most menial positions were filled by officers.

For his balloon crew, Andrée selected two fellow Swedes: Nils Ekholm, his chief from Spitsbergen; and young Strindberg, who would serve as expedition photographer. At Gothenburg, the departure port, a gang of carpenters, two of whom would sail with the expedition, spent the spring prefabricating Andrée's five-story balloon shed. Erected near the piers, its timbers numbered, it would then be taken apart, ready for shipment on board. Axel Stake, the expedition's chemist, ordered fifty thousand pounds of sulphuric acid and seven tons of iron filings from England for his arctic hydrogen plant.

Provisioning consumed much of the winter. Andrée's pemmican mixture was identical to Nansen's on the *Fram*, provided again by Beauvais of Copenhagen. But it was packed in space-saving square cans that were made of copper so that no iron would interfere with magnetic measurements to be made in flight. There were also lozenges of concentrated lemon juice as an antiscorbutic, much celebratory wine and spirits (the beverage of choice for all balloonists is still champagne), and hundreds of rounds of ammunition—"my concentrated food," observed Andrée, who planned to hunt when and if forced down on the ice.

Andrée's arrangement for cooking aloft might have come right out of the patent office. Aware of the hazard of an open flame near hydrogen, he devised a method of operating his Primus stove while it was suspended safely beneath the car on a rope. The flame would be ignited by a string-operated match, cooking would be monitored through an angled mirror, and the flame would be extinguished by blowing smartly down a rubber tube lashed to the stove's supporting line.

The expedition's equipment was loaded in early June. The night before departure, Baron Dickson arranged an elaborate farewell dinner; among the guests was Strindberg's sweetheart, Anna Charlier, who had accompanied the young man's father from Stockholm to see him off. The next morning, the *Virgo*, under command of Captain Hugo Zachau, headed to sea. After calling at Tromsø, the vessel was blocked by ice south of Spitsbergen. Andrée fumed during four days of intolerable delay; finally a change of wind disrupted the floes and they continued north.

Their destination was the Norwegian Islands, a pair of mountainous sentinels lying just off Spitsbergen's northwestern corner on the threshold of the arctic circle and very near Parry's departure point in 1827. The northernmost, Amsterdam Island, had an inhospitable coastline, but on neighboring Dane Island, they selected (and named) Virgo Bay. It was ideal for Andrée's purpose, a good anchorage, open to the north and protected inland by mountains. There was a shelving beach for landing supplies and adjacent flat ground for construction of the balloon house.

Off-loading began at once. The *Virgo* lay 150 yards offshore, separated from the beach by waters filled with ice that dispersed or regrouped at the whim of wind and tide. Captain Zachau put three of his boats side by side and lashed them together as an improvised lighter. It lay alongside to receive the first load, the hydrogen plant. Cumbersome lead-lined vats were hoisted from the hold and towed ashore by steam launch while outriders fended off the ice. Once the vessel landed, carpenters set the factory foundations on low ground so the hydrogen could flow uphill during inflation.

Next, lumber for the balloon house ran the ice-filled gauntlet to shore. The structural framing was all on the outside, leaving smooth inner walls, which had been lined with felt wherever the balloon's equator might chafe. The side facing the water had been designed as a breakaway wall that carpenters could demolish just prior to ascent. Staircase towers added strength at the eastern and western corners.

On July 21, 1896, one month to the day since their arrival at the island, the largest single component, Lachambre's crated balloon, came ashore. It was the size of a farm cart and weighed over two tons, taxing the capacity of their improvised lighter. Ashore, the crate was skidded over greased planks laid on the snow. Then it was opened and the orange silk balloon manhandled with infinite care into its waiting hangar. Once valves had been attached and locked shut, hosepipes were connected, and Stake began hydrogen production. His steam pump hissed into life, and the outflow hose, snaking through wet snow up to the balloon house, fattened as the first cubic feet of hydrogen crept into the waiting folds of *Le Pôle Nord*. It was two o'clock on the afternoon of July 23.

After four days, the top of the inflated craft protruded above the shed's low northern wall. In the working space beneath, rigging crews tied off a tangle of cordage and placed the car in a hole specially excavated in the floor. Andrée had long since spent a token night on board, having temporarily hung the entire contraption from a crossbeam to counterfeit the sensation of being aloft. He had read some pages of Nordenskjöld's *Vega* diary, ceremonially, "to consecrate, as well as I could, the new vessel." Three drag ropes, coated with vaseline, were attached to the bottom of the car by threaded couplings.

Everything was in readiness, all save the right wind. During preparations for the flight, weather conditions had been ideal, with a steady southern wind. But then it had changed direction and Virgo Bay was continually ruffled by a persistent onshore wind out of the north. Andrée lamented in his diary: ". . . if nature will only do its share, we should soon all be set." But nature, perversely, did not and, as the first days of August passed, a sense of bitter anticlimax settled over the Dane Island camp.

Zachau, master of the *Virgo*, reminded Andrée tactfully that his contract would terminate on August 20; the ship's insurance would lapse beyond that date, and he could not remain in Spitsbergen much longer. Time had run out. Andrée gave orders to collapse the balloon. Valves were opened and five thousand cubic feet of precious hydrogen were vented into the chill August air. Then the silk was folded and, together with car and net, loaded on board. The balloon shed was dismantled down to the second tier in hopes that it might survive the winter. Just before they were to leave, another ship slipped into Virgo Bay, the long-lost *Fram*, only just released from the polar ice. The entire crew downed tools and rowed out to greet the returning explorers.

Andrée spent the following winter preparing for another try. The balloon was shipped back to France and enlarged: An extra yard of treble silk was inserted around the equator—more lift but more leakage. The craft was rechristened: *Le Pôle Nord*, Lachambre's choice, was supplanted by the less specific *Örnen*, or *Eagle*.

There was a change in crew. Nils Ekholm opted out, concerned about the problem of leakage. He communicated his fears to Strindberg, but the younger man would not be swayed. Ekholm's substitute was Knut Fraenkel, an engineer rather than a scientist. Like Johansen, he was a gymnast, young, strong, and athletic, considered quite fearless. Andrée's choice of Fraenkel betrays amended priorities: a scientist replaced by a sportsman, wisdom by youthful ingenuity. Fraenkel was sent to Paris for a crash course in ballooning; the names of his practice craft were *Fram* and *Nobel*.

If Strindberg had no doubts about the *Eagle*, he had no

doubts about the future, either. In October 1896 he became formally engaged to Anna Charlier, daughter of the postmaster at Klippan, a village in the South. Before his departure the following spring, he and his fiancée penned projected dates into the almanac he would carry with him. For October 17, 1897, the anniversary of their engagement, Nils Strindberg made a wistful, sentimental entry: "Home 7:05 A.M." It was the arrival time of the Gothenburg/Stockholm night express.

Mortality touched the expedition. Alfred Nobel died at San Remo before Christmas of 1896 and Baron Oscar Dickson died the following June. Andrée's mother fell victim to a fatal illness that spring as well. But there was good news from another quarter. King Oscar put the gunboat *Svenskund*, under the command of Count Ehrensvärd, at the disposal of the expedition. The naval vessel could perform double duty as an ice-breaker and would make short work of any delays en route.

An earlier timetable was established for that summer of 1897. *Svenskund* left Sweden in mid-May, her first port of call Tromsø, where she rendezvoused with the *Virgo*, engaged now as a supply ship. The two vessels sailed at the end of the month.

Though no ice hampered their crossing to Spitsbergen, Virgo Harbor was packed with floes. For thirty-six hours, *Svenskund* reversed and rammed, forcing a passage to an anchorage for both vessels. More suspenseful than their struggle with the ice was anxiety about the balloon shed: Had it survived the winter? Andrée himself first spotted the flagpoles atop each stair-case tower; the hangar, he reported jubilantly, was listing slightly but intact.

By May 30, both vessels were anchored off the beach. It was earlier in the season than the year previous, and the ice was so tightly packed that many of their supplies went ashore on the backs of naval ratings. The balloon crate had to be floated ashore, but the ice obstructed their boats. Dynamite was finally used to open a lead to the beach, the expedition saved, in effect, by the fortuitous application of one of its backer's inventions.

Alexis Machuron, Lachambre's nephew, was subbing for his uncle as the resident balloon expert. He ordered a test inflation with air. After giant bellows had inflated the balloon, eight men armed with pots and brushes stepped into the orange twilight of its interior to daub a final coat of varnish along the

175

seams. They emerged, eyes streaming, choking from the fumes. For three full days, the lifeless silk hung dormant in its drafty prison while they waited for it to dry. Strindberg put his time to good use, designing and constructing a wind indicator with giant copper letters for the hill behind the *Eagle*.

On June 19, Axel Stake put his resurrected hydrogen plant into operation and, once again, the *Eagle* resumed its buoyant posture, tugging at the ballast bags ringing the net. Stake had a new method of pinpointing leaks: Strips of white silk, impregnated with acetate of lead, were laid atop the balloon. Wherever the still-sulphurous hydrogen was escaping, telltale black stains of sulphur acetate appeared. A rope was strung between the two towers' flagpoles, and nimble sailors rode a pulley out to the center before dropping onto the *Eagle*'s yielding convex summit, testing and revarnishing every faulty seam they could find. Men had never walked on top of a balloon before.

The *Eagle* was ready at the end of June, a month earlier than the previous year. Otto Sverdrup reappeared in the harbor, in command of *Lofoten*, an excursion ship sailing regularly between Hammerfest and Spitsbergen. He promised to stop by on his way back to the mainland.

Overnight, on July 6, high winds rattled the shed furiously, endangering the captive *Eagle*. Some hydrogen was lost as the netted globe worked back and forth in its felt-lined enclosure; Stake was up at dawn, putting out more hydrogen. Andrée kept one eye on the barometer and another on the giant weather vane atop the hill, still waiting for the perfect wind.

Three days later, *Lofoten* reappeared and stayed for an hour; Sverdrup and Andrée talked briefly. When she sailed for Hammerfest, her place in Virgo Harbor was taken by a sealing vessel whose captain sought shelter from predicted squalls out of the southeast. His forecast was accurate: At three the next morning, Sunday, July 11, the wind started to blow offshore, gently at first before blustering into a fitful gale. Strindberg roused Axel Stake exultantly: "We shall sail today, the wind is from the south!"

The three expedition members gathered excitedly on top of the creaking balloon shed, the two younger men awaiting their commander's verdict. But Andrée queried them instead: "Shall we try it or not?"

Strindberg recorded the exact words in his diary. They seemed evasive and halfhearted, uncharacteristic of the man whose determination had inspired them all. Years later, Sverdrup revealed that Andrée had told him on board *Lofoten* earlier that week that he did not trust the weather, that he was not optimistic about success, but that he planned to carry the thing through regardless. One senses that now he worried, not for himself, but for his young crew, one of them with a fiancée.

Not until they had reboarded the *Svenskund* did Andrée give any indication of his decision. He told Count Ehrensvärd that he was agreeable to going "although with some reluctance" and that men should be sent ashore to take down the north wall of the shed. With this almost studied obliqueness, Salomon August Andrée gave the signal for his momentous flight to begin.

The Sabbath calm was disrupted. Sailors assembled for church parade changed into working rig and raced ashore. Count Ehrensvärd signaled the neighboring sealer to reanchor, out of *Eagle*'s path. The wind sent clouds tearing overhead, and rippling Swedish pennants on top of each staircase tower pointed the way north. Carpenters demolished the northern wall. Another crew strung additional windbreaks atop the southern wall, lashing flapping canvas to uprights already in place.

Inside, Andrée directed his riggers, shouting over the noise of the carpenters above. The balloon's equatorial links with the shed walls were severed, its upward thrust countered instead by sandbags. Then three restraining lines were added, rove through blocks anchored solidly in Dane Island bedrock, *Eagle*'s only remaining umbilical tie to earth.

Then Andrée gave the command to slacken off. Three crews gave cautious way, paying out inches of taut manila that slipped, triple-turned, about smoking wooden bights. *Eagle* floated up, trembling in the restless wind. When the load ring was ten feet off the ground, Andrée called a halt. The ropes were tied off and the passenger car was attached.

Out in the harbor, two more sealers had appeared. They had a grandstand view of the *Eagle*, like an orange pupa emerging from its cocoon. A flight of small balloons danced aloft from the beach: Strindberg was conducting final tests of the upper air currents.

As soon as the car was attached, more sandbags were hung around its sides. The ends of the three drag ropes, Andrée's rudder, were dragged up from the beach and attached. The sails were hoisted. Andrée listened patiently to Strindberg's weather report; then Andrée made a circuit of his airship, testing and tugging every rope. Earlier reluctance gone, Andrée was calm, assured, forceful, a veritable eagle himself.

"Strindberg and Fraenkel, are you ready to get into the car?" he called. Carpenters, riggers, and sailors crowded around, their labors over at the moment of ascent. There were hurried embraces and handshakes. Someone thrust some bottled beer at Fraenkel. Strindberg handed a letter to his friend Machuron, addressed to Anna, then swung over the canvas railing onto *Eagle*'s flight deck. Andrée dictated a wire for Ehrensvärd to send to King Oscar.

On a signal from Machuron, the three lines were chopped simultaneously. The car rose with the majestic, irresistible finality of a rocket. A spontaneous cheer followed it. "Long life, Andrée!" blurted out the count. Strindberg's response echoed down: "Long live old Sweden!"

The *Eagle* burst into the sunlight. Caught by the wind, she lofted over the beach toward Virgo Harbor and its cheering flotilla. The three guide ropes twisted and flailed through the air as they were drawn up from the beach. Then, suddenly, all three parted in midair and splashed into the shallows. There was no time to ponder the cause, for worse disaster threatened: The *Eagle* was caught in the downdraft sweeping seaward over the humpbacked slopes of the island. She sank down to the water, the bottom of the car actually touching the surface. Watching sailors ashore ran for the boats to rescue the explorers. But Machuron called them back: He and Andrée had anticipated the downdraft, and Machuron had every confidence the *Eagle* would recover. As he spoke, the explorers were seen slashing at clusters of sandbags, jettisoning ballast in a desperate attempt to rise. Rise they did, trailing ballast lines drawing a furrowed wake across the water beneath them. These same lines, suspended from the leeward side of the car, had already exerted sufficient drag on the airship to twist it through 180°, thus negating the effect of the sails. Those on shore saw one of the crew (it was Fraenkel, the gymnast) scurry up the rope ladder to the load ring to detach the temporarily useless sails while the other two, just visible over their canvas baffle, paid out the halyards.

It is interesting to speculate on the *Eagle*'s fate had the drag ropes *not* become detached. The threaded couplings incorporated into their length were there against Andrée's better judgment. Swedish experts had insisted that one of the trailing ropes might easily catch on rough ice. Rather than cutting it free from the car and losing its entire length, the couplings were incorporated so that the balloonists, cranking a geared mechanism from the car, could twist the rope, disengage the coupling, and part it halfway down; the bulk of it could thus be retained for further use. Unfortunately, this fail-safe system had served as the agent of its own destruction: As the *Eagle* gained altitude, the ropes were drawn up and, uncoiling with a gravity-impelled twist (Andrée's precious torque in ironic reverse), disengaged themselves with almost ludicrous precision.

Catastrophic though the accident may have seemed, I would hazard that only *because of* the loss of the ropes and their half-ton weight did Andrée survive his near-dunking. Had more of the car been submerged, it might well have foundered, aborting the expedition within moments of its having begun. But the balloon regained height, and it and its three gallant passengers disappeared into the north over Amsterdam Island.

Ehrensvärd and the *Svenskund* packed up and sailed for Gothenburg. Before leaving Dane Strait, Machuron prevailed upon the Count to put a search party ashore on the eastern tip of Amsterdam Island: Strindberg was to have dropped a final note to his beloved Anna en passant. But nothing was found. (Strindberg's letter was not finished in time for Amsterdam; he released it over Vogelsang Island, a hundred miles farther to the northeast. Presumably it is still there today in its tin box.) So Anna Charlier had only Nils's hasty scribble before boarding the *Eagle*. Machuron also gave her one of the airship's empty sandbags, retrieved from Virgo Harbor.

In all, Andrée carried thirty-six carrier pigeons aloft with him, housed in wicker cages lashed above the load ring. They were the best bred in Europe, Antwerp birds trained for the expedition out of a dovecote in Hammerfest, Norway's northernmost town. Yet the distances involved were overwhelming. Birds released from the balloon faced a grueling sea journey of nearly six hundred miles. Moreover, meteorological conditions most likely to be encountered over water in the arctic summer—mist or rain—make for the worst possible flying for pigeons; their homing instinct is fatally muddled by wet weather.

Andrée released four of his birds each day, by prearrangement. Only one of the thirty-six was ever recovered, and the details of that recovery are extraordinary. Captain Ole Hansen, master of the sealer *Alken*, was awakened at two o'clock in the morning of the fifteenth, four days, had he known it, after the *Eagle's* ascent. One of his crew pointed out an exhausted bird that had taken refuge in the rigging, pursued by a pair of gulls. Hansen clambered up for a closer look, decided it was a ptarmigan, and shot it, point-blank. It fell into the sea. Not bothering to pick it up, Hansen kept the *Alken* on course.

But the following day, after talking with the master of another sealer, he realized that the previous night's quarry could have been one of Andrée's messengers. Hansen reversed course at once and, reaching the place where the creature had been dispatched, sent two boats over the side to search for it. The carcass was found and recovered. When it was examined on board, each wing bore an unmistakable legend: Under the right one was stamped ANDRÉE, and marked on the opposing pinion was *Aftonbladet Stockholm*, the afternoon paper that owned Andrée's Swedish serial rights. Wrapped in oil parchment under the tail feathers was a scrap of paper giving the *Eagle's* position as of midday on the thirteenth. After thirty-six hours in the air, the exhausted bird had traveled south only a hundred miles, erratic progress in the direction of Hammerfest. The pigeon's skin ultimately reached Stockholm, where, after a taxidermist had mounted it as though in flight, it was presented to Anna Charlier. She cherished it for the rest of her life, "a permanent souvenir," wrote Oscar Strindberg, her prospective father-in-law, "from the dearest she has, poor thing."

When the story of the *Alken's* miraculous find had been circulated, thousands of pigeons and near-pigeons all over northern Europe were slaughtered by hunters hopeful of enjoying Captain Hansen's good luck. But there was no further message for two years, until May 1899, when buoy number 7 was found on the northern shore of Iceland. Buoy number 4 washed up in August of the following year at Finnmark, on Norway's northern tip. The message it carried is worth reproducing in full. It

was Andrée's longest communication and gives us a tantalizing glimpse of the balloon's progress as well as the high morale
of its occupants:

Buoy Number 4

The first to be thrown out. July 11, 10 p.m. GMT. Our
journey has gone well so far. We are drifting at an elevation of about 250 metres with a course which at first was
N 10 E True but later N 45 E True. Four messenger
pigeons were sent out at 5:40 p.m. Greenwich time. They
flew westerly. We are now over the ice which is much
broken up. The weather is beautiful. We are in the highest spirits.

ANDRÉE, STRINDBERG, FRAENKEL
We have been over broken ice since 7:45 G.M.T.

Between the lines, one can sense Andrée's contentment on that
calm polar evening: The *Eagle* had been afloat for eight hours,
three of them over the forbidding pack, that icy rampart by
which earthbound ships would long have been forestalled. But
the *Eagle* drifts serenely northward, exactly as Andrée had predicted. The frustration and struggle of Dane Island have been
left behind and Andrée's arctic aeronautical vision has come to
life.

In the absence of further communications, there was no shortage of assistance from all over the world. Citizens of Winnipeg,
in central Canada, saw the *Eagle* quite clearly on July 1, ten
days *before* it had left the ground at Spitsbergen, a forerunner
of a host of inaccurate sightings to follow. First came reports of
wreckage seen in Norwegian waters, none of them subsequently verified. The bark *Ansgar* sighted the remains of a balloon on July 13, east of the North Cape. Four days later, the
captain of a Dutch steamer "saw" the *Eagle* adrift on the
Barents Sea. In October, mysterious screams heard by sailors
off Spitsbergen were attributed to the *Eagle*'s survivors. But
keener eyes still saw the airship aloft. Eskimos at Ivigtut
claimed to have seen the balloon in early August, sailing over
Greenland's southwestern coast. Angmagssalik natives on
Greenland's east coast heard gunshots offshore. A zany named
Bracke, in Germania, Iowa, professed to be in spiritual contact

with Andrée and wired Swedish authorities to search Edam Land for their shipwrecked countrymen—in northeastern Greenland. Ultimately, an expedition under Andrée's colleague Nathorst explored Greenland's coast between latitudes 70° and 75°; they found nothing. Neither did a Siberian expedition under Stadling, one of whose members was Hans Fraenkel, brother of the missing gymnast.

From all over the Northern Hemisphere—from Russia, Canada, Alaska, Scandinavia—the reports proliferated. The heaviest concentrations seemed centered in western Canada and Siberia. Two separate tribes of Indians in British Columbia "saw" the balloon that August of 1897. In April of the following year, an ex-mailman from Dawson claimed that Andrée had turned up in the Klondike and had given him a letter; it was never forthcoming. On the opposite side of the globe, a trio of dead horses was found near Tomsk; but when news of the find reached St. Petersburg, horses' had been distorted into the explorers' remains. Of course, the czar had unwittingly encouraged all manner of peasant enthusiasm by publicizing the Andrée balloon efficiently: broadsides describing the expedition had been widely distributed, and it is not surprising that simple imaginations thus prompted produced a rash of preposterous claims. The wife of the governor of Sakhalin, an island off Russia's eastern coast, saw the *Eagle* float past in September.

One can forgive well-meant cooperation. But gratuitous fraud inflicted needless cruelty on relatives and friends waiting anxiously in Sweden. Bogus bottled notes began washing ashore in Iceland and Norway. Another was picked up along the railroad tracks near Vilna in the Urals. Its message was typical, hardly the work of superstitious peasants: "Andrée's balloon has crossed the Urals" was printed in French. A Russian postscript was added: "Give this letter to the consul or police."

Fellow explorers held out some hope. Nansen was encouraging at first. In February 1898, seven months after the *Eagle's* departure, he announced that Andrée must be wintering in Franz Josef Land and would doubtless reappear in the spring on board a whaler. Such expert reassurance was comforting to Strindberg's family and fiancée. Fridtjof Nansen was, after all, living proof that men could camp through an arctic winter.

But elsewhere, old doubts were raised. Von Payer, the man

who had first explored Franz Josef Land, in 1872, was not sanguine. A month before Nansen's remarks, the Austrian explorer lectured in Kiel, suggesting that Andrée should have conducted balloon tests under arctic weather conditions before committing himself. Nils Ekholm, the Sweedish meteorologist who had parted company with Andrée in 1896, went further: He stated that the *Eagle* could not possibly have stayed aloft for more than a few days. Lachambre responded defiantly from Paris that they should wait for three years before giving up.

Wait was all anyone could do. The winter dragged by. July 11, 1898, the first anniversary of the flight, passed. The Wellman expedition was in Franz Josef Land that summer and reported that traces of men were found near Cape Tegetthoff. But when the party subsequently reached Cape Flora, they despaired, Wellman bemoaning in print the following February, a year after Nansen's hopeful prognosis: "Poor Andrée! Poor, brave, dead Andrée!"

What clinched matters for almost everyone was the discovery of the polar buoy on a Spitsbergen beach in September 1899. Over two years had gone by. The largest of Andrée's buoys, destined to be dropped at the pole, contained no message. Nansen was forced to admit that the buoy's recovery indicated that the *Eagle* was lost, either on the ice or in the sea. Even Anna Charlier began to lose hope. Nils had told her in one of his letters from Dane Island that she should wait for him for at least two years. In fact, she waited for thirteen before marrying an Englishman, Gilbert Hawtrey, who taught at St. Paul's School in Concord, New Hampshire, between the wars. Anna Hawtrey gave generations of St. Paul's boys music lessons. Hung in the window near the piano was the carrier pigeon recovered from the sea off Spitsbergen.

A journalist in England, pondering the fate of the Andrée expedition, did some arithmetic and arrived at a bleak total: By 1897, the quest for the north pole had cost 751 lives, including 23 on the *Jeannette*, 19 with Greely, and now 3 more with the *Eagle*. But in spite of all that, the quest would go on.

9

SOUTH, THEN

*The real severity of the Antarctic climate
is not shown in its low minimum temperatures but in its low maximum temperatures.*

—*Polar Record*, July 1953

Topographically, Antarctica is the reverse of the arctic,
best remembered by picturing the globe as heart-shaped: On
top there is a depression, below a protuberance. The north pole
is in the midst of a frozen ocean; the south pole is two miles up,
in the midst of the world's highest continent. This is Antarctica, the last continent to have been discovered, buried under
90 percent of the world's ice, a glistening white mantle that,
from space, is this planet's most prominent feature. Antarctica
shares with neighboring Australia the distinction of being the
only continent unattached by land to any other.

Such was not always the case. Aeons ago, when the earth's
crust was first formed, Antarctica was part and parcel of a
supercontinent that geologists have dubbed Gondwanaland;
besides Antarctica, it included Brazil, Uruguay, Africa, Arabia,
and Madagascar as well as central and western Australia. But
starting in the Mesozoic era and continuing for hundreds of
millions of years, Gondwanaland fragmented and scattered,
tectonically reshuffled into its present-day configurations. Antarctica was thrust farthest south to occupy the coldest, remot-

est and most desolate arc of the globe. Still locked beneath its frigid crust are fossilized remnants of its tropical past.

In terms of weather statistics, that southern continent qualifies as a desert. Annual precipitation is restricted to twenty-four inches of snow, an accumulation that never melts but is continually redeposited by fierce, scouring winds. At the pole itself, no more than six inches falls per annum. It is bitterly cold, colder than the arctic, for it derives no stabilizing warmth from an underlying ocean. The environment is so hostile that, inland from its game-rich coastal waters, nothing lives or grows save for a species of wingless fly and stunted lichens. For the rest, Antarctica is a lifeless deep-freeze, an inhospitable, barren, but incredibly beautiful wasteland of 5.5 million square miles.

Those of us who live in the Northern Hemisphere are conditioned to think of December as the start of winter; in Antarctica, it is high summer, albeit a chilly one. October heralds the antarctic spring, April ushers in autumn, and winter is at its worst during July and August. Suffering most cruelly from this climatological inversion were expedition dogs, brought south in August with coats that had already molted, to remain out of synchronization with Antarctica's summer and winter.

Antarctica is remote not only from the temperate North but the less populated temperate South as well. Below the Cape of Good Hope, the earth is girdled by an ocean freeway along which cumulatively awesome winds and waves can circle the globe unobstructed by land. Unique to these southern oceans, this belt of maritime ferocity was christened by sailors the Roaring Forties, exceeded in fury only by the Furious Fifties or, worse, the Shrieking Sixties.

Captain James Cook was the first to circumnavigate the globe via this tortuous route, in 1774; though he sailed inside the Antarctic Circle several times, he saw no trace of the rumored continent (Terra Australis) farther south. But he guessed at its presence: ". . . and yet I think there must be some land to the south behind this ice, but if there is, it can afford no better retreat for birds or other animals than the ice itself, with which it must be wholly covered." Captain Cook was not far off the mark.

Sixty-five years would pass before another Englishman would see that continent. James Ross was eminently suited to lead an expedition to Antarctica, having spent eight winters in the arctic. He sailed south in quest of a scientific pole, the southern magnetic one, one of two points on earth where a vertical compass needle will point straight down. Ross had already located the north magnetic pole in 1831.

He sailed from England in the autumn of 1839 in command of the *Erebus* and the *Terror*. Unlike his twentieth-century successors, he seems to have been in no hurry. A year passed before he was ready to leave his final port, Hobartstown, the capital city of Van Diemen's Land or, as it is known today, Tasmania. Ross's host at Government House was an Old Arctic colleague, Sir John Franklin, who extended every help and consideration in reprovisioning the *Erebus* and the *Terror* for their voyage south. It was a rendezvous of eerie coincidence, Sir John waving off the same two vessels that would carry him to arctic oblivion five years later.

Ross sailed east rather than proceed directly toward Antarctica, reaching the 180th meridian of longitude before turning south. He had good reason for this detour: He wished to avoid rival French and American expeditions, under D'Urville and Wilkes, respectively. He hoped also to profit from the report of a British sealing captain, John Balleney, who the year before had spotted open water inside the continental rim of pack ice. Antarctica's winter ice fragments and drifts northward each summer, surrounding the continent with a formidable defense perimeter that, like Melville Bay's Middle Pack, never dissipates. Before Ross, no one had ever penetrated it.

Two days after Christmas of 1840, Ross saw his first iceberg and, on New Year's Day, he crossed the Antarctic Circle at 66½° South. Warm clothing was issued, gratis, to every member of the crew. (It was about time: The temperature on Midsummer's Day, December 21, had been a chilly forty degrees.) Ross forced his two ships through the summer pack. Unlike D'Urville and Wilkes, he was equipped to do so. The *Erebus* and the *Terror* were bomb ships, substantially strengthened and reinforced for that punishing work. After a hard-fought week, the Royal Navy flotilla broke through the antarctic pack, first vessels in history to enter those virgin waters. Ross pressed triumphantly south through an "open polar sea," precisely the geographical fantasy that Kane would hope to find at the opposite end of the globe a dozen years later. On board the

Erebus, all eyes strained for first sight of land to the south, though Ross discounted several eager sightings from his officers of the watch. He was a conditioned skeptic: In 1819 he had been on board the *Isabella* when his uncle, John Ross, had turned back at Lancaster Sound's eastern end, thwarted by a range of mirage mountains fabricated out of arctic clouds.

But on January 11, Ross did see mountains, real ones, which he subsequently christened the Admiralty Range, disposing of a host of naming obligations with one breathtaking discovery, wiping the slate clean of nearly the entire Royal Navy establishment. The first point he sailed past he called Cape Adare after a friend, Viscount Adare, member of Parliament for Glamorganshire. On the twelfth, although threatened by an impending storm, Ross landed on Possession Island and laid formal claim to Victoria Land after his young sovereign. In ensuing years, Clements Markham would wax long and lyrical about the Victoria Quadrant, that quarter slice of the continental pie that he saw as Great Britain's just dessert, a British preserve including, at its narrowing point, the coveted pole.

Ross had been lucky in his choice of meridian. He sailed the optimum sea route south and the first phase of the polar approach. Antarctica is round like an apple, its core resting on the pole, its stem thrusting toward Cape Horn, and most of its 11,000 miles of skin lying neatly along the Antarctic Circle. Two enormous bites are taken out of the apple, one called the Weddell Sea between the tenth and sixtieth meridians and the other, to be named after Ross, skewered by the International Date Line; it was into this second bite that Ross had stumbled. There, almost due south of New Zealand, a massive segment the size of Spain intrudes into Antarctica's circumference for more than 1,200 miles. If it were navigable, explorers could sail to within 300 miles of the pole; but, as Ross would discover, that sea arm was frozen with a vengeance. After having followed the mountainous coastline to starboard south for more than two weeks, Ross spied, directly ahead, an active volcano, looming 12,000 feet into incredibly clear air. (Antarctic visibility in fair weather was to become an exploring constant. Ross saw the volcano distinctly while still 100 miles north of it; Scott would sight it 120 miles away.) As the two ships approached, it flashed angry red at night and its summit was wreathed in smudges of chilled black vapor by day. Ross named it Mount Erebus after his flagship and, to the east, a smaller and extinct volcano after the *Terror*.

But a volcano belching away at the edge of the continent was a harbinger of an even more momentous discovery, what Ross called the Great Ice Barrier. It was just that, a wall of compacted snow rearing over 200 feet out of the sea. Ross had sailed into a corner where the south-trending coastline met that ice wall, hinged, in effect, at Mount Erebus. Further seaborne progress south was impossible. There was no way to circumvent or pass through the Barrier; to do so, Ross commented, was as hopeless as sailing "through the Cliffs of Dover." So, after christening the waters at the corner McMurdo Sound after the *Terror*'s first lieutenant, Ross sailed east, parallel to the Barrier, balked by this antarctic threshold from reaching the magnetic pole. Just as frustrating was Ross's inability to see over its crest. There was no way to land on or scale the sheer ice wall that towered above his main truck. All Ross glimpsed over its top was a splendid mountain range, which he named after his old commander and colleague Sir William Parry.

Obstructing Ross was the face of a vast ice shelf averaging 1,000 feet deep, a glacial extension of the continent's land ice that had been oozing seaward for countless millennia. The immediate dilemma it posed for explorers to follow—Scott, Shackleton, and Amundsen among them—was whether that ice shelf was afloat or aground. Though it looked permanent, its margin could obviously fragment: Ross saw distinctive, flat-topped icebergs clustered along its edge. We know now that the Ross Ice Shelf floats, for scientists have bored through it and, with lowered television cameras, seen fish swimming beneath it.

Ross revisited Antarctica for two further consecutive summers and, near the Barrier's eastern end, in its only indentation, achieved his most southerly latitude, 78°11'. If shy of Parry's northern mark, it was a respectable advance over Captain James Weddell's prior record of 74°15', made in the sea bearing his name in 1823. The point at which Ross sailed farthest south would figure prominently in subsequent exploration. Scott referred to it as the Barrier Inlet and, later, Balloon Bight; it was there where *Discovery* was to tie up and the expedition's balloon would be disembarked for a trial ascent. The inlet was unique along the Barrier's entire length, a permanent fissure in an otherwise consistently forbidding cliff.

Due south of it, along the 164th meridian, was the only large island under the ice shelf, to be discovered and named by Admiral Richard Byrd in the 1930s. Its peak lies 700 feet beneath the Barrier's surface, the only obstacle in the otherwise unobstructed northward movement of the ice. Exactly as a submerged rock affects water flow downstream, so submerged Roosevelt Island distorts the Barrier's form at its margin, 60 miles distant. At that point the face of the shelf is permanently flawed, regardless of how many bergs calve or how much time passes. When Scott first saw the Barrier, its edge had receded 40 miles from where Ross had plotted it on his chart. Nevertheless, the inlet remained, a chronic Barrier fault at the 164th meridian. Whether inlet, bight, or bay, that little indentation in the Barrier's face was to play a significant role in twentieth-century polar exploration to follow.

Ross returned to England in triumph, greeted with a knighthood as well as the acclaim of every learned society. Yet, despite the sensation his four-year voyage evoked, no one save whalers and sealers followed his lead. The unknown continent existed, yes; but it was clearly such a remote and inhospitable place that fifty years would pass before any further attempt was made to explore its hinterland. Benign neglect was Antarctica's fate for the remainder of the nineteenth century: The Duke of Argyll remarked that mankind knew more about Mars than it did about the last of its unexplored continents.

Sir James Ross's great British successor was Robert Scott, although two separate ventures stole some of his thunder in the 1890s. The first was commanded by a Belgian naval officer, Adrien de Gerlache de Gomery, who sailed in the *Belgica*. In 1898, he and his men made the first land excursion on the continent in the Bellingshausen Sea area, far removed from the Victoria Quadrant. They spent a week ashore, manhauling sledges in an attempt to travel inland. Among the fur-clad stalwarts who dragged in harness that January were Roald Amundsen, the *Belgica*'s mate, and Dr. Frederick Cook. Later, de Gerlache pressed his ship to the south, hoping to surpass Ross's record; but the season was too far advanced, and the

Belgica became beset in the Bellingshausen Sea ice for nearly a year. It was March 1899 before she was freed after a harrowing, scurvy-ridden ordeal.

The second preamble to Scott's voyage was made by a Norwegian/Australian schoolteacher with a Dutch name, Carsten Borchgrevink. During his summer vacation in 1893, he had shipped as a hand on the whaler *Antarctica*, during which cruise he and his shipmates landed on Victoria Land for the first time. (Ross had merely set foot on Possession Island, never the actual mainland.) Borchgrevink decided to lead his own expedition, one that would winter over at Cape Adare. He looked in London for backing, trying first at the Royal Geographical Society. Not surprisingly, its newly elected president, Sir Clements Markham, turned him down; he was organizing his own expedition and would not invest in a rival venture.

Like De Long before him, Borchgrevink turned to the fourth estate; Sir George Newnes, a successful magazine publisher, became his sponsor. A Norwegian whaler, the *Southern Cross*, was chartered and, in February 1899, deposited Borchgrevink and nine companions on the reeking shingle at Cape Adare. (Penguin guano accumulates there in noisome quantities.) They spent the winter in a prefabricated hut called Camp Ridley, after Borchgrevink's mother's maiden name. The party survived the winter. Little extensive exploration was accomplished, due to the difficulty of sledge travel over the sea ice around the cape. Before returning north in the summer, Borchgrevink took the *Southern Cross* to the Barrier Inlet and, with two fellow explorers, sledged inland to establish the world's most southerly mark before sailing for home. For years Borchgrevink was a neglected polar figure, an oversight remedied by the Royal Geographical Society three decades later, when they presented their patron's medal to the aging explorer.

But the greatest southern foray was yet to come. Surpassed in the North by Nansen and the Duke of the Abruzzi, Britain's polar instigators sought knowledge and glory in the South. Their reawakened interest in Antarctica stemmed from economic urgency: Once-rich arctic waters had been hunted so efficiently that by the late nineteenth century, Dundee whalers were returning to port with half-empty holds. New fishing grounds had to be developed and, despite the vast distances involved, a move to the virgin southern oceans was inevitable. Armed with new, lethal harpoon guns and serviced by shore installations on South Georgia Islands, British and Norwegian whaling vessels would set about the bloody and profitable business of killing off the great antarctic whales. As in the case of the abortive Northwest Passage, economic opportunism and exploration went hand in hand.

In 1893, Clements Markham was elected president of the Royal Geographical Society and thus was enabled to implement his long-cherished dream of a south polar venture. Two years later he was knighted, reaching the zenith of his influence and power. Although in his sixties, the man had lost none of his fire, his characteristic ardor having neither mellowed nor diminished with age. Much of his hair was gone, but he had cultivated a brace of muttonchop whiskers in its place. Hooded blue eyes gave Sir Clements a deceptively sleepy look, belied by lips that, parted, seemed poised for a withering riposte. There was about him an air of stubborn pugnacity, very much like Winston Churchill's; once embarked on a course of action, Sir Clements persevered unrelentingly. The Herculean task he set for himself was mounting the British National Antarctic Expedition of 1901.

Scorning his government's indifference, Markham joined forces with the Royal Society to raise funds privately. It was this prestigious alliance that gave rise to an alternate name, the Royal Societies Expedition. Markham canvassed the Victorian rich and was gratified to receive a splendid initial donation from a fellow of his Society, Lewellyn Longstaff, a Wimbledon paint manufacturer who pledged twenty-five thousand pounds. Alfred Harmsworth, Jackson's sponsor in Franz Josef Land, offered five thousand pounds; within months, Sir Clements had raised forty-five thousand pounds. Only then was Mr. Balfour, first lord of the Treasury, shamed into promising an equal sum, establishing the projected expedition as a reality. (Years later, Lord Balfour called himself "the father of the expedition," a self-congratulatory inaccuracy that must have made Sir Clements choke with rage.)

His financing assured, Markham turned his attention to the matter of leadership. For years he had compiled a list of potential commanders and their qualifications. "The appointment of a leader to the Antarctic Expedition is the most important step of all. He should be a naval officer, he should be in the regular line and not in the surveying branch, and he should be young, not more than 35; but preferably, some years younger than that." Markham's first choice had been a former arctic hand, George Le Clerc Egerton, who had served under Nares on the *Alert* in 1875. But Egerton's age was against him: He was forty-six in 1898. Markham's second choice had been handpicked years earlier, in 1887, while visiting HMS *Active*, flagship of his cousin Albert, commodore of a West Indian training squadron. A feature of his stay had been a service cutter race for midshipmen, held off St. Kitts. Markham, always on the qui vive for promising polar officers, was particularly impressed with the winner, Midshipman Robert Scott of HMS *Rover*. The competition was demanding: Entrants had to start at anchor, rigged with tropical awnings. At a signal, awnings were struck, mast stepped, sail and anchor raised. The cutters had to sail to a mile-distant buoy, then row back to their original anchorage, mast and sail stowed and awnings rerigged. Markham detected in Scott, both during the contest and at a subsequent wardroom dinner, the precise combination of resolution, initiative, and skill—derring-do, really—that typified a sound expedition commander. Then, too, the older man must have experienced either a bittersweet recall of his own naval career or the promise of the son that Minna had never borne him. In either event, his impulse was sound: Years later, Robert Falcon Scott would serve as the instrument of Markham's ambition.

The young midshipman did not start life as the paragon that Markham first spied from the *Active*'s bridge. Born into a sea-going family in 1868, Scott was the third of six children, with four sisters and a younger brother, Archibald. As a child, young Con was neither healthy nor endearing: He was quick-tempered, untidy, and often disoriented. By his own account, he had inherited indolence from his father, who, by middle age, had squandered the income derived from the sale of a family-owned brewery.

As an adolescent, Scott was prone to long periods of gloomy introspection. During his early years on board the training ship HMS *Britannia*, he was nicknamed "Old Mooney." But by the time he was eighteen, the Royal Navy had worked its familiar miracle on the young dreamer; he owed everything to its stern regime of responsibility and hard work, early imposed.

On the surface, Scott was a model young officer, of medium height and athletic figure. He was handsome, with well-composed, neat features—heavy brows, dark blue eyes, and a finely chiseled mouth. Yet that very composure was almost too controlled, as though masking a psychological turmoil that he (and the Royal Navy) had channeled and, for the most part, kept contained. He was never without a pipe. Pipe smokers radiate wisdom and serenity; violent or impassioned types seldom use pipes. Whatever the narcotic satisfaction, I suspect that Scott's pipe's real value was its calming stability, yet another aid to careful self-control. For beneath that reasoned exterior lurked those familiar demons, violent temper, black depression, insecurity with his peers, and his father's inherent inoccupation.

All of Scott's abbreviated life—he was only forty-four when he died—was a struggle: the battle of wills as a cadet, consuming financial anxiety, assuming command of the *Discovery*, the punishing ordeal of sledging and raising money for his second and last try at the pole. As a result, he aged swiftly; by the time Scott sailed on the *Terra Nova* in 1910, photographs show a tendency to paunch, his features puffy and wrinkled, framed by receding hair and the suspicion of a double chin.

His father had died in 1897, his younger brother, Archie, two years later. As a young, penurious officer, Scott was now his widowed mother's principal support. All four of his sisters went cheerfully to work. Outlands, the comfortable Devonport house in which they grew up, had long since been rented, and Scott's family descended into that netherworld of the strapped middle class, classified sympathetically as distressed gentlefolk. Scott's early naval career, however promising, was haunted by deprivation. He denied himself any extravagance. Even his account at Gieves, the naval tailor, was a modest one.

The geographer and his protégé did not meet for ten years after that pivotal cutter race. Their next encounter occurred off Vigo during Royal Naval maneuvers in the Bay of Biscay; Sir Clements remained impressed. Two years later, in June 1899, his long-cherished expedition a reality, he met Scott by chance near Victoria Station. The two men walked together to Markham's house in Eccleston Square. There, Scott was informed of his selection as Markham's candidate to command the Royal Societies Expedition. Delighted with the news, Scott returned to duty on board HMS *Majestic*, under Captain George Egerton, the man who, but for his age, would have been selected in his stead.

The role of expedition leader, thrust suddenly and providentially upon Scott at the age of thirty-one, came as a heaven-sent opportunity. If all went well, fame and promotion were sure to follow. Up to that moment, unlike Nansen, Amundsen, or Peary, Scott had never had the remotest intention of becoming a polar explorer. But when the opportunity presented itself, he grasped at it, less for glory than reward.

He signed on in time to oversee construction of his vessel. Nansen had recommended that the British duplicate the *Fram*'s design. But the Ship Committee of the Joint Committee decided instead on a conventional whaling hull, mindful of the ominous southern oceans their vessel would have to traverse before reaching its objective. (It is ironic that Amundsen took the *Fram* south without trouble in 1910.) Scott's *Discovery* was the sixth British vessel to bear that illustrious name and was designed along the lines of her most recent namesake, Nares's *Discovery-ex-Bloodhound*.

Finding a yard that would build the new expedition ship was not easy for, by 1900, wooden hulls of that size in Britain had become rarities. When tenders were invited, few builders responded. Sir Clements thought to have her built in Norway by Colin Archer but was reminded by his colleagues that a British yard should build a British expedition ship. The contract was finally let to the Dundee Shipbuilding Company. The keel was laid in March 1900, a year before the ship was launched by Lady Markham.

The *Discovery* took shape as a steam-powered, three-masted bark, 172 feet long, 10 feet longer than her predecessor. She was the first ship ever built in Britain specifically for scientific exploration and cost over fifty thousand of Sir Clements's precious ninety-two thousand pounds. Her massive bows were set up first, severely raked so that, when ramming the pack, they would ride up over the ice margin and crush a passage by deadweight. Aft, the stern frames flared into an alien configuration: Old Dundee hands who gathered daily to watch construction were aghast to see that the *Discovery* had been given an overhanging counter, a radical departure from the whaler's conventional profile; dire predictions were volunteered that it would break off. But William Smith, the Admiralty's chief naval constructor, felt it offered a drier platform for the helmsman in a following sea—sound precaution for the Roaring Forties—and, farther south, protection for rudder and propeller. Smith did borrow from the *Fram*, providing vertical wells into which both propeller and rudder could be withdrawn. The *Discovery*'s wide beam amidships was dictated by inclusion of twin boilers for a five-hundred-horsepower engine. The propeller it would turn was a two-bladed, ten-foot heavyweight that, near the end of fitting out, dropped accidentally and jammed within its well, delaying her departure by several crucial days.

John Gregory, a Melbourne geology professor, was appointed chief of the scientific staff. After one meeting with Scott in Dundee, he wrote to his Royal Society patrons that he feared his work in the South might be compromised by what he termed delicately "naval adventure." The letter brought to a head a long-simmering feud dividing fellows of the two royal societies on the Joint Committee: who, sailor or scientist, should be in charge.

Professor Gregory was clearly unwilling to subordinate himself to a young naval officer, albeit one recently promoted to commander. Sir Clements, on the other hand, was determined that his protégé should do more than transport a party of scientists to Antarctica and back. However impressive Gregory's academic credentials, Markham argued, the geologist did not appreciate the severity of a polar winter, nor have any aptitude for command. Though Scott was a polar beginner himself, he was at least an officer of the same Royal Navy that had been admirably served by a host of arctic "beginners," among them Parry, Ross, and McClintock.

Ultimately Markham had his way and Gregory bowed out. But it was a bloody business while it lasted, and the Joint Committee endured many a stormy session. Sir Clements recalled bitterly of one meeting: "I was attacked and browbeaten, and at last so grossly insulted that I was obliged to leave the room"; this from a man who prided himself on control of temper as well as on the eloquence of his persuasive powers.

In hindsight, it seems unthinkable that any but a Royal Navy man would have been placed in charge. The responsibilities plaguing an expedition leader are varied and unending, afloat or ashore. Polar commanders had to be familiar with all things maritime and meteorological; as at ease with ship as with sledge; familiar with rations, ropes, and regulations; able to dispense tact or tyranny; to be masters of an awesome compendium of skills. If any one man fulfilled this demanding profile, it was more likely a naval officer than a geology professor.

Before leaving this thorny issue of divided command, it is worth mentioning the unpleasantness it created on a contemporary polar venture, the notorious Baldwin-Ziegler arctic expedition, which sailed north just as Scott was sailing south. In fact, as the *Discovery* left Dundee under tow for London, she dipped her colors to the *America,* a forty-year-old whaler under expensive refit at the hands of William Ziegler, an American who had made a fortune in baking powder. Ziegler was convinced that "No-one but an American should win the honor of discovering the north pole." To this end he had chartered a whaler and put an American, Evelyn Baldwin, in charge. Since he was no sailor, Baldwin hired a Swede, Captain Johanssen, and crew to run the vessel. American explorers and Swedish crew were soon at odds, reflecting the instant animosity between Baldwin and Johanssen: The American called him "my sailing master," while Johanssen dismissed the American as a troublesome passenger. After one season in the arctic, Baldwin fired the captain, who refused to quit; it took a Norwegian court to uphold Baldwin's right. Shortly thereafter, Baldwin was recalled to New York and fired in turn, by Ziegler. The poor *America* ultimately came to grief in the ice. (Her original name had been *Esquimaux*—yet another example of ill-advised name-changing, according to Sir Clements!) Although the expedition was flawed from the start, the added burden of abrasive, divided command serves as a sorry object lesson.

Although the British rejected the design of Nansen's polar ship, they had no compunction about copying his sledges. Scott surmised, quite correctly, that he might well encounter surface conditions similar to those on Greenland's icecap. So in October 1900, while Scottish shipwrights were bolting five-inch oak doubling along the *Discovery*'s flanks, Scott, Sir Clements, and Lady Markham embarked for Christiania. For anyone polarbound, consultation with Nansen was inevitable: He was the world's foremost authority on sledging.

Nansen received his British visitors with special cordiality and introduced them to the best Christiania outfitters. They supplied Scott with the same model sledges that Nansen had perfected—long, low, narrow craft that hugged the ground, their runners the width of skis. These had proved successful both in Greenland and on the *Fram;* not surprisingly, Scott ordered them in preference to the McClintock original that Nares had copied in 1875. Those British sledges were more like miniature sleighs, a foot high and a yard wide, shod with narrow iron runners; useful over sea ice, they had a high center of gravity and a tendency to bog down in soft snow. Scott ordered his Nansen sledges in a variety of lengths and would find that the eleven-foot model served him best.

Then he returned to headquarters in London's Burlington House and threw himself into the hectic business of provisioning. So moribund were Britain's polar purveyors that pemmican was no longer manufactured in England, although the Bovril Company would send out an experimental batch on the *Morning,* the first relief ship, dispatched in 1902. Scott ordered foreign brands instead: some from the redoubtable Dr. Beauvais of Copenhagen and what turned out to be an inferior brand from Chicago's Armour. Several British firms, anxious for invaluable publicity, made outright gifts of supplies: Cadbury sent two tons of cocoa powder, Colman donated barrels of flour and cases of mustard, and Messrs. Bird & Sons contributed quantities of their celebrated custard powders. A company called Evans, Lescher, and Webb supplied gallons of lime juice, that woefully inadequate antiscorbutic; as a result, the *Discovery*'s people were subject to brief outbreaks of scurvy. (Scott was convinced that the fault lay in the deterioration of improperly canned meats and would require every can on board to be opened in the presence of one of the expedition's two surgeons.) As his stores accumulated, Scott had them forwarded to a warehouse near the East India Docks, including sledges, skis, and a peltry of reindeer furs that arrived from Norway.

Only three members of the *Discovery*'s wardroom had had prior experience in high latitudes, two in the North and one in the South. Lieutenant Albert Armitage, R.N.R., who had been Jackson's second-in-command in Franz Josef Land, resigned from the P&O Line to assume the same post with Scott. Another Jackson veteran was the *Discovery*'s surgeon/botanist,

Reginald Koettlitz. Louis Bernacchi, the expedition's physicist, had wintered over on the southern continent as one of Borchgrevink's party at Cape Adare. Charles Royds was appointed the ship's first lieutenant. Two of Scott's fellow officers from HMS *Majestic* were signed on: One was Lieutenant Michael Barne; the other was Reginald Skelton, who would become the *Discovery*'s chief engineer. Skelton entrained at once for Dundee. Once the engines were shut down in Antarctica, he would become the expedition's photographer.

The last officer hired was a Merchant Navy man, recommended by Cedric Longstaff, son of the expedition's most generous backer. Traveling on the Union Castle liner *Carisbrooke Castle*, Cedric had befriended one of her officers, Lieutenant Ernest Shackleton. At twenty-seven years of age, Shackleton was four years younger than Scott. Shackleton was an engaging Irishman, solid as oak; although he was only five-ten, he seemed the embodiment of towering bulk, square-jawed and broad-shouldered. He was prone to quoting poetry at the slightest provocation. (Louis Bernacchi would later recall that often, having finished his watch on board the *Discovery* and about to descend to his bunk with a long-anticipated mug of cocoa, he would be forestalled by the relieving Shackleton with: "One moment, old boy, have you heard this?" Reams of Browning would follow, Bernacchi listening through yawns while his mug cooled in his mittened hand.) *The Daily Telegraph* described him later as having "the look of a poet, the face of a fighter"; graced with fair hair and twinkling blue eyes, it was a face as determined as John Bull's. His voice was pleasant, with a ring of nautical command when necessary yet, in the wardroom, full of charm and irrepressible delight in life.

One of the reasons Scott had recruited him was his expertise with sails. Shackleton had left Dulwich College at the age of sixteen for a boy's berth on the *Tower Hoghton*, a windjammer bound from Liverpool to Cape Horn, a harsher introduction to the sea than the Royal Navy cadetship his impoverished father could not afford. Shackleton had survived *con brio;* the master of the *Tower Hoghton* rated him "the most pigheaded, obstinate boy I have ever come across." In addition to serving as the *Discovery*'s most junior officer, Shackleton was put in charge of seawater analysis, wardroom catering, issuance of provisions, and entertainment; he was also to edit the ship's illustrated newspaper and select the library.

Scott welcomed him aboard without reserve, although Clements Markham exhibited disenchantment almost at once, following their first meeting in March 1901. Sir Clements had spent months designing each officer's sledge flag—"to help relieve the eyes of the sledge party from the white glare of the snow and ice"—and was irritated that Shackleton insisted on a square-shaped flag rather than the swallow-tailed banner that Sir Clements had ordained: the cross of St. George at the hoist, its fly emblazoned with the bearer's crest and bordered with the colors of his arms.

In Markham's jaundiced view, Shackleton's insistence on a square flag made him a renegade, "the only one that did not accept the pattern." "Accepting the pattern" counted a great deal in Sir Clements's eyes. Perhaps he was made most uneasy by the Irishman's bluff competence and obvious potential for leadership. He never liked or trusted him. Years later, when Shackleton electrified London by slogging to within ninety-seven miles of the south pole, Sir Clements's only response was that, in so doing, Shackleton was dislodging "his distinguished chief."

Perhaps the most memorable figure on board the *Discovery* was Dr. Edward Adrian Wilson, the expedition's zoologist and second surgeon, junior to Koettlitz. (Two doctors were taken so that both ship and shore parties would be covered in the event of separation; this medical doubling permitted Wilson long absences from the *Discovery* without jeopardizing the health of her crew.) Wilson was tall, bony, energetic, and scholarly. A ginger thatch topped a sunny, wise face in which crinkly-cornered blue eyes predominated over what someone once called a "kindly, twisted smile." The son of a doctor, Wilson grew up in the gentle Gloucester countryside, enthralled by natural history, a hobby enriched by skill with pencil and brush.

The most distinctive thing about Wilson was his faith: He was deeply, joyously religious. It was a conviction, one would have thought, that might have estranged him from the often noisy jocularity of the wardroom. But apparently it never did; on two separate voyages to Antarctica, Wilson—"Billy" on the

Discovery and "Uncle Bill" aboard the *Terra Nova*—was held in affectionate esteem by all, despite his unconcealed distaste for smoking, drinking, swearing, gambling, and those boisterous wardroom discussions known in the Royal Navy as "cags." Wilson seems the archetypal Edwardian Christian gentleman, honest, fair, healthy, and clean. If distressed by the wardroom's hugger-mugger, he would simply don Jaeger, Burberry, and crampons and go for a brisk climb to Observation Hill, weather permitting, or, with numbed hands and nose, try to capture on paper the elusive splendor of the aurora australis that hung overhead, displacing Mount Erebus's night glare from the sky. But if it was blizzing, as the mess deck said, Wilson might withdraw instead to his chilled cabin with a book or, better yet, one of his bride's precious letters. (He and Oriana Souper, the daughter of a clergyman, had been married only three weeks before the *Discovery* had sailed.) In fact, one of the most moving manifestations of Wilson's faith was his habit, each Sunday, after the ship's service, of celebrating a private communion in his cabin, timed to coincide with his family's devotions on the far side of the globe. Shortly after crossing the equator, his fourth Sunday at sea, Wilson wrote in his diary:

> Read through the Holy Communion Service at 8 o'clock, not knowing where anyone would be at home, but I always go in spirit to St Philip's where I can find Ory, at any rate.

Wilson communed, thus, with both his God and his beloved Ory, the two profoundest loves of his life. One of his firmest friends on board was Shackleton, with whom he shared much of his leisure time as well as the great southern journey on which they would accompany Scott.

In March 1901, Sir Clements and Lady Markham traveled north to officiate at the launch of the expedition ship. Minna Markham snipped a white ribbon, releasing a bottle of Australian champagne that shattered against the *Discovery*'s iron-shod stem. As the crowd cheered, the hull slid down the ways into the Tay. Then the official party adjourned to the Queen's Hotel for a late lunch, punctuated by those elaborate speeches without which momentous Edwardian events seemed somehow incomplete. That night, after yet another banquet and more toasts, Sir Clements penned in his diary, in his distinctive, spidery hand, that she was "the strongest ship ever launched." He even remembered to note in the margin that he had tipped Mr. Bates, the societies' inspector, five pounds and the yard foreman ten, reimbursement for which he would solicit the expedition's account.

The *Discovery* was indeed strong but, beneath the businesslike lines of her black hull, there were flaws aplenty or, in Royal Navy argot, much scamped work. Once the ship reached New Zealand and dry-docking (for which there had been no time in the United Kingdom), acrimonious exchanges flew between the Dundee yard and RGS headquarters at 1 Savile Row. Dailey, the *Discovery*'s carpenter, signed his name to a scathing report: Numerous empty bolt holes and defectively clenched bolts were uncovered, and six feet of seawater had seeped into the main hold within weeks of leaving England. One of the Royal Societies Expedition's rare theatrical presentations in Antarctica, produced by Lieutenant Royds ashore in the Royal Terror Theatre, was waggishly titled *The Dish-Cover Minstrel Troupe:* When "Mistah Johnson" inquired: "What am de worst vegetable us took from England?," "Mistah Bones's" response elicited an appreciative howl: "The Dundee leek!"

But there was no leakage during the *Discovery*'s towed passage from Dundee to London at the beginning of June. She carried only one passenger, Sir Clements, in blue serge reefer and yachting cap. Rippling at the mizzenhead was the royal societies' flag he had designed, the cross of St. George at the hoist with the swallow-tailed fly argent and azure (ice and sea) with the globe of the RGS. Despite its overwhelming Royal Navy composition, the expedition was not permitted to fly the White Ensign, even though the sovereign had given his approval. Instead was flown the burgee of the Royal Harwich Yacht Club, of which Scott had been elected a member.

Through the intercession of the British consul in Moscow, twenty-three sledge dogs had been selected by Baron Trontheim, Nansen's supplier of 1893; they were the pick of a vast, yelping entourage of four hundred animals that had been driven overland from Archangel for delivery to Baldwin and the *America*. By contrast, the *Discovery*'s was a pitifully inadequate pack, reflecting limited resources as well as the expedition leader's distaste for dog-driving. Scott had written to Sir Clements: "Conquest is more nobly and splendidly won by man's unaided effort than by forcing dogs to suffer." Scott was sickened by cruelty and blood; in Antarctica he would be aghast at Wilson's continual dissection of seals and penguins, which sometimes turned the ship's decks into an abattoir. Suffering of any kind distressed him. After the birth of a healthy child to one of his sisters, it was Scott who had fainted; hence the token dog pack for an otherwise elaborately equipped expedition. Given all the time and money spent on the *Discovery*, it is ironic that so little thought was given to land travel, the expedition's real mission.

The animals were housed temporarily in Regent's Park Zoo, a source of delight to nannies and children that summer. Joe, a dog of Bernacchi's that had wintered at Cape Adare, was added to the pack. They would be shipped to New Zealand by steamer, and it is regrettable that their food—dried Norwegian codfish called *torsk*—did not accompany them rather than travel in the unrefrigerated holds of the *Discovery*. Passage through the tropics tainted it, contributing, Scott insisted, to the dogs' poor showing on the southern journey.

Shackleton, under the guidance of West End comedian Harry Nicholls, was stocking a property box with greasepaint, costumes, and playscripts for winter theatricals that Sir Clements was anxious to have mounted in the grand tradition. Shackleton also had charge of the library, sorting out a thousand volumes, many of which had been donated. Some had been selected as specifically helpful for readers in high latitude—the memoirs of previous explorers, although, curiously, no works by Nansen, Peary, or Nordenskjöld were included. The books were housed along mahogany shelves bracketing the wardroom's overhead beams. Those same beams were to be used for additional indoor pursuits. As did Parry seventy-five years earlier, Koettlitz would grow mustard and cress in flats placed under the skylights; he even managed to coax crocus bulbs into blossom as well. Wilson monopolized the beam closest to the stove as a defrosting shelf for frozen penguins he wished to dissect. The stiffened, feathered corpse could remain there until the wardroom informed the junior surgeon that the cadaver "was beginning to talk," after which it would be hastened down to an empty coal bunker, where Wilson wielded his scalpel.

The *Discovery*'s wardroom, only twenty by thirty feet, would be crowded. Unlike the messdeck below and forward of it, it did not run the full width of the ship, being flanked on either side by cabins. In this space, ten men were to dine, read, gamble, work, smoke, hang their laundry, and live. Occupying one wall was a pianola, the gift of a Dundee matron. Royds was the ship's only pianist, but other enthusiastic music lovers could pump away, working the player mechanism to their heart's content. Indeed, the wardroom's only drawback was that it would get extremely cold. Insulated on top and to either side, it was situated atop the bitterly cold iron bunkers. In the antarctic cold, floor planking shrunk, and coal dust and drafts worked their way up through linoleum and rug. That same wardroom rug retained within its nap stubborn cold germs. The first time that marine orderlies beat it in Antarctica, every officer succumbed to sore throats and catarrh. Similarly, crates of Jaeger woolens, when opened for the first time, prompted bouts of coughing and sneezing.

The Royal Observer Corps made a last-minute donation of two captive balloons. Several officers and men, Shackleton among them, went to Aldershot for instruction. Despite Andrée's disappearance four years earlier, aerial polar reconnaissance still intrigued. Since the gift had not included any hydrogen, Scott resorted to the letter columns of *The Times* for a special appeal; enough money was raised to equip the *Discovery* with fifty cylinders, which were lashed atop the after deckhouse.

It was imperative that the ship sail from England in August to be ready to enter the antarctic's summer pack in December. Delay was intolerable, and the sorry example of the *Belgica*, which had never penetrated the pack at all, haunted Scott. Toward the end of July, the pace of preparation became feverish; so, too, did the wardroom's social calendar. All London, it seemed, wanted to say bon voyage in person. The expedition's officers were invited to one gala after another, dinner meetings at both royal societies, the Geographical Club, the Kosmos Club, and, inevitably, the Savage Club, which had entertained Nansen before and after his epic drift. For the club's dinner on

July 6, Savage Harrison Hill penned some lighthearted lyrics that were roared to the tune of "Auld Lang Syne":

> So here's to Scott and all his lot
> With all our might and main,
> We'll meet them in the Savage Club
> When they come home again.

Poets all over England were inspired as well. Walter Parker wrote an interminable "Song for the South Pole," the first verse of which ran:

> At the Pole, at the Pole,
> Britannia's pretty sure to reach her goal!
> Her ever-conquering legions
> Will annex those distant regions
> And make a new dominion of the Pole!

It was predictable, jingoistic stuff, echoing the popular sentiment surrounding the *Discovery* and her crew, who were initiating Britain's first polar effort in a quarter of a century. Only an editorial in the *Yorkshire Herald* took a negative stance:

> . . . to reach the south pole is a task as hopeless as the reformation of a female drunkard.

On the ship's final day in the East End—Tuesday, July 30, 1901—the bishop of London added his blessing. Clothed in full pastoral regalia—miter, cope, and staff—he boarded the *Discovery* to lead a service on deck. After the last "Amen," the bishop and the crew's womenfolk filed ashore. Telegraphs shrilled from bridge to engine room. Clouds of rank coal smoke poured from the funnel. Lines dropped from pier bollards, and the tug *Midge* chivvied the expedition ship from her berth. A cheer arose from dockside. Sharing pride of place with wives, parents, and sweethearts was a scenting of Blackwall prostitutes. During the previous weeks, the expedition's bluejackets had become popular figures in the neighboring pubs. Now, after a last raucous pint of cheer, some expedition ratings ran for the ship, vaulting the moving bulwarks. Their painted companions jostled after them, shrieking, "Good luck to the icebergers!"

Rainbowed with signal flags and looking dazzling in the sun—"as trim a vessel," hypothesized *The Sphere*'s correspondent, "as ever rose on an icy wave"—the *Discovery* shed her tug and turned in midstream. There was time for a last wave from the dock before she gathered momentum downriver, her progress heralded by whistles and hoots from workaday Thames traffic. Past Greenwich, the cadets of HMS *Worcester* swarmed up into the shrouds, cheering themselves hoarse.

The final send-off came a week later, after the *Discovery*'s black hull had nosed into the glittering white-and-mahogany anchorage of the Royal Regatta at Cowes. She tied up at a royal mooring in time for King Edward and Queen Alexandra, as well as Princess Victoria, attended by a suite of equerries and ladies-in-waiting, to troop on board. Sir Clements Markham solemnly presented his protégé to his sovereign. Then the royal visitors descended to inspect the *Discovery*'s 'tween decks, Her Majesty prodding at mattresses and peering into the galley. Back on deck, the king addressed the ship's company informally and fished a leather case from his uniform pocket. Inside it was a medal, the Victorian Order of the Fourth Class, which Mrs. Scott was permitted to pin to the breast of her son's frock coat.

It was a complete surprise. Whereas Nansen had been decorated on his expedition's return, Scott was bemedaled before his had begun. (The *Discovery*'s third officer, Ernest Shackleton, could not have guessed that six years later to the day, he would receive the same decoration from the same king's hand on the stained and crowded deck of the little *Nimrod*.) But unexpected or not, the honor cheered not only its recipient but also the entire ship's company, royal endorsement of an expedition that was about to leave England for three long years.

10

THE BARRIER PREVAILS

*Ten years later, within a mile of the
same spot, Wilson and Scott were both
dead and I was still alive.*

—Ernest Shackleton

The day after that royal visit, August 7, 1901, the *Discovery* sailed for Antarctica. The shortest distance to New Zealand—around Cape Horn—was not the fastest. By taking the longer route around Africa, the *Discovery* would profit from the southern ocean's prevailing winds. Clear of the English Channel, Scott set course for Madeira and continued south to latitude 20°. Only then did the *Discovery* turn east. Once past the fitful winds of the horse latitudes, her sails filled with the press of prevailing westerlies that would carry her clear to New Zealand.

They landed at Cape Town by the start of October to test their magnetic instruments and take on coal. Two ratings were disembarked for return to Blighty, one a troublemaker, the other syphilitic following the protracted docking at Blackwall.

By midmonth the ship was headed east again, through the infamous Roaring Forties, her taffrail log registering two hundred damp miles each day. The engines were silent now as the black bark surged along under straining canvas, thundering down the forward slopes of the world's most awesome rollers.

Her radical counter paid off, rising safely above the pursuing wave crests. Languorous tropical sailing days were over: Sunbathing, deck golf and cricket were no more; blizzards alternated with squalls, and green water sloshed in the ship's waist, occasionally deluging those huddled behind the bridge's canvas dodger. It penetrated everywhere, drenching cabins, wardroom, messdeck, and galley alike. *Discovery* rolled abominably, hurling crockery and belongings indiscriminately onto the puddled carpeting. "Nothing breaks," commented a beleaguered Wilson, "because everything breakable was broken long ago."

Scott's initial verdict on his ship's handling had been negative: Under sail in the English Channel, he pronounced her sluggish, shortmasted, and undercanvased. But for the Roaring Forties, these were sound shortcomings. The doughty vessel could weather the worst gales sporting a respectable spread of canvas, bowling stubbornly along before fearsome winds that would have reduced her finely tuned sisters to bare poles. A month after they left Cape Town, the first floating ice was sighted. Some of King Edward's Heidsieck '95, inadvertently left on board following his Cowes visit, was broached in celebration.

At Lyttelton, the *Discovery* was twice put in dry dock, where the Dundee shipwrights' lamentable scamping was corrected as far as possible. Then cargo was reloaded, with so much additional that Dailey, the carpenter, turned a blind eye to the *Discovery*'s submerged Plimsoll line, that painted indicator of prudent loading. Numbered rafters, joists, and beams of Gregory House, the expedition hut that had been prefabricated in Melbourne, came on board, as did a quantity of expedition stores shipped out from England by P&O at reduced rates. Cases of local butter, cheaper than the Danish stuff already in use and unsullied by passage through the tropics, were lowered into the hold. Four dozen reluctant sheep were herded into deck pens aft, as far removed from the dogs kenneled on the fo'c'sle as possible. They would be slaughtered once the New Zealand summer had given way to the chill of Antarctica.

Four days before Christmas of 1901, the *Discovery* sailed through Lyttelton Heads into the Pacific. HMS *Ringarooma* and *Lizard* dressed ship in her honor and, by way of response, the *Discovery*'s crewmen clambered into the rigging. Seaman

Charles Bonner stood atop the main truck, with nothing to grasp save the copper shaft of the wind indicator. He brandished a whiskey bottle and, before the gaze of horrified shipmates, fell suddenly, killed instantly as his head struck the deck. It was a sobering tragedy. All Christmas celebrations on board were postponed. On the twenty-fourth of December, a final call was made at Dunedin, south of Lyttelton. Bonner was buried with full naval honors. The *Discovery*'s bunkers were topped up with twenty-five tons of coal, free of charge; additional coal was stacked on deck wherever space could be found.

Passage through the pack was exhilaratingly brief. The *Discovery*'s iron-shod prow made short work of the ice and, as it had for Ross six decades earlier, only a week elapsed from entry until she bulled her way into the open sea. The explorers landed at Cape Adare to leave their first cairn and continued south, the Admiralty Range passing in majestic review along the starboard railing. Soon Mount Erebus was in sight. With summertime to spare before the necessity of making his winter anchorage, Scott followed his predecessor's example and sailed the length of the Barrier's face. At its eastern end, Shackleton—who was officer of the watch at the time—first verified the peaks of what Scott would christen King Edward VII Land, containing the ice shelf's eastern reaches. Thus Ross's Barrier was bounded within royal domains: Victoria Land to the west and, named after her son, King Edward VII Land to the east. Scott's discovery had extended Britain's antarctic dominion yet farther east. Now the great task remaining was to find what lay at the Barrier's southern extremity.

By January's end, Ross's Parry Mountains, the chain he thought he had seen over the ice shelf's top, proved nonexistent. No mountains lay south of Ross Island, merely a collection of three smaller islands christened Brown, White, and Black islands. On the map, Ross Island has the shape of a sphinx or lion couchant, its northern head a round protuberance dominated by Mount Bird. One dangling paw, a peninsula extending toward the western mountains, is the southernmost point of the island. Scott christened it Cape Armitage after his second-in-command. Because it was a mild summer, he berthed the *Discovery* at its tip, in an indentation called Arrival Bay. His vessel remained anchored offshore for the winter; all other antarctic explorers—Borchgrevink, Shackleton, and Amundsen included—had to be deposited onshore while their ships returned north until the following summer.

Gregory House was off-loaded onto a level patch of gravel. Once erected, the hut never served as more than a potential emergency shelter, to be used in the event of damage to the ship, stocked with coal and provisions. Its greatest value was as a frigid auditorium for the Royal Terror Theatre; subsequent expeditions would use it as a convenient halfway house en route from their hut to the Barrier.

The *Discovery*, meanwhile, was prepared for winter. All boats were removed from their davits and parked on the ice, a common arctic expedient that proved, for the *Discovery*, hideously ill-advised: They were snowed under and filled to the gunwales with ice. Extricating them before the ship's departure was nearly as difficult as disengaging the mother ship from her wintry berth. For the first weeks of autumn, the *Discovery* was made fast to the shore with steel cables and ice anchors, which were repeatedly dislodged before Arrival Bay was frozen solid. A canvas deck awning that had been cut, sewn, and grommeted in Dundee was rigged and lashed overhead.

As secure as their vessel's anchorage was the socioemotional security belowdecks. Despite cramped, noisy, and smoky quarters, life on board seemed a boisterous recapitulation of boyhood. Identical school conditions prevailed: an exclusively masculine company far from home, faced with bracing physical hardship, whether sledging or bruising football matches on the adjacent ice. A cheerful school-like camaraderie permeated the *Discovery*'s wardroom, lined as it was with tiny cabins identical to the cozy studies of their youth. It is an archaeological maxim that a civilization's refuse contains pertinent clues as to its nature. Still to be found to this day among the litter of Scott's second hut at Cape Evans is an assortment of food and books that includes bloater paste, plum jam, and a dog-eared copy of Kipling's immortal schoolboy classic *Stalky & Co.*

Two of the day's meals were consumed in an atmosphere of bumptious informality. Breakfast was lengthy, porridge slathered with treacle (rib-sticking fare about which famished sledgers would later fantasize) followed by fried seal's liver and stacks of toast and jam. Lunch was a midafternoon high tea, with officers crowded around the open stove, toasting forks at the ready. Only during the evening meal did adult formality obtain, an observance of ritual just as natural as the racketing that had preceded it. Though collars and ties were dispensed with, Royal Navy dinner table decorum was not: A mess president officiated, charged with saying grace, keeping order, and proposing toasts. Sir Clements had presented the wardroom with a calendar book listing each officer's birthday, the date of the vessel's launch, founding dates of both royal societies, etc., so there was no shortage of toasts, following the traditional one to His Majesty, whose autographed portrait gazed benignly from the wall.

Dinner menus tended, perforce, to repetition. After a brush with scurvy, canned meats were used only one night a week, a scheme that also allowed Clarke, the *Discovery*'s temperamental and hardworking cook, a night off. For five of the remaining nights, all hands ate fresh meat, either seal steak or penguin breast. Most eagerly anticipated was Sunday's mutton dinner, when one of the precious frozen carcasses was retrieved from the rigging, thawed, and roasted.

Once the wardroom's civilizing dinner had ended, glasses were cleared and the place reverted to a dayroom. Wall quoits, an inspired gift from Oriana Wilson, were in constant use, while chess and whist held sway at the long table. Noisiest were marathon poker sessions that ran into the middle watch, long after nongamblers had retired, either to catch up on diaries or to try and sleep. On mess nights there might be Scots reels, when the thump of booted feet drowned out the pianola. Sometimes there were debates, or lectures about wildlife or sledging from the appropriate expert. All that the *Discovery*'s wardroom lacked was solitude, available only to him whose turn it was to stay awake to take two-hourly scientific observations. This was a time to catch up on laundry (although some officers paid bluejackets for this service), sewing, or reading, a somnivolent vigil accompanied by the rattle of wind in the chimney stove and snores from the cabins. A cherished perk for that watchkeeper was yet another feast, a tin of sardines put to fry on the stove and washed down by cocoa.

There were two coal stoves in the wardroom, only one of which was kept burning full time. Another glowed in the messdeck. A third, the galley cooker, was banked at night. None of the three could burn when gales roared out of the south, for

Launched by Fru Eva Nansen, *Fram* splashes into the water from Colin Archer's yard, October 26, 1892. *Fram Museum.*

Fram's stern in dry dock. Note the wells for withdrawing propeller and rudder. *Universitetsbiblioteket in Oslo, Picture Department.*

ABOVE: Archer's indestructible hull atop the ice. *Fram Museum.*

AT RIGHT: Some of the dozens of wooden knees inside *Fram. Harald Brandsburg.*

BELOW: October 1894, a mild Sunday afternoon on board the beset *Fram: Left to right:* Frederik Hjalmar Johansen, Dr. Henrik Blessing, Otto Sverdrup, Theodor Jacobsen, Sigurd Scott Hansen, and Lars Pettersen. *Universitetsbiblioteket in Oslo, Picture Department.*

Andrée's balloon shed on the day of departure. The north wall has been demolished. *Library of Congress*.

Salomon August Andrée, the gallant Swedish aeronaut. *Library of Congress*.

With some sails rigged and remnants of drag ropes trailing, the *Eagle* disappears into the North, July 11, 1897. *The Smithsonian Institution*.

ABOVE: Sir James Clark Ross, "the handsomest man in the Royal Navy," posed heroically for John Wildman in uniform and bearskin. At the lower right is Ross's dip-needle compass used for locating the magnetic south pole. *National Maritime Museum.*

AT RIGHT: Sir Clements Markham. This bust of the explorer, commissioned by the Peruvian government, stands outside the Royal Geographical Society's headquarters in London. *Collection of John Maxtone-Graham.*

Discovery's officers on the quarterdeck. At the far left is Dr. Edward A. Wilson, then Ernest Shackleton; Robert F. Scott, with three Royal Navy stripes on his sleeve, stands in the center. *Canterbury Museum, Christchurch, New Zealand.*

Discovery sailing out past Lyttelton Heads, December 21, 1901, with Seaman Charles Bonner atop the mainmast. Within moments, he had fallen to his death. *Canterbury Museum, Christchurch, New Zealand.*

The southern journey.
ABOVE: Full of hope and expectation, Shackleton, Scott,
and Wilson, ready to leave on
November 2, 1902.

AT RIGHT: Two months later,
at their farthest south.

BELOW: Within sight of *Discovery* on their return, February 1903. *Royal Society*.

Belgica's officers pose in a Patagonian photographer's studio, 1899. LEFT TO RIGHT: Henryk Arctowski, geologist; Frederick Cook, surgeon; Roald Amundsen, mate. *Library of Congress.*

AT RIGHT: Amundsen's expedition ship, the 70-foot fishing sloop *Gjøa. Norsk Sjøfartsmuseum, Oslo.*

ABOVE: Amundsen on board, January 1908. On the bulkhead behind him is Nansen's portrait. *Odd F. Lindberg Collection.*

Ponies to the south pole: Shackleton's assault party moves off, October 29, 1908. *Radio Times Hulton Picture Library.*

"We have shot our bolt." Ninety-seven miles short of their goal, Jameson Adams, Frank Wild, and Ernest Shackleton pose on January 9, 1909, with Queen Alexandra's flag. *Radio Times Hulton Picture Library.*

RACING SLEIGHS TO THE SOUTH POLE WITH PENCILS IN PLACE OF DOGS AND "DR. COOK" AS ASSISTANT: PLAYING A NEW CHRISTMAS GAME.

"To the Pole With Shackleton:" Hamley's popular Christmas game attested to the national sensation Sir Ernest's near-miss had engendered. *The Illustrated London News,* December 24, 1910.

THE EXCLUSIVES.

NORTH POLE (to SOUTH POLE). "HALLO! ARE YOU THERE? I SAY, OLD MAN, THEY NEARLY HAD YOU THAT TIME."

VOICE FROM SOUTH POLE. "YES, I KNOW. THERE'LL SOON BE NO SUCH THING AS PRIVACY."

[With *Mr. Punch's* best compliments to Lieutenant Shackleton.]

The cartoon above appeared in a 1909 issue of the British humor weekly *Punch,* subtitled: "With Mr. Punch's compliments to Lieutenant Shackleton."

then acrid fumes were driven back down the chimneys, and officers and men alike, clad in greatcoats and gloves, would chew on cold rations. Lighting was supplied by oil lamp or candle. The windmill generator—modeled, once again, on a Nansen original—was toppled and broken by savage winds. During the *Discovery*'s second winter, candles became so scarce that wax drippings were collected and recycled in Wilson's glass test tubes.

On the messdeck, winter routine was less formal and, regrettably, less well documented. Save for a rum ration rather than claret, the crew ate the same food as the officers, a sensible policy laid down by Scott to forestall complaints. Smoking was permitted at all times, contravening standard naval procedure, so that ratings ate, yarned, gamed, and slept in a perpetual miasma of rich, Navy shag. They were far more self-reliant than their arctic predecessors; unlike the sailors of Parry's day, *Discovery* crewmen looked after themselves without the need for diversion improvised by their superiors. Although officers occasionally served as invited lecturers, the sailors retained a measure of privacy, at Scott's specific instruction. The messdeck's consuming passion was shove ha'penny; those not embroiled in this tabletop version of shuffleboard read, sewed, or constructed elaborate ship or sledge models.

Exploration of the hinterland, both Barrier and mountain, was pursued over the next two years. When the *Discovery* had first entered the pack in January, ski lessons were given on the sea ice. Once the crew were in winter quarters, daily practice continued on a neighboring slope, consuming outdoor time not devoted to football. Predictably there were injuries: Scott pulled a knee tendon; and Ford, the ship's steward, broke his leg. But skiing was only part of their antarctic apprenticeship; sledging techniques had to be absorbed as well. The men of the *Discovery* had to learn how to nurse their fragile Primus stoves, how to stow sledges properly so that each night's equipment was at hand, how to pitch tents quickly yet securely, and how to dress in a bewildering wardrobe of specialized fur clothing, some of it impossibly awkward. One Christiania error had been Scott's selection of fur sleeping tunics as a substitute for sleeping bags; in the field, moisture in the fur froze so stiffly that no one could put them on.

The earliest sledge excursion was undertaken with a kind of

Boy Scout naïveté. They had landed at Balloon Bight to make their first (and only) balloon ascent, and a sledge party under Armitage, numbering six in all, had set off on foot to better Borchgrevink's farthest south. This was easily accomplished, but when they camped for that first night on the Barrier, only one three-man tent was found on the sledges; Bernacchi elected to sleep outside. On another excursion, a tent's edge was improperly weighted with snow blocks, and its inhabitants spent a desperate night clutching at flapping canvas to keep it over their heads. On yet another flawed outing, Seaman William Lashley's sleeping bag was blown away in a gale.

Antarctic blizzards strike year-round, generating such a flurry of snow that familiar landmarks simply vanish. Two warrant officers went for a long walk one May afternoon and were caught in a blizzard. Attempting to regain the *Discovery*, they staggered right through winter quarters, atop snow that had already drifted over lifelines strung between gangplank and scientific huts. But at least they found their way back unhurt. An earlier mishap, tragically concluded, involved a nine-man sledging party returning from Cape Crozier under the command of Lieutenant Barne. On the last day, within sight of the ship, cumulative disasters overtook them, each resulting out of a classic instance of ignorance, neglect, or inadvisability. A blizzard enveloped them during a lunch stop in the tents. Neither of their two Primus stoves would light, a legacy of postbreakfast haste. Chilled by the lack of warming food and yet reluctant to struggle into their awkward sleeping furs, Barne and his men abandoned tents, sledges, and dogs for a quick dash to the ship.

Just as small-boat sailors should never swim from their capsized craft, so explorers marooned in a blizzard should never venture away from their camp. Nevertheless, Barne and his men started for the ship. Two of the nine improvidentially retained their warm *finnesko*, the Lapland shoe packed with sennegrass, instead of leather ski boots. Admirable for negotiating the flat, their pliable fur soles were lethally inadequate on the sloping ice that was encountered as they groped their way across the northern (and wrong) side of Castle Rock, later christened Danger Slope. Clarence Hare, one of the two wearing *finnesko*, turned back to get his boots from the sledge, a foolhardy decision that paradoxically saved his life. He became lost at once, and a distraught Barne tried organizing a search. But a new peril assailed them: One by one, the remaining men began sliding down the sheer ice slope toward the brink of a cliff's edge. Seaman George Vince, the other man shod in *finnesko*, could not stop; together with one of the dogs, he glissaded into the sea. Four others, their terrifying descent arrested by a snow terrace, clawed back up the slope with sheath knives and managed to reach the ship.

A large search party set out at once and located a badly frostbitten Barne and two men. Skelton, meanwhile, fired a boiler and set the *Discovery*'s steam whistle echoing into the hills around Arrival Bay. Shackleton launched a whaleboat—fortunately not yet entombed in the ice—to scour the drenching surf under the cliff, in hopes of spotting the two lost men along the icefoot.

Poor Vince was never found, but Hare, astonishingly, survived. Two days later, a solitary figure approached the ship. It was the missing steward. He had never reached the sledge but collapsed in the snow, where, buried at once by drift, he had slept dreamlessly for thirty hours. Once awake, he made his own way back to the *Discovery*. The most astonishing thing about Hare's escape was that he sustained no frostbite and, once roused from what, presumably, could have been a terminal sleep, was able to move. Only eighteen and obviously bursting with vitality, young Hare had been only slightly cramped; he started for the ship on hands and knees but, after a few yards, was able to walk. Two years later, on the day that the *Discovery* was released from the ice, a large Maltese cross, known to this day as Vince's Cross, was erected above Hut Point as a sturdy memorial from his shipmates to the first—and only—man to perish in McMurdo Sound.

In the summer of 1902, the southern journey was at hand, a probe of the Barrier's limit as well as a march for the pole. Scott had initially envisioned taking only one companion with him on the southern journey, and he chose the ship's second surgeon, Edward Wilson. Wilson's selection for this arduous trek would have amazed his mother, who had always believed him a frail child. Indeed, Wilson had contracted tuberculosis only five years before the *Discovery* sailed. But during the expedition's first year, Wilson had proved fitness incarnate; he put on over twenty pounds and became seemingly impervious to cold. But sound health was not the only reason for Scott's choice. Wilson was a doctor, and also his skill with pencil and brush would be invaluable to record the new terrain over which they were to travel. Wilson's watercolors are extraordinary, combining artistic sensibility with an almost photographic exactitude. And, perhaps most telling, he was the steadiest and most even-tempered soul on board.

Approached in June, Wilson accepted at once, flattered to have been chosen. But, in turn, he recommended strongly to Scott that a third sledger be included; three, he pointed out, would fare better than two in the event of sickness or injury to one of them. Moreover, the expedition's tents and tables of organization accommodated trios; the weight of additional rations would be negligible, more than offset by the presence of another man in harness.

Scott concurred and, to Wilson's delight, chose Ernest Shackleton as third of the triumvirate. The Merchant Navy officer was hard as nails; he had also become one of Wilson's closest friends, a friendship cemented over that winter by their joint editorship of the expedition's periodical, *The South Polar Times*.

The strength of the party was thus established: Scott, Wilson, and Shackleton would share the hardships of that slog to the pole. The only flaw was subtle. As in any human triangle, there existed an inherent social trap: Two tend to form an allegiance, excluding the third. Emerson has touched on the matter: "Two may talk and one may hear, but three cannot take part in a conversation of the most sincere and searching sort." The same imbalance would mar the southern journey. When that polar party limped back to the *Discovery* three months later, earlier loyalties had shifted: Scott and Wilson were drawn together, apart from the ailing Shackleton. The apparently indestructible Merchant Navy officer was crippled by a combination of scurvy, malnutrition, and severe bronchial attacks. And it was more than merely the stronger pair united to care for the weaker odd man out. For some reason, that southern journey initiated a rift that would separate Shackleton from Scott forever.

What happened? One can only assume that it started on the journey itself, for Scott would never have chosen a man he disliked. And polar historians have combed the sledge diaries of all three for a clue. But the candor they seek is seldom included in diaries written in the intimate proximity of a three-man tent.

Perhaps it is not surprising that the social and psychological links were weakest between the two service officers. The moody and withdrawn Scott was burdened with command, whereas Shackleton tended to high spirits; he could also be surprisingly stubborn, almost truculent. A trait the two shared was ironclad ambition, already manifested in Scott and revealing itself increasingly in his subordinate. Both relished the antarctic challenge and, even more, the reward that might follow. In this respect Wilson was the outsider, a scientist content with the advancement of knowledge.

But at midday on November 2, 1902, there was neither dissension nor disenchantment. Ready to leave, Scott, Wilson, and Shackleton seemed only gallant companions dedicated to realizing the best that was in them. A support party, a dozen strong under Lieutenant Barne, had trudged off two days earlier, bound for a rendezvous at Depot A, fifty-five miles south. They had manhauled their sledges, whereas Scott's party was taking the entire dog population: Nineteen animals were harnessed in line that morning, restless, fractious, and tangling the traces.

Skelton posed the departing trio in front of their sledges, which had been bedecked for the occasion with the obligatory banners. The three men's faces appear clean and well-shaven, eyes peering out from under wind-protecting brimmed hats. Their Burberry coveralls are spotless, belted neatly at the waist; pristine lampwick secures their wolfskin mittens. Only Scott manages a self-conscious smile; his two companions seem preoccupied, perhaps cold and anxious to be off.

There were final handshakes. The dogs were sorted out for the hundredth time and tore off at a gallop, pulling a train of five sledges. Well-wishers loped alongside the party for the first few miles. The southern journey had begun.

Would that their initial burst of speed had been maintained! After the support party turned back at Depot A, Scott and his two companions were reduced to relaying their sledges, now increased to six. Each morning they set out with half their runnered craft, established a depot two miles ahead, and then slogged back with an empty sledge (to keep the dogs in check) for the remainder.

The dogs' food was the most expendable load, nearly half a ton of dried codfish loaded on sledges 1, 2, and 3 in the event of a crevasse; the tent, sleeping bags, cooker, and fuel—life-support equipment—were carried on sledges 4, 5, and 6. Their paraffin, sixty pounds of it, was stored in gallon containers plugged with corks. Later, when dwindling loads were consolidated, oil and pemmican traveled ill-advisedly together on the same sledge. Scott found that no matter how tightly secured the stoppers, the fuel crept, imparting an oily seasoning to some of their hooshes. Improperly capped fuel cans would haunt Scott years later, when desperately needed supplies that had been depoted were found to have evaporated.

But it was not equipment that failed on the southern journey: It was the animals and, subsequently, the men. Their loads were within reason. Scott's six sledges and all his supplies, down to the last strap, weighed just over two thousand pounds, an appropriate load for a team of nineteen dogs, which are conventionally assigned a hundred pounds of sledge weights apiece. (Men can drag twice that amount.) They were ruthless about weights, as all sledgers must be. The only book they carried—Darwin's *Origin of Species*—had its cardboard covers removed. Admittedly, some frivolous contraband was included: Traveling in the toe of one of Shackleton's spare socks was a tiny plum pudding with a sprig of imitation holly; poached in their Christmas cocoa, this more than justified its illicit inclusion.

But it was the dogs that failed them. Scott's disappointment would have fatal repercussions a decade later, on the *Terra Nova* expedition. Quite simply, he was a reluctant dog-driver. Unremitting harshness is obligatory. Eskimos whipped or clubbed into insensibility dogs that would not pull; unconscious dogs were left with their mouths propped open, facing a north wind. Extreme Eskimo punishment was leaping onto a recalcitrant dog's back and biting off its ear.

Cruelty of this kind was anathema to Englishmen. They recoiled from the expedient of killing and feeding worn-out dogs to the surviving pack or, God forbid, eating them themselves. When Nansen was once lecturing in Lancaster, he mentioned that he and Johansen had left the *Fram* with a hundred days' food for themselves but only thirty for the dogs; a subsequent speaker remarked that "the lecturer could hardly justify his conduct to the dogs, which he treated in a barbarous manner." During an RSG dinner for Amundsen in 1912, Lord Curzon proposed feelingly, "Three cheers for the dogs!"

Dogs in Britain are petted, seldom whipped, and never used for haulage. To do so violates the law. The Cruelty to Animals Act of 1854 specifically forbids the use of dogs "for the purpose of drawing or helping to draw any Cart, Carriage, Truck or Barrow." (Were England's climate less temperate, sledges would undoubtedly have been written into the law as well.) To this day, failure to report to the police the death of a dog in a motor accident is an offense, whereas no infraction is involved in running over any number of cats. An English gentleman, it is said, shows tolerance for his children but affection for his dogs.

Inevitably, this same feeling permeated Scott and his men, just as it had Nares's a quarter of a century earlier. When the dogs had first been unloaded at winter quarters, a sledge race had been held between two teams, one whipped, the other cajoled. Although patently inconclusive and using untrained dogs, the cosseted team had won, and vestiges of this canine indulgence suffused all three travelers on the southern journey. Scott's standard marching orders placed one man ahead with orders to turn and offer encouragement to the dogs; a second man was harnessed to the sledge, pulling in tandem with the animals; while a third—the job Scott hated—had the whip, beating the creatures forward. Neither man at the sledge spoke during the march for, at the sound of a voice, the dogs would slow down, seizing any excuse to stop pulling. Wilson divided dogs into two categories, "pullers" and "sooners"; the latter were those that would "sooner do anything than pull."

A month after their departure, sooners outnumbered pullers by an overwhelming margin. Scott tried day-long halts to re-fresh the dog team, a hopeless prescription. Although dogs cannot contract scurvy (they produce vitamin C within their systems), the expedition's dog food was held at fault; Scott felt it had spoiled during the passage south from England.

By mid-December the dogs were finished, straggling use-lessly along behind the sledges while the men pulled, a tragic inversion of priorities. Yet even pulled by healthy teams and ruthlessly driven, the southern party's sledges still would have been delayed by adverse surface conditions, characteristic of the Barrier, called sastrugi, from the Russian *zastruga*, for groove, a common feature of Siberia's gale-scoured tundra. Sastrugi are formed where snow is carved and burnished by prevailing winds into massive gutters or ripples, like the sandy crenellations left on a tidal flat.

Sastrugi ridges—which serve, incidentally, as fixed wind vanes—are rock-hard, producing a succession of ditch-and-rampart treacherous to men and runners alike. Traveling over sastrugi in either direction is exasperating: Crossing them involves continual jolting over a corduroy road while paralleling them—and prevailing Barrier winds roar out of the south—is scarcely better, for sledges are continually tipped over when runners veer off ridgetops. Blizzards seldom cover or erase sastrugi but merely fill in the depressions between ridges, creating an illusory flat surface. On the southern journey, this fresh snow rarely offered advantage, being either so wet that it clung like cotton wool—"flocculent" was Wilson's word—or so frozen that it was not slippery. Runners, skis, and skates all slide because their pressure produces a thin film of lubricating water. In extreme cold this film cannot form and, in consequence, antarctic sledges frequently move only with massive effort, grating as though through sand. Sastrugi's final bedevilment is that their alternating ice and snow composition makes for a fine confusion about the most suitable footwear—ski boot or *finnesko*—the very confusion that killed poor Vince. At least the men of the polar party were fitted with crampons, detachable boot spikes improvised back at Arrival Bay out of scraps from the shattered windmill.

Long before December, it was apparent that though the southerly record would be bettered (the entire support party sat for that group photograph), the pole remained well beyond their reach. They did pass, for the first time, 80° South, intruding within the blank white disk with which contemporary mapmakers adorned the final ten degrees of southern latitude.

On December 15, a month and half into the journey, a second cache of food and fuel was made, Depot B, after a detour toward the mountains to their right. Scott felt it essential to site it near recognizable terrain; depoting on the featureless Barrier was too risky.

From Depot B they continued south for a scheduled fort-night, pulling only two sledges and grateful to be done with relaying. The year 1902 ended their poleward progress at 82°16' South, 540 miles from their objective. On New Year's Day they turned back, the southern winds now at their backs, sometimes sailing their sledges, with remnants of the useless dog pack trailing in their wake.

The health of the party deteriorated almost as severely as the dogs'. Shackleton had left the *Discovery* with a cold, a rare exception to their generally germ-free environment, caught fol-lowing the beating of the wardroom carpet. It settled in his chest and he coughed persistently throughout the journey. In early December, Wilson recorded the first appearance of scurvy: Shackleton's gums were swollen, leading Scott to or-der an increase in their consumption of seal meat. Over Christ-mas and New Year's the disease seemed to be held in check but, on the homeward trek, it intensified. Shackleton was the worst hit, lameness combining with lassitude and shortness of breath; severe coughing produced a frightening bloody dis-charge from his throat. Both Scott and Wilson suffered excru-ciating pain in the knee joints.

Wilson's other susceptibility was to snow blindness, in-curred from his habit of shedding goggles and sketching in the glare, recording the mountain panorama along their route. So agonizingly was he afflicted that for one day's march he trav-eled blind, his head covered, while Scott kept up a running commentary on the scenery they were passing.

During January the Barrier's temperature rose, creating try-ing conditions overnight in the tent. They slept in individual sleeping bags; three-man bags had proved just as unpopular among the English as among the Norwegians, discomfort out-weighing economy in bulk. Yet, even encapsulated singly, Wilson, Scott, and Shackleton faced an unrewarding night's rest because frozen body moisture stiffened the reindeer fur. Having fought their way down into their sleeping bags, they toggled the flaps over their heads. Thus confined, they were short of breath and had to pant like dogs until heart rate and the need for oxygen subsided. Leaving an air hole was worse, for openings became rimed with ice that melted in turn and dripped onto the neck. After shivering through uneasy sleep, plagued by nightmares of unattainable feasts, all three emerged from their humid cocoons to have drenched clothing ice instantly into such ironclad rigidity that morning conversation was literally drowned out by the crackle of frosted Burberry. Donning *finnesko* was a replay in miniature of entering the sleeping bags: Sweated fur boots left flat or crumpled froze overnight into defiant immobility.

In mid-January, with rations dangerously low, the sledgers came upon the black-flagged haven of Depot B. Jim and Nigger, the last surviving dogs, were put out of their misery and, reprovisioned, the explorers set out on the last 150 miles to winter quarters. Only Scott and Wilson were in harness now, drawing two sledges between them; Shackleton, forbidden to pull because of his weakened condition, skied alone. (Scott and Wilson had discarded their skis some weeks earlier.) Shackleton was lame, slow, and frequently dizzy, subject to violent coughing after the slightest exertion. When sails were bent onto the sledges, he was ordered to ride, ostensibly to slow their progress with a ski pole but in reality to avoid the total breakdown that Wilson feared.

Scott and Wilson were relieved to be manhauling rather than having to drive dogs. They plodded on in tandem, firm friends, delighted at last to be able to talk as they marched but further isolating the sick companion who trudged in their wake. It is not hard to guess at Shackleton's distress, a hollow shell of his robust self, excluded from the former sledging troika as a passenger, hobbling in at the finish.

As haze-cloaked Mounts Erebus and Terror towered in the northern sky, homing beacons of indescribable comfort, they reached Depot A. Confined to the tent for a day by blizzards and also Shackleton's infirmity, they rested, feasting on chocolate, raisins, prunes, and sardines, washed down with port, a gastronomic binge that sickened all three of them. Five days later they were met several miles from the ship by Skelton and Bernacchi.

Wilson could not help remarking how clean the welcoming committee looked. Only on their return did sledgers realize what ruffians they had become: hair matted, beards bleached by the sun where they were not soot-stained, faces and hands the color of mahogany, lips chapped raw and bleeding. (Sledgers' lips were always burned when cocoa or tea was gulped down scaldingly hot to warm chilled extremities.) Barring a ceremonial Christmas wash, they had not bathed for three months.

The two visitors joined the returning sledgers for a last lunch in the field and, after banners had been lashed in place, took over the dragropes for the final run home. Once around Cape Armitage, they saw the *Discovery* rainbowed with flags, rigging dressed with cheering men. On board, the southern party rejoiced in the hot baths, clean clothes, and warmed sheets that Armitage always laid on for returned sledgers. An elaborate wardroom dinner followed. But the rapacious sledging hunger still bound the three returned explorers: Late that night, long after the feast, when all but the night watchman snored in their bunks, Scott was at the stove, calling: "I say, Shackles, how would you fancy some sardines on toast?" Sweetest of all prospects was lengthy recuperation in dry bunks as well as a lazy read of letters and newspapers just arrived from England on the *Morning*.

This marked the first of two summer visits made by Sir Clements's promised relief ship. However, apart from the cherished mail and creature comforts that included Markham's own piano, what she brought was less dramatic than what she took away: Lieutenant Ernest Shackleton was sent home on her a month later. Still weakened, he embarked over his strenuous objection. But both surgeons, Koettlitz as well as Wilson, had recommended his repatriation, as did his commanding officer. Therein lies an intriguing conjecture: Was Shackleton merely invalided home, or had Scott seized on the disabling scurvy as a convenient means of repatriating a troublesome officer? And just how troublesome had Shackleton been?

The answers are not clear. No reliable account of their estrangement is extant, only hearsay long after the fact from Lieutenant Albert Armitage. Two decades later, the *Discovery*'s executive officer would recount an episode of Shackleton's alleged insubordination. But his story, supposedly originating with Wilson (who had perished with Scott), is so farfetched and unlikely that it seems more calumnious than accurate. Moreover, the eye of that particular beholder was irreparably jaundiced: Armitage was unhappy with his part in the expedition's overland achievements and nursed a grudge that promises made by Markham and Scott at the time of his recruitment had been ignored.

Perhaps what most jeopardized the harmony of the expedition was that traditional gap separating Royal and Merchant navies; Armitage and Shackleton were both Merchant Navy officers. Was it only coincidence that eight of Shackleton's fellow passengers also sent home on the *Morning* comprised all the *Discovery*'s Merchant Navy ratings? One of Scott's rare indiscretions, to be published in his *Voyage of the "Discovery,"* was his openly professed satisfaction at their departure. Their return to England en masse had all the earmarks of a purge, and it included the ailing Shackleton.

Another question: Had Shackleton stayed on and overcome his illness as well as Scott's disaffection, would Shackleton still have returned south with his own expedition five years later, determined, it has been suggested, to "show" Scott? I sense that it was inevitable. Ernest Shackleton was driven by the same financial need that spurred Scott. Moreover, Shackleton was seduced by the haunting white wastes that had nearly killed him, victim of the same polar fever that infected all the giants of the heroic age.

The *Morning* brought news of the Royal Societies Expedition back to England. Although equally ambitious sledge journeys were in train, including Scott's penetration of Victoria Land's mountainous interior, it was the polar attempt that caught the public fancy. But there were men in the corridors of power at Whitehall and the Admiralty who wished the explorers home. Further rescue operations were summarily removed from Sir Clements Markham's control, and the following summer the government mounted a two-ship relief expedition. The *Terra Nova*, a Dundee whaler that had just retrieved the remnants of the Baldwin/Ziegler fiasco from Franz Josef Land, was rushed to the Far East (towed partway by relays of Royal Navy warships) to sail south from Tasmania with the *Morning*.

Their joint arrival in McMurdo Sound on January 4, 1904, came as an unwelcome surprise. Scott's crew had spent fruitless weeks trying to saw an exit channel from their mooring to open water. The Admiralty's instruction to abandon the *Discovery* if necessary was one that Scott and his shipmates were loath to obey. By good fortune, at the eleventh hour the *Discovery* was extricated from her two-year imprisonment by a combination of gun-cotton charges and a shift in the ice. Her scarred hull bobbed free in mid-February, floating among the rubble of her frozen berth, ice fragments lined with caulking plucked from her planking.

But another peril threatened her. High seas mounted and, with steam up in only one boiler, the *Discovery* was driven aground in shallows off Hut Point. Heeled to windward by a force-ten gale, she was racked and strained, timbers groaning in a death rattle. Condenser intakes were jammed hard against the gravel below, so that steam power was denied her. But later that same day, the gale blew itself out, and as the tide turned, she began to back off. The only help her grateful people could offer was the time-honored expedient of sallying ship, the crew charging in unison from port to starboard and back repeatedly, rocking their vessel free. She floated off and, the following day, took on coal and stores from the *Terra Nova*. Then, in company with his rescuing flotilla, Scott set sail for New Zealand, arriving off Lyttelton Heads on April 1, 1904. Wilson noted that it was Good Friday, doubly "good" in that his beloved Oriana boarded the *Discovery* from a harbor tug.

Five months later, the Royal Societies Expedition ship tied up at a Portsmouth jetty, her way heralded by acclaim from warships in the roads. A jubilant Sir Clements boarded the vessel for passage around to the Thames and her London dock. An entry from his diary for September 15 is revealing:

> . . . Cheers from the *Cornwall* and we reached the berth in E.I. Docks by 5. Many lady relations came on board and Shackleton. They all went off with their friends, leaving only Scott, Shackleton and I on board. We dined together, us three, and had a very jolly evening. . . .

That cozy dinner in the wardroom seems somehow incongruous in light of past and future recriminations among the three participants. With the expedition over, perhaps Scott kept the peace. Certainly Sir Clements had greeted the invalided Shackleton cordially on his return, and the Merchant Navy officer had been instrumental in organizing and equipping both relief ships for the final trip to Antarctica.

The next evening there was a more elaborate dinner at the Criterion, the Royal Geographical Society's official welcome for the officers and men of the expedition, attended by nearly three hundred guests. Sir Clements was in the chair, flanked by

Scott and Armitage, and the dais was festooned with sledge banners ("some of the sledge flags" runs Sir Clement's diary; was Shackleton's renegade square omitted?). There were toasts, songs, and speeches, for which Lady Markham, Scott's mother, and several other ladies were admitted; it is revealing that Edwardian dinners of this kind were exclusively bachelor affairs, reflecting the expeditions themselves. The whole thing was, according to Sir Clements, "a splendid success."

It heralded, in fact, the finale of a dozen years' reign at the society's head: The following year, Sir Clements Markham stepped down as president, although he was to remain a prestigious and articulate member of its Council. He had reason to be pleased: Almost single-handedly, despite official disinterest and formidable administrative obstacles, he had succeeded in launching history's first great scientific expedition to Antarctica, restoring luster to Great Britain's tarnished polar crown. His protégé, Scott, was promoted to captain; but although decorated by King Edward—a notch up in the Victorian Order, of which he was already a member—he received no knighthood. That was an honor that would come only posthumously, after his second expedition. I suspect that on his return from Antarctica in 1904, he was in bad odor at the Admiralty, doubtless the result of unguarded comments—later denied—made to the New Zealand press about the unnecessary extent of his relief. He spent the next year on half pay, completing the manuscript of *The Voyage of the "Discovery"* before rejoining the fleet. Shackleton took a post with the Royal Scottish Geographical Society, and Wilson went to work for the Board of Agriculture's commission investigating grouse disease.

The *Discovery* was sold to the Hudson's Bay Company for a fifth of her builder's price. During World War I she ran munitions to Russia under charter to the French government but returned to antarctic waters in the 1920s with an Australian expedition under Sir Douglas Mawson. At present she has been returned to Dundee as a museum. The ship's timbers are rotting and their repair is the object of an appeal for public funds. The wardroom and its cabins serve as a small floating museum of the Royal Societies Expedition. The walls are almost bare. All that remain in the cabins are a few dusty relics, fragments of the great undertaking: Scott's wooden snow goggles, a miniature *Gulliver's Travels* (the gift of Sir Clements), a square copper matchbox used while sledging, even some pony snowshoes that must have come from the *Terra Nova*.

I only hope that the *Discovery*'s curators will be able to restore some sense of the life on board in Antarctica. During her incarceration at Arrival Bay nearly ninety years ago, *Discovery* served as a haven of warmth and security for her gallant occupants, a bastion against the polar furies. Wilson described his cabin as "a small sanctuary for happy recollections, lamp soot, and general comfort," a description in microcosm that typifies conditions on board in general, maintained by men whose efforts, if they did not encompass the pole, set a new standard for good cheer and good work in high latitudes. Set on board, too, was Shackleton's and Scott's clash of ambition and, for the latter, together with Wilson, that inevitable white road to failure and death.

11

HIT AND MISS

The prize of the general is not a bigger tent, but command.

—Oliver Wendell Holmes

One August evening in 1903, a laden fishing sloop sailed into an inlet of Devon Island in the Canadian archipelago. At a command from aloft, the helmsman brought the vessel up into the wind. Forward, a crewman released the anchor, followed by two fathoms of rattling cable. Halyards were unlashed, and the flapping mainsail cascaded down over the boom. Emerging through a trap in the bottom of the crow's nest, the captain, a wiry man wearing a black, wide-brimmed hat, clambered down the shrouds and dropped into a small boat that had been lowered from davits over the stern. He was rowed ashore. High atop crates stacked in the bow, a dog whined disconsolately.

The captain stepped ashore on what has been called Beechey Island—in reality, Cape Beechey, connected to the mainland by a spit concealed either by flood tide or, in any month but August, a white mantle. Now the island/cape was devoid of snow, a barren waste of shingle. His sea boots crunching up the slope, the captain reached a framed wooden structure. Beneath a litter of barrel staves and coal were vestiges of order, stone foundations marking the outline of long-vanished tents. Beyond the camp, the captain lingered over three sun-bleached wooden crosses—one of which lay toppled—as well as a formal stone plinth set on a rectangle of flat stones.

The sloop was the expedition ship *Gjøa*—pronounced *ewer* in Norwegian—her anchorage Erebus Bay and her master Captain Roald Amundsen. His solitary excursion ashore was less a matter of curiosity than reverence: Cape Beechey was, in his words, "holy ground," and his detour to that neglected cape a pilgrimage. Sir John Franklin and his men had wintered there half a century earlier and, for years, it had remained the only clue to their whereabouts before they sailed into oblivion. The wooden structure was not Franklin's but Northumberland House, a later rescue base stocked with fuel and provisions in the early 1850s should Franklin retrace his steps. But he never did, either to Beechey or to England. The Norwegian pilgrim would implement his dream instead.

Roald Engelbregt Gravning Amundsen was—first, last, and always—a polar explorer. Whereas Nansen had been a scientist, whereas Shackleton, Scott, and Peary had pursued exploration at the expense of service careers, Amundsen had no other vocation, nor did he wish for any.

He was born near Oslo in 1872. The youngest of four sons of a successful shipbuilder, he grew up wedded to ships. When he was fourteen, his father died. The only child left at home, Roald promised his widowed mother he would become a doctor. But his promise was forgotten within a year. From the moment he read of Sir John Franklin, he was determined to become an arctic explorer. Years later, he recalled that what he had found most compelling was the suffering of their crews. He hoped that by submitting himself to the same ordeal, he might emulate those Royal Navy martyrs and finish their uncompleted voyage. It was that simple. What in another child might have been forgotten, evolved in Amundsen's mind from adolescent fantasy into adult *idée fixe*. Amundsen never married, never thought of anything else, and never was deterred. He would triumph, uniquely, in both arctic and antarctic. It would be safe to say that, of all his rivals, Amundsen suffered the least; moreover, completing the work of British pioneers remained an invidious constant.

Nansen's return from Greenland in 1888 added further fuel to the fire: Amundsen was stirred by Christiana's contagious adulation and trained assiduously. Football, skiing, and rigorous calisthenics were pursued to perfect his body for hardships to follow. He slept with his bedroom window wide open year-round and undertook punishing winter ski trips. The relentless conditioning paid off: When he signed up for army service, the surgeon was so impressed by Amundsen's superb physique that he paraded the recruit, naked and embarrassed, before his colleagues.

When his mother died, he went to sea on a succession of his family's ships, implementing the next phase of training for his exploring career. Amundsen believed that he should be able to command both ship and expedition. His first berth was on the *Magdalena* as a common hand for a five-month sealing cruise in the arctic. To join another ship, the intrepid sailor bicycled across France and most of Spain in time to board the *Oscar*, sailing from Cartagena to Florida. En route home, he landed at Grimsby on England's eastern coast and, although unpaid, invested his remaining pocket money in a secondhand collection of arctic memoirs.

By 1895 he had a mate's certificate and, putting both maritime and exploring qualifications on the line for the first time, journeyed to Belgium with his older brother Leon to apply for a post on board the *Belgica*. De Gerlache signed him on as first mate.

Amundsen's service on the *Belgica*—from 1897 to 1899—was an admirable polar baptism. The *Belgica* became the first vessel—albeit involuntarily—to winter over in Antarctica. Like the *Jeannette* and the *Endurance*, she was beset in the pack; a summer visit turned into an enforced layover at the mercy of the Bellingshausen Sea ice. Belgian ship and crew were ill-equipped for the appalling year that followed. After both de Gerlache and his captain succumbed to scurvy, it was Amundsen and Frederick Cook, the American surgeon, who rallied the crew, prescribing and enforcing a diet of fresh seal meat. Later the same two officers supervised sawing operations that finally freed the vessel. By the time the little *Belgica* had tied up at Ostend, Amundsen was blooded, having coped with a starving, dispirited crew as well as mastered the unwritten manual on ice navigation. In 1900, six months after his return to Norway, he obtained his master's papers. From deckhand to captain in six years—one spent frozen into the antarctic ice—was impressive. He was twenty-eight years old.

A contemporary portrait is revealing. Neither smiling nor relaxed, Amundsen appears solemn, almost brooding, hooded eyes staring out impassively from either side of an imposing beaked nose, topped by eyebrows that, as the years progressed, sprouted in bushy profusion. The total effect is as forbidding as an arctic promontory. Despite a luxuriant mustache and a dashing goatee cultivated on the *Belgica*, Amundsen's features are set in a mold of unforgiving self-expectation: Humor, gentleness, or frivolity have no foothold. Yet letters and diaries belie this bleak impression; there was much good humor and chaff among the men who sailed with him. One is left with the conviction that Amundsen the explorer was determined to create an implacable public image.

The next step was his own expedition. Nansen had crossed Greenland as a maiden venture; Amundsen resolved to complete Franklin's task, sailing from Atlantic to Pacific north of the American continent. Before they died, Franklin's people had shown the way, and a Royal Navy ship searching for them had gone one better. In 1850 Captain Robert McClure, in command of the *Investigator*, had entered the archipelago from the Pacific. Although he was soon able to see, from high ground, a water route that would carry him into Barrow Strait, horrendous ice jams thwarted his ship's progress. After two summers, McClure had to walk his men out, abandoning the *Investigator* to save their lives.

But then, on April 6, 1853, incredible contact was made with another search expedition that had been dispatched from the east through Lancaster Sound. It was a moment of extraordinary drama: McClure and his first lieutenant were walking near the ship, looking for a place to bury a sailor who had died. A solitary figure was seen approaching from the east on foot. McClure thought it was one of his own men but, to his astonishment, heard the apparition—its face blackened by blubber smoke—identify itself as Lieutenant Bedford Pym of the *Resolute*, anchored 150 miles away, at Dealy Island. The encounter between the two officers marked a historic linkup between expeditions that had navigated eastern and western portions of the elusive passage. But though explorers from the two oceans had clasped hands, no vessel had ever negotiated the passage in its entirety. It was this British omission that Amundsen proposed to remedy.

His first requirement was a ship. Although the *Fram* had just returned from an expedition west of Greenland, under Otto

Sverdrup, Amundsen wanted a vessel of shallower draft and greater maneuverability. He bought the *Gjøa*, a forty-seven-ton sloop built in 1872, the year of his birth. She had seen many years' service as a herring boat and had several sealing voyages to her credit. Together with the German *Grönland*, the *Gjøa* has the distinction of being the only major expedition ship with a single mast. Yet despite this rig, she could carry an impressive spread of canvas, thanks to a bowsprit half again as long as her seventy-foot hull. Moreover, she was partially square-rigged, boasting two square foresail yards. The hull was strengthened with a doubling of greenheart, and more iron strapping was added to the cutwater. The world's first marine petroleum engine, a thirteen-horsepower Danish "Dan," was lowered into the engine room.

The *Gjøa* could only carry seven people in all, so everyone on board had to double, triple, or even quadruple in brass: For instance, Lieutenant Godfred Hansen of the Danish Navy, Amundsen's second-in-command, would serve as navigator, astronomer, geologist, and photographer. Amundsen himself became a scientist, for he had decided that in addition to negotiating the Northwest Passage, he would locate and measure the north magnetic pole, last found by Sir James Ross in 1831 on Boothia Peninsula's western coast. To this end, Amundsen took a course at Hamburg's Deutsche Seewarte under Von Neumayer, a world-famous authority on terrestrial magnetism. Gustav Wiik, the *Gjøa*'s only bona fide scientist, was signed on to take the magnetic readings but was obliged to serve as second engineer under chief engineer Peder Ristvedt. Ristvedt, in turn, would be the expedition's meteorologist and veterinarian and would prepare all their pemmican. Anton Lund and Helmer Hanssen signed on as first and second mates, respectively. Sverdrup's gift to the expedition, in addition to six experienced sledge dogs, was Adolf Lindstrom, a cheerful, roly-poly soul, the only man on board with but one job, ship's cook.

As on board the *Fram*, there was no disciplinary structure and no separation of officers from ratings. Some were, admittedly, housed in the foc's'le but only because accommodations aft were so limited; no social inferiority was implied. The six Norwegians were young, resilient, and enthusiastic, devoted to their commander and blessed with that precious Norwegian commodity, instinctive cooperation.

The *Gjøa* tied up at Christiania in the spring of 1903 while supplies, provisions, and borrowed scientific equipment were loaded on board. Thanks to her generous twenty-foot beam, five years' provisions could be stored in the hold; outboard packing cases were ingeniously constructed to match the hull's interior slopes, as were fuel and water tanks.

Amundsen found, as did all explorers, that his most demanding labor was not assembling stores but paying for them. More than fifty contributors had answered his appeal, the king, the Royal Geographical Society, and Lewellyn Longstaff among them. But he was still short of money, and in early June one Christiania merchant threatened to nail a writ to the *Gjøa*'s mast if payment were not forthcoming the following morning. Amundsen's only recourse was what is known among impoverished defaulters in England as a midnight flit: Late that night, with her entire crew and Amundsen's three brothers on board, the *Gjøa* was towed down Oslofjord by a steam tug under cover of a downpour. Once the brothers Amundsen had disembarked at Horton, the voyage was begun. That furtive departure was pure Amundsen—bold, ruthless, and successful.

Within a week they had cleared the Orkneys and, a month later, rounded Greenland's southern tip. At Godhavn they took on more petroleum, sledges, kayaks, and some Eskimo dogs. Melville Bay's infamous ice proved no obstacle, and a last call for supplies was made at Dalrymple Rock. Then, with almost no freeboard, the *Gjøa* tacked boldly into Lancaster Sound, hugging the land along Parry Channel.

At Beechey Island, Amundsen walked that "holy ground" for himself; but there were scientific chores as well. The *Gjøa* stayed anchored in Erebus Bay for two days while, in a tent onshore, Wiik's dip needle was set up. This is a simple compass mounted on a vertical axis, indispensable for tracking a magnetic pole. Wiik's readings indicated that it lay still farther south, in the direction of Amundsen's course. But the magnetic variations were already erratic, and the *Gjøa*'s compass over the next months would move sluggishly or not at all. Navigation by the stars would be hampered by summer fog.

Before leaving Beechey Island, Amundsen deposited a sealed

message inside the cairn, a precaution that his illustrious predecessor had, in haste, neglected to take. Then the anchor came up and the little Norwegian fishing sloop sailed south through Peel Sound, in both Franklin's and McClintock's wake. Passage was unobstructed: That summer of 1903, the ice accumulation happened to be negligible. The *Gjøa* breezed through Peel Sound, continuing unhampered down Franklin Strait and south toward James Ross Strait. In so doing, Amundsen avoided Franklin's fatal error. Cape Felix is the northernmost point of King William Land and, for the British, it marked their point of no return. Franklin had turned his ships to starboard, to the southwest, in the direction of his objective. But in so doing he had run afoul of an overwhelming ice flow spewing out of McClintock Channel. It was an onslaught that turned the waters off King William Land's western shore into a graveyard for the doomed *Erebus* and *Terror*.

Conversely, Amundsen left Cape Felix to starboard and, once into James Ross Strait, was sheltered from McClintock Channel's ice juggernauts. The canny Norwegian had a distinct, crucial advantage over Franklin, intelligence of a new, circuitous route to the west that had been discovered by Dr. John Rae, a Scottish explorer. Most astute of the Franklin searchers, Rae had been treated with scandalous indifference by the Arctic Council, some said because he was employed by the Hudson's Bay Company rather than the Royal Navy. Rae had discovered that water existed between King William Land and the mainland, that King William Land was, in fact, King William *Island*. It was for this virgin waterway that Amundsen was headed.

Assorted hazards lay before them. Matty Island sits like a cork in the bottleneck between King William Island and the Boothia Peninsula and is fringed with satellite islets and treacherous shallows. Although the *Gjøa* had been designed to draw only six feet, her working draft was now two thirds again as much, and she fell afoul of uncharted shoals. Yet whenever the *Gjøa* touched bottom, a determined Amundsen drove her forward rather than backing cautiously off. Under a dangerous spread of canvas, the doughty fishing smack was urged on, bumping and scraping over submerged rocks that threatened to tear her hull to pieces; they escaped one reef by jettisoning six tons of precious deck cargo. One night, a flash fire sent flames licking out of the engine room hatch, a blaze that the desperate crew managed to put out before it ignited their petroleum reserves. September's first storm caught them at anchor off Boothia. Both hooks dragged, and it was only Ristvedt and Wiik's frantic efforts in the charred engine room that enabled the ship to maintain position against a gale that roared from every quarter of the compass.

Although open water lay invitingly to the west, mid-September is no time for a ship to be under weigh in the arctic. Amundsen secured the *Gjøa* for the winter. On September 12, she was made fast in a bay on King William Island's southeastern shore that he christened Gjøahavn. "The finest little harbor in the world!" Hanssen had called from the crow's nest; ever since their near-disaster in the shallows off Matty Island, the Norwegians had conned their ship from the masthead while another man stationed on the bow had heaved a continuous lead.

Gjøahavn was ideal, with an entry so narrow that restless sea ice would pose no problem. It was, conveniently, about ninety miles from the magnetic pole's location, with no nearby mountain ranges with ferrous content that would disrupt their observations. There was adequate fresh water, and game in abundance. Herds of reindeer migrate each fall back to the mainland once the ice freezes over, and their route skirted Gjøahavn, a vital source of fresh meat that, inexplicably, had evaded Franklin's men during 1847 and 1848. Helmer Hanssen, the best hunter on board, killed thirteen reindeer on a single outing; by the end of the month, a hundred carcasses were stacked on the *Gjøa*'s open deck forward.

The vessel was entirely unloaded. Case after case was emptied and refilled with sand, to serve as building blocks for a colony of shore huts. The largest was a general storehouse; another accommodated explosives and ammunition. A third, floored with cement and built exclusively of copper-nailed packing cases, was designated the magnetic variation laboratory. Nearby was a fourth, Villa Magnet, a cozy, one-room dwelling for Ristvedt and Wiik, complete with double bunks and reindeer-skin carpeting. Here the two men would winter in greater comfort than those remaining on board. But they dined each evening on the ship, drawn by Lindstrom's skill in the spacious new galley that had been arranged in the emptied hold.

Although winterized in traditional fashion—decked over with canvas, double-glazed, and boasting supplementary stoves—the *Gjøa* lacked the *Fram*'s sophisticated insulation, and the five men on board suffered from extensive ice accumulation belowdecks. That damp continued through two successive winters at Gjøahavn.

Amundsen first greeted the local Eskimos with a show of force, remembering Kane's problems with fractious tribes at Rensselaer Bay. With loaded rifles at the ready, he, Hanssen, and Lund met them in a skirmish line, three armed Norwegians against five baffled Eskimos. Tension increased as the parties closed, broken, to Amundsen's vast relief, when he heard cries of *"Manik-tu-mi! Manik-tu-mi!,"* a cordial greeting recalled from McClintock's memoirs. The Eskimos were welcomed on board, restricted to the hold to avoid an infestation of lice. Lindstrøm's offer of coffee and biscuits was rejected, but some raw meat proved more appealing to the visitors: All smiles, they produced knives from beneath their furs and devoured an entire haunch of reindeer. Eskimos eat by stuffing their mouths to capacity, then slicing off any excess at the lips with a sweep of the knife. They gorge at every sitting and never stock against the future.

By judicious bargaining as well as firm insistence that his crew refuse all offers of female companionship, Amundsen gained the Eskimos' friendship and cooperation. Within a few weeks, the Norwegians were kitted out in fur regalia, run up by obliging women in return for a pittance in needles and scrap iron. Amundsen also learned how to build igloos. The Eskimo snow house is unique in all architecture, consisting as it does of a single dome erected without benefit of interior scaffolding.

The most demanding preliminary was selecting precisely the right snow, neither too powdery to compact nor too icy to be sculpted with a bone snow knife. Snow blocks should be quarried beneath the site so that their excavation would increase headroom inside. Once a suitable supply was found, yard-long blocks were cut, half as wide and four inches thick. They were placed on edge, end to end, along a clockwise curve, spiraling up and in, wall segueing gradually into roof. The second block had to be canted against the first block, and each block was cemented to its neighbor with snow mortar.

Once the dome was capped (sometimes with a sheet of clear ice as a skylight), a low, vaulted tunnel pierced the lowest course of blocks, its dogleg entrance sited away from prevailing winds. Inside, a lamp would be lit, raising the temperature sufficiently to melt just the innermost surface. Then the flame was extinguished to allow the walls to refreeze into a secure glaze; too thick a glaze would vitiate the snow wall's insulating quality. Finally, the igloo was banked with snow around its lower edge. Amundsen's men found that four men could craft a snow house large enough to accommodate themselves comfortably—ten feet in diameter—in less than two hours.

They put their newfound expertise to immediate good use during the first abortive spring journey. At the end of February 1904—the same month during which Scott was struggling to free his vessel from Arrival Bay—Amundsen and three companions set out in the direction of the north magnetic pole with two sledges. One was drawn by men, the other by dogs. Amundsen's only failing, typically, was heading out too early in the season, an impulsive false start that would be duplicated in 1911, under more imperative time pressures, from Framheim. In addition, there was extreme cold—the mercury hovered at −80° that night. After only a few miles, Amundsen called a halt, and the chilled Norwegians were soon ensconced within a snow house. They pressed on for a second day's run before turning back, depoting provisions in the igloo to await kinder temperatures.

The second start was made a fortnight later, at a mere −40°. Only two men, Amundsen and Hanssen, made up the party, and they did not return to the *Gjøa* until the end of May. They retraced on foot their tortuous sea route back to Matty Island and established the new location of the north magnetic pole.

Of all the polar sagas, Amundsen's conquest of the Northwest Passage most lacks conventional dramatic structure. It is an uneven scenario, short on suspense, climax, or denouement, spread out over three long years. The *Gjøa* was imprisoned at Gjøahavn for two of them. Once Amundsen had freed her in August 1905, he would achieve his goal within two weeks, pressing through the only segment of the passage never before navigated. His triumph is clear from today's map names: Victoria Strait, the waters west of King William Island that doomed Franklin's ships, leads south into a gulf that Amundsen named after the Norwegian Queen Maud. Nordenskjöld Island was named in honor of the Swedish conqueror of the Northeast Passage. But just to the west, British nomenclature is resumed, thanks to Captain Collinson of the *Enterprise*, who had first reached those waters from the Pacific in the early 1850s: Nordic place names give way to Duke of York Archipelago and Wellington Bay.

On August 26, a fortnight after leaving Gjøahavn, glorious confirmation of their feat materialized over the *Gjøa*'s bows. Lieutenant Hansen raced below to alert his commander with unaccustomed formality: "Vessel in sight, sir!" She was the American whaling schooner *Charles Hanson*, out of San Francisco. Captain James McKenna, her master, presented the Norwegians with invaluable gifts, up-to-date charts of waters to the west and California newspapers that told the explorers of their country's final independence from Sweden.

But they were not through yet. Months would pass before the *Gjøa* made her way around Point Barrow. During the summer of 1905, the Norwegians traveled a thousand miles to the west. North of Cape Parry, Amundsen Gulf was named, marking entrance into the open Beaufort Sea. Open on the map, that is, but seldom for navigation: Once clear of Canada's island gauntlet, Amundsen had to pursue his course along an oft-occluded front between the continent and the unhindered thrust of the arctic icepack. Near the Alaskan border, the *Gjøa* was moored off King Point to pass the expedition's third arctic winter. The shore was littered with tree trunks washed down by the nearby Mackenzie River. Five of the ship's crew spent the winter ashore in a driftwood hut; two remained on board.

In March 1906, Gustav Wiik, the expedition's scientist, died of peritonitis. He was buried at King Point, interred within the abandoned magnetic observation hut. His lonely resting place seems a northern equivalent of another explorer/scientist's grave at the other end of the globe, the hill above Cape Adare, where one of Borchgrevink's men, Nicolai Hansen, lies buried. Whalers who heard of Wiik's death promised the Norwegians that they would tend the wildflowers planted on the hut's turf roof.

Amundsen's welcome at Nome was tumultuous. His ship

could barely maneuver: Her propeller shaft had been fatally bent in the ice, and her gaff, repaired countless times, was once more in splinters. She inched toward land under scraps of sail until a steam launch finally towed the battered little vessel in. The town's entire population thronged the shore and, most astonishing to a deeply moved Amundsen, the strains of his national anthem floated over the waters: Otto Sverdrup's nephew, a Nome resident at the time, had laid on an emotional welcome for his triumphant countrymen.

The *Gjøa* ended her historic voyage on the beach at San Francisco, where, for decades, her crumbling hull was a neglected feature of Golden Gate Park. In 1972 she was returned to Oslo as supercargo on a freighter and was restored as part of the comprehensive Norwegian Maritime Museum. She rests in splendid company, near *Fram* and *Kon-Tiki*.

Although the *Gjøa*'s voyage was arctic rather than polar, it begs recounting if only to introduce a formidable competitor into the heroic lists. Though he lacked Nansen's erudition, Amundsen sprang from the same Viking tradition, and this arctic overture foreshadows the antarctic coda that would close the heroic age. Skill and determination were Amundsen hallmarks, and every detail of his outfit was tempered with shrewd foresight. Nothing was found lacking, neither rolls of felt for Gjøahavn's scientific huts nor gauze to keep the summer gnats at bay. Even his shipboard decoration was finely honed; only three items hung on the *Gjøa*'s saloon walls: a portrait of King Haakon, Norway's new sovereign; a photograph of Nansen; and a map of the skipper's completed route through the Northwest Passage.

The same congeniality that had obtained throughout the *Gjøa*'s voyage prevailed on the grubby little whaleship *Nimrod* as she steamed out of Lyttelton Harbor on New Year's Day of 1908. Thirty thousand New Zealanders packed the waterfront to wish her bon voyage, and the thirty-nine men on board responded in boisterous kind. Caps were tossed to sweethearts ashore; all loose change was flung to Alfred Reid, the expedition secretary on the quay. It was considered bad luck to go south with any money at all, and this condition of blithe penury was an accurate reflection of the expedition's account as well. But its commander, who had just that afternoon been referred to as a "human dreadnought" by Bishop Julius of Christchurch, seemed unaffected; puffing a cigarette contentedly on the bridge was Lieutenant Ernest Shackleton. His departure for Antarctica that regatta afternoon, in command of his own expedition, ended four years of humiliation, planning, cajoling, and whirlwind determination.

Long before, in New Zealand's autumn of 1903, still brooding over his repatriation from the *Discovery*, Shackleton had cabled Emily Dorman:

> BROKEN DOWN IN CHEST RETURNING SOUTHERN SLEDGE JOURNEY
> SUFFERING FROM SCURVY AND OVERSTRAIN DON'T WORRY NEARLY
> WELL COMING HOME VIA CANAL ABOUT THREE WEEKS SHACKLETON

It was pure Shackles—blunt but reassuring—yet the kind of cold-shower news that any fiancée might have trembled to read. Within a year they were married and the returned explorer accepted the position of secretary-treasurer with the Royal Scottish Geographical Society.

Like all Shackleton's attempts to settle down, it was foredoomed. He chafed at his post, impatient with office routine and Edinburgh's geographers alike. As in Scott's household, money was perennially short, all the more so once he and Emily had produced young Raymond and Cecily. His pre-*Discovery* vocation—Merchant Navy officer—would have kept him at sea for months, inadequately paid.

He quit the RSGS to launch one money-making scheme after another. He tried marketing Tabards, a brand of luxury cigarette sold from a Jermyn Street shop. He entered into negotiations with Russia to charter it troopships. He even ran for Parliament but, despite easy rapport with his Dundee electorate, lost at the polls. Then he was hired by William Beardmore, a Clydeside shipbuilder and industrialist, who would ultimately subsidize Shackleton's polar ambition.

It was inevitable that Shackleton would never be content with a conventional job. He was restless, a man for whom office, commuting, and home were stifling; he belonged outdoors. Even had he won election to Parliament, even had Tabards or troopships panned out, a return to Antarctica was never in doubt. His entrepreneurial activity—consistently unsuccessful—was a means of providing some kind of financial security so that he could mount his own expedition. He was driven to even the antarctic score.

In February 1907, he made it official. Shackleton announced publicly that he would try for the south pole, the first antarctic explorer ever to be quite so explicit. However, like Amundsen before him, he enriched his prospectus with a scientific mission: locating the south magnetic pole. The venture was called the British Antarctic Expedition; no royal society endorsed him, and no savants or sailors rallied to his support. Alfred Reid ruefully compared the *Discovery*'s top-heavy committee of sixty with the understaffed operation that he and Shackleton—"The Boss"—mounted out of a crowded Regent Street office. The government, still rankling at the cost of having retrieved Scott from McMurdo Sound, viewed this private antarctic venture with indifference.

The entire budget was thirty-thousand pounds, less than it had cost to build the *Discovery*. Despite Beardmore's generous example, finding additional investors was a struggle. In his darker moments, Shackleton felt that he was personally suspect, his image tarnished by having been invalided home in 1903.

He spent cautiously. The *Nimrod*, a forty-year-old Newfoundland whaler, was a bargain at five thousand pounds, but it cost half again as much to make her shipshape. A hasty refit was undertaken at Blackwall the moment she arrived in the Thames. When she sailed at the end of July, her 'tweendecks still reeked of whale oil. A white flag flew at her foremast, symbolizing no-man's-land, an evocative reminder of her objective. But at Cowes, Queen Alexandra presented the expedition with a Union Jack and, like Scott before him, Shackleton was decorated with the Victorian Order, Fourth Class, by King Edward.

A week later, the *Nimrod* sailed from Torquay without her commander; Shackleton stayed behind, lecturing and begging up to the last moment. Even so, by the time he embarked on a steamer in November, the expedition's debts amounted to twenty thousand pounds, a shortfall only partly alleviated by subsequent grants from Australia's and New Zealand's parliaments for six thousand pounds.

Lashed atop the *Nimrod*'s afterhatch was a crated marvel, Antarctica's first motorcar, an Arrol-Johnston. The jaunty two-seater was powered by a four-cylinder, air-cooled engine of a prototype paradoxically designed for service in the Sudanese desert. Oversized steel and hickory rear wheels, ten inches wide, could be changed for different surface conditions, from Dunlop tires for "summer motoring" (as though Antarctica melted dry during the warm months) to wooden-knobbed rims for deep snow or spiked wheels for ice. Both front wheels could be replaced by broad runners. One cylinder had its exhaust routed to warm the carburetor, while the remaining three were piped cozily under the driver and passenger's feet, then rearward to pass through a snow-melting tank.

But if the Arrol-Johnston was a mechanical curiosity, Shackleton had another innovative but more practical means of dragging his sledges. Agents of a Far Eastern bank had been instructed to buy and ship fifteen Manchurian ponies from Tientsin to Port Lyttelton, where they were quarantined conveniently on Quail Island while awaiting the *Nimrod*'s arrival. These were savage, apparently indestructible little beasts, seven years old, none more than fourteen hands high. They were completely wild and were broken to harness by dragging heavy sledge mock-ups around the beaches of their island preserve. Only ten could be accommodated within the *Nimrod*'s deck stalls, so the five most intractable were reluctantly left behind.

Shackleton had been advised that each pony would be able to draw eighteen hundred pounds, an extravagant estimate later revised down by two-thirds. Unquestionably, ponies were less well adapted to live in the polar open than dogs. Though their winter coats grew protectively long, the ponies could not curl up in the snow overnight but had to remain standing in the wind, draped with rugs. Although they never contracted frostbite, snow blindness afflicted them badly. Shackleton surmised that by the time the animals died on the march, they were all quite blind. Scott, who would take ponies to Antarctica in 1910, sometimes led his animals with their heads wrapped in sacking.

An anatomical disadvantage for horses in snow is their weight distribution, substantial bodies supported on relatively small hooves. They invariably broke through the top crust and, even more dangerous, the snow bridges that sometimes concealed crevasses. After a blizzard they would have to flounder through girth-deep snow. Their only advantage over dogs was that, on the march, their heads remained well above what is called in Antarctica drift, not an accumulated depth of snow but a stinging blast of driven snow that scours the Barrier surface at the level of a dog's muzzle.

Ponies presented dietary problems as well. Essentially herbivorous, they will not devour their own kind, thereby lacking that logistical convenience of self-consuming dog teams. Shackleton's animals were fed a combination of maize—ground laboriously at winter quarters in a vast iron mill—as well as Maujoo ration, a pemmicanlike blend of sugar, currants, carrots, and beef.

To conserve coal, Shackleton had arranged to be towed from New Zealand as far south as the pack by the Union Steamship Company's *Koonya*. Fifteen hundred miles and a drenched fortnight later—a vessel in tow is particularly susceptible in dirty weather—they sighted the ice margin. The gallant little *Koonya* cut the tow after her captain had sent over some freshly slaughtered mutton and taken the expedition's final letters in return. Shackleton had been sworn in by New Zealand's prime minister, Sir Joseph Ward, as King Edward VII Land's first postmaster ("duties unique, salary nil"), and his homebound mail bore that historic postmark. In the manner of every traveling papa, he dispatched postcards to Raymond and Cecily Shackleton, addressed to "A. Penguin, Esq.," with the plaintive query, "Is Father there?"

Left under her own power, the *Nimrod* penetrated the pack in a record two days, emerging into the Ross Sea at longitude 178° East. Her position—fortuitously where Antarctica's ice girdle was thinnest—had been dictated by an extraordinary bargain struck months earlier in England, arising out of that prickly issue, territorial prerogative.

Captain Scott had insisted that the entire Ross Sea was his domain. After a prolonged exchange of proposals—smoothed over by Wilson in his traditional role as peacemaker—Scott gave his blessing to Shackleton on condition that *Nimrod* remain east of longitude 170° East: This slices through Cape Adare and includes Ross Island and McMurdo Sound on its western and—to Shackleton—forbidden side. Thus Shackleton would have to establish his base either on the Barrier itself or on the unexplored shores of King Edward VII Land far to the east. In accepting his ex-commander's stipulation, he was denying himself a known anchorage, proven access to the Barrier and, at that date, the only known route to the pole.

Shackleton had every intention of keeping to the bargain. Had he been able to land on the Barrier, he would have profited from the same geographical advantage—sixty miles closer to the pole—that would assist Amundsen four years later. But Balloon Bight was no more: Each headland had calved away as icebergs. The bight was now an unprotected bay, its waters roiled by killer whales, after which Shackleton christened this large new Barrier indentation the Bay of Whales.

Determined not to camp on that obviously impermanent shoreline, Shackleton pressed farther east to his alternative, hopefully terra firma. But the *Nimrod* was halted by unrelenting ice. King Edward VII Land, only glimpsed by Ross and Scott, remained inviolate for Shackleton as well. Balked at the Barrier's center and its eastern end as well, he faced two unpleasant alternatives: return to New Zealand or break his promise. He chose the latter.

In his published account of the expedition, Shackleton's decision is recounted with a kind of detached inevitability:

> . . . I did not give up the destined base of our expedition without a strenuous struggle, as the track of the ship given in the sketch-map shows; but the forces of these uncontrollable icepacks are stronger than human resolution, and a change of plan was forced upon us.

To Emily, he confided in tormented detail (under stress, Shackleton's sentences pour out with punctuation ignored):

> . . . Well child you will have seen about it roughly and in bald facts in the papers and cables, so you can understand what has happened but you I know can read between the lines and realize what it has been for me to stand up on the bridge in those snow squalls and decide whether to go on or turn back my whole heart crying out for me to go on and the feeling against of the lives and families of the 40 odd men on board: I swept away from my thoughts the question of the Pole of the success of the Expedition at that moment though in doing so I know now in my calmer moments that I was wrong to even to do that. . . .

At the end of January 1908, Shackleton steered the *Nimrod* into the sacrosanct waters of McMurdo Sound, a decision that would invoke a storm of suspicion, mistrust, and personal enmity as well as cost him the friendship of his *Discovery* comrade Wilson. But it is as difficult to accept the principle of Scott's proprietary claim as to condemn Shackleton's trespass. Indeed, as a test case, the affair is at variance with historical precedents. Was Nares obligated to obtain permission from Charles Francis Hall's executors before wintering at Discovery Bay? Should Greely have had clearance from Nares prior to occupying Fort Conger? And was Peary delinquent in not steering clear of Kennedy Channel in the event that Greely chose to return? Close to the scene of the crime, when Scott moored the *Discovery* at Balloon Inlet in 1902, did he violate territorial imperatives established by Borchgrevink? In 1911, should he not have turned back at the Beardmore Glacier, which was Shackleton's discovery?

Shackleton was no more at fault in reneging than Scott in having laid down his presumptuous ground rules. Even though Scott was planning—*privately*—a return to McMurdo Sound, he could not very well expect the world to await his pleasure. The polar campaign in both hemispheres had always been waged with cumulative attacks, explorers improving on their predecessors' best, regardless of locale, timing, or nationality. It seems shabby treatment of a former comrade and fellow Englishman and in stark contrast to Shackleton's generosity in reverse: Writing to Scott Keltie, secretary of the Royal Geographical Society, before leaving England, he suggested: "Scott's expedition should be announced before I draw back so that the foreigners cannot get in." Elspeth Huxley pointed out in her definitive biography of Captain Robert Scott that the issue was less geographical than personal: Scott and Shackleton were rivals not because they sought the same prize but because they were very different men. Therein lies the rhubarb over McMurdo Sound.

Scott's winter quarters at Hut Point were iced in that summer, so that the sensitive issue of occupying them was rendered academic. Shackleton settled instead for Cape Royds, twenty miles farther north. However, the icefoot ringing Cape Royds was too solid for the ship to penetrate yet too fragile for use as a permanent quay. The *Nimrod* burned precious tons of coal shunting from Front Door Bay to Back Door Bay to Derrick Point to land all her cargo. More than once, supplies offloaded onto storm-weakened ice were salvaged just in time, prompting Shackleton's immortal reassurance to those on board: "Never mind, we have saved the Browning!"

But disquieting events other than storms clouded that frantic disembarkation: So worrisome were triple priorities of saving ship, supplies, and dwindling coal that, on more than one occasion, Shackleton differed violently with the *Nimrod's* sailing master, Rupert England, an old friend who had been first officer on board the *Morning.* When the *Nimrod* sailed for New Zealand on February 22, Dunlop, her chief engineer, carried with him sealed instructions from "The Boss" that would relieve England of his command at Lyttelton, to be replaced for the spring return by Captain Evans of the *Koonya.*

The vaunted snow car was a fiasco. On soft snow, the Arrol-Johnston was stymied. Even after mechanic Bernard Day, an employee from the motorcar company, stripped all the car's superfluous hardware, the engine, directly over the front wheels, consistently buried her axle-deep whenever soft snow was encountered; churning rear wheels only dug the grave deeper. It was determined in the end, ironically, that conventional tires wrapped in chain gave the most satisfactory service. Obviously, the era of motor-drawn sledges had not arrived by 1908; tracked rather than wheeled vehicles were necessary for Ross Barrier work. Scott would include three snow tractors on the *Terra Nova,* as well as the indefatigable Bernard Day to oversee their operation.

The Manchurian ponies proved more successful, though vulnerable to illness. Two died during the *Nimrod's* stormy passage from New Zealand, one so badly chafed along its flanks from struggling to remain upright in its pitching stall that Shackleton ordered it shot. The remaining eight were landed at Cape Royds. But half those survivors succumbed to their insatiable voracity, consuming lethal quantities of sand from what was henceforth called Dead Pony Beach. By the time the British Antarctic Expedition settled into winter quarters, only four of the original ten taken on the voyage—Quan, Grisi, Socks, and Chinaman—remained in figurative harness for the momentous work to come. With the car a dud and only a handful of dogs at his disposal, Shackleton gave strict orders that the ponies—his only remaining polar trumps—be cosseted accordingly.

Winter quarters ashore—whether Fort Conger's drafty barracks, Nansen's walrus-skin hut in Franz Josef Land, or Amundsen's packing-case villa at Gjøahaven—had one overwhelming limitation: They had to be infernally crowded. The *Nimrod*'s detachment would fare better than the nine men who had wintered over with Borchgrevink. That pioneering shore party, Antarctica's first, had a dwelling only 225 feet square, affording each man a scant 22½ square feet. (Since a bunk occupies a minimum of 15 square feet, the space-per-explorer remaining amounted to little more than the area of a bathmat.) Borchgrevink had had the hut's berths equipped with sliding doors so that each man could retire to cramped privacy. Amundsen would install thick woolen curtains on his men's bunks at Framheim in 1910. But Shackleton and Scott were less concerned with privacy, opting instead for cubicles and dormitories, respectively. In the large *Terra Nova* winter quarters, which one occupant, Apsley Cherry-Garrard, was to rate "the Ritz of Antarctic huts," all the officers were bunked together in claustrophobic double-deckers, separated from the ratings by a packing-case wall.

Shackleton's fifteen-man party at Cape Royds enjoyed a space-per-man ratio double that of Borchgrevink's, in a building 30 feet by 19 feet. The cork-insulated hut, prefabricated by a Knightsbridge firm, had merely four walls and a roof. The explorers subdivided the space into eight bedrooms—seven doubles, and a single for "The Boss." A central alleyway ran the length of the building. This combined living, dining, and work room was restricted at the far end by the stove and, inside the entrance, a contrivance for producing illumination. This was the acetylene plant, moved indoors when it was discovered that the water tank, a vital component, froze solid in the anteroom at the hut's entrance.

Although that interior approximated the *Discovery*'s wardroom and cabin arrangement, the traditional storage nooks worked into a ship's joinery—drawers, shelves, and lockers—were unable to be duplicated in a hut partitioned with canvas. As a result, each bedroom was unbelievably cluttered. The polar wardrobe, with Jaegers, Burberries, *finnesko*, felt boots, mufflers and thick woolens, ran to bulk. In addition, a vast assortment of tools, instruments, books, and equipment erupted unchecked on every side.

Hammocks, those nautical beds that vanish by day, could scarcely be slung in canvas-walled cubicles. Most of the men made do with mattresses on top of provision boxes, although some improvised bunks out of lashed bamboo. (Tropical bamboo, paradoxically, was in plentiful supply on polar expeditions, for use as supple, lightweight trail markers.) Very much like Thomas Jefferson's vanishing bed at Monticello, the dining table at Cape Royds was suspended on ropes; once the meal had been cleared, the table was hoisted up against the ceiling, trestle legs folded neatly out of sight. Invaluable open space remained for chores, games, and inevitable festoons of laundry clustered above the stove. Storage capacity improved as winter progressed: Permanent partitions had been built out of packing cases laid on their sides; as provisions within them were consumed, the crates became much-needed lockers.

There were two windows along the hut's leeward side. However, they admitted no light, for the ponies were stabled along that protected exposure. (Global inversion again: In Antarctica, the northern side is the most sheltered.) They were housed more spaciously than their masters. Cases of maize provided two of three stable walls, while the third consisted of compressed fodder bales. The ponies proved only occasionally tiresome. Grisi poked his head through one window, necessitating a ponyproof wooden hoarding in place of the shattered glass. The ponies' halters were attached to a long, transverse wire. But Quan, who resented being left alone for the night, had the last word, frequently disrupting the sleep of his neighbors, both equine and human: He would seize the wire in his teeth, pull it back, and let it snap with an ear-splitting crash against the galvanized iron sheeting that lined the stable wall, a late-night ritual that, when first attempted, brought the night watchman on the run.

Although Shackleton elaborated on nearly every detail of life at Cape Royds, he never mentioned the excretory functions. Discussion of elimination was either taboo or cloaked in abstruse euphemism. Nancy Mitford, in her admirable essay on Scott's last expedition, wondered how explorers on winter journeys, "as the Americans say, went to the bathroom." (It is irresistible to counter this swipe at Yankee gentility by rephrasing Miss Mitford's query in her parlance: "What had Scott's men done when they wished to wash?") Yet whatever the metonym, we are seldom told, at least not by the men at the top.

Few Edwardians and fewer Victorians were outspoken on the subject. A rare exception was an unnamed bishop, notorious for imparting wisdom to any who sought it. A young prince once asked the prelate a good rule by which to live. His Lordship's legendary response: "Never, sir, miss an opportunity to pass water," sound advice for one who would endure endless ceremonials. But how, one wonders, were bowels moved or water passed in high latitudes? In subzero temperatures, when exposed hands or faces sustained frostbite, were not private parts or buttocks equally vulnerable? How were arctic lavatories constructed, either at winter quarters or on the march? Alas, turn-of-the-century polar diarists revealed almost nothing.

William Smith, the Admiralty's chief constructor, dismissed the problem: Writing about the *Discovery* in *Transactions of the Institute of Naval Architects* for June 1905, he touched on sanitary requirements:

> . . . Owing to the severe climatic conditions, these matters were very important both afloat and ashore. The arrangements ashore were especially difficult, and Captain Scott met them in the resourceful manner characteristic of British seamen.

Intriguing yet baffling!

An anonymous officer who sailed with Nares in 1875 used the revealing term "ice closet," polar usage for the temperate Briton's water closet. This same explorer allowed, too, that an upturned sledge served for what his fellow Victorians referred to as a chamber utensil or close stool.

American explorers were no more forthright than their British colleagues. Adolphus Greely's memoir confirms the existence of a "urine tub" within the invalid's tent at Camp Clay; emptying this vessel served as punishment for the obstreperous. Lieutenant Robert Peary, his countryman, remarked that for sledge travel he wore Eskimo regalia, with the exception of its birdskin undershirt. In place of it he recommended a flannel vest with a double layer stitched across the lower back "so as to prevent too active a stimulation to the kidneys." In all his considerable polar output, this is Peary's single oblique reference to either bladder or bowel. Shackleton was equally reticent: He and Wild signaled the *Nimrod* from Hut Point with desperate ingenuity by igniting a carbide flare with their own urine, triumphantly surmounting Antarctica's chronic water shortage. But no acknowledgment of their enterprise appeared in the official record.

By contrast, a "nightstool" was listed solemnly on the manifest of the Swedish polar balloon *Eagle*, although on at least one occasion its use was foregone. An entry of unique candor in Andrée's diary reads: ". . . We lightened ship. Tee-hee." By 1910, men on the *Terra Nova*'s lower deck were even more explicit. Francis Davies, the ship's carpenter, recalled that whenever trawl nets were lowered over the stern, the bosun closed down the crew's forward head. But some ignored the edict, and occasionally, undesirable cloacal specimens were drawn up and tumbled out on deck, to the irritation of the scientific staff. From the same earthy pen comes the intelligence that crewmen sometimes were detailed to retrieve from the *Terra Nova*'s deck and rigging "telegrams," the messdeck term for fragments of used toilet paper that garnished the ship with a following wind.

Recently, Sir Charles Wright, Scott's physicist on the *Terra Nova*, recalled that urinating into the snow inside the tent had been commonplace save when assigned to the commander's tent; Scott's rule was "outdoors," regardless of the temperature. This was not easy. How, lamented one exasperated officer on Admiral Byrd's first expedition, did one coax a two-inch penis through six inches of clothing? Frostbite of that particular member apparently is not a problem: A correspondent from Alaska writes that private parts exposed to subzero temperatures sustain no damage due to body warmth of both urine and groin. (The groin or fork, as he called it, was the only part of Cherry-Garrard's body that never grew cold during his celebrated winter journey.) The U.S. Navy, incidentally, passes along an urgent Antarctic *caveat* to novice personnel not to urinate close to sledge dogs that have not yet breakfasted: Cold, hungry animals have been known to leap savagely for exposed genitalia unbuttoned within range. Let it be noted, too, as final observation about this neglected subject, that urine voided in low temperatures has the appearance of boiling water. In fact, Eskimos hunting arctic reindeer often track their quary by the cloud of white urine vapor that remains suspended in the chill long after the creatures have decamped.

By the time the *Nimrod's* shore party had established itself in the Cape Royds hut, no time remained for autumn sledging. Instead, a successful ascent was made to the summit of Mount Erebus, a challenging adventure that produced one casualty: Sir Philip Brocklehurst, a young man who had secured a berth on the expedition by investing in it, fell down a slope while wearing no boots. Clambering back up, he sustained such serious frostbite that a big toe later had to be amputated by Eric Marshall, one of the two surgeons. Undaunted, the patient hobbled proudly around winter quarters carrying his detached extremity preserved in a bottle of alcohol.

His injury disqualified Brocklehurst from inclusion in the polar party, as did the poor health of another, Ernest Joyce, a petty officer candidate. (There were few other undertakings in Edwardian times for which a baronet and a petty officer were equally eligible, an interesting sidelight on the practical democracy of polar sledging.) Moreover, Shackleton's plan had had to be revised in the light of his ponies' attrition: The four surviving animals could drag only enough food for four explorers. The quartet would include, in addition to Shackleton, surgeon Marshall; Jameson Adams, a merchant sailor; and Frank Wild, whose antarctic career had been and would remain closely interwoven with his leader's. Yorkshireman Wild, although only an able seaman, was a direct descendant of Captain Cook and had served in both Merchant and Royal navies; he had first sailed south with Scott on the *Discovery* and would be named second-in-command of the *Endurance*.

In late September 1908, depot-laying began. Ponies, preserved against the day of the journey itself, were left behind as six men, including the polar party, set out to establish Depot "A" 120 miles to the south. Although they were to manhaul for the entire round trip, they started off in motorized *luxe*, sledges drawn by Bernard Day at the wheel of the temperamental motorcar. Once onto the Ross Barrier, they were in for a bitterly cold slog. By October 6, Shackleton and his five companions had persevered to 79°36', where a modest depot was left: 167

pounds of maize—four days' rations for four ponies—and a gallon of paraffin. It was completely out of sight of land, a speck in the Barrier's void marked by an upturned sledge topped with a black flag.

By the time they returned to Arrival Bay, their rations were nearly exhausted, a haunting déjà vu of things to come. On the sea ice near Cape Royds, the Arrol-Johnston met them again and took both sledges in tow. Only two weeks later, four of the exhausted men would turn back south for a try at the pole. A support party, including Brocklehurst and Joyce, were to accompany them as far as Depot A.

Shackleton's southern journey began in brilliant sunlight on October 29, four days earlier than the one on which he and Wilson had accompanied Scott five years earlier. After Day's motorcar had chugged off with the advance party's sledges, the polar party departed in comparative silence. Leading horses over firm snow is placid, a far cry from the cursing, yelping turmoil of driving dogs. With a man trudging at the head of his charge, the flotilla of sledges moved in dreamlike quiet. There was no rataplan of landbound hooves: Jackson had discovered that ponies were surer-footed unshod, and Shackleton followed his example. Nor was there the jingle of harness; all buckles had been wrapped in leather to prevent irritation of the animals' skins.

As the ponies sweated along, ice clad their shaded flanks and they risked chafing galls. An especially designed, broad leather band traversed their chests, attached to the sledge's whippletree by alpine rope traces.

For the entire month of November, conditions were salutary. The party progressed three hundred miles due south, reeling off a respectable fifteen miles each day. Occasionally, blizzards confined them to tent and sleeping bag, animals and men alike devouring precious rations with no progress to show for it. (One advantage of motorized haulage is that idle machines consume no fuel; animals eat regardless.) But they reached Depot A by the morning of November 15. During the redistribution of supplies that followed, a small can of black-currant jam and another of sardines, earmarked as Christmas treats, had, reluctantly, to be left behind; those few ounces of inessential luxuries were, among nearly a ton of supplies, considered superfluous.

Shackleton found the Barrier surface "as wayward and changeful as the sea." Whether burnished sastrugi, breakable crust, or deep snow, the terrain was invariably a hindrance to the ponies. Either they skidded and slipped, plunged through one or more successive layers of crust, or floundered girth-deep. Breakable crust was tormenting, not only from the effort of extricating hooves after each pace but from the abrading and wounding of their fetlocks against the jagged ice edge as well. All of them developed galls just above the hoof. Overnight they fared little better, tethered between two sledges along a wire rope. Too cold to lie down, they were caparisoned in wool rugs and huddled through the night, frosted hindquarters turned into the wind. Each morning before they were harnessed up, compacted snow had to be scraped from under their hooves, frozen accretion from the night's pawing and stamping.

It seems curious that simple expedients were not followed to improve the ponies' lot. Traveling by night rather than day (a common arctic practice) would have made for a firmer crust, less glare, and warmer camping while the sun was up. Apparently Shackleton preferred the slicker surface of the wet daytime snow. Never once did his men erect snow walls, wind barriers that would have protected their animals from blizzards. Though the labor at each halt was exhausting, the men on Scott's second expedition did as much for their ponies. Perhaps most inexplicable was Shackleton's failure to have equipped his animals with *hester-trugers,* Norwegian snowshoes designed for horses in deep snow. No mention is made of these invaluable devices anywhere in the *Nimrod* memoirs. Mentioned, instead, in Shackleton's diary were entries such as: ". . . the ponies struggling gamely . . . constantly broke through the crust . . . surface . . . appallingly soft . . . sinking in up to their hocks . . . the ponies, who, poor beasts, had to plough through a truly awful surface . . ." Compassion is a poor substitute for foresight. Shackleton's shortsighted omission of *trugers* may have compromised the pole.

Poor Chinaman gave out first, fetlocks galled and pathetically crippled. On the evening of November 21, he was taken out of sight and shot, then butchered by Wild and the surgeon in haste before his dripping flesh chilled into stone. The following morning, four men and three ponies trudged on, leaving behind Chinaman Depot; two hindquarters lay buried at the foot of his upturned sledge, guyed by his redundant harness. From that day on, fried pony appeared on their menu, and slivers of Chinaman, warmed in the midday sun, served as invaluable thirst quenchers on the march. A week later (two days after they had passed Scott's farthest south), Grisi gave out and was shot, followed three days later by Quan. There is no telling how long Socks might have lasted; although he nickered and whinnied mournfully tethered alone at night, the resolute little beast stayed in harness for an additional week. His end was very nearly the end of the southern party.

It was the afternoon of December 7. The weather was good, almost too good; the men marched in pajama jackets. For three days they had been toiling up what Shackleton had first called "an open road to the south"; subsequently he would christen it the Beardmore Glacier, after his most bountiful patron. Fortuitous chance had brought Shackleton's party directly to the foot of an enormous sloping ice sheet that pierced the mountain chain crossing their path. Ascent of this "road" was not without hazard: The Beardmore is one of the world's largest glaciers. Where it meets the immovable Ross Barrier, both ice masses buckle, truncate, and fracture into a maze of crevasses.

Shackleton, Adams, and Marshall were in the van, pulling the first sledge. Wild, following deliberately in their tested tracks, led Socks and the second sledge. Wild walked ahead of, rather than beside, the animal, urging it up the slope, a precaution that saved his life. Suddenly the halter was whisked out of his mittened grasp; with "a rushing wind," the pony vanished. The sledge lay stopped at the edge of an abyss. A snow bridge that had borne the separate weight of four men and the first sledge had given way under Socks's hooves. So precipitously did the pony drop that the shock shattered the whippletree, the swiveling wooden bar to which the traces were attached. Pony, harness, and traces had vanished. Wild barely escaped a similar fate: Falling backward across the crevasse, he hung on to its northern edge and was rescued by his three companions. Neither sight nor sound of poor Socks came from the black depth that yawned in front of his sledge. Had the sledge gone, too, half their fuel and supplies, and two irreplaceable sleeping bags, would have been lost as well.

With no ponies left, Shackleton and his men continued

manhauling up the glacier. Despite low rations, superhuman exertions, and the increasing altitude, their health was tolerably good. They did suffer from the standard polar discomfort, split and bleeding lips—an affliction, recorded a deadpan Shackleton, that kept them from laughing too much. They were never *not* hungry: Socks's loss, both in harness and in the stewpot, had been keenly felt, even though the remnants of his maize fodder, ground between two flat stones, proved an invaluable if less digestible substitute. Another irritant was snow blindness. Their eyes, curiously, were most susceptible during the shadowless white glare of overcast days. Although equipped with orange-tinted goggles, they were often compelled to remove them: Prospecting for crevasses or the snow bridges that conceal them was difficult with goggles. Yet taking them off hastened incapacitating snow blindness. In its severest stage, the eyes drip ceaseless tears (which consolidate in the beard as ice) until the eyes close up altogether. Cocaine or a wash of zinc sulphate relieved the pain and swelling. (One of the best treatments, perfected four years later by Birdie Bowers, was a poultice of used tea leaves; tannic acid proved most soothing.)

Yet with or without goggles, the Beardmore's crevasses continually hampered them. All four men broke through continually, saved from death by their harnesses; Wild compared their progress to strolling across the glass roof of a railway station. Somehow they still averaged ten miles a day, a hard-fought ten miles up icy slopes for which they had no crampons. Often they had to chop a level patch for their camp and, in the absence of loose snow, weight the tents' skirts with ration boxes. Every one of Shackleton's diary entries for the second half of December predicted that the next day should see them over the glacier's crest, onto the polar plateau, surfaced with the same hard snow that Scott had found atop the Western Mountains in 1903.

On the twenty-fifth, a Christmas feast was improvised: first an amplified hoosh of maize, pemmican, Oxo, and ground biscuit, followed by a tiny plum pudding, cocoa, a spoonful apiece of medicinal brandy and crème de menthe, and, from some jealously guarded hoard, four cigars. There was much to celebrate besides Christmas: They were camped at nearly 86° South. Warmed and encouraged by a full stomach, Shackleton predicted that night that they would reach the pole by January 12.

But, alas, the plateau toward which they had been struggling proved just as trying as the 130 miles of glacier they had surmounted: Temperatures plummeted and summer blizzards raged. Deep snow dragged at their sledges, and a cutting wind roared out of the south into their faces. The savage weather on the long-awaited plateau might have sprung full-blown from Shackleton's favorite poem, Browning's *Prospice:*

> When the snows begin, and the blasts denote
> I am nearing the place,
> The power of the night, the press of the storm,
> The post of the foe.

Without doubt, they were "nearing the place." But could their health and equipment hold out? Everything was breaking down. Want prevailed—want of food, want of warmth, want of rest. Rations were grotesquely inadequate, their Christmas hoosh a haunting memory. They were dragging only 70 pounds apiece, but to their weakened bodies it felt just as arduous as the 250 pounds they had wrestled up the Beardmore just after Socks had been killed. Their body temperatures, Marshall discovered, hovered at about 94°. Frostbite was commonplace. Atop the plateau, two miles high, they suffered from migraine headaches and nosebleeds. The sledges moved obstinately; all spare parts had been depoted back with their heavier clothing; worn and split runners crabbed the sledges sideways. Sennegrass was running low, and their *finnesko*, as well as the lamp-wick that bound them to their feet, were disintegrating.

This deterioration in well-being worked insidiously on the most gallant of wills. A week before Shackleton would turn back, less than a hundred miles short of his goal, the changing tone of his diary entries anticipated the decision. Entries became cryptic; cold and exhaustion abbreviated style into a shorthand of despair. There were syntactic indications as well: Intent turned into speculation about what could or should have been done, into advice for those who might follow, from the need for more food to the necessity for scissors to trim beards so they would not ice so painfully to their collars.

There was a shift, too, in anticipated distances, less concern with how far to latitude 90° than how far back to Cape Royds. On New Year's Day 1909, at 87° South, Shackleton wrote that they had only "three weeks' food and two weeks' biscuit to do nearly 500 geographical miles." He faced the explorer's Catch-22, that each poleward mile carried with it a diabolical matching grant of return slogging, requiring just as much food and effort. This double jeopardy tested the resolve of all polar commanders, whether Nansen struggling north over the frozen sea, Amundsen forcing his vessel west through the Canadian shallows, Nordenskjöld persevering around Cape Chelyuskin, or Shackleton plodding south over that bleak white plain at the bottom of the world. At the moment when his logistical mainspring was wound to breaking point came time for Shackleton's toughest decision: reward or return?

He called it quits on January 6, temporizing that if he did not get back alive, then "all results will be lost to the world." He did promise that, the next day, he and his men would leave everything behind for a rush south to "plant the flag." (They carried two Union Jacks, one of their own and the other a present from Queen Alexandra.) But even this compromise would be dearly bought. They awoke the next morning to a fearsome blizzard. Gale-force winds tore at their tents, forcing a fine swirl of driven snow within. Again at the mercy of the plateau's capricious climate, they endured a limbo of neither advance nor retreat for two and a half days, consuming precious rations. The tent became increasingly confining as the canvas bowed inward from snow accumulation outside. Four cold, hungry men lay in their damp sleeping bags for sixty hours with nothing to read and little more to eat, their feet continually drifting over that numbing threshold of frostbite, roused to aching sensation only when warmed against a comrade's body.

It stopped snowing at one o'clock on the morning of January 9, though the gale sustained its fury. After a meager breakfast, the polar party raced south—literally running partway—over fresh-burnished snow with no sledges at their heels. At nine they stopped and thrust a tentpole into the crust, letting both flags in turn ripple and snap in the blast. Shackleton held the camera, posing his three companions for the historic photograph: Adams, Marshall, and Wild stood in line, looking like goblins with their bulky, windproof anoraks, *finnesko*-shod feet wrapped in lampwick, and, withdrawn inside Burberry hoods, white-frosted beards. They might have been in a photographer's studio, arrayed before a white cloth draped from floor to ceiling. But they stood, in fact, at 88°23′ South, only ninety-seven geographical miles short of their coveted objective, nearer to either pole than man had ever stood before.

After claiming the plateau for his sovereign, Shackleton rolled up both flags and stood for a moment, eyes squinting painfully through binoculars into the compelling desolation ahead. He saw nothing. Then, for the first time in more than two months, he turned his men back north.

Their return to McMurdo Sound was made in desperate haste, a keen wind at their backs. With a sail bent onto their one remaining sledge, the party raced from depot to depot, failure to find any one of which would have doomed them. On January 19, their last day on what Shackleton called "that awful plateau," they made a record run of nearly thirty miles. A week later, still retracing their outward tracks, they bucked horrendous odds with only ounces of food to carry them forty miles to the next depot. Half a mile short of Lower Glacial Depot, Marshall had to press on alone to retrieve rations for his three famished companions. They were back on the Barrier.

Some of the depoted pony meat had become tainted, and the explorers suffered crippling attacks of dysentery. During a subsequent respite at Depot A, the Christmas can of black-currant jam was mixed with crumbled biscuit to produce a splendid pudding. But the great glut came later, at Bluff Depot, established in their absence by the conscientious Joyce. With only cocoa and crumbs remaining, they saw a flag-bedecked heap of plenty stacked atop a snow mound ten feet tall. Shackleton clambered up and rolled down an avalanche of luxuries—biscuits, jam, fruit, even eggs from the recently arrived *Nimrod*—so much food that the explorers improvised a second cooker from an empty biscuit can. Five days later, Shackleton and Wild left Marshall, still plagued with dysentery, in Adams's care; they reached Hut Point and contacted the waiting *Nimrod*. The southern was the last party in. The British Antarctic Expedition was over, south magnetic pole achieved, south pole an incredible near-miss. If his ponies had been properly shod, even for the crevasse that swallowed poor Socks, Shackleton might have brought it off. For want of sixteen *trugers*. . . .

Worldwide release of Shackleton's stunning exploit came in late March 1909, first appearing in the columns of London's *Daily Mail;* they had paid for exclusive rights to his story. Shackleton contented himself with a triumphant signal to Emily (far briefer than the distressing one sent from the *Morning* in 1903):

ABSOLUTELY FIT HOME JUNE VIA INDIA

(*"India"* was, in this case, a ship rather than the colony.) Among hundreds of cables that deluged him in New Zealand, none pleased Shackleton more than one from his old school, Dulwich College: The entire student body—720 boys—had contributed a penny each to finance a congratulatory wire to their suddenly most famous old boy. From Major Leonard Darwin, the new president of the Royal Geographical Society, came an invitation to address a general meeting, with its implication of a gold medal. Sculptors at Madame Tussaud's rushed a fur-clad likeness of the explorer to exhibition, photographs of which several impatient newspaper editors published in lieu of actual pictures.

The man himself landed at Dover's Admiralty Pier in June, as promised, to be met by Emily. The two children remained in London, in an enormous crowd waiting at Charing Cross Station. During the weeks that followed, Shackleton was lionized, the recipient of all the kudos denied Scott in 1904. The press hailed Shackleton as "the Nansen of the South." "It is difficult," wrote one reporter, "to sing the praises and feats of a man like Lieutenant Shackleton without risk of gush."

For his first great lecture, the first polar expedition recorded on motion picture film, Royal Albert Hall was packed. The Prince of Wales awarded him the RGS Patron's Medal, "from one sailor to another." It had first been proposed by Sir Clements when word of the farthest south had reached London.

In the ensuing months, the aging ex-president tempered his earlier enthusiasm, questioning the accuracy of Shackleton's observations. In an unpublished critique of Shackleton's book *The Heart of the Antarctic,* Sir Clements unburdened himself in part:

So that there is nothing remarkable in Shackleton's journey up the glacier and over the icecap. What makes his feat remarkable is the hurried return over 300 miles of ice barrier with insufficient food, owing to faulty arrangements. . . . The object was to make a dash to the highest latitude he could possibly reach. This was not business and not exploring. . . .

Between the lines, it is not hard to see the old man's displeasure that Shackleton had eclipsed his protégé. But another member of the RGS, Scott Keltie, wrote:

You have done more in a few weeks than Peary has been able to do in 12 years.

Scott and Shackleton met several times that summer, first at Charing Cross Station and, five days later, at a Savage Club house dinner. Scott introduced the guest of honor:

If I had a hand in rocking his antarctic cradle, I am very proud of it, and I think you will allow that he is a healthy product of that cradle. . . .

Shackleton responded tactfully:

I cannot forget that the pioneer of antarctic travel is sitting in the chair here tonight. . . .

He then accepted his election to an honorary life membership because "when the oil ran low, I ate raw pony."

That summer, while the *Nimrod*, on display in London and Liverpool, drew record crowds, Shackleton toured the Continent. In Paris he addressed a large gathering at the Sorbonne in bold if execrable French. Nansen was present in Oslo when Norway's king decorated Shackleton with the Order of Saint Olav, and Amundsen led a torchlight procession in his honor that night.

On his return to London, Shackleton was greeted with the electrifying news that Parliament had voted a twelve-thousand-pound Treasury grant that almost wiped out his expedition's deficit. In November came His Majesty's ultimate accolade: On the birthday list appeared the name of Sir Ernest

Shackleton, the first antarctic knighthood since Sir James Ross's, an honor withheld from Scott because of the controversy surrounding the *Discovery*'s relief.

Then followed a triumphant tour on the other side of the Atlantic. He arrived in Halifax during a blizzard with no carriage to meet him at the station; undaunted, Sir Ernest lashed his luggage and slides to a borrowed sled and trudged through snow drifts to the auditorium. At Carnegie Hall in New York, Robert Peary introduced him: "Ladies and gentlemen, a man!" Just before an Explorers Club dinner at the Belleclaire Hotel, a distraught manager reported that dinner would have to be canceled because the waiters were on strike. Shackleton's response brought the assembly to their feet: "Do not worry about us. Most of us are explorers and we can not only find any food you have concealed about the hotel but we are accustomed to waiting on ourselves."

Back in England, Hamley's, the Regent Street toy shop, was doing a brisk trade in a new drawing room game called "To The Pole With Shackleton." It was played on a large, circular papier-mâché board, painted white and grooved with concentric ridges of miniature sastrugi. Each player assumed the identity of a famous explorer and, equipped with special magnetic pencils, coaxed miniature sledges through a maze of tracks toward a central pole. False leads led to dead ends, and any player thus stymied could extricate his sled only by using a magnet of reversed polarity marked "DR. COOK."

That Frederick Cook was given this backhanded acknowledgment in a child's game mirrored a furor in the adult world that winter of 1909. Attention had shifted abruptly from antarctic to arctic, from Shackleton to two rival Americans: one was Cook, last encountered as de Gerlache's surgeon on board the *Belgica;* the other was Robert Peary. Their acrimonious dispute over who had reached the north pole first—or, indeed, reached it at all!—lingers to this day.

12

RUCKUS OVER THE NORTH POLE

*There is but one way to find the pole
and that is to go, go, go until you find it.*
—Captain Bradley Osborn
at an Arctic Club dinner in 1906

The two men had started as colleagues. Fresh out of medical school in 1891, Cook had answered Peary's newspaper advertisement for the post of surgeon and ethnologist on a major expedition to North Greenland. This was the Brooklyn-born doctor's first arctic venture and the second of its commander: Peary's only prior experience in the North had been his reconnaissance of the Greenland icecap behind Disko in 1886. Now he and Cook embarked on the whaleship *Kite*, together with four other explorers, one of them, astonishingly, a woman.

The only spouse ever to accompany her husband to high latitudes, Josephine Diebitsch Peary, established herself as undisputed chatelaine of Red Fern House, Peary's winter quarters above the icefoot of McCormick Bay. She was not universally popular with her husband's subordinates. One of them, John Verhoeff, who had paid for the privilege of joining and would perish in a crevasse, found Mrs. Peary overbearing, especially during her husband's extended absence inland. But both Pearys felt it was a success and, in 1893, on another North Greenland expedition, went one better: When they embarked on the *Falcon* in June of that year, Josephine was six months pregnant. A daughter, Marie Louise Ahnighito, was born that September in Anniversary Lodge at latitude 77°40′ North. The child was delivered with the combined assistance of surgeon Edward Vincent and Mrs. Cross, a midwife brought north to care for mother and child. Young Marie flourished and, among Eskimos who flocked to marvel at her extraordinary complexion, was known as the Snow Baby.

Cook seems to have done well on the earlier expedition, but one must guess at this, for Peary was uncommunicative about the performance of his men. One senses that Peary expeditions were all business, without many jokes or games. Peary admitted that he preferred few colleagues in the field, the fewer the better; the thirteen crowded into winter quarters in 1893–94 he rated too large a company. They were apparently an unhappy company as well: Several complained later of sharing short commons at one chilly end of Anniversary Lodge while their commander and his family kept themselves comfortably apart at the other. Morale was parlously low. The following summer, the *Falcon* took all but Peary and two male companions south, including Josephine, Mrs. Cross, and the Snow Baby; but morale remained low. Even on all-male expeditions to follow, Peary seemed remote from his subordinates, far more gregarious with the Eskimos than with his fellow white men.

His most faithful companion was not white at all. This was the legendary Matthew Henson, to whom Peary referred, in the patronizing terms of the period, as "my colored man, Henson, a dark-skinned, kinky-haired child of the equator." Henson was handsome, slim, and dapper, a skilled carpenter as well as a crack sledge driver. His background had been nautical; he had sailed as a cabin boy and been taught to read and write by an enlightened sailing master. After a spell ashore as a stevedore on the Baltimore docks, he became a clerk at B. H. Steinmetz & Sons, the Washington outfitters. It was there, in August 1887, that young Lieutenant Peary came in to buy a pith helmet for his Nicaraguan tour. Mr. Steinmetz himself had recommended Henson as a first-class body servant, and Peary offered him the post. Guided by, as Henson termed it, "the instinct of my race," he accepted Peary's offer and stayed on with him for three decades, service that would take him, ultimately, to the pole.

Dr. Cook's arctic appetite had only been whetted after his return from North Greenland in 1892. He started his Brooklyn practice with sights set longingly on further polar work. He favored the south pole rather than north, convinced that further northern undertaking would lead to inevitable entanglement with his former commander, an accurate foretaste of problems to follow. After formally announcing plans for an antarctic expedition to the American Geographical Society, he set about raising money.

Two summer outings resulted. First, he sailed north on the yacht *Zeta* in 1893, returning that fall with a trunkload of artifacts and, like Charles Francis Hall before him, an Eskimo couple, Mikok and Kalahkatah, whom he renamed Willie and Clara. Cook took them on a lecture tour, playing to packed houses who came to gape at kayaks, harpoons, and perspiring, fur-clad Eskimos while listening spellbound to the lecturer's gripping arctic scenarios. He was an amusing and attractive speaker, with all the charm that Peary lacked; open, friendly features were framed by a crew cut and beard. After several lectures, he had raised some of the money for his proposed antarctic expedition, and he turned tour leader the following summer to raise the balance.

Cook chartered the British-built eleven-hundred-ton steamer *Miranda*—"as safe or safer in this vessel as in an Atlantic liner"—and offered berths at five hundred dollars apiece for a summer's cruise in the arctic; ports of call would include historic sites—Polaris Bay and Hall's grave—as well as Peary's latest encampment on Bowdoin Bay. Cook advertised for four classes of passengers, "tourist, sportsman, scientist, and artist." Over fifty men responded, largely hunters and academics, one of them only thirteen years old, and the *Miranda* sailed from New York on July 7, 1894.

Had any of her passengers bothered to probe the history of their cruise ship, they would have uncovered her uncanny propensity for collision, one off Point Judith and another, in the East River's Hell Gate, that had only recently sent her to the bottom. Leaving her East River pier, the *Miranda* plowed forward rather than out into the stream, colliding with some lighters; undismayed, Captain William Farrell set his course for the arctic. En route to Newfoundland, every seal or whale that came within range was peppered with fusillades from dozens of expensive sporting rifles. Later, mutinous crewmen belowdecks broke into the wine stores and went on an ugly rampage.

The *Miranda*'s next collision occurred in the Strait of Belle Isle. Running at full speed through thick fog, she struck an iceberg and had to return to St. John for repairs. While there, some of Cook's more apprehensive clients caucused, proposing an alternate cruise around the United Kingdom instead; but a majority outvoted them, opting to continue on their promised arctic itinerary.

Bow plating restored, the ship sailed for Greenland in late July and suffered her final collision, with a reef. She was so badly damaged that Cook dispatched an open boat south for help. A Gloucester fishing schooner was summoned, the ninety-two-foot *Rigel*, whose master agreed to relinquish the balance of his season for four thousand dollars. Cook paid up and his passengers were transferred to the *Rigel*, accommodated in the afterhold on mattresses laid atop a bed of salt. Then the schooner was taken in tow by the faltering steamer. Two days later, the *Miranda* sank. The tow rope was severed and her crew rowed aft to the already overladen *Rigel*. In three weeks she reached Halifax, where a sister ship of the *Miranda*, the *Portia*, had arrived to take the arctic tourists back to New York. She seemed just as jinxed as her late sister: On the ninth of September, fogbound off Martha's Vineyard, she ran down the *Dora M. French*, cutting her in half and drowning all but one of her crew.

The most astonishing aftermath was that the day before the *Dora M. French* was rammed, Cook's apparently resilient tourists, although described by a *New York Herald* reporter as "pinched and haggard," had gathered in the smoking room to form The Arctic Club, inviting officers of both the *Miranda* and the *Rigel* to join as well.

Although founded lightheartedly to commemorate a summer's misadventure, the club grew swiftly in both numbers and prestige. Students of the period will recognize this as typical of pre–World War I boiled-shirt bonhomie, when prosperous, newly urban Americans, inveterate joiners, embraced everything with the right outdoor vibes. Within a few years, its membership comprised a kind of "Who's Who in Arctic America": Generals Greely and Brainard, Admiral Schley, Admiral George Melville, and Amos Bonsall, last surviving member of Kane's expedition on the *Advance*.

The club's business was serious as well as informative. A newsletter advised members of arctic and antarctic affairs. Honorary members from abroad—Shackleton, Scott, Amundsen, and the Duke of the Abruzzi—dined whenever passing through New York. Although initially academic, the membership grew to include merchants, explorers, service officers, and bankers—indeed, anyone who either had a stake in or cared passionately for exploration in high latitudes. Cook and Peary were both members in good standing.

Dr. Cook did finally get to Antarctica, but not in command of his own expedition. For three years after the *Miranda* debacle, he continued practicing medicine in Brooklyn, serving as one of The Arctic Club's guiding lights. In the summer of 1897 he read in the *New York Sun* that the *Belgica*'s proposed surgeon had bowed out. Cook cabled de Gerlache, suggesting himself as a replacement. The Belgian wired his acceptance and, that fall, Cook joined the ship in Montevideo.

Meanwhile, Peary was plugging away in the arctic. Twice—once in 1892 and again in 1894—he slogged across North Greenland to its undiscovered northeastern coast, establishing its insularity without question. In 1899, using Fort Conger as a base, he followed in Lieutenant Lockwood's footsteps, trekking past America's farthest north to establish his own record 83°39'. Miles past Cape Washington, the farthest headland that Lockwood had seen, Peary and Henson planted their flag on what they called Cape Morris Jesup. Written word, wrapped in burlap inside a tin box, was left in a cairn, signed by Peary on behalf of the Peary Arctic Club, a name very similar to that chosen by the amiable alumni of the *Miranda* cruise but, in fact, a very different organization.

Morris Ketchum Jesup, a rich New York banker and philanthropist, was president of the American Museum of Natural History. Together with other influential Americans on the order of J. P. Morgan and Joseph Choate, he had been one of the museum's original incorporators in 1869. As Markham was to

Scott, so Jesup was to Peary. When Josephine Peary was looking for funds to send a ship north for her husband during the
winter of 1894–95, Jesup was on her list of potential donors.
He promised help: two thousand dollars toward the cost of
chartering a whaler as well as introductions to other benefac-
tors. Jesup admired Mrs. Peary's spunk. Moreover, by contributing to her cause, he effected an advantageous quid pro quo
for his museum: In return for his assistance, Mrs. Peary promised him the bulk of her husband's specimens and artifacts
from North Greenland. It marked the start of a profitable relationship between explorer and collector. In 1896 and again in
1897, the American Museum of Natural History sponsored two
additional Peary expeditions, mounted to excavate and retrieve a trio of Cape York meteorites, first located by Sir James
Ross in 1818. Two of these—"the dog" and "the woman"—
were relative lightweights, but the third, called "the tent," was
a massive one hundred tons of celestial iron that taxed Peary's
ingenuity to the utmost before it was laboriously jacked up and
winched on board the good ship *Hope*. The three meteorites are
on display to this day at the museum, historical symbols of
Peary's fortitude and Jesup's acquisitiveness. Peary never forgot his benefactor: On his last polar march, in 1909, his northernmost camp was named after the Peary Arctic Club's
founder/president, who had died just over a year before his
protégé's lifework was to be achieved.

Jesup had organized the club in the spring of 1898, specifically to provide some measure of financial continuity to
Peary's polar work. The original conception—twenty-five
members who would contribute a thousand dollars a year for
four years—fell short of the mark by two thirds: Only eight
men signed up before Peary sailed that summer, the first of
four brutal sledging seasons that would see the end of his involvement with Greenland as a route to the pole and the loss,
by gangrenous frostbite, of all but one of his toes.

In fact, the Peary Arctic Club was less a club than a syndicate
of rich, determined men who were betting on Peary's ability to
reach the pole. Most had never traveled north of the arctic
circle; their concern for polar exploration was surpassed by
their ability to write large checks on demand. Just before
Peary's final gambit in 1908, for instance, Zenas Crane, a Mas-
sachusetts paper tycoon, volunteered a ten-thousand-dollar

gift, munificence that guaranteed him the vice presidency of the club.

This unique polar consortium was a very real necessity. Despite his naval commission, Peary never received any federal money for his arctic work. In fact, exploration cost him money, for during all but his last expedition, he was on leave of absence at half pay. Unlike Scott, he did not serve as an officer of the line; Peary moved in the less glamorous, workaday Navy of the Bureau of Yards and Docks. But even had he commanded a dreadnought, he would have fared no better. Quite simply, Congress evinced no interest in polar exploration following the triple disasters of Hall, De Long, and Greely. Half a century would elapse before Admiral Byrd would rekindle his country's polar ambition. So Peary had grubbed for backing by publishing, lecturing, and wringing grants from geographical societies before Jesup came to his aid.

Peary was a quintessential diamond in the rough. Whatever he was to garner in the way of international prestige, he never lost Maine's reassuringly rural stamp; indeed, his involvement with his home state continued throughout his life. He was a loyal Bowdoin alumnus; the *Roosevelt*, his polar vessel, was built in a Rockport shipyard; his snowshoes came from Dunham; his first U.S. port of call after reaching the pole was Portland; he retired to an island in Casco Bay, in a house literally lashed to the rugged coastal rocks he loved; and in Arlington National Cemetery, his tomb is marked by a massive globe chiseled out of white Portland marble.

Peary looked the part as well, boasting a homespun look that never left him. As a young man, his taste in civilian clothes verged on the raffish, all patent leather and loud checks encouraged by provincial haberdashers. He sported a long walrus mustache.

But despite his country airs, Peary fitted in well, a bona fide member of the Peary Arctic Club by instinct if not income. When he was president of the Explorers Club, Peary introduced Shackleton at a club dinner in 1910, welcoming him as "a man of our class." Did he mean "our class of explorer" or "our *social* class"? Most probably the latter. As pronounced as the maleness of the heroic age was its adherence to class. The men in polar command were cut from the same cloth as the men who backed them. Black body servants or able seamen as seconds-in-command were all very well, but the leaders had to be officer material. However arduous the trek, however brutal the conditions, however prolonged the absence, when he returned home, the commander had to belong, breaking bread and making the right small talk with those on whose behalf he had sailed. It was perfectly acceptable in the field to wear the same shirt for months on end, but it was essential at home to don a stiff shirt with ease at a testimonial dinner.

An important aspect of Peary's personal life was the nature of his relationship with the two women who meant most to him. It has been said that he grew up as a mother's boy. Certainly, classic psychological forces shaped his childhood: He was the only son of a mother widowed when the boy was three years old. She never remarried, dedicating herself single-handedly to raising Robert. There was just enough money to keep up appearances. Mary Peary was all things to Robert—mother, father, and sibling. He remained a shy, friendless boy, a loner. When he went to Bowdoin, his mother came with him, settling for four years in Brunswick to be near her son. Peary was a serious, self-contained, and ambitious scholar. He shunned team sports in favor of solo feats demanding strength and endurance, always testing himself against punishing physical odds (shades of Amundsen!).

Peary's transition from son to husband was not without pitfalls. After ten years in the Navy, he married Josephine Diebitsch, a pretty Washington girl. She learned to steer a tactful course through the complexities of her husband's and mother-in-law's ancient alliance. It could not have been easy: Mrs. Peary accompanied the couple on their honeymoon to the New Jersey shore. (Small wonder that Josephine sailed to the arctic with her Bert, as she called him; at least Mama stayed at home.)

No polar wife ever served her husband more faithfully, as lecturer, writer, and fund-raiser. Her most demanding role was that of single parent. The Pearys had two children, Marie (the Snow Baby) and, born in 1903, Robert, Jr. Marie wrote her father plaintively and said her friends thought of her as an orphan, since Peary was away so frequently. Whereas Nansen had relinquished polar work for his family, Peary never did.

The ironic result for his children was that he passed on to them the dominant omission of his childhood: They grew up in the same fatherless household he had known in Maine.

But those punishing years served him well as an explorer. By the time he reached the pole in 1909, more than half his adult life had been spent grappling with the arctic. He had survived eight northern winters, sledging hundreds of miles under all conditions and absorbing the Eskimos' skill and ingenuity. In terms of arctic travel he had no equal, and, from the very beginning, had been in command. Unlike Nansen, he was not a *skilöbber;* but he was comfortably at home with the cold and made none of the neophyte's mistakes or, at least, if he did, we are not privy to them.

He adapted to snow and cold like a native. Additionally, he had proven theories about every aspect of polar sledging. He preferred a minimum number of colleagues in the field, and those selected were, by his own criterion, "small, wiry men." He had devised a height/weight formula: no more than 2½ pounds for every inch of height. (Six-foot Matthew Henson was at pains never to exceed an optimum weight of 180 pounds.) Smaller men, Peary pointed out, eat less and take up less space in an igloo. He also preferred sledgers who neither smoked nor drank, sparing himself an addictive and hence dependent companion. The only exception to this rule was pipe-smoking Bob Bartlett, skipper of the *Roosevelt* and as tough a sledger as Henson.

Polar travel obsessed Peary wherever he was. He once bought some war surplus boarding pikes that, when shortened, proved admirable for breaking trail. In a steelyard, he found just the right width and tensility of steel to serve as sledge runners. The Peary sledge was his own invention, adapted from a shorter Eskimo original; it was higher than the Nansen sledge and so avoided too much punishing contact with ice pinnacles. He never made dog harness from walrus hide because the dogs were forever eating it; instead, he made do with canvas banding, his traces made from braided linen. Even the venerable Primus stove came under his relentless scrutiny: He perfected an improved burner that brought a gallon of icy slush to a boil in five minutes flat.

In the matter of clothing, Peary borrowed, as had Kane, his famous arctic forebear, from the Eskimos. Peary dressed from head to foot in seal, fox, reindeer, and bear fur. Only animal skins, he insisted, kept out the wind; in addition, they were less likely to absorb stiffening moisture. The most notorious accumulators of moisture were tents and sleeping bags. Peary never used either, even though some of his men did. He slept in the open like his dogs, curled up in the lee of a sledge, torso encased in traveling fur, arms withdrawn inside his sleeves, Eskimo fashion, and legs encased in fur leggings. Only in the bitterest cold did he build an igloo.

Deviating further from the polar norm, Peary seldom warmed his pemmican, preferring to gnaw on frozen chunks of it instead. Anything eaten uncooked on a sledge journey saved fuel consumption, and the absence of fuel as well as tent and sleeping bag meant that he could carry many more days' rations. Peary suggested that had Shackleton followed his example, he would have had sufficient food to reach the south pole.

In 1902, his sixteenth year in the arctic, Peary abandoned his lifelong preoccupation with Greenland and set out instead from the northern shore of Canada's Grant Land, over the same ice that had defeated Lieutenant Beaumont twenty-six years earlier. He carried neither kayak nor cutter. He, Henson, and two Eskimos sledged north of 84° before turning back, farther north than the Cape Morris Jesup try of 1899 but short of the Duke of the Abruzzi's record northing of 1900 in Franz Josef Land, news of which greeted the American on his return to the United States.

Peary's spirits at that homecoming were uncharacteristically low. Four years in the arctic without a break had left their mark on him: At forty-six, he was feeling his age. He had stayed on to the limit of the Navy's five-year leave of absence, loath to return without the coveted prize that both he and his backers felt his due. Now, Matthew Henson signed on temporarily as a Pullman car porter while Peary entered the hospital to have the stumps of his mutilated toes put right with corrective surgery. During a long recuperation, some of the old fire returned, and exploratory letters, dictated to the ever-faithful Josephine, reestablished contact with the patient investors of the Peary Arctic Club.

Some were disillusioned and begged off making any further "subscriptions"; even Morris Jesup seemed anxious for relief from the pressure of funding Peary's polar exploits. But others continued their support. Typical was Herbert Bridgman, publisher of the *Brooklyn Standard Union* and secretary/treasurer of the club. One of his fund-raising broadsides to his fellow members ran:

> We are simply undertaking to enable a friend in whom we have firm faith to achieve the greatest geographical feat, and to stand by him to the end in his effort to plant his country's flag where it can never be approached, much less hauled down. . . .

From his hospital bed, Peary assured them that he had evolved a foolproof means of reaching the pole. But an integral part of that plan was purchase of a more powerful ship. Up to that time, Peary had made do with a series of chartered or borrowed vessels, all of them inadequate for the task of getting him far enough north. One of the non-American club members, Alfred Harmsworth, had promised to reengine the old *Windward;* but he had reneged, and the whaler had never made it north of Cape Sabine in 1902. Josephine reported scathingly in a letter that "the ship cannot be sold even for firewood." (In fact, a Norwegian broker gave Peary eight thousand dollars for her.)

With those modest funds, Peary tried for a full year to buy a secondhand polar ship. He pestered the British Admiralty about purchasing Nares's *Discovery* and corresponded with Sir Clements Markham about the performance of Scott's *Discovery*, as well as the specifications for the *Morning*, just recently dispatched to bring the expedition home from Antarctica. He wondered if he could buy the Duke of the Abruzzi's *Stella Polare*, or the *Belgica* from the Belgians.

But always he dreamed of building his own. On April 1, 1903, he wrote to Bridgman:

> What a pity it is to be poor! I long for the good old days when souls were a marketable commodity and always in high demand by the devil. . . .

But by late summer, Bridgman's indefatigable prose had worked its magic, and sufficient new members had been enrolled to enable Peary to return to the arctic (for the seventh time) and to build his own vessel as well. Christened by Josephine Peary the *Roosevelt*, she would be a steam yacht auxiliary schooner, the first and only ship ever built specifically for polar exploration in the United States.

The Bucksport yard of McKay & Dix took the contract and, in October 1903, construction began. She would be the first polar ship that was not merely a sailing auxiliary but a full-fledged steamer with sails. Shorn of triple masts, Peary's vessel had the look of a small liner. A single funnel, nine feet in diameter, dominated her profile, promising massive reserves of power belowdeck. A 12-inch shaft carried at its after end an 11-foot screw that, together with the rudder, could be withdrawn up into the hull.

The *Roosevelt* was short—only 184 feet—for better maneuverability. She was immensely strong. The hull was steel-plated at either end, and her staunch flanks were sheathed in greenheart. Belowdecks she was braced transversely with 14-inch balks and specially wrought steel scantlings.

The vessel's looks were not helped by the addition of a trio of railway boxcars bolted to the deck, one forward and two aft. These would house his crew. Peary's plan was to avoid any possibility of belowdeck damp as well as allow himself sufficient bunkering space to carry 500 tons of coal. Moreover, both times that the *Roosevelt* headed north she would be accompanied by a coaling ship plodding in her wake. She was needed: Peary's "arctic ice-fighter," as he called her, burned 12 tons of coal a day, twice the *Fram's* figure.

Only days after the ship had been launched into the ice-filled waters of Penobscot Bay, on March 23, 1905, her builders found themselves "in financial embarrassment." Peary ordered his hull towed to Portland for engining at another yard. She was finally ready by the summer of 1905, at a cost of seventy-five thousand dollars delivered to her East River pier in New York.

With a ship at his disposal powerful enough to guarantee him an Arctic Ocean base, Peary unveiled his new sledging plan, designed specifically for efficient and fast travel over frozen ocean ice. Depoting supplies in advance the previous autumn, Ross Barrier style, was out; provision caches might not remain in place on sea ice longer than a few days, let alone the entire winter. Anywhere along the 430 miles separating the continent's northernmost tip, Cape Columbia, from the pole,

Peary's trail might shift or vanish; Peary would have to carry everything with him as he traveled.

His solution—which he called "the Peary system"—was an organization of continuous resupply. A succession of sledges, each driven by a four-man team of one American and three Eskimos, would be dispatched daily from the mainland. The first team, carrying only tools and subsistence rations, would hack a trail for their sledge as well as for those who would come panting along in their tracks every twenty-four hours. When the first team was exhausted, the second team, spared thus far any arduous pioneering, would replace it at the point. The second team would, in turn, be relieved by the third team and so on until the polar assault team, with Peary in command, would assume the lead within striking distance of the pole. Recuperating teams in his wake would keep the trail intact and open, each charged with ferrying rations along prescribed portions of the route. It was an innovative concept, an arctic post road across the ocean, complete with igloo way stations along its length, ready-made housing for parties proceeding in either direction.

Peary's new ship and sledging system were first put to the test in the summer of 1905. The *Roosevelt* bulled her way north the length of the American route, in spite of serious damage to both water-tube boilers. By September 5 she was made fast in a secure winter anchorage at Cape Sheridan, the first vessel that far north since Nares's *Alert* in 1875. The following February, Peary and his men hauled provisions along the coast to Point Moss, sixty-five miles distant and his chosen jumping-off place for the pole. The assault began in earnest on the first of March: the first team, Henson and a trio of Eskimos, set off, hacking their way north from the land.

Within a fortnight, the flaw in Peary's post-road strategy became apparent: The same open water that had permitted the *Roosevelt's* painless passage north raised hell with his sledging schedule. What had worked in theory on the *Roosevelt's* cabin table, with matchbox sledges and percussion cap rations, was aborted in practice by the restless Arctic Ocean ice. At 84° North, four assault teams were stranded on the southern bank of a huge lead—Peary christened it the Hudson River—that balked any progress for a week. Scouting parties sent east and west found no crossing place; in any event, Peary carried no boat of any kind.

Half the teams were dispatched back to Point Moss to conserve rations. When new rubber ice finally bridged the lead, Peary and his men were stranded on the northern bank for an additional week by a blizzard. After it had abated, they struggled on, rations shortened by the disrupted supply train. On April 12, with dogs and men alike feeling the pinch, Peary gave up at 87°6'. He was heartbreakingly close, having surpassed Nansen and the Duke of the Abruzzi. Since this preceded Shackleton's triumph in Antarctica, the exhausted Americans stood closer to either pole than any man ever had before.

Peary set course for home, an agonizing and extended voyage. Just inside the American route, near Cape Union, the *Roosevelt* was beset, thrust against the land ice with such force that rudder, rudder post, and propeller were severely mauled. There was also a gash in her hull large enough for a man to fall through; its healing plug of oakum and cement was repeatedly pushed inward by subsequent encounters with the ice. Finally, Bartlett had to station a man at the leak full time to monitor its condition. Then ashes clogged the engine room pumps; engineers had to hack their way through a seven-inch pine bulkhead forward, letting accumulated water flow into the main hold and its unclogged main pumps. Although two of four propeller blades had been sheared off, coal ran low nevertheless, and the *Roosevelt* limped south along the Labrador coast burning wood scraps from both cargo and ship's structure, leavened with walrus blubber. Passage south, from Cape Sheridan to Sydney, consumed four and one half grueling months.

If Peary's return that Christmas of 1905 created a sensation for the public, there were members of the Peary Arctic Club who were less sanguine. His near-miss guaranteed a return engagement the following year, and Peary would have no footdragging in the business of mounting yet another expedition. Once more, Herbert Bridgman returned to the hunt, beating the financial bushes for new members with new money. It was uphill work. There was little financial return without the prize in hand, even from as high a latitude as 87°6'.

Massive costs were necessary to restore the *Roosevelt* to fighting trim. She was not returned to Portland but to a yard at

Shooter's Island, close to Elizabeth, New Jersey. In early January she was put into dry dock so that her planking, propeller, and rudder could be fixed. However, while those relatively straightforward repairs proceeded outside the hull, Dickey, the yard's owner, recommended work of a far more serious nature belowdeck. He advised the Peary Arctic Club that both Almy water-tube boilers had to be replaced. The damage had been sustained on the way north in 1906 after two successive fires in the engine room. Although the flames had been quickly extinguished, both boilers had sustained mortal damage. Bartlett recalls that they "blew up"; Peary is vaguer. In retrospect, it is remarkable that the *Roosevelt*, with only half her steam output, still had been able to reach Cape Sheridan. The cost of the refit was forty-two thousand dollars, nearly two thirds of the vessel's original cost. Grudgingly, Bridgman ordered the work done.

The most damaging cost, it turned out, was time rather than dollars. Throughout the six months remaining before Peary's projected departure the following summer, the work dragged interminably. Peary fumed throughout an anxious spring and, by June, was forced to postpone for a year; 1907 was a dead loss. Furious at "the diabolical delays of ship contractors," Peary wrote Bartlett in Newfoundland, canceling his contract for that year. (More expense for the Peary Arctic Club: He would have to be recompensed for a lost whaling season.) Eleven thousand dollars' worth of pemmican from Armour had to be consigned to a New York warehouse for storage. Sledge dogs, survivors of the punishing trek of 1906, were offered once more to the New York Zoological Gardens for the winter. But a distraught director, already surfeited with yapping Ziegler/Fiala dogs, declined: "Dogs in Zoological Parks are always noisy," he advised Bridgman wearily, "because they see so much at which to bark."

While Peary languished, Cook was active. Since his return from the *Belgica* in 1899, he had found that he still lacked the exploring clout necessary to finance his own expedition. For two restless years, he tried settling down in Brooklyn; but the arctic still called. He sailed as expedition surgeon on the *Eric*, one of Peary's relief ships. Later there was talk that Cook might succeed Evelyn Baldwin in command of Ziegler's Franz Josef Land fiasco, but nothing came of it.

In 1903 Dr. Cook forsook high latitudes for high altitudes, turning his attention to Alaska's Mount McKinley. His motive seems transparent, a grandstand play, first ascent of North America's highest peak. It was a climb that had already defeated no less a distinguished explorer than the Duke of the Abruzzi in 1897. If Cook could only conquer McKinley's dizzying peak, he might then be able to raise money for his own expedition to the pole.

He led two separate expeditions to Alaska. During the first, in 1903, he conducted a systematic reconnaissance of McKinley's lower slopes. Three years later, in the midst of his second expedition, Cook claimed sudden and dramatic success via the mountain's notoriously difficult southern face. The circumstances were as follows: Cook had separated from the main party in company with only one other man, an Alaskan guide named Edward Barille. After a brief absence Cook reappeared, informing his astonished companions that he and Barille had reached the top on September 16.

His account was received with skepticism and, by one subordinate, outright disbelief. Belmore Brown was a New Yorker who had accompanied Cook on both expeditions and who would subsequently climb the same mountain successfully in 1912. He had several reasons to believe Cook a liar: Both Cook and Barille were wearing rubber shoe packs, unlikely footwear for scaling icy cliffs. Additionally, they had not been gone long enough to have accomplished an assault of that duration. Finally, the guide seemed evasive. "You'll have to ask Dr. Cook about that" was his equivocal response to questions put to him by Brown.

It was Brown, in fact, who was to unmask the deceit. Back in New York, together with several other members of the expedition, he proceeded with well-advised caution: They were dealing with a respected figure who, prior to Mount McKinley, had enjoyed a solid reputation. He had twice been Peary's surgeon, had emerged unscathed from both the *Miranda* and the *Belgica* ordeals, and was the only American explorer to have had both arctic and antarctic experience.

But beneath that facade lurked Cook's fatal doppelgänger, the furtive, calculating charlatan. Brown suggested that during the second 1906 McKinley expedition, Cook had been broke, too broke to return to New York without having

275

achieved the summit. Yet Cook's second wife, Marion, was rich, widow of a prominent Philadelphia surgeon. Apparently she had approved of her husband's Alaskan adventure and had accompanied him in 1903; unless her patience had worn thin over the intervening three years, there was no reason to presume that her husband was financially embarrassed. It seems more likely that Cook saw and seized the opportunity for a fraudulent mountaineering coup. It was not hard to expose: Four years later, Belmore Brown found and photographed Cook's published "McKinley summit," the false peak on which the doctor had posed coconspirator Barille with the Stars and Stripes.

But for a heady moment, Cook had New York at his feet. *To the Top of the Continent* was serialized in *Harper's* before publication by Doubleday. He was elected president of the Explorers Club. In December he was among the distinguished guests at a National Geographic Society dinner given at Washington's Willard Hotel; Robert Peary was to be awarded a gold medal for his farthest north of the previous summer. Cook was greeted with acclaim, chatted with Peary (for the last time), and even delivered an impromptu address, cut short when Alexander Graham Bell, in the chair, called for silence at the approach of President Roosevelt. Two weeks later, Cook returned to Washington to address the society on the subject of his Alaskan climb.

But time was running out and Cook apparently knew it. In June, a heaven-sent opportunity arose. He was lunching with John R. Bradley, a fellow member of the Explorers Club. Bradley was a rich Floridian who had subsidized a portion of Cook's first Alaskan expedition. Bradley hunted big game and, having scoured Asian and African jungles, was planning a summer trip to Greenland to enter walrus, seal, musk-ox, and polar bear into his game book. He suggested over lunch that Cook accompany him. Then he added, as an almost casual afterthought, "Why not try for the pole?"

Cook prevaricated for only a moment. It would cost an additional ten thousand dollars, he countered; Bradley dismissed that as no obstacle. He had already bought a ship, a Gloucester fishing schooner he had painted white, engined, and rechristened the *John R. Bradley*. The two men agreed that the "Bradley Polar Expedition"—as it was later called—would remain a secret before departure; that way, Bradley suggested, in the event of failure, the polar attempt could be forgotten and it would revert to a hunting trip.

As far as Cook was concerned, any extended absence from New York suited him perfectly, whether hunting or exploring. Only four weeks after this lunch, he set sail from Gloucester with his wife and two children on board; Bradley would rendezvous with them in Labrador. The schooner's captain was Moses Bartlett, formerly the *Roosevelt*'s first officer and Robert Bartlett's uncle. Though he was left in the dark as to the exact purpose of Cook's expedition, he reported later that he wondered why there was so much pemmican in the hold and so much hickory on board, apparently to be used for building sledges.

Marion and the two children were left on Cape Breton Island for the summer while the *John R. Bradley* continued north to Smith Sound. Hunter and explorer disembarked north of Etah, Bradley to shoot game and Cook to establish his base, recruit Eskimos, and build sledges.

In September the doctor's family sailed back to New York on the returning schooner. Just before Christmas, Marion received a letter from her husband. In it he announced that he had "discovered a new route to the pole" and that with 100 dogs would start in January. Bradley, despite their agreement, could not resist making some noise himself: Cook, he announced to anyone who cared to listen, had 150 dogs and was in charge of "my polar expedition." Having violated his pledge of secrecy, Bradley set off for a fall hunting trip to the Rockies.

The news rocked the Explorers Club, even though Cook's absence since June and whispers of a "secret" expedition had long been common knowledge. One recently elected member was appalled: Robert Peary felt betrayed. He had originally been disinclined to join the club; aloof from explorers in the field, he saw no reason to mingle socially with them in New York. He had accepted membership provisionally, reserving the right to withdraw after having scrutinized the bylaws. Now it appeared that his early suspicions had been correct. When Henry Collins Walsh, one of the club's cofounders, asked Peary to accept the presidency to succeed Cook, Peary temporized, unburdening himself to his (and Cook's) old friend:

. . . To avoid misunderstanding in the matter, I will
say that I regard the action of Dr. Cook in going off "sub
rosa" this summer, while professedly engaged in plans
for Antarctic work, for the admitted purpose of stealing
a march on me, and appropriating my field of work, and
the services of my Eskimos, whom I have been training
for years, as one of which no man with a high or even
average sense of honor would be guilty. . . .

His distress was understandable. The *Roosevelt* was incapacitated at Shooter's Island; by the time she could carry Peary
north the following summer, who knew what Cook might have
accomplished with a year's head start? Peary was fifty-two, ten
years older than the doctor, and getting no younger. That the
prize he had so nearly grasped might now go to another, a
supposed friend and colleague who had crept off to the arctic
without so much as a by-your-leave, was intolerable.

Cook's "new route" was curiously indirect as well as challenging for an inexperienced sledger. In choosing it, he was
abandoning the traditional American way, that water route
between Greenland and Ellesmere Island that Hall, Nares,
Greely, and Peary had all used. Admittedly, Cook had no ship
at his disposal. Bradley, however sporting, was not about to
risk his vessel; she was merely a Gloucester fisherman, not a
whaler, and had no strengthening for the ice. But Cook could
have sledged up the American way's western coast along the
icefoot, very much the way Peary had in the spring of 1902 on
his first serious bid for the pole.

But Cook did not, and one is left with the suspicion that he
chose his "new route" with an eye to its remote novelty. The
very qualities that made it indirect also guaranteed its obscu-
rity. The frozen hinterland west of Etah was off the beaten
polar track, only partly mapped by Greely, Sverdrup, and even
Peary himself. One of the landmasses that Sverdrup had
named was Axel Heiberg Land, which we now know to be an
island just west of Ellesmere. It was the northernmost tip of
this island, named Cape Thomas Hubbard by Peary, after one
of his backers, for which Cook made during the early arctic
spring of 1908.

Cook had with him only one American companion, a bum-
bler named Rudolf Francke, who had elected to stay with him

rather than continue as cook on board the *John R. Bradley*. Together with eight Eskimos, Cook and Francke set out in mid-February. If it was later than he had anticipated, it was earlier than most explorers would have chosen to leave their winter quarters. But with good reason: Cook had a long way to go. He reached the other side of Smith Sound with ease, effecting in reverse the crossing that had stymied Greely's starving command at Camp Clay twenty-four years earlier. Once on Ellesmere Island, Cook and his party cut across its narrowest part, struck up Eureka Sound, and reached the northern tip of Axel Heiberg Island in early March. Once camped there, he sent back all but two Eskimos, Etukishook and Ahwelah. (Francke had given up weeks earlier. He had returned to the base camp and was found there, riddled with scurvy, when Peary arrived at Etah the following spring.)

After a long, circuitous western detour, Cook began the crucial northern leg of his "new route." On March 18, together with his two Eskimos, he committed his sledges to the polar ice. No land lay between him and the north pole. But Cape Thomas Hubbard lay at 81°22', two full degrees south of either Cape Columbia or Cape Sheridan, and had no advantage as a jumping-off place. Cook faced a grueling 1,000-mile round-trip to the pole over the notoriously difficult surface of the frozen Arctic Ocean. He had with him two sledges, twenty-six dogs, and two Eskimo companions; but he had food for only eighty days. That would mean that he would be obliged to average 12½ miles each day, an unlikely rate of progress over ocean ice, as every polar traveler, from Parry to Nansen to Nares, could testify. Even with remarkably good weather and surface conditions, Cook's timetable was improbable.

Whatever his actual accomplishment north of Cape Thomas Hubbard that spring of 1908, he was a long time at it. More than a year later, a month after Peary had reached the pole, Marion Cook hosted a bridge, whist, and euchre party in Brooklyn, the proceeds of which were to underwrite "the rescue of Dr. Cook." Dillon Wallace, of the Explorers Club, had been appointed expedition chief. (This modest fund-raiser hints at Mrs. Cook's reduced circumstances. However rich her first husband, the residue of his estate obviously did not permit, as in the case of another arctic wife, Lady Franklin, the instant charter of relief vessel and crew.)

The *Roosevelt* sailed from New York on July 6, 1908, a year since Cook had left from Gloucester. Just after noon, she backed out from her East River berth. Members of the Peary Arctic Club, as well as wives and children of the explorers, thronged the humid decks—New York was stifling that day—for the trip upriver to City Island. Peary enjoyed himself immensely on the bridge, acknowledging salutes from other vessels, including the presidential yacht *Mayflower*.

The next day, Peary lunched with the president at Sagamore Hill. Then the two men descended with their families to Oyster Bay Harbor for an official visit. No other American arctic expedition had ever enjoyed this special cachet. Both men, Peary as well as his commander in chief, were heavily mustachioed and portly in rumpled white linen. The weather continued unbearably hot. President Roosevelt shook hands with all the expedition members and appeared highly pleased.

No sooner had the presidential party disembarked than Peary and several other expedition members did so as well, returning to New York to complete last-minute preparations while their ship plodded north without them to Cape Breton Island. Sydney was the scene of the final departure from civilization: On July 18, the *Roosevelt* sailed, her deck and 'tween-decks packed with coal; the little collier *Erik* sailed in her wake, bursting at the seams with more coal. When the first rolling started at sea, loose coal on the *Roosevelt*'s deck clogged the scuppers, allowing water to accumulate in the ship's waist and wash over raised doorsills, flooding the deckhouse cabins.

It was a harsh baptism for the new members of the expedition. Peary had recruited six men to head his sledge divisions, three old hands and three untried. The veterans included Captain Bob Bartlett; Ross Marvin, a Cornell engineer who had been on the 1905 expedition; and the redoubtable Matthew Henson. A trio of tenderfeet made up the balance: Dr. John Goodsell, the expedition surgeon; Donald Macmillan, a schoolmaster from Worcester Academy who would later head his own expedition; and George Borup, an immensely strong and spirited Yale graduate who made up in keenness all that he lacked in wisdom.

A month later, on August 18, there occurred a third and final farewell, this time from Etah, home of the Smith Sound Eskimos and headquarters of the Bradley-Cook expedition.

Francke, the man Cook had left in charge, had had enough of the arctic and begged Peary to let him sail home on the *Erik*. Peary consented, and Bradley's cook took the place of the *Erik*'s northbound passenger, one Harry Whitney, a sportsman like Bradley who had come north to spend a year hunting.

Although only three hundred miles away from his projected anchorage in the polar sea, Peary left a large cache of supplies at Etah and detailed two crew members from the *Roosevelt* to stand watch over it. Then the *Roosevelt* set off north again, a floating pantechnicon of over two hundred moiling dogs, stacks of rancid whale meat to feed them, and an Eskimo contingent fifty-strong. The Smith Sound Eskimos were Peary's ancient comrades and had welcomed him back to the arctic for years. Those enlisted for this latest expedition camped on the fo'c'sle head, complete with wives and children. (The two Eskimos who had accompanied Cook—Ahwelah and Etuki-shook—were also Peary's friends.)

Two and a half weeks later, the *Roosevelt* was anchored at Cape Sheridan. Depot-laying began almost at once, as soon as the ship, always vulnerable to a fatal nip in that unprotected anchorage, had been emptied of all her supplies. Eight tons of whale meat were stacked on shore, coralled within a dogproof palisade of coal sacks. By September 16, sledging began. Rations were depoted at Cape Columbia, ninety miles to the northwest and starting point for the polar thrust. The new men had to learn fast: Borup and Macmillan set up a grisly "shooting gallery," an empty biscuit-can "sledge" behind eight frozen dog corpses (*piblokto* had struck already) over which the two novice sledgers practiced cracking walrus-skin whips until they could unerringly target any one of eight malingerers.

Typical of Peary's ease with polar conditions, he refused to remain imprisoned on board the *Roosevelt* during the dark months. Throughout the winter, during periods of vivid moonlight—ten days each month—sledge expeditions went out in all directions, depot-laying and hunting. Peary's men, including his three tenderfeet, lived in the open throughout the winter, the same season during which Royal Navy sledgers remained cooped up in their vessels. The only difference between Peary's winter as opposed to autumn travel was that tents were replaced by igloos. Sleeping bags still were not used. The men slept like their commander, in Eskimo sledging clothes on a two-by-four-foot mat of musk-ox fur, arms withdrawn from the sleeves of their deerskin *kooletah* or anorak, its drawstring tight around their hips.

The polar assault would begin very early in the season. All sledge divisions and supplies were ready and in position at Camp Crane, beneath Cape Columbia's twin peaks, by the end of February; in 1876, Markham and Aldrich had not even left the *Alert* before April. It was bitterly cold, colder than any of Peary's Eskimos could remember. The expedition thermometers registered 58° below zero. It was so cold that the alcohol for their stoves would not light and had to be coaxed to the vaporizing point. But the snow crust was granite hard, overwhelming compensation for the bone-chilling cold.

Peary's Arctic Ocean post-road system had been refined to circumvent another disastrous backup at the "Big Lead," open water he was convinced lay permanently at 84° latitude. Rather than have his divisions strung out behind him, sustaining the fragile trail, Peary decided that all six, his own included, should travel together. Each sledge, carrying five hundred pounds of provisions, could feed the entire party for five days; once depleted, empty sledges and their men would turn back. Peary, last in the field, would return from the pole consuming his previously untouched rations as far as Camp Crane; there he would continue with depoted rations awaiting him. The arrangement still was the Peary System with the same end result: Peary, Henson, and their four Eskimos, spared the work of trail-breaking, would be fresh for the final assault on the pole.

The weather that Sunday, February 28, was cloudless and slightly less cold. Two divisions (a division was made up of one American and several Eskimo helpers), commanded by Bartlett and Borup, left the land first; Peary and the remaining four would follow the next day. Their progress was thwarted almost at once by an open lead just offshore. But it closed after twenty-four hours and Peary's main party continued in Bartlett and Borup's tracks. But the opening and closing of the lead played havoc with the trail, shifting portions of it laterally to the east, so much so that Borup, returning south for fresh instructions from Peary, missed him completely; he returned all the way to Cape Columbia without meeting anyone.

His failure to meet Peary nearly proved disastrous. The commander and his main party were already in need of one crucial item of resupply from Camp Crane: more cooking fuel. Of all Peary's equipment, like Scott's, it was his fuel containers that fell most abysmally short of the mark. Alcohol was carried in its original gallon containers, cans with soldered seams and screw tops, made of metal so light that it buckled, dimpled, and leaked badly after a few days on sledges tackling that roller-coaster trail.

Peary sent Ross Marvin back with instructions to find Borup, load additional fuel, and catch up with him while he continued north. Marvin reached Camp Crane, found the waiting Borup, loaded both their sledges with fuel, and started back north in hot pursuit. Almost at once, they were stymied by yet another lead, four hundred yards wide. Miserable, not even cheered by the return of the sun (it was March 5), the two men and their Eskimo teams camped on the lead's southern margin. Peary, they fretted, was gaining on them. (Had they but known it, Peary was also stopped by open water forty miles to the north.)

After five days, the lead closed and they set out again on the tenth of March. The following day they found one of Peary's cairns, telling them to expect surgeon Goodsell, who, having fed the party for five days as planned, was returning to land. Borup and Marvin pressed on, determined to catch up. The pace was brutal. Lunch, customarily omitted on Peary's expeditions in favor of larger breakfasts and dinners, was reinstituted as a means of helping the two young explorers "keep the steam in our boilers up to the 200-pound mark and win out." (Borup's diary syntax is pure turn-of-the-century undergraduate. On March 12 he recorded irrepressibly: "Only one day behind the main party. Yea! Touchdown!") It was two grueling days before they met Goodsell panting south; Peary's camp, he informed them, lay only a short distance ahead.

Within a few miles, they could hear the welcome yelping of dogs and, exhausted but happy, sledged into Peary's camp, "men and dogs," recorded their relieved commander, "steaming like a squadron of battleships." Peary had spent a gloomy week, tormented by one of those logistical dilemmas endemic to polar travel: Waiting for fuel would have delayed his progress; proceeding regardless risked losing it altogether. If a lead between the parties had not closed, it could have doomed the whole expedition.

Borup and Marvin had made exceptional time: 90 miles in 4½ days, almost unbelievable speed on ice over which Markham's bluejackets sometimes had measured progress in yards. The secret of their improved performance was threefold: It was still only mid-March with a better surface, they were traveling along an established trail, and they used Eskimo dogs and sledges rather than manhauled McClintock sleighs.

Less than a week later, on March 20, Borup turned back, the third division leader to do so; Goodsell and Macmillan had preceded him. Borup was heartsick, although typically he leavened his dismay with a simile straight out of the Yale Bowl: "It was part of the game. When the captain of your eleven orders you to go to the sidelines . . ."

Marvin went back next, then Bartlett, just south of 88°. Long afterward, Peary was criticized for sending south any who might have contradicted (or supported) his sightings. Peary's response was that Henson was his best sledger and, after years of loyal service, deserved a crack at the pole. A sound reason for retaining Bartlett was that, since he was an experienced navigator, his verification of Peary's observations would have proved invaluable. Rather than replace Henson, might Bartlett not have been added to the polar party as a seventh member? Peary's response was that Bartlett would be needed back at base on board the *Roosevelt*, skippering her home in the event that the expedition never returned. Perhaps, too, the fact that he was a Canadian made him unacceptable in Peary's eyes, sullying the Americanness of the achievement. In any event, it would have been ill-advised for Peary to have amplified his polar group on impulse, the error that Scott would make three years later on Antarctica's polar plateau.

Social rather than polar historians argue that Peary's motive in sending Bartlett back had nothing to do with his expertise. Peary would be asked: "Why did you not want a white witness at the pole?" Peary's reply: "Because after a lifetime of effort, I wanted the honor for myself." What about black Henson and the four Eskimos? Did Peary's "myself" mean that he wanted to be the only white man at the pole? Whatever the commander's reason for excluding Captain Bartlett, it seemed bound to provoke future controversy.

During the next days of early April, the six men's progress was incredible: twenty, sometimes twenty-five miles each day.

On the ninth, forty days since leaving land, Peary's calculations indicated that he was within latitudinal minutes of 90° North. This was the first of thirteen separate observations taken with numbed fingers and snow-glared eyes, focused on that trembling orange image of the polar sun, seen inverted in the artificial horizon's mercury pool, warmed and poured into its trough by the patient Henson. No other sextant in history nor sum of its figures had ever produced those coveted results. Peary had reached the pole.

"The prize of three centuries. My dream and goal for twenty years . . ." he wrote later with strangely inaccurate recall: The year 1884, twenty-*five* years previously, was his acknowledged date of polar infatuation. Sadly, Peary did not remember—or saw fit not to record—the exact words he must have cried out to Henson once his first reckoning had been computed. The often trivial yet spontaneous solecisms that slip out are often more poignant than the loftier prose formulated after the fact. Bell's first words over the telephone wire—"Mr. Watson, come here, I want you"—carry far more immediacy than the "What hath God wrought?" that Samuel Morse flashed over his first telegraph wire. In our time, how electrifying to have overheard the Apollo astronauts' routine transmission "Tranquility Base to Houston, the *Eagle* has landed" in addition to Neil Armstrong's overripe pronouncement about a "giant leap" as he first trod the lunar dust.

But Peary only recalled that moment with the kind of cliché customarily inscribed on marble plinths. Indeed, perhaps Peary's great flaw was his lack of humanity. It was Borup, for instance, who informed us that at one point during the northern journey, while Peary was hacking a trail with a pickax, he accidentally struck his foot, piercing his boot at the point where his big toe would normally have been. Had Peary *had* a big toe, the injury might well have changed polar history; but this kind of fascinating, vulnerable minutiae Peary ignored, preferring instead the predictable platitude.

He did comment in his diary that April 6 seemed no different from any other day, nor the pole any different from any stretch of arctic wilderness. As a site, the pole remains disappointingly anonymous: there is no peak, no geographical feature of any kind—indeed, nothing that will look the same the next day. There was nothing distinctive to photograph. Peary arranged his men on the crest of a rafted floe, each holding a flag. There were five: Josephine's silk taffeta Stars and Stripes (fragments of which were already deposited at past farthest norths), the Navy League banner, the Red Cross flag, the flag of the Daughters of the American Revolution, and Delta Kappa Epsilon's fraternity flag. Curiously, neither Explorers Club nor Peary Arctic Club were represented.

Glorious mission accomplished, the six men raced back to Cape Columbia at an astonishing (unbelievable, for Peary's detractors) speed. Peary left the pole on April 7 and reached land on April 23. A journey that had consumed forty days outbound was completed in only sixteen days inbound, Peary claimed, because the trail was already broken.

Once back among his fellow explorers, Peary was curiously closemouthed. He told them that no one was to know if he had reached the pole until he had first informed his fellow Peary Arctic Club members by wire from Labrador. It seems improbable that during the intervening four months the subject was not discussed on board. Would Bartlett, Borup, Macmillan, Goodsell, and Henson have remained silent on the subject? (Poor Ross Marvin was dead. He had never made it back to Cape Columbia. On April 10, two days' march from land, he fell through the ice and drowned, despite the presence of two Eskimo companions. Years later, one of them confessed before dying that he had murdered the American explorer; but many dismissed this deathbed sensation as irresponsible.)

Peary was inconsistent about what he told his men. Bartlett remembers congratulating him for having reached the pole. Peary replied: "How did you guess it?" When Macmillan and Borup congratulated him, his response was: "When I get home, I can tell you all about it." But he ignored the mysterious charade in another fashion. George Borup was dispatched back to Cape Columbia with instructions to build an enormous cairn at the point of departure from land. Atop it he was to erect a signpost, fabricated on board the *Roosevelt;* the arm pointing north was inscribed: "North Pole, April 6th, 1909, 413 miles."

On September 6 the *Roosevelt* dropped anchor in Indian Harbor along the coast of Labrador, the northernmost link in the international cable net. Four messages flashed south, one to Josephine, one to *The New York Times,* one to the Associated

Press, and one to the Peary Arctic Club. Only then, Peary informed his patient crew, were they free to tell the world the same news but with one caveat: No mention was to be made of Frederick Cook.

But Peary was too late. Five days earlier, from the Shetland Islands, Cook had cabled the *New York Herald* that he had reached the north pole nearly a full year earlier, on April 21, 1908! What Lincoln Steffens would call "the dispute of the century" had begun.

Peary had heard rumors of Cook's claim long before. At Etah, on the way home, he had cross-questioned Cook's two Eskimos. Passing Cape York on August 25, a Dundee whaling master had alerted him to the news. Peary was enraged, determined that nobody, least of all this Judas-like colleague, was going to snatch the pole from him.

Acting with an imperious hauteur never far below the surface, Peary denounced Cook to all who would listen. And at the *Roosevelt*'s next stop, appropriately named Battle Harbor, there were listeners aplenty: Tugloads of reporters fanned the flames of Peary's anger. This squabble over priority at the pinnacle of the world was a journalist's delight.

Of the two, it was Peary who made the first tactical blunder, trying to flatten his rival's credibility with one salvo. He cabled *The New York Times* that "he [Cook] has handed the world a gold brick"; it misfired badly, tipping the scales of public opinion in his opponent's favor. Without having examined Cook's records—which he had left, Cook claimed, at Etah—Peary was branding him a fraud.

Conversely, Cook's public demeanor was ingratiating. News of Peary's polar claim reached him in Copenhagen. "If he says he has been to the pole," he murmured disarmingly, "then I believe him." Cook went on to offer his congratulations, assuring reporters that there was room enough for two at the pole.

Cook had returned from the North in May 1909, a month after Peary had reached the pole. At Etah, Cook found that Rudolf Francke was gone. In his place the doctor was pleasantly surprised to find American sportsman Harry Whitney. Having wintered in the open, Cook was weak from malnutrition and exposure and stayed with Whitney long enough to regain his strength. As he recuperated, he begged Whitney to lend him dogs and provisions so that he could continue south and catch a ship. Whitney demurred; the provisions were Peary's. Cook then asked for a loan, and Whitney obliged with a check for one thousand dollars, drawn on a New York bank. Twenty-four hours later, Cook departed abruptly, taking Peary's dogs and provisions that Whitney had denied him.

Six hundred miles to the south, Cook reached Upernavik and sought admittance to Governor Kraul's residence. The governor, who apparently had known his share of explorers *in extremis*, greeted his visitor warily on the threshold. The dialogue that followed speaks volumes for the fastidiousness of colonial administrators.

"Are you suffering from vermin?" he demanded.

"No, sir," Cook replied.

"Then you can come in."

Kraul called his servants to prepare a tub. "For every good reason," he recommended, "it will be best for you to take a bath."

After a bath and some food, Cook produced a map and traced the extent of his travels.

"You have been to the north pole?" gasped the incredulous Kraul.

"Yes" was all that Cook responded, almost sotto voce.

Days later, Cook reached Egedesminde in time to catch the Danish steamer *Hans Egede*, bound for Copenhagen. During a call at Lerwick in the Shetland Islands, he dispatched his momentous wire to the *New York Herald*:

> REACHED NORTH POLE APRIL 21, 1908. DISCOVERED LAND FAR NORTH, RETURN TO COPENHAGEN BY STEAMER HANS EGEDE. FREDERICK COOK

The steamer tied up in Copenhagen on September 5. Scores of reporters and stringers were waiting, so many that the curiously reticent doctor held a press conference in the ship's dining saloon. One young reporter, Peter Freuchen, who would make a name for himself in the arctic later, smelled a rat almost at once; so did several others. Cook regretted that he had no diary or records with him; he said he had left them in Greenland with Harry Whitney for fear that his sledge journey south to Upernavik might have jeopardized their safety. It was not lost on anyone that this kind of precaution was unusual and unlikely; explorers are seldom parted from their records, in no more danger on the icefoot between Etah and Upernavik than en route home from Axel Heiberg Land.

But the press's occasional reservations were lost in an outpouring of affectionate welcome from Denmark's establishment. The crown prince escorted Cook ashore, and the king himself lent him a tailcoat for a dinner in his honor that evening. Cook accepted the offer of a gold medal from Denmark's Royal Geographical Society and an honorary doctorate from the University of Copenhagen. After ten giddy days in the Danish capital, Dr. Cook embarked for New York on the *Oscar II*.

On September 21 there were two separate welcoming ceremonies in North America. While Cook came triumphantly home to Brooklyn, Peary tied up in Sydney, its waterfront filled with cheering Canadians; Captain Bartlett recalled, "You couldn't spit without hitting a silk hat." At the same moment, Cook was riding through the streets of his native Bushwick in an open carriage, garlanded with flowers. But, significantly, no one from Washington, Albany, or even City Hall was part of his welcoming committee.

That autumn, the Cook/Peary feud intensified. Charges and countercharges filled the columns of the warring *Herald* and *Times*. Editors all over the world joined in. "POLAR TOURIST" shouted British headlines. A cartoon in Mexico City's *Herald* showed Shackleton approaching the south pole confronted by Cook: "I discovered this a year ago," ran the caption, "I've just been hiding here behind this pole all the time." During one of Shackleton's American lectures that winter, he referred to Captain James Cook and then convulsed his audience with the aside "No relation."

The Explorers Club was split down the middle. Peary and his adherents derided Cook's claim, asserting that Ahwelah and Etukishook, his Eskimo companions, had confessed to Peary that they had never been out of sight of land. The Cook faction rebutted this revelation with the explanation that Cook had told his Eskimos that every cloud they passed was land to allay their fears of venturing onto the sea ice. Peary himself knew about the Eskimos' nervousness when forced onto the ocean: He had bribed his Smith Sound tribesmen with weapons and tools before they would accompany him north of Cape Columbia.

But, in truth, Cook seemed equally confused about which were clouds and which was land. He reported seeing mountainous terrain to the west, which he had christened Bradley Land, after his patron. But did Cook *really* see Bradley Land, or had he pretended to to conform with Peary's discovery—equally specious, it turned out—of Crocker Land in 1906? No one can ever know for sure what really transpired north of Axel Heiberg Land that spring of 1908; events were cloaked in a haze of myopia, confusion, inaccuracy, and, alas, subterfuge. And if Peary lacked credible witnesses supporting his presence at latitude 90° North, those he did have behaved more loyally than Cook's: Ahwelah and Etukishook declared that Cook had merely posed them on top of their igloo with a flag, two days' march from land.

Even to his most ardent supporters, Cook's inadequate supplies, the mint condition, according to Whitney, of his undamaged sledge, and his lack of sledging experience argued against his achievement. Most unsettling was his lack of documentation. Whitney said no diaries had been left with him, only some instruments. Peary told reporters that he had left all of Cook's equipment in Greenland; had he brought it home on the *Roosevelt*, he suggested wisely, he might have been accused of tampering with any diaries of sightings. In the end, Cook never produced any figures, either for Mount McKinley or the pole. In a Montana courtroom he suffered an embarrassing confrontation with Edward Barille on the subject of the bogus ascent. Publication of *My Attainment of the Pole* did not help; inaccuracies and inconsistencies abounded and, stylistically, the narrative leaned heavily on the lyric rather than the scientific.

As the chorus of doubt peaked, Cook vanished. Rumor had it that he was submitting his diaries to the University of Copenhagen, but the captain of the vessel on which he was supposed to have booked reported that he had no Frederick Cook as a passenger. One of his *Belgica* shipmates, engineer Max van Rysselberghe, said that he ran into Cook on a street in Santiago. A British newspaper report placed the missing explorer as a patient in Heidelberg's Roggenau Sanatorium. Like Andrée's balloon, though Cook supposedly popped up in unlikely quarters of the globe, his actual presence was never confirmed. It seems most likely that he had gone to ground somewhere in Brooklyn as his house of cards collapsed around him.

And collapse it did. Two New Yorkers, one of them a sea captain, admitted that Dr. Cook had approached them, offering to pay handsomely for some convincing navigational data that might have been taken at the pole. Angered at never having been paid for their work, the two went disastrously public. Scholars at the University of Copenhagen waited in vain for Cook's promised records; all they received were typewritten accounts that gave results but no computation. In the end, the Danish gold medal and honorary doctorate were withdrawn.

On Christmas Eve of 1909, the Explorers Club dropped Frederick Cook from its rolls for his part in the Mount McKinley deception. They had no choice: The doctor had failed to deliver any documentation. But although Cook's credibility may have been destroyed, his popularity remained undimmed. Throughout the dispute, Peary's arrogance rivaled Cook's duplicity, and a host of the commander's enemies gleefully embraced the doctor's cause. Cook's underdog role was a natural, the outsider challenging the prestige of a sometimes abrasive front-runner. Whereas Cook had charm, Peary had little, and there was some truth in Peter Freuchen's oft-quoted bromide that "Cook was a liar and a gentleman, Peary was neither." Moreover, Peary's long polar campaign was perceived as having been sustained by a clique of rich men who had the president's ear. And elsewhere in Washington, at the Navy Department, there was professional jealousy: Peary's promotion had continued despite years of absence on half pay. Two flag officers, both Old Arctic warriors, lined up against Peary for other reasons. Greely backed Cook because Peary had once been critical of his handling of affairs at Cape Sabine. Admiral Winfield Schley, who referred to Peary witheringly as "civil engineer Peary," took umbrage at his subordinate's removal of the name Schley from an arctic feature and so declared for Cook. Even Amundsen was torn: Cook had been his old shipmate from *Belgica* days. But he did finally support Peary.

Perhaps Cook's greatest disservice to his rival was fomenting a mood of official skepticism. When Shackleton had come home to England in 1908, he never experienced the grilling to which Peary had to submit in Washington; but then, the Irishman was not claiming the pole and, in any event, had had with him a trio of competent observers. Peary was taken to task for his extraordinary figures; whereas Cook had produced none,

Peary's seemed too good to be true. Congress and even the National Geographic Society could not have been unaware of a growing aura of mistrust, especially in Great Britain. In 1911, W. Henry Lewin, writing under the pseudonym "An Englishman in the Street," wrote a volume called *Did Peary Reach the Pole?*; it was followed by another, Thomas Hall's *Has the North Pole Been Discovered?* That both titles terminate with question marks typifies a polite but persistent sense of disbelief. Both authors articulated the doubts of a growing host of Peary critics. What bothered them all was his phenomenal speed over ocean ice, especially from the moment Bartlett turned back to Cape Columbia: From seventeen miles a day, Peary's rate jumps incredibly to twenty-nine. Similarly, on the party's return from the pole, it peaked to an astonishing thirty-three miles daily, four times the best mean average of Nares and Lockwood.

Peary continued to defend his records, insisting that a small party with lightened sledges traveling over a broken trail could achieve those impressive speeds. But there were other omissions and disparities. Peary took no longitudinal sightings, insisting that east/west ice drift that year had been negligible. Then again, shadows in his polar photographs indicated to some a solar elevation of 30° rather than the reported 7°. Henson inadvertently muddied his chief's waters in a memoir of 1912 (foreword by Peary) in which he recalled with awe how the sun at 90° North had moved regularly up and down in the heavens; in fact, the north polar sun stays at a fixed height above the horizon, neither setting nor climbing.

The famous feud remains a rather dusty and tattered *opera buffa* production that is periodically sent out on the road for another try. Polar historians love to pick at it, submitting new hypotheses and theories, adding additional volumes to an already substantial bibliography. Cook is vindicated as predictably as Peary is pilloried; the underdog's attraction seems irresistible. But these revisionists face a formidable task, fully as heroic as the age concerning them: Not only must Peary's final expedition be debunked, Cook's must also be legitimized—to my mind, an impossibility. After eighty years, it seems unlikely that any new proofs will emerge, and speculation seems pointless. Either one must believe Peary—and I do—or one does not; regardless, his possible dereliction cannot improve Cook's credibility.

The National Geographic Society, which had contributed to Peary's expedition, set their seal of approval on his figures and substantiated his claim, as did the Congress of the United States. Peary was promoted to admiral—the promotion dating from April 6, 1909, tacit acknowledgment that his story was accepted. In May 1910, Peary addressed the Royal Geographical Society in Royal Albert Hall; he was presented with the society's gold medal, designed by Kathleen Scott, wife of the British explorer. In presenting it, Major Leonard Darwin, president of the society and son of the famous naturalist, informed the gathering that Peary's medal recognized not only achievement of the pole but also two decades of arctic endeavor.

Although well meant, Darwin's addendum gives the added impression that his society was hedging its bet on the polar sweepstakes: Was Peary's unqualified win being relegated to place? Officially, the Royal Geographical Society had sidestepped the Cook/Peary affair and left it for the Americans to settle Peary's legitimacy for themselves. But one RGS member remained unconvinced. Sir Clements Markham, then in his eightieth year and about to retire from the council, made it no secret that he doubted Peary's observations just as much as Cook's. The artificial horizon, he pointed out in a letter to J. Scott Keltie, was not reliable for use on floating ice; he criticized Peary for not employing a theodolite instead. "I do not believe," he concluded in that familiar crabbed script, "that either of them have been near the pole."

But Sir Clements would soon adjudicate a more poignant competition in the South. Among those in Royal Albert Hall that May night was Captain Robert Scott, only weeks away from departure for his second polar attempt. In the wake of Shackleton's near-miss of 1908, Scott was determined for another try at the remaining pole. His renovated whale ship *Terra Nova* would sail for Antarctica that summer.

One half of the polar riddle had been solved. But Cook had poisoned the north polar well: To this day, mention of Peary's triumph brings to mind a legacy of confusion and deceit. To bury the Edwardian dispute with a latter-day metaphorical epitaph, Peary's record is forever wedded to a flawed flip side.

13

TRAGEDY AT THE SOUTH

The Victoria Quadrant, which Captain Scott has made peculiarly his own, had to be explored to its very apex, which happens also to be the south pole.

   —Sir Clements Markham

Great God, this is an awful place and terrible enough for us to have labored to without the reward of priority.

   —Robert Scott at the south pole

Peary was thrice forestalled by Norwegians. First, in 1886, when his planned crossing of Greenland was preempted by Nansen; in 1898, when Sverdrup invaded the American way on board the *Fram;* and in 1906, when, having struggled north to 87°, Peary returned home to find his thunder stolen by Amundsen's conquest of the Northwest Passage.

But Peary would have his revenge. For it is doubtful that anyone in the world, with the possible exception of Frederick Cook, was more discommoded by his reaching the pole than Amundsen. Indeed, the heroic age's two great pivotal events were these: Shackleton's miss of 1908, which set the stage for Scott's second expedition; and, inextricably interwoven in a way that no one guessed at the time, Peary's attainment of the north pole, which turned Amundsen's sights south.

In 1906, Amundsen had disembarked from the *Gjøa* at Seattle and traveled home to Christiania. There, after a welcome that rivaled Nansen's, he wrote his obligatory book while accepting the plaudits of the world's geographical societies. He was an established explorer—no longer an impoverished dreamer but a Viking in Nansen's tradition who had stolen a march on the British and first navigated the fabled—if useless—waterway.

But the Northwest Passage had been merely a prelude; the north pole was Amundsen's next objective. He decided to approach Nansen for permission to borrow the *Fram* for a second drift over the Arctic Ocean. Strictly speaking, its owners of record were three Christiania investors—Axel Heiberg among them—and the Storthing, Norway's parliament; but a token call on Nansen was the first step. Nansen had entered public life with his appointment as his country's first ambassador to the Court of St. James's and, to Eva's relief, had renounced any further polar excursions. He gave his blessing to Amundsen with only one condition: that he take with him as a member of the expedition Hjalmar Johansen, his old comrade from the ship's first voyage. Amundsen agreed, and the *Fram* was his.

She was still the only ship in the world that could survive that hazardous ice drift. Amundsen's projected voyage would be longer than Nansen's and, it was hoped, innovative: He planned entering the polar ocean the way De Long had, through Bering Strait, then turning northeast as far as Point Barrow before surrendering to the pack. By locking himself in above the North American continent, Amundsen hoped to investigate the fringes of the Arctic Ocean—known as the "zone of inaccessibility"—and, succeeding where Nansen had failed, to drift directly across latitude 90° North.

In June 1908, Amundsen and Colin Archer made a thorough examination of the vessel, laid up at the naval yard at Horten since Sverdrup's return in 1902. Although invaluable against arctic ice, polar ships are less useful in conventional waters: They have unwieldy hulls, a modest spread of canvas designed for a limited crew, and are burdened with more displacement than is profitable for commercial use. So the stout old *Fram* had languished at her moorings until 1905. Then she had been put into service as an ammunition storage hulk for the Navy. From the shore, the *Fram* seemed derelict, naked masts towering above her littered decks. Rig replacement would be a necessity, for cordage, canvas, and spars had been destroyed in a warehouse fire.

But the hull was sound. The Navy had added zinc plating below the waterline to protect the greenheart sheathing from a voracious boring worm, the teredo. But damp had worked its insidious damage on the cabin insulation. The sandwich of felt, reindeer hair, and cork between inner and outer walls had rotted, and the infectious decay had spread to adjacent timbers. Nansen's original steam engine would be replaced by a motor from the A.B. Diesel Company of Stockholm. (It would prove so reliable that, after the *Fram*'s return, its makers rechristened the model "Polar Diesel.") Bunkers were torn out and oil-storage tanks inserted in the bilges, outboard tanks shaped to conform to the hull's saucerlike configuration. Topside, the ship's profile remained identical save for a new bridge amidships forward of the mizzenmast.

Amundsen's appeal for funds was greeted with sober enthusiasm in geographical circles. By February 1909, the Storthing had voted seventy-five thousand crowns toward the expedition. Britain's Royal Geographical Society authorized a five-hundred-pound grant, an investment they would come to regret.

Amundsen's plan was for subordinates to sail the *Fram* around Cape Horn while he traveled overland from Norway to Nome. All was in train for departure in early 1910 when Peary's cable from Indian Harbor burst on the world in September 1909.

The rug was pulled out from under the Norwegian. Since childhood, the north pole had been his ambition; now it was lost before he had even had a shot at it. The raison d'être for his arctic voyage had evaporated: Interminable years spent drifting across a polar ocean, the central riddle of which had been solved, no longer appealed. Within hours of hearing Peary's news, Amundsen made an abrupt change of plan. If the north pole were taken, he would go for the south. He had a partially subscribed expedition, a first-rate crew, and a ship sturdy enough for the southern oceans.

Amundsen's volte-face was quite in character, the same instantaneous expedient of seven years past when, threatened with ruin, he had sailed regardless, embarking inexorably in hopes that success would right all wrongs left behind. But now, rather than a vindictive merchant, Amundsen was planning to deceive—indeed, deceive—an august international body of contributors who were committed to expansion of Dr. Nansen's pioneering arctic work rather than an impulsive gamble for the south pole.

Amundsen sensibly kept his decision to himself, telling only Leon, his brother/manager, as well as the *Fram*'s senior officers. Subsequent crewmen signed on in ignorance of their true destination. Several money sources did dry up on receipt of Peary's news, paradoxically those investors who might well have relented had Amundsen shared his bold alternative with them. But he could not risk offending his scientifically oriented backers, including his own government.

Obviously, even though a handful of Norwegians were in on Amundsen's secret, it was vital that no one across the North Sea be apprised; for Captain Robert Falcon Scott had, by bizarre coincidence, announced *his* intention of going for the south pole, on September 13—only a week after Amundsen had privately resolved to do likewise. This second expedition of Scott's—cable address ONWARDNESS—was known as the National Antarctic Expedition. Despite its quasi-official title, the undertaking would have no formal endorsement from the government or from either of the two prestigious royal societies. Having declared openly for the south pole, Scott was on his own. Parliament contributed only twenty-thousand pounds, and the staggering task of raising the balance as well as mounting the expedition rested on the shoulders of a still penurious Royal Navy officer. By 1910 Scott had pressing family commitments, with now a wife and child as well as a mother and sisters to support. He had married Kathleen Bruce—a sculptress and unconventional free spirit—in September 1908. A year later, the couple had produced a son, christened Peter Markham in deference to his two godfathers, James Barrie—whose *Peter Pan* had captivated London in 1904—and Sir Clements.

Despite the expedition's primary polar mission, ancillary polar work would be pursued. Edward "Bill" Wilson, Scott's *Discovery* comrade, was completing his massive report for the

Grouse Commission and accepted the post of chief of scientific staff, a position he had refused on board the *Nimrod*. Markham, keen as ever, agitated for a pledge of support from the Royal Geographical Society. But he was no longer in power, and the taint of the *Discovery's* relief debacle still lingered. Try as he would, Sir Clements could no longer stir his fellow council members to action with the kind of persuasive rhetoric that had launched the *Discovery*:

> Captain Scott's Antarctic Expedition is now in very urgent need of funds . . . the continuation of the Society's work in the "Victoria Quadrant" which could not be properly completed by one expedition. . . . Dr. Wilson, the splendid artist and *beau ideal* of an Antarctic Scientific Director, is also one of the Society's Officers, and Cheetham, Evans, Lashly, Crean, Heald, Williamson and others are all [the] Society's men. The great work to be achieved is the work undertaken by the Council and left incomplete. . . .

Yet, argue as he would about the "Society's" officers and men completing the incomplete, it was clear to his colleagues that they were no longer the society's people at all but ticket-of-leave Royal Navy personnel signed on with Scott.

Raising money was discouraging; it came in small, grudging amounts, with no donations larger than a thousand pounds. Two members of the expedition assured berths for themselves by contributing as well. Captain Lawrence Oates of the 6th Royal Iniskilling Dragoons, a professional soldier as well as an amateur yachtsman, contributed a thousand pounds. "No Surrender" Oates, a sobriquet earned during the Boer War, was a surprisingly gentle, accommodating man who was taken on to look after the expedition's ponies. The other thousand-pound-paying member was a friend of Wilson's named Apsley Cherry-Garrard. Although professionally unqualified for anything, he was a tireless worker who served as assistant zoologist to Wilson. Had Cherry-Garrard done nothing else, his book *The Worst Journey in the World*, published in 1922, serves as ample return on his—and Scott's—investment. It remains the most readable account of the lot, extraordinarily sensitive and compelling.

A third newcomer to polar exploration was an indomitably

competent officer of the Royal Indian Marines, Lieutenant Henry Bowers. Referred to Scott by Sir Clements Markham, he had been signed on originally for the ship's staff only. But his genius at organizing stores as well as his splendid physique and seeming imperviousness to cold were to earn him a berth ashore. His cheerful, ruddy face was dominated by a beaklike nose, and he was known immediately as Birdie.

Eight thousand ratings, mostly from Royal Navy messdecks, volunteered to accompany Scott to Antarctica in 1910. Even urchins from London's East End used to camp on Scott's doorstep at 174 Buckingham Palace Road in hopes of being recruited. It was a measure of the intense south polar fever of the period. Throughout the United Kingdom, patriotic fervor permeated all levels of society and the services, in hopes that the Union Jack, thwarted at the north pole, should wave first at the South.

In compliance with his stringent budget (which was, in its entirety, what the royal societies had spent building the *Discovery*), Scott chose as his vessel the *Terra Nova*, a sturdy whale ship that was already a polar veteran. She had sailed once to McMurdo Sound as a relief ship in 1903. By 1910 she was a quarter of a century old, a far cry from the sleek *Discovery*, with a distressing tendency to leak above and below the waterline. Throughout the voyage from Cardiff to Ross Island, the *Terra Nova*'s crew spent protracted daily periods at the pumps. In rough or rainy weather, leakage through the supposedly caulked main deck drenched those berthed below. (Forward, ratings who slung their hammocks beneath the fo'c'sle stables suffered a far more noisome seepage.) But at twelve thousand pounds she was a bargain.

Scott's ponies, like Shackleton's, were bought in Manchuria. Rather than trust their selection to a bank agent, Scott sent two of his men out to buy both ponies and dogs. Unaccountably, cavalry officer Oates did not go, but Cecil Meares and Wilfred Bruce—the latter was Scott's brother-in-law—met in Vladivostok in July. From there they traveled inland to Harbin (now the Chinese city of Haerhpin). Two young Russians were enlisted not only to help select the best animals but to accompany the expedition as well. Anton Omelchenko was a jockey, and Dimitri Girev was a knowledgeable dog-driver. The party traveled with their four-footed charges, both canine and equine, to Lyttelton, arriving there on September 15, one month in advance of the *Terra Nova*. Larger than the *Nimrod*, Scott's ship would accommodate nineteen ponies in admittedly cramped quarters forward. Most of them were white— Shackleton had suggested that they seemed hardier than the grays.

No more than a token pack of dogs, thirty-three in all, comprised the expedition's entire kennel. Scott was banking heavily on ponies and a trio of expensive motor sledges. These were an improvement over Shackleton's motor car—tractors, really, with eighteen-inch cogged wheels driving chain treads; every section of tread had bolted to it a diagonal batten to grip the snow. The chassis was built largely from aluminum, and the engines were four-cylinder Wolseleys. Each came equipped with a plywood cover lined with quilted canvas batting, enormous tea cozies that were designed to protect brittle engine components from the cold. Part of the tractors' prohibitive expense was the cost of two separate testing sessions, one in Norway and the other in the French Alps. Each tractor required the services of two operators, one on board juggling the engine controls, and another walking alongside, who steered by hauling on a rope attached to a projecting bowsprit.

Scott had no hope that his motor sledges would reach the pole, but he assumed they would repay their investment while unloading and setting out depots. But it turned out that their greatest value was psychological: Their presence at Scott's winter quarters would be a source of uneasy concern to Amundsen. In fact, his fears were groundless: The motors petered out very soon and offered no return for the money they cost as well as the deck space they took up when loaded on board at Lyttelton.

Welsh coal merchants offered the expedition a shipload of patented fuel, so Scott decided that Cardiff would be his final port of call. The coal (oil-impregnated compressed brickets) was loaded on board during the second week of June 1911. Then the *Terra Nova* sailed, not to be seen again in that port for exactly three years, under the command of Lieutenant Teddie Evans, R.N., Scott's second-in-command. Scott would join him in South Africa. *Punch*'s farewell wished "*Terra Nova* a safe landing in *Terra Scotta*."

At the same time that the *Terra Nova* sailed, the *Fram* was still in Norway, her antarctic destination top secret. It is astonishing that no one from the British or Norwegian press put two and two together to divine Amundsen's change of plan. The arithmetic was transparently simple. Just as lunar rockets must find a specific "window in the sky" to achieve crossover from earth to moon orbit, so polar expedition ships had to observe a rigid schedule of departure for either arctic or antarctic. If Amundsen were indeed planning a summer entry into the arctic ice off Point Barrow, he should have sailed no later than February to reach Bering Strait by August. (The *Jeannette* had taken five months to get from Le Havre to San Francisco.) Yet February, March, April, and May passed before the *Fram* stirred from her Horten berth. Then, months after she should have departed, Amundsen merely transferred her to Christiania to load stores and equipment. He deflected queries by announcing that he planned extensive zoological experiments through the South Pacific.

Then there was the mystifying business of the dogs. Amundsen ordered one hundred through the auspices of the Royal Greenland Trading Company. They were shipped to Norway free of charge on the *Hans Egede*. But what a curious way to select an *arctic* pack! Why not take Siberian dogs or, better still, pick them up in Alaska on the way? Was Amundsen going to subject his animals to two needless voyages, one from Greenland and another around Cape Horn to the arctic, passing twice through the tropics? Again, Amundsen forestalled the incredulous by announcing that he preferred Greenland dogs over the Siberian or Alaskan variety.

There was yet a third arctic anomaly: the sturdy, prefabricated hut constructed by Jorgen Stubberud and his brother on Amundsen's lawn at Bundefjord. As will have been noted, polar expeditions bound for Antarctica took huts so that the explorers could winter on dry land; for arctic explorers on board the *Fram* (designed specifically to accommodate them throughout a long drift), a living hut was redundant. When asked why he needed it, Amundsen prevaricated yet again: The structure, he said, was "my observation hut." But obviously this was no mere shelter for magnetic instruments but an ambitious, twenty-six-foot structure with a kitchen, double-decked bunks, and triple-glazed windows.

The existence of that hut betrayed Amundsen's antarctic destination just as clearly as his insistence on Greenland dogs and a midsummer departure. Yet no one tumbled, no one save Sir Clements, who divined exactly what the Norwegian was up to. But none of the reporters who came to see Amundsen off saw through what seems, in hindsight, a transparent ruse.

Amundsen did find, with the north pole discovered, that some of his investors backed off. Armour reneged on their proposed gift of free pemmican, so Amundsen had to make his own in an abandoned Christiania bakery. He economized, too, on his men's clothing, using surplus Navy blankets as material. *Fram*'s rigging felt the pinch: Amundsen could not afford a full set of sails, canvas sorely missed when he reached the southern oceans. But in the matter of tents, furs, and skis, he ordered the best there was: Amundsen might compromise with sustenance and comfort but never with efficiency.

In June, the fully laden *Fram* had royal visitors: King Haakon and Queen Maud boarded the vessel and presented its company with a silver pitcher. Then *Fram* sailed to Bunderfjord to load the components of "the observation hut," then back to Horten for gun cotton and ammunition.

The next month she was dispatched on a shakedown cruise before returning to Bergen for a final engine refit, additional supplies, and, taken on reluctantly at the last moment, those Greenland dogs. *Fram*'s topsides were literally smothered with animals, housed under temporary awnings wherever there was room; 14 were chained at intervals across the bridge, and the crew resigned themselves to handling lines covered with dog feces. During the long voyage that followed, it only got worse— 97 dogs embarked in Norway, 116 disembarked in Antarctica. The expedition finally sailed for good on August 9, perfect timing, as even a child of that polar-conscious world of 1909 would have guessed, for a December penetration of the ice ringing Antarctica.

A month later, she dropped anchor in Madeira's Funchal Roads, Amundsen's final port of call before vanishing south. His brother Leon was waiting for him. On the ship's last day in port, the crew was told of their momentous change of destination. Telling them was one thing; telling the world was another. But Amundsen had worked it all out methodically. Leon would carry the news back to Norway. To the chairman of the *Fram* expedition, Amundsen wrote:

. . . You ought to have been told long ago but I did not venture to. The *Fram* goes direct south from Madeira into the antarctic regions in order to compete with the Englishman for the South Pole. . . .

A long apologia went to Nansen, another to King Haakon. Two cables would also be dispatched from Norway, one to New York's Arctic Club and the other to Scott, the man most affected by the stunning news:

BEG INFORM YOU FRAM PROCEEDS ANTARCTIC AMUNDSEN

Amundsen gave no clue as to his base or estimated landfall, only a gauntlet flung down.

Tactical diameter is a nautical term that describes the perpendicular distance between a ship's position before and after turning through 180°. Since this was the psychological maneuver Amundsen had executed, we should evaluate his personal tactical diameter worldwide once his decision was common knowledge. All Norway was ecstatic. But in Stockholm, Nordenskjöld had misgivings about the propriety of the move. In Paris, Charcot insisted that Amundsen's trail would doubtless be fresh, "not trail-blazed for him by Shackleton." Shackleton himself was lecturing in America and wondered to reporters whether the Norwegian was following "the dictates of polar etiquette"; he went on to assure them that Scott would reach the pole first because he had superior equipment. But a former *Nimrod* shipmate differed presciently from "the Boss": Amundsen, said J. R. Davis, "was the hardest nut in all Norway, born to work as no Englishman could." It would be safe to say, then, that Amundsen's tactical diameter was supportable although he was seen to have violated the sensitive principle of territorial prerogative.

The Madeiran press reported without surprise that the Norwegians were headed for Antarctica. This was not due to lax security: All the crew's mail as well as Amundsen's letters and cables were kept in Leon's scrupulous care, to be dispatched from Christiania later in the month. That the Funchal reporter had stumbled inadvertently on the truth was sheer conditioned apathy: The *Southern Cross*, the *Discovery*, and the *Terra Nova* had all stopped at the islands en route to the south. Yet another vessel, outfitted for the cold, was presumed, mistakenly, to be headed in the same direction. But no word of the Madeirans' oddly accurate inaccuracy leaked to the outside world.

Amundsen had written Nansen that his antarctic base was not yet selected, only that he planned to avoid Scott. (Amundsen later contradicted himself in his memoirs: in *The South Pole*, the author states unequivocally that the Bay of Whales had always been his first choice.) In fact, he had only two clear choices, either McMurdo Sound or the Bay of Whales; with Scott at the former, only the Bay of Whales was left. Of course, there was always the challenging possibility that the *Fram* might penetrate far enough east to land in King Edward VII Land; three British predecessors—Ross, Scott, and Shackleton—had been unable to: Antarctica's immutable seasonable timetable made it almost impossible. There just was not enough time to get that far east with impunity and still leave time to secure a winter base. Each ship's itinerary had been consistent: through the pack, south past Cape Adare, east along the Barrier, past the Bay of Whales, and into increasing congestion near King Edward VII Land; then, inevitably, a hasty retreat back to known waters and a haven at which to unload before winter set in. The *Discovery* had done just that; so, reluctantly, had the *Nimrod*. Amundsen, profiting from their experience, set his sights firmly and boldly on the Bay of Whales, virgin and perhaps dangerous territory for a base and, incidentally, as far south as a ship can sail.

From northern Europe, sixteen thousand sea miles had to be traversed, more than half a global circumference. Amundsen's and Scott's contrasting progress reflected their differing priorities: Amundsen's was secrecy; Scott's, money. The *Fram* took five months and made no stops after Madeira. Two more were planned, but both were aborted by rough weather. At Gough Island, Amundsen had planned filling his water tanks, and at Kerguelen Island, where the *Erebus* and the *Terror* had called in 1840, he hoped to recruit additional crew members from the Norwegian whaling station there. Once his nine-man shore party had disembarked in Antarctica, only ten would remain on board for the *Fram*'s demanding trip around Cape Horn. But he managed without either call, and he cut down on soup as a means of water rationing. There was no problem with fuel:

The *Fram* sailed most of the way with the propeller drawn up into the hull, a slow but economical passage to her destination.

Scott could have made better time had he not scheduled extensive delays en route. But, in fact, his only real deadline was departure from New Zealand by Christmas. So he followed the *Discovery*'s example, calling at Trinidad to paint his upperworks before reaching Simonstown at the Cape of Good ·Hope, calculated showmanship to attract investors. Scott rejoined his vessel there and, after a hectic fortnight of speeches and fund-raising, sailed with only an additional thousand pounds.

The *Terra Nova* was kept under steam for most of her voyage. There were plenty of extra hands in the wardroom, and they served stifling tropical watches in the stokehold. Yet this abundance of manpower cut both ways: Scott's ship carried three times as many as the *Fram*, so his need for water and coal made a succession of stops inevitable.

In October, the *Terra Nova* rode a squall into Melbourne's Port Phillip Bay, her first Australasian stop; among the waiting mail was Amundsen's cable.

Although shaken, Scott kept his feelings about it, even news of its existence, to himself. This conduct has recently drawn criticism. Roland Huntford, in his encyclopedic yet curiously anglophobic *Scott & Amundsen*, suggests that Scott's lack of public response betrayed a kind of paralytic funk, that by apparently ignoring the message's import the Englishman was playing ostrich in the sand. In so chiding his fellow countryman, surely Huntford ignores the British explorer's characteristic persona. Scott's credo was control: control of temper, control of inner turmoil—control, in short, of everything. Moreover, the watchword of Britain's officer corps has always been "Never explain, never complain"; by maintaining silence, Scott was, personally and professionally, adhering to that code. Though his silence makes sense to me, to Huntford it does not: For discretion, he reads fear; for reticence, inertia.

In fact, nothing could have been gained by venting anger or frustration in public with only one exception, as Huntford himself points out: Perhaps Canberra's Parliament might have been shamed into doing better than the grudging twenty-five-hundred-pound grant they voted. An appeal on nationalistic grounds might have raised the ante. But as it was, apart from calling the whole thing off, Scott had little other choice. Amundsen's news came too late for him to effect any change in his plans. Scott was harnessed to those plans as inexorably as he would be harnessed to his sledges.

Had he chosen to share his news with colleagues on board, at least two would have proved disappointingly unsupportive. Edward Wilson, his closest friend, made no diary reference to the Norwegians until much later, on hearing that the *Fram* had been encountered in the Bay of Whales. Then, in a revealing entry, he expressed doubts about the safety of the Norwegian camp, then worried about their dogs' suitability for sustained Barrier travel (typically, Wilson cites the "monotony" involved for them!). Then, a full half year before the fact, Wilson offers a dispassionate prognosis:

> However, he may be fortunate and his dogs may be a success, in which case he will probably reach the pole this year, earlier than we can, for not only will he travel much faster with dogs and expert ski runners than we shall with ponies, but he will be able to start earlier than we can as we don't want to expose the ponies to any October temperatures. . . .

It was an imperturbable statement of probabilities that would prove only too accurate.

Another wardroom member who saw every possibility of Amundsen's success was Lieutenant Oates (or Titus, to use his nickname). He was as loose as Scott was taut and had no patience with Royal Navy ceremonial trappings. Early on, he perceived that his commander's inexperience and penchant for show might lose the pole to the Norwegians. But then, candor was Oates's strong suit; there was no pretension about the man at all. He dressed with a raffish disregard for rank, favoring a disreputable slouch hat and moving affably from quarterdeck to messdeck like an eccentric guest at a country house party. Blessed with impeccable social credentials, an upper-class traveler on a middle-class outing, Oates brought to the wardroom a brand of debonair, detached wryness, seeming to care less for the pole than for his beloved ponies.

By the time the vessel reached New Zealand, the press was in full cry about a race. Scott's race, if there was one, was more

Shackleton *(right)* poses with Peary in New York. *Library of Congress*.

Peary's "arctic ice-fighter," *Roosevelt*, the most powerful polar vessel ever launched. *National Geographic Society*.

A close call for the vessel on her first trip north, 1907. Capt. Robert Bartlett inspects the shattered rudder post. *National Geographic Society*.

The awful arctic terrain that had defeated all of Peary's predecessors. *National Geographic Society*.

Matthew Henson *(center)* and four Eskimos at the north pole. Curiously, Peary never published a picture of himself at the pole. *National Geographic Society*.

Dr. Frederick Cook posing in arctic regalia in a Brooklyn studio. The two "Eskimos" are patently not, nor is the collie a sledge dog. *Library of Congress*.

Commodore Robert Peary in furs on the *Roosevelt*'s bridge at Sydney. *Library of Congress*.

WAX FIGURES OF THE EXPLORERS COOK AND PEARY ARE ABOUT TO BE PLACED WITH LIEUTENANT SHACKLETON'S AT MADAME TUSSAUD'S. IT IS HOPED THAT A CAREFUL WATCH WILL BE KEPT OVER THEM, OR SOME SUCH CATASTROPHE AS THIS MAY OCCUR.

Punch cartoonist Toy worried what might happen overnight at Madame Tussaud's. *Punch*.

ABOVE: Bay of Whales encounter, February 1911: *Fram* moored on the right, *Terra Nova* departing on the left. *Library of Congress.*

AT LEFT: Dogs, skis, and sledging expertise characterized Amundsen's rapid pace to the pole. *Library of Congress.*

BELOW: Amundsen takes a sextant reading at the south pole. The artificial horizon has been set up on one of the Norwegians' packing cases. *Library of Congress.*

Members of the *Terra Nova* expedition pose before sailing from Lyttelton, New Zealand, on November 26th, 1910. Captain Scott stands just to the left of the white pole; Edward Wilson is at his right shoulder. *Canterbury Museum, Christchurch.*

Runners-up to the Norwegians, the five-man polar party at their goal. Left to right: Wilson, Scott, Evans, Oates, and Bowers. *Library of Congress.*

Charles Dollman's painting of Captain Oates's death, entitled "A Very Gallant Gentleman." The figure of "No Surrender" Oates was posed by Seaman Mackenzie of the expedition. The canvas hangs today in London's Cavalry Club. *The Cavalry Club.*

Hester-trugers, Norwegian equine snowshoes. These practical devices—which Oates scorned—might well have amended south polar history. *Norsk Sjøfartsmuseum.*

Above: The end of *Eagle*'s flight: A photograph of Andrée's downed balloon, found with his body on White Island in August of 1930. *Below:* From the same roll, Andrée, Fraenkel, and Strindberg manhandle their laden sledge/boat across the arctic ice. *Library of Congress.*

Two years after Scott's death, Sir Ernest Shackleton embarked for the south polar regions aboard the doomed *Endurance*. His plan—never realized—was to cross Antarctica via the pole. Shackleton stands in the peaked cap on the left; to his left is George Marston, a member of the expedition. Shackleton is about to be presented with a bunch of heather for good luck by the unnamed woman on the right. *Library of Congress.*

with the fates. Meanwhile, his ship had to be completely un-loaded at Lyttelton and dry-docked to find a leak, the same dry dock for the same problem that had plagued the *Discovery*. Then dogs, ponies, sheep, tractors, and coal were loaded on board in addition to tons of additional foodstuffs.

When they sailed, they were dangerously overloaded; a last-minute offer of three barrels of beer from a Dunedin brewer had to be—regretfully—refused. At latitude 52° South, a storm nearly finished the *Terra Nova*, a gale out of the southwest that would have tested any vessel, especially one as old and low in the water as Scott's. Mountainous seas thundered on board, loosening bags of coal that were dashed repeatedly against crates of Shell motor spirit with such force that their wooden battens disintegrated. Officers and men repeatedly waded into green water on deck to retrieve coal sacks and loosed gasoline cans that, had they fractured, would have added the hazard of fire to the chaos.

An even worse peril lay belowdecks. Months earlier, during a storm off the African coast, oil had spilled beneath the engine room into the bilges. Now, green water pouring through the main deck found its way into the coal bunkers, washing coal dust into the bilges as well. It mixed with the residual oil to form a lethal slurry that choked the pumps. The only way to get at the pump intakes was through the main hold; but if it had been opened from above, the ship would have foundered. So while all hands bailed, engineers had to pierce an iron bulk-head forward of the stokehold.

It seems hauntingly reminiscent of that night on the ice-bound *Jeannette*, thousands of miles and dozens of years away, when Melville had risked lighting cold boilers to pump dry and save his ship. But the *Terra Nova*'s predicament was worse, at the mercy of hurricane-force winds and deprived of all engine power.

After twelve hours, once the bulkhead and pump well had been breached, indestructible Birdie Bowers, lungs filled to bursting, managed to clear the valves of their encumbrance of coal dust and oil. Those at the pump handles on deck cheered when an inky discharge spewed suddenly from the outflow. Later that morning the wind dropped, and the crisis was passed. Two ponies were dead.

That storm incapacitated one of the seven new hands embarked at Lyttelton. This was Herbert Ponting, the expedition's photographer or, as he preferred to be called, a "camera artist." A combat photographer during the Russo-Japanese War, "Ponco" had been bitten by the Antarctic bug while reading *The Voyage of the "Discovery"* when confined to a Trans-Siberian Railway compartment. He was a terrible sailor, so prostrated by the storm that he had not been able to participate in the bucket brigade. And even after it was over, he used to work in his little darkroom with a basin of developer in one hand and a basin for vomiting in the other. But his pictures were impressive: No other polar expedition has ever been blessed with comparable photographs.

When the *Terra Nova* entered the pack on December 9, Ponting was well enough to clamber out onto a plank lashed just to starboard of the ship's chaste, white figurehead to make movies of their iron-shod prow butting its way through the floes. Although his footage is splendid, the ship's speed through the pack was abysmal: Three weeks and tons of precious coal were consumed before the *Terra Nova* entered the Ross Sea. This was the first of several delays that would play havoc with the expedition's timetable.

Scott found himself once more in the familiar waters of McMurdo Sound. There was too much ice for the ship to get as far south as the *Discovery* had, so Scott settled for a sheltered cape farther north; known formerly as the Skuarry, a nesting place for skua gulls, it was rechristened Cape Evans after the *Terra Nova*'s commander. The vessel was secured with ice anchors and, in beautiful weather, unloading began.

The camp was built onshore, over a mile from the *Terra Nova*'s icy quay. The only casualty of that hectic fortnight's unloading was one of the three motor sledges. While being pulled toward shore by a line of men, it broke through weak ice and sank like a stone, dragging its towline after it; as each man was drawn, protesting, near the hole, he relinquished his hold, thereby accelerating the approach of his fellows still hanging on. Then all let go and, with a rush, the rope vanished. A thousand pounds' worth of sledge was gone, a hopeless, aggravating loss; Scott termed it "a day of disaster."

The hut came ashore in pieces and was assembled on Cape Evans's volcanic sand beach. It was larger than Shackleton's, fifty by twenty-five feet, divided at midpoint by a wall of packing cases to separate other ranks from officers. Empty sledges bound back for the *Terra Nova* carried tons of antarctic rock to put in the hold as ballast.

Scott was pleased with their progress and declared Sunday, January 15, a day of rest, the first since their enforced idleness in the pack. The ship's contingent trudged ashore, assembling with the shore party for outdoor divine services. Afterward, in a holiday mood, men scattered on various excursions. Scott and Meares took a dog team for a look at Hut Point.

As long as the intervening bay was frozen, negotiating the fifteen miles separating Scott's old and new winter quarters was straightforward. One sledged due south over the ice. But if the ice broke up, accomplishing the same journey by land was well-nigh impossible: The shoreline between Cape Evans and Hut Point was a precipitous switchback of icy slopes over which sledges drawn by men, ponies, or dogs could not travel. When the ice broke up, north/south communication stopped; worse, beyond Hut Point, access up onto the Barrier was challenging.

But on that calm Sunday afternoon in mid-January, Scott, Meares, and the dogs made the crossing without incident. The only blemish on their overnight outing was that the interior of his *Discovery* hut was packed with snow. Shackleton's people had not repaired the window through which they had forced an entry, and the desolate, snow-filled interior distressed Scott intensely.

He would have been even more distressed to know that at that very moment, four hundred miles east of Cape Evans along the Barrier face, Amundsen's men were unloading the *Fram* at the Bay of Whales. On his first approach, Amundsen had found it full of ice but, the next morning, a change of wind cleared it and the *Fram* was moored to an ice quay. Amundsen and three companions put on skis and set off in search of a campsite. A short distance inland they found an ideal location, which became Framheim. Any thought that the ice on which it was built might fragment and carry them out to sea was ignored. Amundsen guessed that the Barrier was aground at or near the Bay of Whales and would prove, away from the margin, as substantial as terra firma.

Dogs were hitched into teams, and unloading was begun. After months at sea, the animals were so spoiled that when first harnessed, they refused to pull; drivers were hoarse with shouting, getting supplies inland. The weather was splendid: The thermometer hovered about zero, what the Norwegians called "a grand summer temperature." The "observation hut" was erected. Carpenter Stubberud dug foundations down into the snow so that a third of the structure's height would be below the surface. Over the winter to come, the hut would be almost completely buried, with only its entrance, chimney, and ventilating trunk protruding above the snow. The dogs were picketed nearby, tied at intervals to a line staked out in the snow.

From the beginning, the Norwegians' antarctic progress was charmed. Sailing or sledging, they breezed past obstacles against which the British repeatedly bogged down. The *Fram* had negotiated the pack in a week, the *Terra Nova* in three. Amundsen had sailed to his landfall chosen from half a world away and, contravening all prudence, established a splendid base from which to march on the pole; Scott's access to the Barrier would be formidably difficult from Cape Evans. This marked, one-sided contrast—good fortune for Amundsen, setback for Scott—typified the contrasting Norwegian/Anglo experience in Antarctica in the months to come. And although, for the Norwegians, timing and good luck played their part, those providential factors were buttressed by their inbred familiarity with cold, darkness, and snow. If they were new to the Barrier, they were scarcely new to what made it challenging.

In early February there was a brief, congenial encounter, the only one that ever took place, between men of the two expeditions: The *Terra Nova* steamed unexpectedly into the Bay of Whales. The British had been attempting to complete one last mission before the vessel's return to New Zealand. Under the command of Lieutenant Harry Pennell, the *Terra Nova* was returning from another fruitless attempt to land a subsidiary eastern party in King Edward VII Land. Six men, headed by Lieutenant Victor Campbell, had been given two of Oates's precious ponies and were to have fulfilled Britain's long-cherished dream of exploring that virgin territory, hitherto only glimpsed from a ship. But once again, the pack had blocked their way, and Pennell had regretfully turned back. (In fact, it was the Norwegians under Lieutenant Prestrud who would first reach King Edward VII Land on foot: While Amundsen was capturing the pole, a Nordic eastern party would capture King Edward VII Land, in December 1911.)

So Pennell, acting on orders from Scott, had fallen back to his secondary objective, to land the eastern party at the Bay of Whales instead. Nothing would have pleased Scott more than to have had his men succeed where Shackleton had failed. If Campbell's party could winter there, Scott could offer a mute rebuke to his British rival who had funked it in 1908 and, in consequence, trespassed in McMurdo Sound.

Amundsen and his companions saw the masts of a strange ship as they started the day's first run from Framheim, en route for further unloading. They chose the moment for a race. Dragging empty sledges at breakneck speed, the dogs tore off. Well-disciplined after two weeks in harness, they drew up with a flourish under the *Terra Nova*'s poop, halted by piercing whistles. Amundsen added a showy touch, bringing his team up short by flipping his sledge on its side.

The three senior British personnel—Pennell, Campbell, and surgeon George Levick—joined the Norwegians for one of Lindstrom's pancake breakfasts. Amundsen, brimming with hospitality, insisted that his guests set up camp anywhere they liked; he even offered them a gift of dogs. Campbell, politely but firmly, declined; for the Britishers, the bay was now forbidden territory. Later in the day, the Norwegians lunched on board the *Terra Nova;* after they had disembarked, the British cast off. Before departing, Pennell took the opportunity of surreptitiously besting the Norwegians on at least one score: While maneuvering his vessel away from the ice, he made sure that her bow crossed a yard farther south than the *Fram*'s. (To no avail: The *Fram*'s Barrier dock fragmented shortly thereafter, and the Norwegians moved their ship three miles south.)

As the *Terra Nova* returned along the Barrier, on messdeck and in wardroom alike the talk was of the Norskies (a bluejacket pejorative that stuck) and their obvious toughness and skill. Petty Officer George Abott, one of Campbell's party, wrote his uncle:

> . . . Lieutenant [*sic*] Amundsen is their leader, Johansen who was with Nansen, is also with him so it will be a race! . . .

Back at Framheim, every Norwegian caught a cold, the *Terra Nova*'s most persistent legacy.

The British vessel returned to Cape Evans and left off the two ponies; they had to swim ashore because the ice dock had broken up. Once ashore, they were revived with a straw rubdown and a large dose of medicinal whiskey. En route to New Zealand, the eastern party, renamed the northern party, spent two winters ashore on the ice below the Admiralty Range.

Explorers at both camps began laying depots. This autumn ritual was essential, not only to establish outposts of resupply along the intended line of march but to test men, animals, sledges, and systems as well. For expedition leaders it was a time of anxious expectation. Lists, notes, and tables formulated in heaving cabins on the long voyage south (that blessed hiatus between soliciting at home and slogging in the field) would be submitted to conditions of harsh actuality.

For the British, it was frantic. McMurdo's ice—optimistically called "the Southern Road"—was breaking up; Erebus Bay was already puddling and fragmenting. Depot-laying had to begin at once. From out of a welter of cases and boxes littering the shingle at Cape Evans, loads were gathered and lashed onto sledges: Oats, pemmican, candles, sleeping bags, shovels, diaries, tents, ropes, instruments—the list seemed endless; perhaps it was inevitable that one critical item of supply for the ponies was overlooked.

The departure was made just in time. The next day "the Southern Road" was no more, not to refreeze until mid-April. That vanished expanse of ice aborted any possible use of the two remaining snow tractors. But they would prove nearly as disappointing as Shackleton's snow car. Internal-combustion engines of 1912 were just not up to antarctic demands. Poor Bernard Day and stoker William Lashley nursed their fragile engines from breakdown to breakdown. In November both tractors reached the Barrier, but they ran only a few days before their unpredictable engines were stilled forever.

Scott's goal that autumn was 80° South, approximately the same latitude as both *Discovery*'s and *Nimrod*'s Depot A's. The party left Cape Evans on January 24; three and a half weeks later, southward progress was halted. Over a dozen intervening camps had been built and abandoned en route, each numbered consecutively from winter quarters. Camp number fifteen was the southernmost; because of the amount of provisions it contained, it would become known as One-Ton Depot. It lay at 79°28½', over thirty miles short of its intended position. In Britain's polar annals, One-Ton Depot is a name associated with haunting despair, pivotal shortfall for the returning polar party, as we shall see.

Establishment of that final depot was a struggle. If ever there was writing on the wall, if ever an ominous foretaste of things to come, it was the instant superiority of dog over pony. The *Terra Nova* teams, well trained by a Russian, Dimitri, were vastly superior to the untrained pack that had so disappointed Scott on his Southern Journey of 1903. Wilson now drove a dog sledge, amazed at their speed and vigor over the same surface that proved impossible for the horses.

They had started well enough over the sea ice, pulling quarter-ton loads with ease; but once on the Barrier, they bogged down repeatedly, floundering through soft snow. Tethered overnight, they suffered from the cruel winds that the dogs escaped by burrowing into the snow. Even the advantages of night travel—harder surface for their hooves and sun-warmed rests by day—were nullified at Corner Camp (number six) by a three-day blizzard that saw the animals tethered outside while the explorers, impatient but at least sheltered, chafed within their green Willesden cloth tents. Scott felt the ponies' distress cruelly, and it was at Corner Camp that he first built those protective snow walls that became his campsite hallmarks for the rest of the ponies' lives.

Their rate of progress was never more than eleven miles each day, slightly above Scott's anticipated speed. But the blizzard at Corner Camp exacted a fearful toll: Three of eight ponies had to be taken back to Cape Evans, they were so done in; only one reached home. Most curious of all was the failure—whose, it was never made clear—to bring more than one set of *trugers*, equine snowshoes that Scott had ordered in Norway, concentric rings of bamboo laced with wire radii. Within moments of trying on that single set, Scott was so impressed that he ordered Wilson and his dog team back to Cape Evans to retrieve the rest; but the ice had already broken up. Their one set saw noble service: when five ponies became hopelessly ensnared in a drift, they were unhitched from their sledges and brought out. Then Weary Willie, Bowers's pony, shod with the precious *trugers*, was taken into the white morass from which he easily retrieved all five sledges, one after the other.

It is not clear why they were left at Cape Evans, nor who should have taken the responsibility for bringing them: Was it the overworked and harried Bowers, a preoccupied Scott, or, most likely, Titus Oates, nominally in charge of everything relating to the ponies? We do know from his diary that he felt Scott unqualified to be dealing with draft animals. Also, as a cavalry officer, he disliked the idea of ponies shod with snow-shoes. Perhaps he was the culprit. Certainly they could easily have been brought. Each pony carried a twenty-five-pound item called "pony furniture," including feed bag, rug, extra halters, and puttees, even a fringed eyeshade to reduce glare; the addition of four lightweight *trugers* would have paid mean-ingful dividends, dividends not to be guessed at, regretfully, at the time of that depot-laying journey of 1911. They would have improved progress dramatically, perhaps ensuring establish-ment of One-Ton Depot at its anticipated location. In the cele-brated dog-versus-pony controversy, perhaps Scott was less at fault for having selected horses than in providing for their best employment.

In addition to the two ponies that died en route home to Camp Evans, three more were lost during a perilous descent from the Barrier. Eight had left, the expedition's best; only two returned, leaving eleven still alive for the southern journey. It had been a gloomy overture.

The first southern probe out of Framheim went like a breeze. Amundsen had less reason for haste, for he was already on the Barrier and had had no water to cross before getting there. Four weeks after having landed, on February 10, he and three companions set out, also for latitude 80°. There had never been such a swift polar journey. Lieutenant Prestrud took the point on skis while each of the remaining explorers drove a sledge, drawn by six dogs apiece. Within five days, averaging eighteen miles per day, they arrived at their destination, cached three quarters of a ton of dog pemmican, and turned back to Framheim after lunch. With empty sledges a record run was made, more than ninety miles in two days. (Peary would have applauded this bravura Norwegian performance, for it lent antarctic credence to the speed with which he and his comrades had raced home from the north pole.)

Predictably, contrast with the British debacle was staggering. Amundsen had achieved his objective *and* returned to base within a week; Scott took more than three times as long before calling it quits thirty miles short of the same latitude. A third of his ponies had perished; all Amundsen's dogs romped home. During that record-breaking run from 80° back to Framheim, the sledges had been empty of cargo but laden with passengers instead; in a rare exception to custom, the exultant Norwegians had ridden most of those ninety miles. Their only chore during that exhilarating return had been to drop off trailmarkers of frozen fish—the same *torsk* that Scott felt had poisoned his dogs in 1903—every half kilometer.

A week later, eight men—the entire party save Lindstrøm—set out to lay more depots, at 81°, 82°, and 83°. This second outing proved less lighthearted. Fresh snow blanketed the trail and dragged at the sledge runners. It continued snowing through much of their journey, a not unwelcome phenomenon, for Ross Barrier blizzards meant warmer temperatures; the Norwegians marched right through them. (The British never could: For Shackleton and Scott, blizzards meant stops because the ponies could not take them.)

At the 80° depot, the temperature began to fall dramatically, until their thermometers registered 80° below freezing. The Norwegians' speed dropped with the temperature, and the performance of the dog teams deteriorated. They became so hungry that the *torsk* signposts marking the trail were eaten as a supplementary ration. It did not help. Each morning, bone-thin and trembling, the dogs had to be lifted from their snow holes and whipped into reluctant movement. However hard the drivers lashed their teams, the wretched beasts seemed beyond caring; the weakest simply lay down in the traces.

It was, Amundsen recorded, the hardest sledging of the entire expedition. They did not reach 83° but halted at 82°, established their southernmost depot, and turned home. Johansen later added a load of dead seal to the 80° depot: Amundsen was determined, after the dogs' frightening failure, that polebound sledges in the spring would be pulled at the start, at least, by dogs surfeited with real red meat.

When the last sledges were back at Framheim, three substantial depots, containing an aggregate of two tons of seal, dog pemmican, and paraffin, stretched toward the pole. To ensure that no depots would be inadvertently lost in mist or blizzard, the Norwegians fashioned an ingenious fail-safe: East and west of every cache stretched a line of ten flags, each a kilometer apart and numbered as to its position in the row. Errant sledgers deviating to either side would be able to re-establish their position and be guided back to both trail and depot.

Amundsen's first priority over the winter was a reduction in fixed sledge weights. Rather than dispense with tents or sleeping bags, as Peary had done, he talked the matter over with Olav Bjaaland. Bjaaland was Framheim's genius—carpenter, violinist, and instrument maker. The two of them agreed that expendable weight could be trimmed from both sledges and provision cases.

Though the British carried sledge rations in compartmented canvas bags, Amundsen stored his in rigid containers, four of them lashed permanently to a sledge. Each box had its top pierced by a six-inch hole, plugged with an aluminum lid like a milk can's. When camp was set up, rations could be fished out of one case without removing it from the sledge. The walls of these provision cases were made of venesta, an early form of plywood, and it was in their thickness, as well as the thickness of sledge structural members, that Amundsen and Bjaaland felt reductions might be made. It was risky: If lightening things weakened them, there might be disastrous consequences on the march.

Where to accomplish the work? The hut never served as anything more than living quarters. Even though it had nine men in a space originally designed for ten, it remained extraordinarily cramped. Only Lindstrøm, the cook, had any room for chores, either in the kitchen or the snow-covered passageway surrounding the hut's exterior. The possibility of their round, bell-shaped tents was discussed, but the dogs were already ensconced in them.

An April blizzard solved matters. A drift built up on the side away from the wind, and the Norwegians were faced with the task of removing it. Only then did they discover that their shovels were finished: The only two brought from Norway had been broken while excavating the hut's foundation. So Bjaaland wrought a dozen blades from sheet iron, and carpenter Stubberud fitted them to stout hickory handles, pirated from sledge spares.

Thus equipped, the explorers started to work, tunneling into rather than removing the drift obstructing their entrance. Within a week they had hewn five separate chambers off a central tunnel: a carpenter's workshop; a smithy; a cesspool for kitchen slops; a lavatory; and, at the farthest end, a Primus-powered sauna. Another tunnel gave access to the fuel store. To the northwest, striking off from the little alcove where Lindstrøm hacked off ice blocks for water, the tunnelers fashioned two large additional rooms: a clothing store and, beyond that, a space dubbed the Crystal Palace. Thanks to the limitless depth of snow on which Framheim was situated, they could tunnel ad infinitum. Amundsen's men spent the winter in a complex of interconnected caves. Lindstrøm, for example, could empty slops, find provisions, refuel his stove, and carry in water without ever putting his head aboveground.

Three of the underground workrooms were of standard length, a minimum of fifteen feet, so that sledges could be stripped and planed in the carpentry shop, relashed in the clothing store, and transferred to the Crystal Palace for loading. The caves were colder than the hut, for Barrier snow had long been compacted into heat-conducting ice. So, in all three chambers, occupants worked well bundled up. Amundsen had brought plenty of Primus stoves and fuel to fire them so that, in each glittering white cavern, a Primus roared, raising the temperature to a bearable 0°. Warmer rooms might have improved working conditions (all that precise carpentry meant bare hands), but the stability of the ice walls might have been endangered.

Oskar Wisting found this out for himself. In a curtained nook off the clothing store, he worked at his sewing machine, perfecting a whole line of specialized tents, sleeping bag covers, and clothing. The Primus at his feet heated the confined space to an astronomical 50° (about the temperature of a modern refrigerator), and the walls dripped perpetually. Meltwater was run off by an ingenious system of drains and baffles into a tank, where it was hoarded as a reserve for washing. (Near either pole, bathwater is invaluable.)

The work of reducing sledge weights was undertaken in the carpentry shop. Bjaaland and Stubberud worked back to back, each at his own workbench, planks laid atop ice shelves chopped along each room's long dimension. Underfoot, a carpet of aromatic shavings, the fruits of their winter-long labor, insulated booted feet against the chill. Stubberud took apart each provision case and shaved down each side, not along its edge but across its entire surface. It was mostly cross-grain work, obstructed by knots, but by frequent sharpenings of his tools—he used both plane and a razor-sharp adze—he removed a uniform depth of wood from each side, top and bottom. Once all six elements had been pared down, they were reassembled, save for the top with the hole in it; that would stay off until the case was packed. Then the outside was painted black, an invaluable visual aid against polar whiteness. Each original case had weighed twenty pounds; Stubberud's patient work removed a third of that, a saving of twenty-eight pounds a sledge.

Behind him, Bjaaland reduced each sledge to its components. This was a simple matter, for all the elements, save the platform slats, were lashed rather than screwed together to ensure sinuous movement over rough terrain. Once the lashings had been removed, Bjaaland clamped each runner, stringer, and slat in turn to his bench; a smoothing plane shaved spiraling white millimeters from noncritical dimensions; only the arched cross supports retained their original size. By the time Bjaaland's relentless plane had finished its work, a third of each sledge's weight had been cut away. After both runner and bowed towing yoke had been rebent into their new configuration—in a patented steam kettle powered by Primus—the bundled parts were taken along the icy passage to the clothing store, where Wisting and Hanssen reassembled them.

Johansen reigned supreme in the Crystal Palace. Despite an oil lamp at his elbow and the inevitable Primus that, he discovered, radiated more heat with a brick parked on top of it, his breath frosted white in the room's frigid atmosphere. He devoted himself to packing sledge rations into the lightened cases. Each was filled to scrupulous perfection. Pemmican was cut into cylindrical blocks two inches high, and the interstices between rounds were stuffed with what he called sausages, cloth tubes of milk powder. These stood vertically in a field of pemmican, centrally arranged so that a gloved hand groping through the opening could retrieve any number at will. Empty crannies were filled with an excelsior of chocolate fragments. When the case was full, Johansen nailed down the top, numbered it—"Sledge IV, Case #3"—and entered its contents in Sledge IV's provision log. Then he would start work on the next one. Johansen's only curious omission was his failure to subpackage the expedition's biscuits. They traveled in separate cases on each sledge, arranged in neat rows. Each man's daily ration would be forty, yet no convenient unit of this or, indeed, any amount was ever devised. Twice at resupply points during the polar journey, thousands of biscuits had to be recounted by sledgers with freezing fingers.

Due in large part to an innate, national compatibility, the Norwegians' winter passed cordially, with only one exception. By choice or design, Johansen worked in the chill solitude of the Crystal Palace. Since returning from that celebrated arctic adventure of 1897, apartness and alienation had characterized his existence. Alcohol had become a crutch, and it is not clear which came first, drinking or a host of problems. Johansen's life had disintegrated: He left the Army, his marriage failed, and he lived alone in a state of continual financial distress. For years he was kept afloat by the generosity of Fridtjof Nansen. And when Nansen had requested that his old shipmate be signed on, Amundsen privately regretted it. Despite his seniority and experience, Johansen's debilitated condition could be a liability. He was included at Framheim on sufferance.

It was insubordination that would prove his reluctant commander right. Johansen's downfall was triggered by Amundsen's only antarctic aberration. It began with a duplication of an error made years earlier in the arctic: On the first spring journey out of Gjøahaven in search of the north magnetic pole, he had set off too early in the season, when it was too cold. Now, with a geographical pole at stake, Amundsen was determined to take an early lead over Scott. Although surmising that their ponies would hold the British in check until November, he agonized over the threat of Scott's motorized transportation.

At the end of August, Amundsen ordered the sledges brought up onto the surface. They had been fully packed and waiting for weeks. Over the freshly excavated entrance to the clothing store, Stubberud erected a stout wooden tripod from which a block and falls was suspended. With a team of men hauling and another shoving from below, fully laden sledges were hoisted up into the dazzling Barrier light. It was a reassuring test of the winter's work: Dangling upright at the end of a line, not one box or biscuit budged an inch.

In September, the eight-man polar party began the trek, leaving Lindstrom once again in sole charge at Framheim. But the weather was merciless to men and animals alike. By the time they had reached the 80° depot, Amundsen called it quits, ordering an immediate return to base. The polar sledges were left in place and, already suffering from frostbitten feet, the explorers tore back to Framheim.

It was an unprecedented spectacle, Norwegians in full retreat. Unusual, too, was what seemed the naked edge of Amundsen's panic. In his haste, he outran his men, leaving some of them in potential jeopardy, unequipped to pass a night in the open. It was an isolated lapse from sound, precautionary practice and one that Scott would never have tolerated from himself or any of his commanders. All the explorers did ultimately reach home safely, among them Johansen, who had spent an anxious time shepherding a frostbitten Prestrud back along the trail.

The next morning, Johansen lost his temper and upbraided his commander in front of the entire party. Amundsen's response—had he welcomed the outburst as an excuse?—was a drastic reorganization: Prestrud, Johansen, and Stubberud were summarily detached from the polar party, assigned instead to explore King Edward VII Land. Pointedly, Lieutenant Prestrud, although younger and greener than Johansen, was given command.

In his published account of the expedition, Amundsen trivializes the episode in one offhand sentence: "Circumstances had arisen which made me consider it necessary to divide the party into two." Yet there are other indications of disfavor: Throughout *The South Pole*, Johansen remains a ghostly figure, mentioned only sparingly and excluded by the author from the tightly knit Norwegian fraternity. For Johansen, dismissal from the polar party was to prove the ultimate disgrace.

The real start was made on October 20. Hanssen, Wisting,

Bjaaland, Hassel, and Amundsen, to list them in their customary order of march, left Framheim riding on empty sledges. In
four days they reached the 80° depot and dug out the loaded
sledges as well as a ton of cached seal carcasses. For an entire
day, fifty-two dogs gorged themselves on granite-hard shards
of meat. Then, on the twenty-fifth, pulling sledges at top speed,
they galloped south along the flag-marked trail. The Norwegians were truly away at last, embarked on what Roland Huntford has called "the last great terrestrial journey." Four men
drove sledges, while Amundsen remained unencumbered. He
was, by his own admission, a poor sledge driver, and for the
entire journey he skied alone.

It is an interesting coincidence that both Norwegian and
British polar parties numbered five, last-minute totals determined by each commander's arbitrary choice. Amundsen had
intended originally to take eight from Framheim, although not
all would continue to latitude 90°; some would turn back short
of the goal. Scott did the opposite, increasing his projected
polar party from four to five at the eleventh hour.

The Norwegians, who had twice ridden on their sledges between Framheim and that first depot, indulged in a rare polar
practice. Explorers seldom traveled on sledges: Outbound, the
loads were too heavy and, at journey's end, the dogs would
have been too debilitated to be so abused. Sledges at both
Framheim and Cape Evans were modeled on Nansen's original
and had no driving handles or upstanders. Peary was the only
explorer to use these sturdy devices so that his drivers could
help the dog teams wrench their loads over rough ice. Moreover, his drivers could travel behind the sledge because they
wore snowshoes; ski-shod, the Norwegians ran alongside and
to the left of their sledges, within easier reach of the animals
and handily positioned in the event their top-heavy vehicles
encountered rough sastrugi or skirted the lip of a crevasse. The
Norwegian dogs were harnessed in the Eskimo fan formation,
each independent trace toggled to the yoke at the front of the
sledge. Although this broad configuration crowded a narrow
trail, its precautionary advantage was obvious: If a dog fell
into a crevasse, it would not necessarily drag in its fellows.

Seven hundred pounds of cargo were carried on each sledge,
most of it distributed within the black provision cases. Lashed
on top was the day-to-day camping equipment—fuel, tent,

sleeping bags, cooker, instruments, and spare clothing. Fully loaded, each sledge was almost as tall as its driver, resembling, rather than low-slung racers, cumbersome chests of drawers. Extraordinary care was taken to keep things firmly in place. Although the sledge itself was designed to be supple, the load remained as rigid as possible. Four provision boxes wired in place made for a splendid foundation.

It is safe to say that no sledges ever moved with more dispatch than Amundsen's that astral spring of 1911. Progress was phenomenal. In less than a month, with the clockwork precision of a suburban train, the Norwegians reeled off more than half the distance to the pole, from their first depot at latitude 80° to their last on the Ross Barrier itself just south of latitude 85°. Every four days they built a depot at a new degree. In between they left square snow beacons, higher than a man, topped by black flags or the stiffened corpse of any dog that had died.

The efficiency of their travel by day was equaled by the comfort in which they passed each night. At Framheim, Wisting had taken a pair of the expedition's original, round three-man tents and sewed their door panels *en face*, creating a single, lozenge-shaped structure that easily accommodated five men in sleeping bags, even though its center was obstructed by a pole. Held up by this single pole, Amundsen's tent needed extensive guying around its canvas perimeter.

British expedition tents were draped over a free-standing framework of five bamboo poles, held together at the top by a leather cap. Although heavier, it offered the tepee's advantage of a support-free central area. The British did not, as the Norwegians did, attach their ground cloth to the skirt of the tent, preferring to keep the canvas square available for use as a sail. Tents of both expeditions were double-layered, making them measurably warmer. To reduce glare, the Norwegians' inner tent was colored blue—thanks to ink dye—while on the outside it was covered with red fabric pirated from the bunk curtains at Framheim. It worked very well, and interior rime deposits were reduced. The only other shelter they carried was a small, elegant silk tent that Martin Ronne, the *Fram*'s sailmaker, had stitched on the way south. Very compact and weighing only two pounds, it had been brought along not only for emergencies but to mark the pole as well.

When it was coldest, Amundsen's men slept in triple bags, a soft inner shroud of young deerskin, then a conventional reindeer fur bag enclosed by an outer shell of canvas. Moreover, the Norwegians managed to avoid the traditional British bogey of accumulated moisture. Their secret was simple if Spartan: They slept with their heads outside their bedding. How they did so without freezing their ears or noses was never made clear; either they slept wearing their fur hoods, or they were just inherently more resistant to cold. Exhaled breath congealed as rime on the outer canvas layer of their bags only, from which it could be brushed each morning.

From his winter base at the Bay of Whales, Amundsen had proceeded poleward along longitude 164° West. He did not head for the Beardmore: Having risked camping on the Barrier, the Norwegian commander dared again, chancing that where the Barrier ended, he would be able to blaze a new trail up onto the polar plateau. The Transantarctic Mountains range diagonally athwart the Barrier's end. When Scott reached the Beardmore—Shackleton's "white road to the south"—he would be at a latitude of approximately 83½°; Amundsen, however, would not have to commit to his uphill trek until past 85°, a hundred miles closer to the pole. The route that he pioneered—he called it the Axel Heiberg Glacier—he found on November 17. The second phase of the Norwegian journey had begun. On that same date, Scott was only a dozen miles south of One-Ton Depot, with Mounts Erebus and Terror still visible over his shoulder.

Passage up the glacier was steep yet abbreviated, a shorter ascent than the long, gentler slope of the Beardmore. His dog teams still intact, Amundsen made short work of it. His camp at the summit was called the Butcher Shop because it heralded a ruthless reduction of dogs. Amundsen retired inside the tent, in hopes that the roar of his Primus would drown out the slaughter, two dozen pistol shots as each driver methodically thinned out his team. Only three sledges would continue south, each now pulled by six animals. During a two-day layover, the surviving teams feasted on their fellows, their first red meat since the seal glut at 80°. Inside the tent, dog was on the menu, too, as the explorers varied their pemmican diet with husky cutlets.

Because of fog as well as the two-mile altitude, the Norwegians resumed course more slowly. (The glacier ascent had necessitated a brief detour to the southwest.) They found themselves crossing another glacier along the plateau's tortured fringe. The pull of an eastbound glacier to their left, stretching the ice at their feet, had created a wasteland of crevasses and chasms, which they called the Devil's Glacier. Hassel, who had relinquished his sledge at the Butcher Shop, was roped to Amundsen in the van now, the two of them on ski, searching out a safe route for the sledges proceeding gingerly in their wake. Crampons, depoted atop the first glacier, were sorely missed; as sledge runners slithered laterally, drivers followed in awful, involuntary glissades.

For a terrifying finale, they encountered acres of glistening, windswept ice roof—what else but the Devil's Ballroom?—fragile, double-domed ice that shattered repeatedly under men and dogs. Those sudden-death plunges through the ice sheets were terrifying, a sickening drop to waist and elbows, followed by the noise of ice splinters skittering musically over yet another glazed surface a yard below. Sometimes their feet burst through that subsidiary ice as well, revealing only chill black depths of oblivion. After hours of this, the Norwegians threw caution to the wind and lashed their sledges across the treacherous, glasslike flats. Miraculously, they all got across.

Within ten days, they arrived. Helmer Hanssen, once again driving the lead sledge, beckoned Amundsen to the fore so that he should be first upon the south polar snow. Half a mile later, Amundsen halted and called for the flag, already fluttering from Hanssen's sledge, bent onto a pair of ski poles lashed together.

It was a glorious, sunny morning, two years and eight months after Peary had stood astride the coveted antipode in the arctic North. The five Norwegians doffed their mittens, grasped the improvised flagstaff in barehanded concert, and thrust it into the snow. Amundsen spoke for his comrades: "Thus we plant our beloved flag at the south pole, and give to the plain on which it lies the name of King Haakon VII's Plateau."

The ease with which the surface was pierced told the tale. For the last hundred miles, conditions and consequently progress had improved dramatically: sun constant, cold abated, mists evaporated, sledging superlative. To those who had penetrated the full ninety degrees of southern latitude, these incredible travel conditions came as a kind of reward, the sunny final episode of a paradigmatic Nordic fable from their childhood. The spell was broken: At its polar heart, past concentric rings of trial—pack, barrier, glacier, blizzard, fog, chasm—the forbidding continent was benign.

Ronne's silk tent, immaculately clean and well crafted, was broken out and erected. Atop the bamboo pole at its peak, flew the Norwegian flag and, beneath it, a pennant inscribed *Fram*. This was Polheim; after Amundsen, each of the others crawled inside to sign their name to the record. Also left was a note addressed to King Haakon and another requesting Scott to deliver it.

The British had been much on Amundsen's mind. Throughout the final approach, he had despaired of reaching his goal first. Vastly relieved, he set about establishing his find with indisputable exactitude; the recent specter of confusion and bickering over the arctic prize warranted his utmost care. Pinpointing the south pole was easier than the north, for this was no wandering, oceanborne marker but a fixed location on terra firma.

One of Stubberud's packing cases served as a base for the artificial horizon. Like Peary, Amundsen would use sextant rather than theodolite. Over separate twenty-four-hour periods, two sets of observations were taken as the obligingly clear sun revolved serenely in its unique polar orbit. Flankers were sent out on skis to bracket the area; they carried spare sledge runners tagged with flags that, thrust deep into the yielding snow, proclaimed the Norwegian triumph. On their last night at the pole, they feasted on seal meat. Tobacco cherished since Framheim was passed around, and watches, knives, and rings were engraved with the date and latitude, sanctified trinkets that would be much cherished at home, the Edwardian equivalent of moon rocks.

On December 17, the Norwegians started back north. The worst of the Devil's Glacier was detoured and, once down onto the Barrier and plentifully resupplied from their depots, the polar party rushed back to their winter quarters, arriving at 4:00 A.M. on the morning of January 25. They had traveled 1,860 miles in 99 days. Back in May of that year, Shackleton had told an Indianapolis reporter:

> It is quite impossible for an expedition such as his [Amundsen's] to reach the pole and return under four months from the time it starts out. . . .

If it seems absurdly easy in the telling, that extraordinary journey had been accomplished, in truth, by an awe-inspiring combination of foresight, diligence, and luck.

Their ship had already returned for them and, at the end of the month, they sailed for Hobart, leaving Framheim abandoned. When the polar team first clambered joyfully back on board the *Fram*, there was a coincidental reprise of Peary's closemouthed return to the *Roosevelt:* At least an hour passed before Lieutenant Thorvald Nilsen got around to asking if they had reached the pole.

The British polar party arrived belatedly at Polheim a full month after the Norwegians' departure. A rule of travel for which Scott had always been a stickler was clarity about numbers of men. Sledgers returning from long journeys had standing orders to spread out so that watchers could ascertain through a glass that the party was returning intact. Yet the five manhaulers dragging those last miles to the pole belied themselves an equally vital precept of the commander. Throughout the winter, in the pipe fug of his cubicle at Cape Evans, Scott had based all calculations on fours: four men to a tent, four to a sledge, units of rations for four, four pannikins nested inside a cooker. From the glacier's summit south, eight men—two teams of four—had trudged southward over the plateau. The fixed understanding was that four would continue while four would retire, the last support party. There had never been any confusion on this point, merely suspense as to just how the division would be made. Of the three expected to accompany their leader to the pole, Wilson was a certainty; that left a pair of slots to be filled from a pool of six. Two were named Evans: Lieutenant Teddie Evans, the *Terra Nova*'s commander; the other that Gibraltar of a man, Petty Officer Edgar Evans, who had shown his worth aboard the *Discovery*. Oates and Bowers were the remaining commissioned candidates, while Lashley and Crean represented the messdeck.

On January 3, just short of latitude 88°, Scott made a startling announcement: Five would continue, three would turn back. Going for the pole would be Scott, Wilson, Bowers,

Oates, and Petty Officer Evans. Evans was the addition, if we are to believe a Ponting portrait taken back at Cape Evans of "the south polar party" showing only the first four. Scott was violating his scrupulous quadripartite projection: One of the four expected to turn back with the last support party would march instead with the polar party, an unplanned imbalance that would hamper both groups.

Lieutenant Evans, the returning shorthanded commander, was crippled with scurvy on the way back; Lashley and Crean only just managed to save him. A fourth man would have made their task immeasurably easier. And Scott's fifth man would prove more a liability than a help. Petty Officer Evans was exhausted, having manhauled since Corner Camp; moreover, he had cut his hand fixing a sledge, and the wound had festered. He kept it secret until it was too late.

Scott sledged on toward the pole, convinced that his decision had been sound. He recalled from one earlier depot-laying journey that five men had managed in a four-man tent. Five men, moreover, would pull more strongly than four and, at that point in early January, there seemed enough food for one more. (What there was *not*, left out of his hasty recalculations, was sufficient fuel to cook rations for five.) Perhaps Scott felt there was a ceremonial rationale: The expanded polar party included a spectrum of the British services: Royal Navy—Scott, Royal Marines—Bowers, Army—Oates, Wilson for science and Evans for a host of other ranks. Within a few days, they would pass Shackleton's farthest south.

Meanwhile, withdrawing down the Beardmore far to the north, the mood of the last support party was bleak. Crean had wept openly when, in Royal Navy jargon, he had been "told off." Tormenting each of the three privately was their relegation from explorer to supporter, second-stringers whose contribution would forever be ranked short of fulfillment. On a scale of comparatives, to have sailed with the *Terra Nova* was creditable; to have wintered ashore, enviable; to have sledged onto the polar plateau, heroic; but to have reached the pole, incomparable. This they would never achieve. Teddie Evans, Lashley, and Crean would remain eternally disqualified, in company with greatness but not at its core. Both Lashley and Crean could have completed the polar journey with ease.

At the polar threshold, it was the sharp-eyed Bowers who

spotted one of Amundsen's peripheral markers, fluttering atop an upended sledge runner. There is a puzzling discrepancy here: Amundsen wrote that it was made of brown Burberry and included a note inside a bag of the same material. But Wilson recorded a black flag—and his painter/scientist's eye was seldom mistaken—and certainly no note. In fact, none was needed. The mere presence of that claim in what the British had hoped was still virgin territory indicated all too clearly that "the reward of priority," to use Scott's pungent euphemism, had eluded them. The Norskies had won; the pole was Polheim.

They spent only one night there, with little to do but record their own observations. The following day, they posed for the camera. Another of Scott's rules on returning to base was the routine display of sledge flags, to reassure those who waited that all was well. Now, at the apogee of his southern journey, paradoxical success and failure combined, sledge banners were unfurled for a full-dress, ceremonial photograph. There were four flags—Evans did not have one—two of them relics from the *Discovery* expedition: Scott's *Ready Aye Ready* and Wilson's *Le Bon Temps Viendra*. Neither of Sir Clements's jaunty mottoes could ever be credited with anything save the most horrifying irony.

While the others erected a modest cairn, Bowers attached his camera to the theodolite tripod. It was a hasty business. Polar weather that had smiled on the winners had turned symbolically bitter for the runners-up: a drop of 20° in temperature, patchy sun, frigid winds, and, throughout their stay at latitude 90° South, a damp, penetrating chill. The explorers lined up in two rows, a parody of the team portraits of their youth; the pair seated in front might well have been clasping tennis rackets. Three photographs were taken. In the first, Evans and Oates flanked their leader, while Wilson and Bowers sat in the snow at their feet, Bowers barehanded to operate the remote shutter release. Then the four subordinates changed places; Evans managed the camera string with his mittens on.

That afternoon, they started their eight-hundred-mile trek home. Near its end, Scott would refer to "the steps of my downfall." He was talking about his frostbitten feet, but his imagery of incremental calamity serves as an epitaph for the expedition as a whole. A chain of circumstances, some unforeseeable, others not, had combined to spell disaster: the ponies and their absent *trugers*, unseasonable weather, the inclusion of the fifth man, leaking fuel containers, the shortfall of One-Ton Depot, and, a familiar scourge that closes the circle of British participation in the heroic age, scurvy.

For each of those five desperate sledgers straggling back down the glacier, the unspoken question haunting them was what would happen if any one of them could not march. Twice, matters were mercifully resolved, once by natural causes, once by suicide.

Evans deteriorated most swiftly. Normally a strong, competent man, he grew increasingly helpless and slow. His infected wound refused to heal. Frostbite attacked both hands and feet. On February 17, near the bottom of Beardmore, he degenerated within the space of one day. During his tragic, final march, his skis kept coming adrift and he fell continually behind, unable to cope or keep up. Finally the others sledged him up to the tent where, an hour later, he died without regaining consciousness.

Reduced now to its projected size, the polar party struggled on. They were halfway home. Evans's death had, in one sense, relieved them; yet it had also been terrifying.

Oates was next. During the winter at Cape Evans, he and Ponting had discussed the ethical responsibility of a failing sledger, Oates declaring flatly that any man unable to keep up should kill himself. The hideous irony was that Oates would put his conviction to its ultimate test. The trouble was in his feet, one so badly frostbitten that it had swollen to twice its normal size. A pair of his *finnesko* found later had been slit up the back, the only way their owner could put them on. His predicament was no secret to the others, who were themselves only degrees removed from an identical desperation. Scott observed on March 5: ". . . We cannot help each other, each has enough to do to take care of himself." It was the only record being kept by then; Wilson had stopped writing his diary a week earlier, fully preoccupied with nursing Oates.

Although Wilson had, at Scott's suggestion, distributed opium tablets, enough to kill each of them, Oates chose a different way. On the morning of March 17 or 18—Scott was losing track—after his companions had refused his request to abandon him, he left the tent forever, remarking, "I am just going outside and may be some time." It was both exit line and epitaph. Did he take the pills, or was he still carrying the revolver with which he had killed the ponies? Scott's diary does not record any shot. "No Surrender" Oates probably just hobbled away, fell, and died.

Two down, three left. Scott, Wilson, and Bowers were so weak, cold, and lame that Scott's diary acknowledged bleakly that "amputation is the least I can hope for." But they stumbled on, roped to their one remaining sledge, progress reduced to pitifully few miles each day. Four days after Oates's death, they stopped forever, nearly out of fuel and only eleven miles from One-Ton Depot, which was meant to be farther south.

There, at that terminal camp, a third, fatal blizzard ended all hope. Their last planned contingency had been for Bowers and Wilson or just Bowers alone—still the strongest of that mortally incapacitated trio—to push on, obtain provisions, and return. But they woke each morning to the ceaseless, battering roar of the blizzard, an impenetrable white blast that made travel impossible.

By March 22 they had sorted out their options. The pills were not for them. "We have decided it shall be natural—we shall march for the depot with or without our effects and die in our tracks."

Their fuel ran out that day, so there was nothing more to eat or drink and no more heat. Only some methylated spirits remained, for which Scott improvised a makeshift lamp of tin with a scrap of lampwick from his *finnesko*. He used it to write to the end.

He had thought to close his diary with a signed apologia: "It seems a pity, but I do not think I can write more. R. Scott." But, added perhaps hours or days later, scribbled in the green twilight of the lampless tent, was a remorseful addenda in an agitated hand: "Final entry. For God's sake, look after our people."

Then Scott closed his diary, returned it to the green canvas pouch normally carried at his belt, and pillowed it beneath his head. As the tent answered to the wind—"the gentle flutter of our canvas shelter," he had written once—three shrouded figures slept and died in their reindeer fur coffins. Drifting snow accumulated outside, so that after each shortening autumn day, there was less and less light inside.

14

ENVOI

*The pole . . . is a mere point without
height, breadth or thickness and therefore
without special interest.*

—Sir Clements Markham
(1875 at the RGS)

*They are not the men to scamper to the
Pole and scamper back for the reward.*

—Sir Clements Markham
(1913 letter)

The heroic age of polar exploration ended in anguish.
The denouement was long in unfolding. Such was the timetable of antarctic accessibility—reentry through the window in
the sky—that almost a year passed before the enormity of Britain's loss reached civilization. So, following that climactic battle of what Sir Ernest Shackleton would call "the warfare of
the South," there was an extended phony war while the British, smarting from Norway's victory, awaited the return of
their champion.

The *Fram* reached Hobart on March 7, 1912, after a rough,
five-day passage from the Bay of Whales. (On that same day,
Scott recorded in his diary that poor Oates's "crisis is near.")
Amundsen's news flashed around the world. If it was greeted
with jubilation by his countrymen, outrage was the order of
the day in England. The first London paper to headline the
news was *The Daily Chronicle. The Daily Graphic* dismissed

Amundsen's feats as "a dash, pure and simple, at the Pole";
subheads like "The Stolen March" peppered the columns of
gray type. The stance of *The Brixton Free Press*'s leader typified
Britain's response: "We could have wished that the honor had
fallen to the British flag."

On March 16, *The Spectator* grasped at straws:

> It still seems possible, however, that Captain Scott may
> have reached the South Pole before Captain Amundsen,
> for although Captain Amundsen found no traces of his
> having done so, it is to be remembered that the Pole is a
> vague point and it would be possible in a region of mists
> and snowstorms for such fragile tokens . . . to be totally
> obscured unless later visitors happen to stumble across
> them.

Readers of *The Glasgow Record* were also advised to withhold
their verdict: "Captain Scott's ship will bring more information shortly." But another ship intervened: Within a month,
the *Titanic* disaster crowded everything off the front page.

There was a frisson of anxiety within the boardroom of *The
Times*. Editor Brookville wrote to Keltie, inquiring discreetly if
Scott's obituary should be prepared:

> But will you kindly inform the Editor where there is
> likelihood of the party's meeting with disaster?

Amundsen's book was raced into print. No more *farthest* or
nearest—*The South Pole* was the second of two ultimate titles.
Peary had already used the other, *The North Pole*. January's
issue of *The Geographical Journal*, published by the Royal Geographical Society, carried a review. Sir Clements's response
was predictably choleric:

> I was sorry to see more absurd laudation of the "bril-
> liant" gadfly in the February number. Surely these exag-
> gerated praises of such a dishonorable trick ought to
> cease now that the time is approaching for Captain
> Scott's return. . . .

The more he brooded, the more furious he became. In a later
memorandum to the council, written but not submitted, he
harked back to a familiarly ironic theme:

His journey was not exceptional. It was much the same as Peary's across the Greenland inland sea, both with dogs. It is not for a moment to be compared with Captain Scott's journey without dogs. . . . They and their men dragged their own sledges instead of trotting along and only carrying themselves, sometimes sitting on the sledges.

Poor Sir Clements! He could not have guessed that *The Geographical Journal's* next issue would appear with black-bordered pages.

The hard news reached London in February 1913, more than a year after Scott and his men had reached the pole and months after a search party had found their bodies. For three consecutive Januarys, the British expedition ship *Terra Nova* had sailed into McMurdo Sound: in 1911, to disembark the explorers; in 1912, to resupply them during Captain Scott's absence at the pole; and in 1913, to bring them home. That last landfall was traumatic. With her wardroom table set for a gala reunion dinner, the ship rounded Cape Royds and was spotted from shore. Over the intervening water went the routine maritime greeting: "Are you all well?" It came from Teddie Evans, fully recuperated and once more on the bridge. A shouted response delivered the appalling news.

Within two days, Cape Evans had been abandoned. The remaining explorers were embarked, and the *Terra Nova* sailed for New Zealand.

At three o'clock on the morning of February 10, Pennell and Atkinson were rowed surreptitiously ashore at Oamaru, a town south along the coast from Lyttelton. Grim, coded messages went out over the wires to London while those on board waited in their offshore limbo for the cables' impact. The master of a passing ferryboat spotted them and pestered Evans for news; none was released. The New Zealander was naturally suspicious; the *Terra Nova* had come back too early.

The next day, when she did steam past Lyttelton Heads with her ensign at half staff, every flag was similarly lowered. At noon, the bells of Christchurch Cathedral were tolled, a tocsin of sorrow that would echo around the world.

New Zealand marked the expedition's return to civilization, the start of decompression after Antarctica's long immersion.

The explorers had been at the bottom of the world for three years, and resurfacing brought a host of disremembered strictures, from neckties and celluloid collars to the unfamiliar pinch of leather shoes. But the hardest adjustment was the necessity for emotional regression. The men of the *Terra Nova* were no longer National Antarctic Expedition members but survivors, survivors who found themselves out of step with what was, for them, the extraordinary scope of the public's grief. The explorers had lived with the reality of their loss since November, when a search party had found the bodies and diaries just south of One-Ton Depot. In fact, they had known even earlier that death was inevitable: All hands at Cape Evans knew to the ounce how much food and fuel had been carried south. Once past April there was no expectation of survival, no Nansen/Johansen miracle on the gameless Barrier. That the polar party was dead was not in question: only why and how.

On November 12, a search party under surgeon Atkinson had spotted the tent, almost completely obscured by snow. He dug down to the entrance, cut open the tunneled sleeve, and found the trio of bodies inside. Bowers and Wilson were, as Cherry-Garrard recorded it, "sleeping" in their bags. Scott's was flung open, his face contorted, one arm resting across Wilson. The diary was found beneath his shoulders. Some of them in tears, only whispering to each other, each man of the search party crawled inside to examine that pathetic interior. It was remarkably neat, as though its occupants had been determined to sustain a shipshape regimen in camp to compensate for the chaos of their aborted march.

Letters, diaries, film, and possessions were gathered up. The tent was removed but its lining left in place and collapsed onto the bodies. An enormous snow cairn was erected over it, topped by a pair of crossed skis. Farther south, the party searched in vain for Oates's body; all that could be found was his discarded sleeping bag. Another cairn was left, bearing a note that began: "Hereabouts died a very gallant gentleman . . ."

One of the men who built both cairns, Cherry-Garrard, would sum up his feelings about the expedition ten years later. In the final chapter of *The Worst Journey in the World* he remarked:

> I now see very plainly that though we achieved a first-rate tragedy, which will never be forgotten just because it was a tragedy, tragedy was not our business. . . .

To be accurate, the tragedy was less first-rate than the response it triggered. In stark, majestic horror, Scott's death matched the age it ended, as though supreme effort should, perforce, conclude with supreme sacrifice.

From Portugal, where frail Sir Clements was taking the sun in Estoril, came an anguished letter to Keltie:

> . . . I am plunged in grief: to think that such a man should have been annoyed by wretched, self-seeking charlatans like Shackleton and Amundsen . . .

Sir Clements was not alone. The tragedy struck a responsive chord everywhere. London's grief focused at St. Paul's Cathedral. Keltie replied to Sir Clements, telling him of the memorial service where "ten thousand were turned away." Inside, King George and Queen Mary were part of the vast congregation; the band of the Coldstream Guard joined with the organ to play "The Dead March" from Handel's *Saul*. Scott's mother and sisters were there, but his wife, Kathleen, was somewhere in the South Pacific, on board the SS *Aorangi* between San Francisco and New Zealand, en route to greet her husband home. The vessel was contacted by wireless and the newly made widow informed. Another widow, Oriana Wilson, already knew, for she had been waiting for the *Terra Nova* in New Zealand.

Later, mourning was supplanted by curiosity. People were obsessed with minutiae of the disaster, as though by reliving those awful, final days on the Barrier, they might somehow alleviate the pain of what had become both a national and a personal loss. The tent itself, complete with Royal Navy honor guard, was exhibited to vast, silent throngs at Earls Court. The routes of the two expeditions were reproduced everywhere, the Victoria Quadrant overlaid with dotted tracks to the pole and back, one incomplete, terminated by a cross flagged "Final Camp."

The polar photographs, developed in Ponting's darkroom at

Cape Evans, achieved worldwide circulation. Invariably, they were captioned then (as they have been ever since) to support the popular theory that the subjects were broken by despair. It seems an inaccurate analysis. Admittedly, all five faces bore the black stigmata of frost and wind. Bowers alone stared into the lens; all the others, save Scott, had lowered their balaclavas to minimize cold or glare. Scott's eyes, in both photographs, are concealed, once by a blink and, yet again, because apparently he had ignored the imminent click of the shutter and was caught turning toward Bowers, as though to rearrange something. But these are mere hazards of mistiming, frozen into filmic permanence, that do not necessarily betray the hopelessness that they have traditionally been accorded.

Endless permutations of rescue were fantasized. Would a relief effort mounted from Cape Evans have saved them? If Bowers had struggled on to One-Ton Depot, could he have completed the twenty-two-mile round-trip in time? Had all three explorers reached One-Ton Depot, would there have been enough fuel and provisions to see them safely back to Cape Evans? There was a morbid compulsion, too, to determine the order of dying. In his letter to Oriana Wilson, Scott's intermingling of present and past tenses makes it tantalizingly unclear:

> My dear Mrs. Wilson:
> If this letter reaches you, Bill and I will have gone out together. We are very near it now and I should like you to know how splendid he was at the end—everlastingly cheerful and ready to sacrifice himself for others. . . . He is not suffering, luckily, at least only minor discomforts. His eyes have a comfortable blue look of hope and his mind is peaceful. . . . I can do no more to comfort you than to tell you that he died as he lived, a brave, true man—the best of comrades, the staunchest of friends. . . .

Was Wilson dead or alive as Scott wrote? Perhaps Scott hoped that deliberately vague chronology might comfort the recipient.

Kathleen Scott was given her husband's diaries in Wellington by Teddie Evans. She had no doubts at all. She wrote to Keltie:

> My man was the last to go. B and W died in their sleep but he had raised himself up and put his arm about Wilson.

Perhaps some clue to Wilson's last thoughts, if they included aught but his beloved Ory, might be found in a diary entry from June 1910 as he was passing through the Orkneys en route to join the *Terra Nova*. At twilight, he had stopped at Kirkwall's red sandstone cathedral to sketch the monument and tomb of John Rae, the arctic explorer who had first guessed at Franklin's true whereabouts:

> . . . a lifesize figure lying asleep wrapped in a buffalo sleeping bag . . . The whole thing looked rather natural and nice . . . honored by his own people and caring nothing about the rest. . . .

But perhaps the most cherished legacy of that "first-rate" tragedy was Scott's message to the public. Since the National Antarctic Expedition had been largely a publicly subscribed venture, it was only natural that among the documents composed by the light of the spirit lamp that flickered at Scott's elbow was a letter to everyone. It is neither polemic nor expiation, merely a discussion of his problems with the ponies, the surface, the weather, and his disabled comrades. Amundsen is not mentioned. But it is the peroration that stands out, with its classic conditional that was precisely the eloquent reassurance his countrymen craved:

> We are weak, writing is difficult but for my own sake I do not regret this journey, which has shown that Englishmen can endure hardships, help one another, and meet death with as great a fortitude as ever in the past. . . . Had we lived, I should have had a tale to tell of the hardihood, endurance, and courage of my companions which would have stirred the heart of every Englishman. These rough notes and our dead bodies must tell the tale. . . .

It was Scott's articulate grace in the face of death that illuminated his failure while at the same time eclipsing the victorious Norwegians. He had come second at the pole, but his harrowing, gallant exit would indeed "stir the heart of every Englishman" forever.

The public's financial response was everything their dead hero asked. Seventy-five thousand pounds were subscribed to pay off the expedition's debts, provide a fund on behalf of the dependents of the polar party, and establish a most fitting memorial that flourishes to this day, at Cambridge, the Scott Polar Research Institute. Twice daily, the *Terra Nova*'s brass bell summons staff and visitors to midmorning coffee and to tea in the afternoon.

The title that had eluded Scott during his life was awarded posthumously to his widow, and she became Lady Scott. Among the thousands who wrote offering sympathy, the most ardent was Fridtjof Nansen, who eventually proposed marriage. She refused him and, nine years later, married a politician, Edward Young. During the First World War, Sir Clements unveiled her statue of Scott that stands today in Waterloo Place. Her next commission was Captain Edward J. Smith, the late commander of the *Titanic*.

Amundsen was lecturing about the south pole in America when the news reached him. He was stunned. Later he wrote a long, rambling piece for a Chicago newspaper, describing in imaginary detail how Scott must have died:

> . . . The scurvy, the not-to-be-conceived-of cold and low provisions began their deadly work. The scurvy slacked the circulation. The blood, heavy with poison, did not do its work and the cold penetrated right through. One of the men finally fell, exhausted. There were no dogs to pull him on the now nearly empty sleds. . . .

Of course, he was right about scurvy as well as the dogs. But it seems nothing more than transparent wish fulfillment, an effort to convince himself as much as his readers that Scott had not died of a broken heart.

Amundsen was riven with other guilt, the awful business about Johansen. Amundsen had fired him from the expedition after several drunken incidents in Australia; he returned alone to Norway in disgrace. A year later, he shot himself in a Christiania park.

Even as the winner, fortune evaded Amundsen to the end. He finally did accomplish his arctic drift on board the *Maud,* a vessel of his own design named after his queen. Seven years were consumed drifting through the Northeast Passage, duplicating Nordenskjöld's feat of half a century earlier. He got nowhere near the north pole, at least with a ship.

So he took to the air, first with Lincoln Ellsworth, a rich American who bankrolled a close but nearly fatal try by seaplane. However, a dirigible flight on board the *Norge,* an Italian airship, did cross the north pole. For the second time, Amundsen was lionized in Nome, although Umberto Nobile, the airship's owner, aroused Amundsen's bitterest enmity by claiming equal credit for the flight. It set the stage for Amundsen's third and fatal arctic flight, again by seaplane, to find Nobile and the downed *Italia.* Amundsen and the pilot were lost somewhere over the Arctic Ocean, their bodies never recovered.

Peary was interested in exploration by air as well but was cut down by pernicious anemia in 1920, too soon to follow the illustrious exploits of his naval successor, Richard Byrd. Peary's nemesis, Dr. Cook, fell on hard times. In the early 1920s, long after he had been publicly discredited as an explorer, he was convicted of an oil-stock swindle and sent to prison. Judge John Killits pronounced sentence with relish:

> You have reached a point now where you can't bunco anybody. You have come to a mountain and reached a latitude both of which are beyond you.

Cook stayed in Leavenworth for seven years of a fourteen-year sentence and, once released, spent the rest of his life in an attempt to legitimize his polar claim, a struggle that was continued by his daughter long after her father had died in 1940.

But the last word in that celebrated dispute was that neither Cook nor Peary reached the north pole first; Peary's black servant had instead. Matthew Henson claimed as much in an interview published in 1954, when he was eighty-seven and near death. According to Henson, he had gone on ahead near latitude 90° North, ignoring orders from "The Boss" to stop and wait.

Nansen died in 1930, just before he would have found out the fate of Salomon August Andrée and his companions. In August of that year, thirty-three years after the balloon had lofted north from Dane Island, a sailor from an expedition ship, in search of water, went ashore on White Island, a desolate speck of land east of Spitsbergen. Something glimmering in the arctic sun turned out to be the top of an aluminum cooker; nearby a folding boat was still lashed to its sledge. He had stumbled onto Andrée's last camp. Waterlogged diaries told the tale. The *Eagle* had stayed aloft for three days and, once forced down by the weight of ice accumulation, its three passengers had walked south, following the example of Nansen and Johansen. But they got only as far south as White Island, approximately the same latitude from which they had begun. There, Strindberg had died and been buried; Andrée and Fraenkel were found nearby, presumably asphyxiated within their tent by fumes from their Primus. Their bodies were taken back to Stockholm for a state funeral, carried on board the *Svenskund*, the same gunboat that the king had lent Andrée in 1897.

In New Hampshire, when widower Gilbert Hawtrey heard that Strindberg's remains had been recovered, he had the body of his late wife, Anna Charlier Hawtrey, exhumed and her heart sent to Sweden to be buried with her first love. Postmaster's daughter and her gallant aeronaut were finally reunited.

Today, tourists from New Zealand can board a jet and fly on special excursions to the south pole, circling Mount Erebus on their return. Both locales are distinctively different now. There is an underground complex at latitude 90° South (the Scott-Amundsen Base, as the U.S. Navy calls it), and marking the actual spot is a barber pole as well as a seriocomic signpost pointing to an infinity of norths. At Hut Point there is an airfield as well as a nuclear generating station and a proliferating sprawl of shore establishments. Among all the detritus of midtwentieth-century technology, three huts—two of Scott's and one of Shackleton's—still occupy their original locations on the shores of McMurdo Sound. They are preserved by New Zealand's Canterbury Museum, and the weathered matchboarding, littered dog kennels, and refuse heaps tell only the faintest tale of their intriguing histories. Inside, mattresses have swollen and burst; remnants of reindeer sleeping bags molder; chipped enamel cups and coffeepots line the walls;

and, framed in Shackleton's hut, are the royal portraits presented to the *Nimrod* when she sailed bravely out of Cowes.

In the North, there is still no settlement or life save for those elaborate ice stations manned by Americans or Soviets that occasionally drift, *Fram*-like, across the arctic wastes. If the ice beneath them fragments, inhabitants and instruments are easily evacuated by helicopter. Three nuclear-powered vessels have visited the pole, two of them U.S. submarines and one a Soviet icebreaker, the *Arktika*, which battered her way through the frozen ocean with a thousand times more horsepower than the *Roosevelt*. Others, on foot, have reached the north pole as well, some with sledges but others riding snowmobiles, all of them supplied by air and in comforting contact by radio.

It is a far cry from the heroic age, when men were wanted for those hazardous journeys. The wages aren't so small now, although the cold is just as bitter, the danger as constant. Return, however, is seldom in jeopardy, and the honors and recognition have long since been awarded. The ancient polar frontiers have been pushed out into space, an even bleaker wasteland with no north or south, no gale, ice, or snow, but from which safe return can be just as doubtful.

Bibliography

Amundsen, Roald. *The South Pole*, vols. I and II, trans. A. G. Chater. New York: Lee Keedick, 1913.

Anderson, William, with Clay Blair, Jr. *Nautilus 90 North*. Cleveland and New York: The World Publishing Company, 1959.

Armitage, Albert B. *Two Years in the Antarctic*. London: Edward Arnold, 1905.

———. *Cadet to Commodore*. London: Cassell and Company, 1925.

Astrup, Eivind. *With Peary near the Pole*, trans. J. Bull. Philadelphia: J. B. Lippincott, 1898.

Bain, Arthur J. *Life and Explorations of Fridtjof Nansen*. London: Walter Scott Ltd., n.d.

Barron, William. *An Apprentice's Reminiscences of Whaling in Davis Strait*. Hull: M. Waller, 1890.

Bartlett, Robert A. *The Log of Bob Bartlett*. New York: Blue Ribbon Books, 1928.

Bernacchi, Louis C. *Saga of the "Discovery."* London: Blackie & Son Ltd., 1938.

Bertram, Colin. *Arctic and Antarctic: A Prospect of the Polar Regions*. Cambridge: W. Heffer & Sons Ltd., 1939.

Blake, E. Vale, ed. *Arctic Experiences*. New York: Harper & Brothers, 1874.

Borchgrevink, C. E. *First on the Antarctic Continent*. London: George Newnes Ltd., 1901.

Bradford, William. *The Arctic Regions*. London: Sampson, Low, Marston, Low, and Searle, 1873.

Brent, Peter. *Captain Scott and the Antarctic Tragedy*. New York: Saturday Review Press, 1974.

Brown, Rudmose. *The Polar Regions*. London: Methuen & Co. Ltd., 1927.

Cameron, Ian. *The Last Continent*. Boston: Little, Brown and Company, 1974.

342

Caswell, John Edward. *Arctic Frontiers*. Tulsa: University of Oklahoma Press, 1956.

Cherry-Garrard, Apsley. *The Worst Journey in the World*. London: Chatto & Windus, 1965.

———. *Postscript to the Worst Journey in the World*. Privately printed, 1951.

Chidsey, Donald Barr. *Shackleton's Voyage*. London: Tandem Books, 1967.

Clark, Ronald W. *Men, Myths and Mountains*. New York: Thomas Y. Crowell Company, 1976.

Cook, Frederick A. *Through the First Antarctic Night*. London: William Heinemann, 1900.

Cook, John A. *Pursuing the Whale*. Boston: Houghton Mifflin Company, 1926.

Craig, Hugh. *Great Arctic Travelers*. New York: George Rutledge & Sons Ltd., 1898.

Danenhower, John W. *Lt. Danenhower's Narrative of the "Jeannette."* Boston: James R. Osgood and Company, 1882.

De la Croix, Robert. *Mysteries of the North Pole*, trans. Edward Fitzgerald. London: Frederick Muller Ltd., 1954.

De Long, Emma, ed. *The Voyage of the "Jeannette,"* vols. I and II. Boston: Houghton Mifflin Company, 1883.

Dodge, Ernest S. *The Polar Rosses*. London: Faber & Faber, 1973.

Du Toit, Alexander. *Our Wandering Continents*. London: Oliver & Boyd, 1937.

Elder, William. *Biography of Elisha Kent Kane*. Philadelphia: Childs & Peterson, 1858.

Ellis, A. R., ed. *Under Scott's Command: Lashley's Antarctic Diaries*. London: Taplinger Publishing Company, n.d.

Ellsberg, Edward. *Hell on Ice*. New York: Dodd, Mead & Company, 1938.

Ellsworth, Lincoln. *Search*. New York: Brewer, Warren & Putnam, 1932.

Euller, John. *Arctic World*. New York: Abelard-Schuman, 1958.

Fiala, Anthony. *Fighting the Polar Ice*. New York: Doubleday, Page & Company, 1906.

Fisher, Margery and James. *Shackleton*. London: James Barrie Books Ltd., 1957.

Freuchen, Peter. *Vagrant Viking: My Life and Adventures*, trans. Johan Hambro. London: Victor Gollancz Ltd., 1954.

Friis, Herman, ed. *The Arctic Diary of Russell Williams Porter*. Charlottesville: University Press of Virginia, 1976.

Gilder, William. *Schwatka's Search*. New York: Abercrombie & Fitch, 1966.

Greely, Adolphus. *Three Years of Arctic Service,* vols. I and II. New York: Charles Scribner's Sons, 1886.

Green, Fitzhugh. *Peary: The Man who Refused to Fail.* New York: G. P. Putnam, 1926.

Hall, Thomas. *Has the North Pole Been Discovered?* Boston: Richard G. Badger, 1917.

Hanssen, Helmer. *Voyages of a Modern Viking.* London: George Routledge & Sons Ltd., 1936.

Herbert, Wally. *Across the Top of the World.* New York: G. P. Putnam's Sons, 1971.

Hilderbrandt, A. *Airships Past and Present,* trans. W. H. Story. New York: D. Van Nostrand Company, 1908.

Hoare, J. D. *Arctic Exploration.* London: Methuen, 1906.

Hoehling, A. A. *The "Jeannette" Expedition.* New York: Abelard-Schuman, 1968.

Holmes, Bette Fleischmann. *Log of the "Laura" in Polar Seas.* Cambridge: The University Press, 1907.

Hoyer, Liv Nansen. *Nansen: A Family Portrait,* trans. Maurice Michael. New York: Longmans, Green and Co., 1957.

Huntford, Roland. *Scott & Amundsen.* London: Hodder and Stoughton, 1979.

———. *Shackleton.* New York: Atheneum, 1986.

Huxley, Elspeth. *Scott of the Antarctic.* New York: Atheneum, 1978.

Jackson, Frederick G. *A Thousand Days in the Arctic.* New York: Harper & Brothers, 1899.

James, Bessie Rowland, ed. *Six Came Back.* New York: The Bobbs Merrill Company, 1940.

Johansen, Hjalmar. *With Nansen in the North,* trans. H. L. Braekstad. New York: New Amsterdam Book Company, n.d.

Kane, Elisha Kent. *Arctic Exploration in Search of John Franklin.* London, Edinburgh, and New York: T. Nelson & Sons, 1890.

———. *Adrift in the Arctic Icepack.* Oyster Bay, N.Y.: Nelson Doubleday, 1915.

Keely, Robert N., Jr., and G. G. Davis. *In Arctic Seas: The Voyage of the "Kite."* Philadelphia: Rufus G. Hartranff, 1893.

Lachambre, Henri, and Alexis Machuron. *Andrée's Balloon Expedition.* New York: Frederick A. Stokes & Company, 1898.

Laing, Samuel. *Journal of a Residence in Norway.* London: Longmans, Green and Co., 1866.

Lamont, James. *Yachting in the Arctic Seas.* London: Chatto & Windus, 1876.

Lanman, Charles. *Farthest North.* New York: D. Appleton & Company, 1885.

Laursen, Dan. *The Place Names of North Greenland.* Copenhagen: C. A. Reitzels Forlag, 1972.

Leslie, Alexander. *The Arctic Voyages of Adolf Eric Nordenskiöld, 1858–1879.* London: Macmillan and Co., 1879.

Lewin, W. Henry. *The Great North Pole Fraud.* London: The C. W. Daniel Company Ltd., 1935.

Lingstrom, Freda. *This Is Norway.* New York: Loring & Mussey, 1933.

Loomis, Chauncey C. *Weird and Tragic Shores.* New York: Alfred A. Knopf, 1971.

Lunn, Arnold. *A History of Ski-ing.* London: Oxford University Press, 1927.

Manning, E. W. *Igloo for the Night.* Toronto: University of Toronto Press, 1946.

Markham, Captain Albert Hastings. *Life of Sir John Franklin and the North-West Passage.* New York: Dodd, Mead & Company, n.d.

———. *Northward Ho!* London: Macmillan & Company, 1879.

———. *The Great Frozen Sea.* London: Daldy, Isbister & Co., 1878.

Markham, Clements R. *The Arctic Navy List.* London: Griffin & Co., 1875.

McClintock, F. L. *A Narration of the Discovery of the Fate of Sir John Franklin and His Companions.* London: John Murray, Albemarle Street, 1859.

McClure, Robert Le M. *The Discovery of the Northwest Passage,* ed. Commander Sherard Osborn. Rutland, Vt., and Tokyo: Charles F. Tuttle Co., 1967.

Mill, Hugh Robert. *The Record of the Royal Geographical Society, 1830–1890.* London: Royal Geographical Society, 1930.

Mirsky, Jeanette. *To the Arctic.* New York: Alfred A. Knopf, 1948.

———. *Elisha Kent Kane and the Seafaring Frontier.* Boston: Little, Brown and Company, 1954.

Mitford, Nancy. *The Water Beetle.* New York and London: Harper & Row, 1962.

Morris, Charles, ed. *Finding the North Pole.* Copyright W. E. Scull, 1909.

Moss, Edward L., M.D. *Shores of the Polar Sea.* London: Marcus Ward & Co., 1878.

Murray, James, and George Marston. *Antarctic Days.* London: Andrew Melrose, 1913.

Nansen, Fridtjof, ed. *The Norwegian North Polar Expedition—1895–1896.* New York: Longmans, Green and Co., n.d.

Nares, Captain Sir George. *Narrative of a Voyage to the Polar Sea.* London: Sampson, Marston, Searle, & Rivington, 1878.

Neatby, Leslie H. *Conquest of the Last Frontier.* Athens: Ohio University Press, 1966.

Neider, Charles. *Edge of the World.* Garden City, N.Y.: Doubleday & Company, 1974.

Nordenskiöld, A. E. *The Voyage of the Vega,* trans. Alexander Leslie. New York: Macmillan & Company, 1882.

Parijanine, Maurice. *The Krassin,* trans. Lawrence Brown. New York: The Macaulay Company, 1929.

Partridge, Bellamy. *Amundsen.* London: Robert Hale Ltd., 1953.

Peary, Josephine Diebitsch. *My Arctic Journal.* New York and Philadelphia: The Contemporary Publishing Company, 1893.

Peary, Robert E. *Secrets of Polar Travel.* New York: The Century Co., 1917.

———. *The North Pole.* New York: Frederick A. Stokes Company, 1910.

Powell, Theodore. *The Long Rescue.* Garden City, N.Y.: Doubleday & Company, 1960.

Prentiss, Henry Mellen. *The Great Polar Current.* Cambridge: Riverside Press, 1897.

Putnam, George P. *Andrée: The Record of a Tragic Adventure.* New York: Brewer & Warren, 1930.

Randles, Slim. *Dogsled.* New York: Winchester Press, 1976.

Schley, W. S., and J. R. Soley. *The Rescue of Greely.* New York: Charles Scribner's Sons, 1885.

Scott, G. Firth. *The Romance of Polar Exploration.* Philadelphia: J. B. Lippincott Company, 1906.

Scott, J. M. *Portrait of an Ice Cap.* London: Chatto & Windus, 1953.

Scott, Captain Robert F. *Scott's Last Expedition, Being the Journals of Captain R. F. Scott, R.N., C.V.O.,* arranged by Leonard Huxley, vols. I and II. London: Smith, Elder & Co., 1913.

———. *The Voyage of the "Discovery,"* vols. I and II. New York: Charles Scribner's Sons, 1905.

Seitz, Don Carlos. *The Famous Gordon Bennetts, Father and Son.* Indianapolis, Ind.: The Bobbs Merrill Company, 1925.

Shackleton, Sir Ernest. *The Heart of the Antarctic.* Philadelphia: J. B. Lippincott Company, 1914.

Smith, William D. *Northwest Passage.* New York: American Heritage Press, 1970.

Stefansson, Vilhjalmur. *Unsolved Mysteries of the Arctic.* New York: The Macmillan Company, 1939.

Story, Dana. *The Building of a Wooden Ship.* Barre, Mass.: Barre Publishers, 1971.

Sverdrup, Otto, and T. C. Fairley. *Sverdrup's Arctic Adventure.* London: Longmans, 1959.

Swedish Society for Anthropology and Geography. *Andrée's Story,* trans. Edward Adams-Ray. New York: The Viking Press, 1930.

Thomson, George Malcolm. *The Search for the Northwest Passage.* New York: The Macmillan Company, 1975.

Turley, Charles. *Roald Amundsen.* London: Methuen & Co. Ltd., 1935.

Tweedie, Ethel. *A Winter Jaunt to Norway.* London: Bliss Sand & Foster, 1894.

Von Payer, Julius. *New Lands Within the Arctic Circle.* New York: D. Appleton & Company, 1877.

Weems, John Edward. *Race for the Pole.* New York: Henry Holt & Company, 1960.

Wild, Frank. *Shackleton's Last Voyage: The Story of the "Quest."* London and New York: Frederick A. Stokes Company, n.d.

Wilkins, Sir Hubert. *Under the North Pole.* New York: Brewer, Warren, & Putnam, Inc., 1931.

Willis, Thayer. *The Frozen World.* London: Aldus Books Ltd., 1971.

Wilson, Edward. *Diary of the "Discovery" Expedition, 1901–1904*, ed. Ann Savours. London: Blandford Press, 1966.

————. *Diary of the "Terra Nova" Expedition, 1910–1913*, ed. H. R. King. London: Blandford Press, 1972.

Young, Sir Allen. *The Two Voyages of the "Pandora" in 1875 and 1876.* London: Edward Stanford, 1879.

Index